SUCCESSFUL SPORT MANAGEMENT.

Edited By
GUY LEWIS
HERB APPENZELLER

THE MICHIE COMPANY
Law Publishers
CHARLOTTESVILLE, VIRGINIA

essential materials. Once these needs are satisfied on at least an acceptable level, needs for social affiliation and personal accomplishment become of primary concern. Opportunities to fulfill these needs are the motivating factors which are available in the work environment.

Motivating factors can be classified into organizational factors and individual factors. Organizational factors are those which are provided through affiliation with the larger work unit. The most obvious of these are salary and fringe benefits. Additional organizational factors affecting motivation include the desirability of the work environment, the amount of job security, affiliation with the organization and acceptance by co-workers. Individual factors motivating job performance include the opportunity to achieve, to receive recognition, to feel pride, to work autonomously, to obtain intrinsic pleasure from the job and to provide a challenge. In situations where the work is redundant and offers little challenge and few opportunities for self-expression, the major motivation must come from organizational motivational factors. Attractive salary and benefit packages, pleasant office furnishings, up-to-date equipment, positive social climate and reasonable job security make these jobs more desirable and thus motivate employees to attempt to hold their jobs. The individual motivating factors, all related to self-esteem and accomplishment, however, are the more powerful factors for affecting most employee performance. Many employees actively seek new opportunities which provide challenges and the means to achieve promotions, status, acclaim and power, even if these are not directly associated with salary increases.

The individual nature of human behavior necessitates that supervisors understand that each employee is a unique person motivated by a different array of organizational and individual factors. The more familiar managers are with their employees, the better able they are to provide the incentives which will be important to that employee.

Employee motivation is directly influenced by the respect they hold for their supervisors. An ineffectual, unrespected manager produces a work climate fostering uninspired employees. Several suggestions for positive supervision leading to motivated employees include:

1. *Accept the responsibility of the administrator.* Make the decisions which are necessary and take the credit and blame for those decisions. Employees are frustrated when decisions which directly affect them are avoided or unnecessarily delayed. Never allow an employee to shoulder the blame for a decision which was made by the administrator.

2. *Delegate both responsibility and the authority to accomplish assigned tasks.* Allow employees some freedom and creativity in their means of accomplishing their duties.

3. *Give credit for staff accomplishments.* Never allow the misconception to remain that an employee's achievements or ideas were those of the administrator.

4. *Be an understanding supervisor.* Attempt to see situations from the employee's perspective. Be sensitive to what is happening in his total job and life at that moment in time.

All managers must remember that they are responsible for a job far too big for them to accomplish alone. They can only achieve success through effectively motivating others to perform the necessary job tasks.

Occasionally it is necessary to reprimand an employee. This can be thought of as negative motivation. Typically threats, corrections, and expressions of displeasure are necessary either to ensure acceptable employee behavior or to communicate expressions of inadequate performance.

Reprimands should be factually based and directed at the act or behavior, not at the individual's personality. Statements such as "you are a poor worker," "you have no commitment to the organization," "you just don't measure up" or "you are a poor reflection of our team" attack the person rather than the undesirable behavior. Attempts to describe the specific behavior as undesirable usually prove more productive. Some examples might be: "we expect all our staff to be at their work site by 8:00 a.m."; "office staff shall refer all questions from the media to the sport information office; never comment on player-coach conflicts." These statements focus the criticism on the behavior rather than the personality of the employee. The tone and emotionality of the reprimand should be sincere, controlled and factual. Often reference to policy, procedures or job specifications is all that is necessary to remind employees of their expected performance. It is unnecessary and often unproductive to "blow-up" or show excessive emotionality.

Reprimands should generally be given in private. They should be rather short in duration but should allow the employees an opportunity to express their side of the issue. Often it is a desirable practice to begin by asking the employee to explain the situation from his viewpoint. Once the reprimand has been given, the supervisor should not hold the incident against the employee on future occasions unless the same mistake is repeated. The manager might wish to monitor the recently reprimanded behavior with the goal of reinforcing the new, desired behavior, when it is exhibited. This will help solidify this behavior and provide the employee with the feeling that the supervisor does notice when the job is done correctly.

§ 1-14. Personnel Records.

A personnel file should be established as a depository for all pertinent information concerning the employment status and productivity of each employee. These files serve the purpose of recording all aspects of employment status including: position title, contract provisions, an accounting of benefits, accumulated sick leave and vacation time. The files often also include sufficient personal information to enable the organization to contact the employee at home, to notify his physician, spouse or next of kin in an emergency and to complete required social security, income tax and other salary-oriented financial matters.

The personnel file may also serve as a record of the employee's significant accomplishments, and as a documentation of any disciplinary actions which may have been taken. This latter use is especially important when justification may be required in a case of dismissal. Normally all official performance appraisals should become a part of the employee's personnel file.

Personnel files are considered confidential. Care should be exercised to protect the confidentiality of the employees. It is general practice that only an employee's supervisors have access to personnel files. Employees are usually permitted access to their own files, upon request. In some specific instances, evaluation materials which are a part of the employee's personnel file or personal notes made by a supervisor may not be made available to the employee. Most organizations establish guidelines for the handling and accessibility of personnel files.

§ 1-15. Resolving Conflict.

Whenever a group of people work together toward a goal there exists considerable possibility for differences of opinion as to means for goal achievement and the definition of roles. This is especially true when one employee's work relies heavily on the previous performance of other employees. The personnel of sports organizations are typically achievement-oriented, strong-willed leaders who are required to interact on many matters. These organizations will produce multiple opportunities for conflict situations.

Many potential sources of conflict exist in any organization. The most common conflicts exhibited in sport organizations are conflicts which occur between athletes and coaches, between coach and administrators and between two coaches or two athletes. Clearly defined job descriptions and lines of authority will eliminate many potential conflicts; however, disagreement will still result from unclear expectations, reliance on others and interpretation of goals, policies, practices and assignments. Many other conflicts result from behavioral or personality factors which one employee finds offensive in another employee. Techniques utilized when conflict exists among two persons of equal status in the organization (i.e., two assistant coaches or two athletes) may be different from those used in situations involving different status levels. In all instances, attempts should be made to reach a solution at the lowest appropriate administrative level. If satisfactory resolution is not achieved, then higher administrative levels may be involved.

One technique for resolving conflict is nonaction; that is, simply ignoring the problem and allowing employees to work out their differences. This is sometimes appropriate in minor conflicts which are simply the result of someone having a bad day. The administrator cannot become involved in every minor conflict which may surface. In many instances, all that is needed is a little cooling-off time or space for the employees to resolve their own conflict. This does not imply that all conflicts should first be ignored, but rather, that many minor problems work themselves out if given a little time. However, it is often unlikely or impossible for the involved employees to solve major or long-standing conflicts without assistance from a supervisor or another uninvolved employee.

The most obvious method for quick resolution of a conflict is administrative decree. The administrator simply uses the formal power of position and dictates how the problem will be resolved. This option has the benefit of a rapid response and may be most appropriate when direct violations of policies and procedures are involved. Since this process does not directly involve the conflicting parties in the resolution process, it may create resentment, feelings of unfair treatment and arbitrariness which could contribute to future conflicts or reduction in job performance.

A more people-oriented approach to conflict resolution involves bringing the parties together, hearing both sides of the issue and attempting to come to a rational solution. Various alternative solutions might be discussed and the consequences of each noted. The process often results in a compromise in which both parties give in and also gain something. One advantage of this process is the heightened awareness of the position and role of each of the conflicting parties. Often, as they become aware of the other person's situation, a compromise solution is apparent. This process can also have long-term positive benefits due to greater understanding and empathy among the employees. If the administrator is not directly involved in the conflict, he can act as the negotiator or arbitrator in the resolution of these disputes. If the conflict is an administrator-employee conflict (or coach-player) the basic process of talking through the situation and seeking alternative solutions acceptable to both parties remains a possibility. In these instances, it may be helpful to involve a third party who is not directly affected by the situation as an additional source of input and to provide an unbiased viewpoint.

There remain situations in which compromise is either not possible or is clearly inappropriate. In these instances, the conflict must still be resolved and the administrator must take the initiative to implement decisive action to correct the situation. It is likely that one or both parties will be unhappy with the resolution, but for the good of the organization, some resolution is necessary. Unpleasant feelings will be lessened if the parties feel that the administrator has been open and fair in reaching a decision.

In even the most harmonious organizations, conflict situations are to be expected as employees interact to achieve their individual roles. The administrator should help foster a climate in which conflict resolution is viewed as a positive process resulting in more satisfied employees and enhanced organizational effectiveness. Staff members should be encouraged, in fact, expected, to suggest potential solutions to the problems and conflicts which arise. This is an obvious technique for requiring people to think through the problem and how a potential solution will affect others. In addition to identifying alternative solutions, this demonstrates to employees that they do have input into the decision-making process.

It is important for employees to identify areas of conflict and for administrators to attend to the prompt resolution of conflict situations. Ignoring conflict and allowing it to fester will cripple an organization and result in an eventual eruption of negative feelings and behaviors.

§ 1-16. Summary/Conclusion.

Personnel management is a challenging area of supervisory responsibility. It represents the heart of the organization since productivity relies primarily upon the individual achievements of the staff of the organization.

Efficient organizations are characterized by:

1. Clearly articulated goals, lines of authority and well-defined job descriptions.
2. Carefully selected and trained employees.
3. The regular use of performance appraisals which provide both feedback as to accomplishments and a focus for future actions.
4. Employees who are motivated and challenged to complete their assigned tasks.
5. The ability to resolve personnel conflicts in a manner which fosters individual and organizational growth.

Appendix 1

JOB DESCRIPTION

Job Title: Equipment Manager

Primary Duties:

1. Devise and administer a procedure for distribution, collection and control of all athletic equipment and supplies.
2. Conduct an annual inventory of equipment and supplies.
3. Order all regular inventory items in a timely manner to prevent depletion of stock.
4. Assist coaches in orders of special equipment needs.
5. Supervise the maintenance of and records of all vehicles.
6. Accommodate special equipment and supply needs of visiting teams and for special events.
7. Supervise locker room and equipment room staff.
8. Supervise laundry and laundry room staff.
9. Work directly with the business manager in preparation of all equipment purchases.
10. Other duties as assigned by the Assistant Director for Operations.

Appendix 2

MANAGEMENT BY OBJECTIVES (MBO)

DATE:

Job Title: Business Manager   Supervisor: Athletic Director

Priority Objectives   Evaluated 3-6-9-12 Months

1. Keep all accounts posted to enable up-to-date budget reports on the 19th of each month.   3—6—9—12

2. Prepare monthly reports showing current receipts and projected receipts for the remainder of the year. Identify the source of any projected receipts which were unrealized.   3—6—9—12

3. Prepare a budget for the upcoming year showing total expenditures no greater than 5% above the current year.   9

4. Make all disbursements within 30 days of billing.   3—6—9—12

5. Monitor all major categories of the budget monthly and anticipate if fund transfer will be necessary. Clear all transfers with the Director.   6—12

6. Supply monthly budget summaries to each head coach.   6—12

Appendix 3

BEHAVIORALLY ANCHORED RATING SYSTEM (BARS)

Job Title: Ticket Clerk
* Job Dimension: ticket sales to public
Rating: Typical Behaviors

1. Customer is greeted with pleasant "hello, may I help you" or similar greeting. Clerk recognizes many customers. Clerk smiles at customer. Tickets are prepackaged and arranged for quick service. Offer is extended to show location of seats. Each customer thanked. Obvious effort is made to move line fast if people waiting. Special requests are handled in a responsive manner which does not significantly slow service to others.
2. Opens window on time, has tickets arranged and cash box prepared. Is generally helpful. Makes change correctly and quickly. Moves line rapidly.
3. Clerk performs all assigned duties but does not go out of way to be helpful. Is occasionally rude or curt with customer. Does not generally greet customers or thank them. Makes no special effort when lines are long.
4. Does not help other clerks when they are busy. Takes extended breaks. Has trouble balancing cash box. Fails to exhibit helpfulness or efficiency.
5. Customer must request service. Clerk chats with friend or on phone while customer waits. Clerk is disorganized and often late in opening. Unfamiliar with stadium seating.

---

*Ticket sales to the public is only one dimension of the total job. Others might include: record keeping, telephone orders, office security, etc. A separate BARS would be developed for each of the job dimensions.

Chapter 2

TIME MANAGEMENT

By

William Brooks

§ 2-1. Introduction.

Effective time management is the single, most-critical skill that a success-ful sport manager can develop. The surprising thing is that very few professional preparation programs for any field of endeavor deal with the topic of time management to any great depth or length.

Success in a well-managed sports program or well-administered business need not be measured by the finite number of hours that one invests on a daily basis. What really counts is how the minutes, hours and days are maximized for peak output. The effective use of time is the key to administratively competent, professional, technically proficient and educationally meaningful programs.

§ 2-2. The Pareto Principle (The 80/20 Rule).

The Pareto Principle implies that 80% of one's results comes from 20% of one's activities. The famous 80/20 rule that "those critical elements in any set usually constitute a minority of elements" is absolutely critical to any meaningful discussion of time management. If one could consciously devote 80% of one's time to the accomplishment of activities that have a value of 80% (those activities required to accomplish clearly defined objectives), one could achieve peak effectiveness at least 80% of the time.

If the day is filled with too many items having a value of 20%, there will not be enough time to work on those activities with a "payoff" of 80%. It makes sense, therefore, to concentrate on those few activities that will yield 80% of the results. An incredible amount of the time every day can be spent on trivia unless the following single, straightforward statement is asked: "What is the payoff of this activity, 80 or 20%?"

§ 2-3. Developing Positive Habits.

Planning and managing time in a daily, weekly, monthly and yearly basis is nothing more than applying self-discipline to develop positive work habits. It is essential to determine the status of current work habits and resolve every day that time will be used wisely. With practice and self-discipline, effective time management can become a positive habit enabling the sport manager to become the master of his/her destiny.

§ 2-4. Guidelines for Time Management.

A. *Setting Objectives.*

In time management it is essential to set objectives to know what is to be accomplished. Objectives must be specific and measured on a quantitative basis. John Billing describes goal setting as a popular management technique in "Management By Objectives" (MBO). The principles of MBO, Billing notes, can be utilized in the process of time management. "This system incorporates the setting of specific goals or objectives to be accomplished, specifies an appropriate time frame and evaluates staff effectiveness based on the degree of goal attainment." He continues by saying that: "The management by objectives format serves to focus the employee's efforts on what management considers to be the most important functions (objectives) and emphasizes measurable results as the basis for success."

Billing concludes:

> Management by objectives does not deal directly with the employee's specific behaviors or the means that may be used to accomplish the objectives. Rather, desirable goals are identified and the employee is allowed the freedom of various means of achieving these goals. Often an employee, such as an assistant coach or fund-raiser may appear busy all the time with piles of work, but in reality, little is actually accomplished. Management by objectives forces the employee to focus on the end results, the accomplishments.

For example, a sport manager may establish an objective to involve no less than 70% of all students in the intramural program by March 30 of a specific year. It is critical that these objectives are realistic, placed in a time frame (the March 30 deadline for intramural involvement fits nicely here), and attainable.

It is important that objectives are compatible with one another and, perhaps most importantly, are recorded. Written objectives tend to be attained on a more regular basis than those committed to memory. There is a tendency to forget things entrusted to memory and remember those that are recorded, written and placed in front of one on a daily basis. In short, there is difficulty in remembering things not known.

It is helpful to identify those specific activities that must be undertaken, on a step-by-step basis, so that each objective can be reached. Related items should be grouped together and ranked in priority order. For example, group together academic concerns, facility matters, staffing and staff developments, personal development, long-range planning and public relations in order of importance.

B. *Planning.*

Once the goals and objectives are set, it is necessary to develop a plan to implement them. The difference between success and failure is often the use of time through planning. Planning is nothing more than looking ahead in a systematic way. The paradox is that most people simply do not plan. There is a significant difference between planning and scheduling since a plan tells what is to be done while a schedule tells when it will be done. Sound advice, therefore, suggests that nothing is planned unless the time in which it is to occur is scheduled. Most positive things, as a rule, do not happen by accident. They are generally planned and the more carefully they are planned the better the results.

Plan, think, organize, direct, control and manage time. Remember to review the day at its end and set objectives and priorities for the next day. Write out a daily to-do list and at the end of the week write out a weekly plan. Within that plan build in specific periods with a personal priority system. The plan should then be placed where it can be seen.

C. *Eliminating Major Time-Wasters.*

Interruptions that steal time are led by meetings, telephone calls and drop-in visitors. No single profession is exempt from poor use of time. Sales groups, service organizations, educational administrators, the legal profession, manufacturers and hundreds of other groups all join the sport manager in facing this staggering group of time-wasters.

D. *Meetings.*

It seems that administrators at all levels spend an inordinate amount of time in meetings although many meetings are a complete and total waste of time. Several practical suggestions may prove helpful in reducing the ineffectiveness of meetings.

1. All meetings should begin and end on time.
2. There should be a prearranged agenda distributed prior to the meeting with each agenda item given a specific time for discussion.
3. Certain questions should be asked before any meeting is held, such as: "What is the purpose of this meeting?"; "What will it solve?"; or "Can it be solved with a memo or telephone call?" Individuals should ask "What can I contribute to the meeting?" "Why have I been invited?"
4. If there is little reason to attend, ask to be excused.

E. *Telephone Calls.*

Most telephone calls have very little to do with anything except asking trivial questions, socializing and stealing valuable time. Unfortunately, many managers presume that persons are calling for legitimate reasons, when, in fact, they are calling for exactly the opposite reasons. Needless to say, many of the reasons for the telephone calls are things that are not related to high-priority items.

It is important to set certain hours to take incoming telephone calls. Train a secretary, work-study student, graduate assistant or even fellow administrators to screen incoming calls. Watch a clock during calls to hold "on the phone" time to an absolute minimum. Return all calls at a specified time, plan calls in writing, and try standing while on the telephone.

F. *Drop-In Visitors.*

Most drop-in visitors, like telephone calls, have little to do with high priority matters. Too often the visitors talk about the latest staff gossip, job openings, or other unimportant items. To keep those interruptions to a minimum, try some of these tips:

1. Meet visitors outside the office, stand up if they should enter the office and simply escort them out the door;

2. Don't be afraid to close doors occasionally;
3. Remove extra chairs from the office; and,
4. Go to the other person's office for meetings.

G. *Allow for Unscheduled Time.*

Activities should be scheduled around key events by limiting or completely avoiding spending time on those activities that are not related to the attainment of predetermined objectives. Allow sufficient time to think, plan, reflect and organize. Ideally, it is good practice to allow between 25 and 40% of every day to unscheduled time to handle crises and emergencies that inevitably arise despite one's best intentions.

H. *Record Every Activity.*

A time log or time record is the best way to objectively determine how one *really* spends time. This exercise is admittedly time-consuming and can appear to be burdensome and painstaking. At times it may even take one longer to record actual time use than it takes to carry out the function one is recording. It is absolutely imperative, however, that one conducts a time log for a one-week period several times a year to determine if work habits need changing. The time log records every activity, no matter how trivial, and is the only way to develop an accurate awareness of the use of time. One cannot wait until noon to record what one did all morning or wait until evening to remember what was done in the afternoon. For many people, a day-to-day log of actual time use is quite revealing and, in many instances, shocking. Rank each activity by importance, identifying each interruption and its specific source and content. Many sport managers conduct a time log during peak periods and again in off season. This gives an accurate evaluation of time utilization at varying periods under different conditions and pressures.

At the end of each day, when the log is kept, review the log and ask several questions. "What time was the task completed?" "How many times, and for what reasons, was it interrupted?" "What was the most productive and least productive period of the day?" "Why?" "Who or what activities can be ignored, delegated or eliminated?"

The real key is to stop a dozen times a day and ask if what is being done at the moment is the most productive and the thing that needs attention. "Is the activity a high-priority activity?" "Is it related to a high-priority objective?" Do not confuse activity with productivity by getting caught up with the trivia that can engulf and limit potential results and professional growth.

I. *Provide a "Quiet Hour".*

There is an old adage in time management that says, quite simply, "As the first hour goes, so goes the rest of the day." Unfortunately, many people tend to use the important first hour on very low-priority items such as drinking coffee, reading newspapers, shuffling papers and other unimportant matters. The more one accomplishes by noon, the greater the opportunity to have a productive day. Many successful sport managers develop a daily habit of setting aside a large block of uninterrupted time. This is often referred to as the "Quiet Hour" when there are no telephone calls, drop-in visitors, meetings or other distractions. It is amazing how the "Quiet Hour" can lead to the achievement of the really important things (primary objectives). Research reveals that the average manager is interrupted every six to nine minutes of the working day. It is estimated that it takes three times as long as the actual interruption to get back in track if one gets back at all. The use of the "Quiet Hour" can maximize time needed for important tasks.

J. *Evaluating Work Habits.*

Make a concerted effort to evaluate the job's functions very critically. Identify those activities, both productive and nonproductive, that need attention on a daily basis and analyze the amount of time that is spent on each function. Many administrators find, when they evaluate their job-related habits, that they are devoting much of their time to relatively unimportant tasks by attempting to do more than it is possible to get done.

§ 2-5. Summary/Conclusion.

It is essential that the sport manager remember that all of us have time allotted in equal amounts. Time cannot be purchased, marketed or saved; it can only be spent. The secret, then, is to make the use of time a positive expenditure by disciplining oneself to develop positive time-use habits. A professional cannot afford to give it away cheaply or frivolously. By a system of evaluation, the sport manager can attempt to determine positive habits and incorporate them into a plan for a set of objectives for which one is accountable. In many ways successful sport managers do the things that the rest of us never got around to doing. Time management can become a positive habit that will build confidence and lead toward professional and capable leadership.

Chapter 3

STRESS COSTS AND BENEFITS

By

Lynne Gaskin

§ 3-1. Introduction.

The event in our arena wasn't over until almost midnight last night and an elderly woman fell down the stairs as she was leaving. It was almost two o'clock before I got home. The alarm didn't go off this morning, and then my dog ran off when I let her out. By the time I had captured her and had finished dressing, I was late leaving the house. The fuel indicator on the car was below "E", so I had to stop for gas and got in line behind three people using credit cards.

Walking into the office 45 minutes late, I'm confronted with a memo to return a call from the lawyer representing the woman who fell last night, the maintenance engineer who tells me our cooling system is malfunctioning, an audit showing our profits are down, and a reporter who wants to interview me about our security during the fight which broke out at the end of the regional basketball game yesterday afternoon. Just as I am ready to begin confronting these situations, my secretary rushes in to let me know that the tickets for next week's game have been printed incorrectly and hundreds of people are downstairs waiting to purchase these tickets which go on sale in two hours.

As I pace the office trying to decide what to do first, I can feel my heart thumping, the dryness in my mouth, the general weakness in my body, and the nervous twitch in my left eye. I feel sick to my stomach, and my head is pounding. I have an overpowering urge to run out the door.

The previous account is a vivid description of stress — too much stress — built up to the point of becoming harmful (distress). Such reaction to acute or chronic stressful situations is predictable and results in the "fight or flight syndrome" so appropriately labeled by the Harvard physiologist Dr. Walter B. Cannon. When we are confronted with situations which require adjustment in our behavior, we undergo this involuntary, but predictable response. We experience an increase in our blood pressure, heart rate, rate of breathing, metabolism, and blood flow to the muscles preparing us to fight or run.

In the days of our primitive ancestors, it was appropriate for man to deal with enemies by fighting or running away in order to survive. Today's rational man, experiencing the same fight-or-flight response, has no such alternative. However, he must learn to use the response to his benefit or ultimately experience chronic health problems and job inefficiency.

§ 3-2. Understanding Stress.

We all have experienced stress and know something about its origins and effects. Some stress is necessary to function at one's best, but there is an optimal level of stress for each person. Stress becomes a problem when it becomes too severe and when one feels that he has lost control over his life.

Individuals react differently to stress and need different techniques to relieve distress. Each person should determine his optimal level of stress and develop techniques for relieving distress. There is no universal formula available. Each of us has to know himself — what stressors affect him most adversely and how to deal with them effectively to function at his optimal level.

Stress cannot be viewed solely as a negative factor, for different people react differently to similar situations. A flat tire on a school vehicle may be perceived as an unfortunate occurrence and as an inconvenience to the bus driver, but to the coach whose team is on the way to an important game it is a stressful situation. The key aspects are perception and mental appraisal. What may be viewed as stress by one person may be viewed even as vitalizing for another. A snowstorm may be perceived as a harrowing experience by the sport manager with 200 boys and girls in attendance in his gymnasium for a youth soccer clinic, but it may bring a sense of euphoria to the downhill skier. Regardless of the stressor, when stress becomes excessive or builds up over a period of time, reduction in a feeling of well-being or lowered job effectiveness may result.

Stress should not be viewed solely as a personal problem, but rather as a managerial challenge for each person. Half the problem in managing stress is identifying the causes. In today's society of accelerated pace and change, technological advancement, and instability in economic and educational systems, the more fully we can understand the meaning, causes, and symptoms of stress, the better prepared we will be to use it to our advantage — both in our personal and work environments (as a manager and as an employee). The goal, then, is not to avoid stress but to understand it, consider how it affects us adversely, and determine how to control potentially stressful situations.

There are several key areas to consider. One's personality and lifestyle habits are highly related to how one perceives stress and is affected by it. Assessing the stressors in one's life, recognizing the high costs of stress, and formulating a plan for reducing the harmful effects of stress are paramount in successful stress management.

§ 3-3. Assessing Personality.

Many forms of stress are rooted in personality. An important first step in managing stress is to acknowledge that one's personality is the key to how he reacts to stress and that some of us may actually create too much stress for ourselves. A person with a Type A personality is described as relentlessly driven, restless, impatient, irritable, aggressive, competitive and overly ambitious (Ref. 1). This individual has a compulsion to overwork, is always confronting time deadlines, and often neglects other aspects of his life such as family, social occasions and recreational activities. In contrast, Type B personality types are easygoing, relaxed and patient. They are less competitive, less achievement-oriented, less hurried and more likely to engage in leisure pursuits.

What type personality best describes you is an important question to consider. You may have a good indication from the previously mentioned characteristics, but stop now and respond to the checklist below. You might as well start right now to learn more about yourself and your ability to handle stress.

ASSESSING PERSONALITY TYPE

(Ref. 2)

Yes	No	Don't Know		
___	___	___	1.	I'm frequently in a hurry.
___	___	___	2.	I'm typically doing several projects at the same time.
___	___	___	3.	I'm always pushed by deadlines.
___	___	___	4.	I usually take on as many (or a few more) projects as I can handle.
___	___	___	5.	I really seek recognition from my boss and/or peers.
___	___	___	6.	I believe it's important for a person to push herself or himself for success, and I seek opportunities for promotions and advancements.
___	___	___	7.	I enjoy competition in all areas.
___	___	___	8.	I really enjoy winning and hate to lose.
___	___	___	9.	My job is the most important thing in my life.
___	___	___	10.	I sometimes feel I neglect my family by putting my job first.
___	___	___	11.	I'm usually too busy with my job to have time for many hobbies or outside activities.
___	___	___	12.	When I'm given a job, I really feel personally responsible for its success — i.e., even though others may be involved, I feel that it just won't come out as well unless I'm personally involved from start to finish.
___	___	___	13.	I have trouble trusting people easily.
___	___	___	14.	I tend to talk fast.
___	___	___	15.	When speaking, I believe in giving special emphasis to my meaning with strong vocal inflection and gestures.
___	___	___	16.	I feel some impatience in most meetings and conversations — I just wish they would speed up and get on with it.
___	___	___	17.	I tend to get irritable and lose my cool easily when obviously simple things don't go right.
___	___	___	18.	I make a list of things I must get done each day.
___	___	___	19.	I generally have strong opinions on most things.
___	___	___	20.	I don't seem to get much time to keep up with my reading.

If you answered yes to at least 15 of these statements, you probably are falling into the Type A behavior pattern.

It is important to recognize that a person's work environment often encourages and rewards the Type A behavior. Even more important, however, is the point that employees with Type A traits are approximately three times more likely to have heart attacks than employees with Type B traits. Type A individuals, of necessity, must gain control over their own lives in order to reduce their stress level and find the optimal stress level where they function best. Otherwise, they are prime candidates for heart attacks. Of utmost importance is the fact that behavior is learned and can be modified. The first step, however, is to identify those aspects of one's behavior which he wants to change and then begin focusing on those areas with specific plans for accomplishing change.

§ 3-4. Lifestyles.

In addition to considering basic personality type, one must consider stress and his ability to manage stress in regard to lifestyle habits. Smoking, drinking and eating in excess, irregular exercise, improper nutrition, inadequate relaxation and inability to talk with others openly about problems or concerns are just a few of the health behavior problems which can contribute to poor health and chronic stress. Obviously, these behaviors must be addressed honestly and a decision made to regulate those perceived to be most hazardous to one's well-being. Each person must face these himself, for no one can improve another's health. One may seek the help of others, both personal support and professional assistance, to help effect change in any of the areas mentioned or in others; but, ultimately, each individual will decide whether he will attack these concerns and what techniques are most beneficial for him.

Specific steps are necessary in managing stress related to lifestyle. Identify those lifestyle habits which need change. Share concerns with a member of the family, a close friend, or a colleague at work. Determine the best approach to attack the problem and solicit another person's support to help break the habit or at least get it within the realm of reasonable control. As is the case with personality and behavior, lifestyle habits are learned and can be modified.

§ 3-5. Assessing Stress.

There are many assessment scales which have been developed to determine degrees of stress. Managers and employees who are interested in further information should consult some of the better known instruments. Probably the best known and most frequently cited assessment is the Holmes and Rahe Social Readjustment Rating Scale (1967) developed to measure the impact of life change events.

A shorter and more easily scored way of assessing one's vulnerability to stress has been developed by Lyle H. Miller and Alma Dell Smith, two psychologists at Boston University Medical Center. Consider each item and score it from one to five according to how much of the time each statement applies to you.

ASSESSING YOUR VULNERABILITY TO STRESS

(Ref. 3)

1 = Almost always
2 = Usually
3 = Sometimes
4 = Rarely

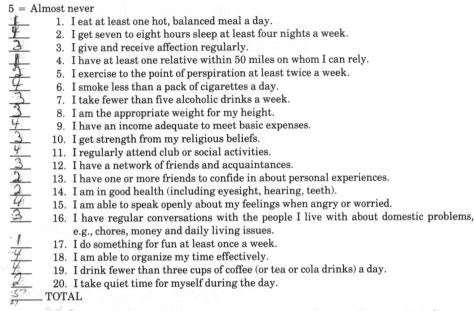

5 = Almost never

1. I eat at least one hot, balanced meal a day.
2. I get seven to eight hours sleep at least four nights a week.
3. I give and receive affection regularly.
4. I have at least one relative within 50 miles on whom I can rely.
5. I exercise to the point of perspiration at least twice a week.
6. I smoke less than a pack of cigarettes a day.
7. I take fewer than five alcoholic drinks a week.
8. I am the appropriate weight for my height.
9. I have an income adequate to meet basic expenses.
10. I get strength from my religious beliefs.
11. I regularly attend club or social activities.
12. I have a network of friends and acquaintances.
13. I have one or more friends to confide in about personal experiences.
14. I am in good health (including eyesight, hearing, teeth).
15. I am able to speak openly about my feelings when angry or worried.
16. I have regular conversations with the people I live with about domestic problems, e.g., chores, money and daily living issues.
17. I do something for fun at least once a week.
18. I am able to organize my time effectively.
19. I drink fewer than three cups of coffee (or tea or cola drinks) a day.
20. I take quiet time for myself during the day.

TOTAL

To get your score, add up the numbers and subtract 20. Any number over 30 indicates a vulnerability to stress. You are seriously vulnerable if your score is between 50 and 75 and extremely vulnerable if it is over 75.

§ 3-6. Costs of Stress and Techniques to Manage Stress.

The costs of stress are real threats to the effectiveness of any organization. School systems, recreational programs, community agencies, and other such groups of people who sponsor sports programs are all affected adversely by stress-related cost — absenteeism, high turnover in personnel, alcoholism, depression, medical costs, job dissatisfaction and even lowered job effectiveness. Stress has been related to many diseases and physical ailments. Among the most commonly mentioned are coronary heart disease, asthma, arthritis, neckaches, backaches, tension headaches, migraine headaches, allergies, kidney problems, indigestion, insomnia, diabetes mellitus, ulcers, high blood pressure, constipation, muscle spasms, sexual difficulties, diarrhea, muscular tension and even cancer. Managing stress effectively can help prevent many of these job-related ailments.

There is no evidence that sports managers and others working in sports programs are any more susceptible to chronic stress than others in similar non-sport positions. There is also no evidence to indicate that sport personnel are any less susceptible. It is acknowledged, however, that the higher number of interpersonal relationships a person encounters in his work, the more likely stressors will present themselves (Ref. 4). People who work with things such as computers, typewriters and other similar types of equipment will not experience the same kind of stress nor the number of stress-related situations as those whose work involves consistent interaction with people — participants, coaches, spectators, officials, media representatives, salesmen, parents and other members of the public who are consumers of sports programs. Sport managers, beware!

No one way to manage stress is best. Each person must determine the best technique for himself and his life. Assessing one's personality and lifestyle is mandatory. Equally important is learning about and engaging in interventions to help take control of one's own body. Based on personal interest and preference, one should at least consider engaging regularly in physical exercise, progressive relaxation, meditation, rhythmic breathing, self-hypnosis, biofeedback or autogenic training. The bibliography at the end of this chapter provides a good resource list for more extensive coverage of these techniques and others which one might choose to incorporate in his life. All these techniques are self-regulated and will not be effective unless the individual is motivated and chooses to practice them consistently.

Whether a sport manager is employed by a college or university, public or private school system, community agency or municipal complex, he must work with others to get the job done. Every sport manager will encounter some stress and can use it to his advantage to become a more effective and efficient manager of both sports and stress. The key to stress management within the organization (regardless of the type of work situation) lies in clearly defining the workload, accepting responsibility for those things which can be controlled, and striving to enhance interpersonal relationships.

The implications are clear for the sport manager and employee. The effectiveness of the organization is undermined drastically when those who plan, organize, conduct and assess sports programs are subjected to excessive stress in the work environment. Conscientious attention must be given to help all workers meet such situations head on.

Sport managers who are directly responsible for others working within the organization should consider specific tactics to help employees function under less stressful situations.

1. Identify a specific job description for each employee. Delineate exactly what the job is and what is expected of the employee.
2. Set up conferences with employees to discuss their goals for the year, job satisfaction and dissatisfaction, and suggestions for constructive change.
3. Give employees who are changing their job focus time to retool or retrain so they can move into the new job with confidence.
4. Encourage employees to express their opinions openly and give them the rationale for your decisions.
5. Involve employees in decision-making and change.
6. Give employees consistent feedback for successful job performance as well as unsatisfactory performance.
7. Encourage employees to develop strong on-the-job support systems.

The sport manager who incorporates these concerns will help employees function more effectively and perceive their job as a constructive and satisfying part of their lives. Each sport manager should carefully examine his own situation and develop managing techniques to fit the specific job-related stressors of his organization.

Although the sport manager must be concerned with helping employees manage their stress, his first responsibility is to himself. No manager can work effectively with others until he has learned to function at his own optimal stress level.

The goal of the sport manager is to gain control of his own life and in turn to convert potentially stressful situations or conditions to his advantage and to the advantage of his employees. There is no doubt that a wise sport manager can gain a definite advantage by learning how to handle stress effectively. Many stress-laden areas can be avoided by anticipating and planning for them.

1. Establish realistic personal goals and reorganize your life. Prioritize!
2. Identify the job-related situations which cause you the most stress.
3. Pace yourself and manage your time wisely.
4. Determine the stress reduction programs or stress management techniques that work best for you and use them consistently.
5. Recognize the limitations of management. Hire competent employees and delegate responsibility.
6. Be assertive and learn to stand up for yourself. Act in your own best interests as you continue to be concerned with others. Maintain a strong support network.
7. Take time for yourself.
8. Accept the uniqueness of your situation and make things work for you and your employees.
9. Be concerned about the well-being of employees.
10. Use stress positively by working together with employees to meet deadlines.
11. Seek your own stress level and live accordingly.

One can and should anticipate stressful situations in the work environment. How can one "work smarter" and counteract the effects of too much on-the-job stress? Burke (see Ref. 5, cited in Adams, pp. 170-71) surveyed a large number of managers, and the ten most frequently mentioned responses to job stress were identified. These responses were later ranked by managers according to frequency of use to protect their health when under stress. The five most effective coping strategies with the fewest symptoms of chronic ill health associated with them were related to "working smarter" — building resistance through healthful lifestyle habits, compartmentalizing work life and home life, engaging in regular physical exercise, talking it through on the job with peers and withdrawing physically from the situation. Five other strategies were identified as effective in coping with job stress but were less effective in regard to the number of chronic symptoms of ill health associated with them — changing to engrossing non-work activity, talking it through with spouse, working harder, analyzing the situation and changing strategy and changing to a different work task.

Regardless of one's personality, lifestyle habits, and assessment of stressors, each person must take responsibility for managing his own stress and cannot let others manage his stress level for him. A sense of control over one's own life is the central purpose in managing stress effectively.

§ 3-7. Summary/Conclusion.

The single, most-important factor in producing harmful stressful situations is the individual's perceived loss of control of his own destiny. Managers and employees not only can tolerate stressful situations, but can actually function effectively in potentially stressful environments. To function effectively, however, they must know that the situations and conditions are under their control.

There are several points which sport managers must consider. Become aware of what causes stress in your life and take the initiative to control your own stress. Stress reduction involves observable action. Practice stress reduction techniques and take more responsibility in managing your own stress. Recognize your needs and be realistic about your abilities. Be alert to ways in which your body reacts to stress, be aware of situations which produce these reactions, and take appropriate steps to protect your health and life.

The initial scenario described in this chapter depicts a vivid picture of harmful stress and a situation in which the sport manager had lost control in regulating stressful situations. How would the description have been different for the sport manager in control of his life?

> The event at our arena wasn't over until almost midnight last night and an elderly woman fell down the stairs as she was leaving the facility. By the time our emergency medical team had completed their report and we had made sure the woman wasn't seriously injured, it was almost two o'clock before I left the building. Knowing I would be working late last night, I had arranged to go in later this morning so I didn't set my alarm. Since the dog scampered over to the neighbor's yard again when I let her out and I had to stop for gas on my way in to the office, I called my secretary to say I would be later than I had expected. Also, I wanted to know what had happened thus far at the office.
>
> My secretary is quite good at his job and always follows the procedures we have established to help us function more effectively. He related several occurrences to me over the telephone.
>
>   1. The lawyer representing the woman who fell last night has already called to inquire about our medical procedures and to ask when it will be convenient for him to come over to check lighting and exit routes.
>   2. Our cooling system is malfunctioning. The maintenance engineer has ordered the necessary equipment and will have it installed by noon.
>   3. I have an appointment at 11:00 with a newspaper reporter who wants to discuss the fight which broke out yesterday afternoon. Fortunately, we have an alert security force, but we do need to be more attentive to groups once they leave the building and are out in the parking lot.
>
> On the way in to the office, I have to stop for gas and am glad to have the extra time to gather my thoughts about how I will respond to the reporter. Also, I want to be sure to commend our medical team, our maintenance engineer and our security force for their effectiveness and

efficiency. I do have to make sure, however, that the security force is aware that they should have been able to prevent the disturbance in the parking lot before it occurred. I will ask them to come up with recommendations for avoiding such situations in the future.

Walking into the office, I am greeted by my secretary who informs me that the tickets for next week's game have been printed incorrectly and hundreds of people are downstairs waiting to purchase these tickets which go on sale in two hours.

I can feel my heart rate speed up, the dryness creep into my mouth, and the twitch start in my left eye. Asking not to be disturbed for ten minutes, I go into the office, close the door, sit down in the chair by the window and begin my deep breathing exercises. It's amazing how much better I can think after I have regained control over my body.

REFERENCES

1. M. Friedman & R.H. Rosenman, *Type A Behavior and Your Heart* (New York: Alfred A. Knopf 1974).

2. M.C. Giammatteo & D.M. Giammatteo, *Executive Well-Being: Stress and Administrators* (Reston, Virginia: National Association of Secondary School Principals 1980). Used by permission of the authors and the publisher.

3. L.H. Miller & A.D. Smith, "Vulnerability Scale," *Stress Audit* (Boston, Massachusetts: Biobehavioral Associates, 1983). Used by permission of the authors and the publishers. Also located in C. Wallis, "Stress: Can We Cope?," *Time* 48-54 (June 6, 1983).

4. R.C. McSwain, "Stress Management: A Burnout Prevention Technique" (paper presented at the meeting of the Southern Association of Physical Education For College Women, Gatlinburg, Tennessee, October, 1982).

5. *Understanding and Managing Stress* (J.C. Adams ed. San Diego, California: University Associates 1980).

Part 2

PROGRAM MANAGEMENT

Chapter 4

SCHEDULING FOR INTERCOLLEGIATE SPORTS

By

John Swofford

and

Patricia Miller

§ 4-1. Introduction.

Effective scheduling is a distinguishing characteristic of every successful athletic program. This is the case because scheduling impacts upon every aspect of the athletic operation. Unless high agreement between the mission of the various teams and schedules generated is obtained, the athletic department will suffer the consequences of less than adequate performance. The success level of each team rests, in part, on the construction of a well-planned schedule.

At the Division I level of intercollegiate athletics scheduling of major spectator sports is vital to the welfare of all programs conducted by the athletic department. One reason for its importance is that football, and in some instances basketball, in most institutions must not only be financially self-sustaining but must also generate funds needed for other sports. Without successful football and basketball financial stability will be virtually impossible to achieve. Scheduling also impacts upon recruiting, post-season competition, championship possibilities, season ticket sales, contributions from the private sector, student interest, faculty support and institution and department images. Consequently, it is imperative that administrators be adept at handling the requirements of scheduling for the athletic program.

Returns to be realized from scheduling are neither limited by sport nor level of play. However, returns are not likely to materialize for any sport, department or institution unless the athletic director has planned carefully and practiced skillful implementation of the plans. The principles to be applied to scheduling are basic and universal, and are thus applicable to programs of varying magnitude, including programs that have profit-making sports, revenue generating sports, nonrevenue-producing sports, and women only, men only, women and men, varsity, junior varsity and club teams. This chapter is devoted to a discussion of those things that are necessary to the development of an organized and effective approach to scheduling for intercollegiate athletics.

§ 4-2. Philosophy and Policies.

Philosophy and policy provide the beginning place for any and all matters related to scheduling. Both may be set by the board of trustees, an athletic board, the president, or left to the discretion of the athletic director. It is essential that statements are established and that they are available in writing. The authority for the statements must be documented.

The philosophy makes clear the place of the athletic program within the institution. What is to be accomplished through athletics and why the things being sought are important to the welfare of the institution are questions that, when answered, create a framework for addressing scheduling and other matters. The philosophy will also bring institutional expectations into agreement with conference and National Collegiate Athletic Association (NCAA) or National Association of Intercollegiate Athletics (NAIA) regulations.

Policies provide guidelines that address the specifics of actions. They exist within the framework established by the philosophy. Policies act to further define the approach to scheduling and set standards to work with while making the schedule. Policies should include specific guidelines as to finance (e.g., a minimum guarantee requirement for away games, or the maximum guarantee for home games); home and away balance (e.g., always play at least six home football games, but not more than seven); types of opponents (e.g., a Division I basketball school may have a policy of scheduling only Division I opponents); geography (e.g., an East Coast team may have a policy of not traveling beyond the Mississippi River for an away contest); academics (e.g., not playing during an exam period); and time (e.g., some institutions will not play a night football game at home).

Institutions that are similar in approach to athletics will often have similar policies. However, each institution is unique and will therefore have policies particular to its needs. Policies cannot cover every circumstance and a mechanism needs to exist for the athletic director to deal with situations that are not addressed in the formal statement. This mechanism could range from simply exercising the use of judgment to gaining the approval of the president or athletic board. This, of course, is an institutional matter and should be known to the involved individuals.

Following are samples of institutional policy questions that might be addressed by the athletic director:

1. What is the standard of competition for each program? What is the expectation level of success at the conference, regional and/or national levels?
2. What is the participation level? What combination of intercollegiate varsity and junior varsity as well as club teams is the institution willing to support?
3. What are the financial parameters governing the construction of the schedule?
4. What geographical/travel limitations exist? Are there conference affiliations to be considered? If an institution supports junior varsity or club teams, are their geographical and travel limitations different than those for varsity teams?

5. What is the policy governing the mode of transportation utilized for trips? Does this policy vary from sport to sport?

6. Is it necessary or desirable to arrange schedules to enable two different teams from the same institution to travel together to a common opponent?

7. Relative to some sports, is there a limit on how many contests per week are academically permissible? Is there a difference or a preference for weekday versus weekend day contests?

8. Are contests permitted or prohibited during final examination periods?

9. Are contests permitted to be scheduled during vacation periods which fall within the athletic season?

10. Are teams who qualify permitted to participate in post-season championship competition? What are the ramifications if post-season participation falls during exams or after the academic year is concluded?

If an institution is a member of a conference, there will most certainly be guidelines and agreements relative to scheduling that should be understood by those making the schedules. Likewise it is quite important for the athletic director to be aware of scheduling parameters set forth by the national athletic governing body to which the institution belongs.

§ 4-3. Roles of Athletic Director, Scheduler, and Coach.

The director of athletics is the institutional officer responsible for enforcing all policy relative to athletics. Where scheduling is concerned the task is to generate instruments (schedules for the various sports) that will aid the department in fulfilling its mission, while following practices that are in complete agreement with policies.

The athletic director is also the chief administrative officer of the athletic department. As such, he heads a staff that has vested interests in the schedule. In the case of coaches, the schedule impacts upon the status one enjoys as a professional. While all coaches recognize the importance of the schedule to their welfare, concepts of how best to use the schedule to advantage differ greatly. Another difficulty is that on occasion coaches will insist upon scheduling practices that serve self-interest at the expense of departmental welfare.

The vast majority of athletic directors actually arrange the schedules. At some institutions scheduling responsibilities are handled by an assistant athletic director or by a scheduling officer. No matter the title of the scheduling officer, functions performed are the same. The basic arrangements are as follows:

1. Schedules for revenue-generating sports are handled independently of scheduling for other teams. This method requires much communication and coordination between coaches of revenue-generating or profit-making sports and the athletic director.

2. Depending on the structure and the needs of the department, the assignments for scheduling men's sports may be handled by one department

administrator while the scheduling of women's sports is handled by another department administrator. Again, coordination and communication are necessary.

3. Some athletic departments schedule by utilizing a single scheduler. From a coordination and consistency standpoint this system works well and is dependent upon the administrative structure.

Whatever the mode of scheduling used, it is critical that final approval rest with the athletic director.

Communication between coaches and the athletic director or scheduler is a very important aspect of the scheduling process. Working within the established policy guidelines the athletic director/scheduler and coach should discuss several questions prior to the construction of the schedule. Notes of the conversations should be made part of the scheduling file.

Information gathering sessions should resolve the following matters:

1. What facility considerations exist? Is the facility shared by men's and women's teams, varsity and junior varsity teams? What other programs utilize the facility; e.g., recreational or physical education? If the facility is shared, what priorities for usage have the department or institution established so that equity exists and conflicts can be avoided?

2. What are the goals of the program? These should be incorporated in department policy and reflected in the schedule. A large majority of contests should be scheduled within the division declaration of the institution. How many contests, if any, should be scheduled in a different division? If scheduling against a lower-division opponent, how strong is the opponent? What effect would a defeat to a lower or higher-division opponent have on the team ranking, and on morale?

3. What days of the week are preferred for scheduling of contests? Is spectator attendance an important factor and how is it affected by day or time of contest?

4. Should contest days and times be consistent from week to week? Do the athletes on the team tend to have one day per week when it is better not to schedule contests because of academic reasons; e.g., labs or classes?

5. Does the institution have a policy about scheduling a contest on the Sabbath?

6. Is Monday a good day to schedule a contest, particularly if it follows a weekend of no competition or practice?

7. Should longer trips be scheduled on weekends in order to cut down on missed class time?

8. What are the vacation periods and holidays that fall during this season? How should the schedule relate to these?

9. When is the first permissible contest date of the season?

10. What opportunities and possibilities exist for post-season competition at the conference, regional and national levels? Some schedulers prefer to plan from the end of the season and work forward from that point.

11. Which opponents should be scheduled early in the season?

12. How should the strong opponents be spread throughout the season?

13. What kind of home and away balance is desired?

14. How does a long trip affect the next competition? What are the considerations of a long trip and how should long trips be balanced from year to year?

15. What considerations exist for contest starting times?

There are three occasions when basic schedule considerations might be discussed between the athletic director and coach. Prior to the schedule-making process, which is during the early fall of the preceding year, scheduling strategies should be planned. Once the schedule has been developed, prior to the budget process, which is usually before the close of the first semester, a second meeting to discuss any divergence from the original schedule plan should take place. If possible, an evaluation at the end of the season of schedule considerations by the coach with the scheduler can assist in an improved schedule for the future. It is extremely important that coaches understand, appreciate, and accept the fact that final decisions rest with the athletic director. Encouragement of involvement in planning should never be handled in ways that would suggest the transfer of responsibility for the entire schedule or any part of it to a coach or to coaches. However, without meaningful involvement of coaches in the planning the idea of schedules that are acceptable to both athletic director and coach cannot be attained.

§ 4-4. Characteristics of a "Good" Schedule.

A good schedule is the end result of meeting the stated philosophy and policies of the institution. Thus, a good schedule for one institution may differ from that of another institution. Even at the same institution, good schedules vary according to sport.

At the University of North Carolina, a good (ideal) football schedule is one that accomplishes the following:

1. Includes all members of the Atlantic Coast Conference (ACC), seven games;
2. Includes four non-conference games that encompass:
   a. one probable win,
   b. one or two top-twenty-type opponents,
   c. one or two respectable opponents that have name identification and are toss-up competitive situations;
3. Includes six home games;
4. Generates maximum financial rewards;
5. Includes at least four games that are potential television possibilities;
6. Includes no more than two games at home or two games on the road consecutively;
7. Creates fan interest;
8. Gives a fair chance to:
   a. have a winning season,
   b. win the ACC championship,
   c. receive a bowl invitation;
9. Includes opponents that have reasonably similar academic standards;
10. Is reasonable in terms of travel;

11. Maximizes geographical exposure, institution and individual players; and

12. Contains no more than one open date after the initial game and concludes before Thanksgiving.

The basketball scheduling philosophy for the University of North Carolina involves a similar approach, with emphasis on travel for recruiting purposes (basketball travel is much less expensive than football on a per-trip basis because of sheer numbers) and a national flavor because of the unusual national basketball tradition that the University of North Carolina enjoys. Academics and class time missed become greater factors in basketball scheduling because 28 games are played, many of them during the week. Agreement with the policies of minimizing class time missed can be accomplished while emphasizing appealing and educational travel by working this travel into vacation periods and by chartering return flights when necessary rather than waiting for commercial flights. These strategies keep players on campus during academic sessions and return them quickly to campus if classes are meeting.

By playing two "home games" per year in two different cities in North Carolina two objectives are satisfied. Gate receipts are increased and those parts of the state have an opportunity to see the team play. This arrangement has become even more necessary because of continued sellouts on campus.

§ 4-5. Time-Frame for the Completion of Tasks.

If meetings between the athletic director and coach take place in the early fall, construction of the schedule should occur through the fall and be ready for the budget process in December. Good knowledge of the budget is necessary so that the athletic director can work within its parameters and avoid difficult schedule changes after commitments have been made.

An aid to planning is a time-frame for the completion of tasks. Items to be included will vary according to requirements that are specific to the institution and department but the following notations are likely to appear.

1. September	With basic knowledge of the budget, athletic director meets with the coach to discuss the schedule for the following year.	
2. Oct.—Dec.	Athletic director contacts opponents to negotiate and firm-up the schedule.	
3. December	Second athletic director-coach meeting to review the schedule. For budget purposes the schedule for the following year is basically intact.	
4. Jan.—Feb.	January is generally a difficult time to contact other athletic directors. During the end of January and the month of February, the athletic director negotiates any minor changes agreed upon when meeting with the coach.	
5. Feb.—April	Finalization of the budget.	
6. Feb.—April	Firm-up and completion of junior varsity and club team schedules.	
7. April—May	Mail out contracts for entire year.	

§ 4-6. Mechanics of a Sound Schedule.

Organization is the key to success in almost any administrative function. Scheduling is no exception. Scheduling is a complex task and to complete the task successfully it is important to keep sound records of ideas, thoughts, phone calls, correspondence, future schedules, agreements to play and contracts. The first step is to develop a list of possible institutions which would help meet the objectives of your scheduling philosophy and policies. Then, put together sample "ideal" schedules which fit objectives using the institutions listed. It will take time to generate "ideal" schedules but identifying teams that satisfy selection requirements will greatly ease and facilitate planning. Once the possibilities have been examined and preferences determined, the next step is to establish contact with administrators at other institutions. If time permits, initial correspondence by mail is one approach. The telephone is a more effective tool plus it saves time. It has the added benefit of permitting discussions with other athletic directors about various "what-if" situations, objections and complications which are everyday problems in the scheduling process. Notes should be made on each telephone call. An administration principle to adhere to when scheduling is to follow all verbal agreements in writing. Standard scheduling procedure is that once an agreement is met, a contest contract is issued by the host institution to the opponent, which is in turn signed by the administrator of the opponent and a copy returned to the host. It is also important to remember that time and date changes made verbally after the initial contract is signed should be followed up in writing.

An important skill for a good scheduler to develop is negotiating ability. A spirit of cooperation and compromise is essential. It is often not possible to construct the perfect schedule, but the closer to the ideal one comes, the higher the return to the program.

A record of contracts sent, received and returned should be maintained. It is important that before a contest takes place, both institutions possess a copy of the contract. Some institutions prefer to send a form to the opposing institutions stating that a contract has either not been received or returned for X contest, approximately one month before the start of the season.

Because there are many people and various operations within the athletic department and the institution who deal with the athletic schedule, many athletic departments develop a day-by-day schedule after the schedule has been completed and distribute this to all who work with athletic teams. Day-by-day schedules should be sent to coaches, other athletic administrators, equipment managers, travel personnel, sports information, operations and maintenance directors, the ticket office, university or college information office and anyone else who should receive such information.

If a schedule is well-planned and well-negotiated, schedule changes will be a rarity. There are times for various reasons that a change in date or time is requested and the scheduler is responsible for negotiating these changes. If such a change occurs after the schedule has been published, it is necessary to alert those involved of the exact change. It is probably appropriate to notify all those who received a day-by-day schedule in addition to the officials.

As correspondence, notes from telephone conversations, agreements to play and eventually contracts develop, it is critical to have an organized system for detailing this information. A dual-file system provides a particularly useful solution. One system would have a file for each institution contacted with regard to football and basketball — an institutional football scheduling file as well as an institutional basketball file. For example, the "Florida State-Football" file would include a complete history of correspondence, phone calls, notes, agreements to play and contracts — past, present and future — between the University of North Carolina and Florida State University in football. The "Kentucky-Basketball" scheduling file would contain the same for basketball. This type of information is invaluable. One file drawer is maintained for each sport and as new institutions are added to the schedules, new files are created. In addition, a contract-file system is established for each sport for the current year plus one year in advance. Example: the 1984 football contract file would contain all 11 contracts for the 1984 football season. Copies of these 11 contracts would also be in the 11 institutional files referred to above. This system provides both a history of scheduling discussions as well as a cross check of contracts by institution and by season. Therefore, it is easy to check the scheduling processes for a particular institution or summarize the contracts for an entire season.

As automated systems develop, some of which are specifically designed for intercollegiate athletic programs, some of the above information could be kept in a computer rather than in a file cabinet, although filing of certain written documents may remain necessary.

Establishing a system to organize your schedule for current and future years is a must. Long-range scheduling forms developed by Ernie Casale, former Athletic Director at Temple University, assist greatly in the accomplishment of this task. These forms are designed so that you can get a complete long-range view of your schedules over a period of years. Corresponding dates are also easy to spot from one year to the next. It is helpful to have your own code to insert into the forms beside each institution that is listed in a particular date. This code would include home (H), away (A), or a neutral site (N), plus the status of the agreement: Agreement to Play (A), Contract Sent (CS), Contract Complete (CC) — meaning the contract has been completed and signed by both institutions.

Completed forms are important records, making them a source of valuable information. Four copies should be maintained. One is kept in the athletic director's master schedule notebook in the office; another is on file with the athletic director's secretary; the third copy is passed to the director. Because of the ongoing nature of the scheduling process, the fact that athletic directors travel extensively and the fact that scheduling opportunities often come up while at NCAA conference or committee meetings, a fourth copy of the long-range schedules should be kept in the briefcase. Its availability makes it possible to take advantage of unexpected opportunities.

The final "closing the sale" aspect of scheduling is the contract itself. It should be signed and dated by the appropriate representatives of each institution, then filed in the dual-filing system and properly coded on the long-range scheduling forms. A checklist for what needs to be included in a basic football agreement includes:

1. dates the agreement is entered into;
2. site of game;

3. date of game;
4. time of game;
5. eligibility regulations of participants;
6. financial agreements, including date visiting team will be paid;
7. auditing requirement;
8. complimentary ticket arrangements for both teams;
9. number of sideline passes for both teams;
10. number and location of visiting teams;
11. how home students and faculty will be included in the game financial audit;
12. admission of band and cheerleaders;
13. control of ticket prices;
14. admission of game workers;
15. radio broadcast agreements;
16. programming concession rights;
17. game officials;
18. special event rights (e.g., Band Day, if any);
19. additional games to be played as part of the original contract agreement;
20. conditions of failure to comply with the contract; and
21. additional miscellaneous agreements.

Financial terms of the contract are, of course, very important. This may be a flat guarantee, a percentage of the gross (usually after a 15-20% operating expense has been deducted for stadium operations), or a minimum guarantee against a percentage of the gross. Whatever the agreement, it should be spelled out specifically and precisely so that problems or misunderstandings do not occur later. People change positions, and particularly with football where scheduling is often done as many as ten years in advance, it is important that all aspects of the contract be established so that it will be clear to all parties whether or not administrative changes take place.

The long-range scheduling of football games requires that tentative arrangements be completed. It is impossible to know what economic and other conditions will be five or ten years in the future. Therefore, for games scheduled that far in advance, an "Agreement to Play" is used instead of a contract. This is done in letter form and simply states the dates that the two institutions are to play and indicates that a contract specifying the financial and other terms will be negotiated within two years of the event. This agreement is then filed accordingly, and the event listed and coded on the long-range schedule.

Basketball contracts are usually shorter, but should be just as precise. A checklist for what needs to be included on a basic basketball agreement includes:

1. dates agreement is entered into;
2. site of game;
3. date of game;
4. time of game;
5. eligibility regulations of participants;

6. financial agreement and date visiting teams will be paid;
7. complimentary ticket arrangements;
8. number of seats for team parties;
9. officials' agency to make the assignment;
10. radio broadcast agreements;
11. television broadcast agreements;
12. conditions for failure to comply with contract; and
13. any miscellaneous additional agreements.

Although basketball games are generally not scheduled as far in advance as football games, agreements to play may also be used here. Guarantees are normally considerably less in basketball on a per-game basis, but the same options exist in basketball as in football — for a flat guarantee, a minimum guarantee against a percentage of the gross, or a pure percentage of the gross.

In the Atlantic Coast Conference (ACC), for example, there is no exchange of money for conference basketball games; the home team keeps all receipts. In football, it is a minimum guarantee against a percentage of the gross in the ACC.

Schedules for the entire department are maintained in a schedule book. The layout styles of schedule books vary from institution to institution. Some athletic directors prefer the entire season of one sport on one page, others would rather see all sports for a one-month period on one page. The style and organization are decisions for the athletic director to make based on what works best for him or her.

Usually, one task of the scheduler is to provide for assignment of officials. Some sports are assigned officials through the conference, if the institution is a member of a conference. Some officials are assigned via a regional bureau. If neither conference office nor regional bureau exist, the host institution is responsible for securing the game officials.

As in all other aspects of scheduling, it is imperative to follow up all communication to officials' office or bureau with written confirmation of contest date, time, place and any change in plans. The fee-structure should be established and other required plans in place for expediting payment for service and reimbursement for expenses.

The development of a good schedule requires good planning, good communication and attention to detail. The greater the number of sports to be placed on the calendar, the more important these elements become. It is possible for a scheduler to accomplish this task well, especially if he or she works diligently within a planned, reasonable timetable.

§ 4-7. Importance of Sound Scheduling.

Revenue from football and men's basketball generates a large percentage of the total revenues of most intercollegiate athletic programs. Therefore, successful scheduling should maximize those revenues. However, maintaining balance in scheduling will best benefit a program over the long term. Far too often certain programs, particularly football, have scheduled strictly for dollars with little regard given to overall opportunity for success on the field over the course of a season or several seasons. Maintaining a balance of financial rewards and giving the coach and team a reasonable opportunity to enjoy a successful year will benefit a program more over time than "over-scheduling" from a competitive standpoint simply to balance the budget. This is not to minimize the importance of revenues but is offered to propose that a program will be better off over the long haul by playing balanced schedules. The risk in "over-scheduling" for tremendous financial reward is that the number of victories will be reduced. Consequently, over a period of time the recruiting effort will probably suffer — thus leading to weaker teams. Attendance will probably suffer, eventually reducing revenues. Opportunities for post-season competition will suffer, thus reducing revenues, exposure and recruiting benefits. Contributions may fall and fan interest may diminish. In short, "over-scheduling" for immediate financial reward may be necessary at times, but if continued it can send a program into a negative spiral that can have devastating effects.

Scheduling can also affect recruiting. Success begets success and if the schedule doesn't afford an opportunity to be successful and consistently losing seasons are experienced it will be difficult to attract top recruits. On the other hand, if the schedule is not attractive enough — and other schools have an advantage over you in terms of travel to attractive sites and/or competing against name opponents — recruiting can also suffer.

§ 4-8. Summary/Conclusion: Why Some Administrators Are Better Than Others at Scheduling.

All administrators are not equal in terms of scheduling. Some are better than others and there are reasons for this. What do administrators that are good at the scheduling process do that others do not do? Characteristics that set apart successful schedulers from other administrators are as follows:

1. They and their institutions have a known and specific philosophy and set of policies. These serve as guidelines in the scheduling process. It is not a hodgepodge, but a systematic approach.
2. After the philosophy is established they make it a workable and active philosophy in following the policies consistently.
3. They work at the scheduling process on an *ongoing* basis. It is a never-ending puzzle.
4. They give it high priority and much time realizing the ramifications are extremely important.
5. They work with their coaches. It is important for a coach to have input into the scheduling process. In today's high pressure world of major college athletics, his job may well depend on scheduling decisions. It is important for the coach and athletic director to understand each other's concerns and thinking when developing a schedule.

Chapter 5

FINANCIAL AFFAIRS

By

Al Rufe

§ 5-1. Introduction.

Management of financial affairs for an intercollegiate athletic program has two important dimensions. One is to oversee disbursements thereby making certain that each operational unit does not exceed in expenditure its budgetary allocation. A second function is development of a budget that will make it possible for the entire athletic program to realize the highest return on monies that are available.

Preparation of the budget is the creative part of the business manager's job. When effectively accomplished, the business manager not only expands the purchasing power of the entire program and each of its operational units, but also greatly eases the task of overseeing disbursements. It is for this reason that a discussion of financial management should begin with the consideration of those elements that impact upon costs.

§ 5-2. Institutional and Departmental Policies — Employment and Travel.

The financial manager must know institutional regulations as they apply to financial affairs. The following are actual examples of state, university and departmental policies that govern an intercollegiate program.

A. *State Policy.*

State law in Massachusetts regarding travel per diem dictates that:

> When a person is engaged in travel, reimbursement shall be allowed for actual meal expenses incurred, including tips, not to exceed the following: Breakfast, $2.50; lunch (mid-day meal) $4.00; supper (evening meal) $7.00.
>
> For travel of one day's duration starting two hours or more before regularly scheduled workday, the person subject to these rules will be entitled to the breakfast allowance. For travel of one day's duration ending two hours or more after regularly scheduled workday, such person will be entitled to the evening meal allowance. In no event will the midday meal be allowed for travel of less than twenty-four hours duration. Voucher must state hour of departure or return as well as a statement giving the regularly scheduled work hours. Normal work day is considered to be 8:30 a.m. to 5:00 p.m.

The law is specific and dictates the dollar per diem limits for staff travel. It is much easier to project per person travel expenses when specific limits are set. It is equally helpful to audit and review expense accounts when detailed policies are in force.

45

If the institution does not have specific travel policies for staff travel, it is recommended that a policy be developed and implemented, if only for the sports department. The results will produce solid fiscal control, substantial savings and in general will make fiscal management much easier.

B. *Personnel Policy.*

Personnel policy regarding employment security requires that:

> Members of the professional non-academic staff and coaches who are employed full-time in permanent positions, whether funded from state appropriations or continuing trust funds (i.e., a trust fund without a terminal date) will be eligible for contracts of increasing duration after a reasonable period of satisfactory service to the University. Based upon this policy, an employee can normally expect to be eligible for the following as a normal practice.

NORMAL PRACTICE

Years of Satisfactory Service	Duration of Next Contract	Notice of Reappointment/ Non-Reappointment*	Minimum Notice of Resignation
0	1 year	3 months	30 days
1	1 year	6 months	60 days
2	2 years	6 months	60 days
4	3 years	6 months	60 days
7	5 years	12 months	90 days

*Stated in months prior to expiration of then current contract; these are minimums and may be increased if appropriate.

This policy deals with the length of employment contracts and has a significant effect on the department's personnel budget. It allows the fiscal officer to accomplish short- and long-range salary planning at a glance.

C. *Policy Regarding Team Travel for Athletics.*

The Athletic Department at The University of Massachusetts/Amherst has established policies that regulate critical aspects of team travel. The statement has a major impact on the entire intercollegiate athletic budget.

POLICIES GOVERNING TRAVEL FOR INTERCOLLEGIATE ATHLETICS

SIZE OF PARTIES

Baseball, Varsity	25	Gymnastics, Varsity-Women	12
Baseball, JV	21	Lacrosse, Varsity-Men	36
Basketball, Varsity-Men	18	Lacrosse, JV-Men	27
Basketball, Varsity-Women	18	Lacrosse, Varsity-Women	21
Cross Country, Varsity-Men	14	Lacrosse, JV-Women	18
Cross Country, JV-Men	12	Ski, Varsity-Men	11
Cross Country, Varsity-Women	14	Ski, Varsity-Women	10
Field Hockey, Varsity	20	Soccer, Varsity-Men	25
Field Hockey, JV	16	Soccer, JV-Men	22
Football, Varsity	64	Soccer, Varsity-Women	25
Football, JV	55	Softball, Varsity	22
Golf, Varsity-Men	8	Swimming, Varsity-Men	22
Golf, Varsity-Women	8	Swimming, Varsity-Women	22
Gymnastics, Varsity-Men	15	Tennis, Varsity-Men	12

Tennis, Varsity-Women	13	Track, Outdoor, JV-Men	17
Track, Indoor, Varsity-Men	32	Track, Outdoor, Varsity-Women	32
Track, Indoor, JV-Men	17	Volleyball, Varsity	15
Track, Indoor, Varsity-Women	32	Wrestling, Varsity	15
Track, Outdoor, Varsity-Men	32	Wrestling, JV	12

CONSTITUENCY OF PARTIES

1. Travel party includes coaches, players, equipment personnel, managers, trainers, physicians when necessary.
2. Lodging, meals and transportation will be budgeted according to travel squad figures.
3. The above limits do not apply to championship play.
4. The above limits do not include van drivers.

CHAMPIONSHIP EVENTS

	14	Men's Varsity Programs
	14	Women's Varsity Programs
Total:	28	Varsity Programs eligible for national championships
	8	Men's Junior Varsity Programs
	2	Women's Junior Varsity Programs
Total:	10	Junior Varsity Programs

A financial manager must know or at least be familiar with all the institutional policies and regulations that regulate the programs the manager is dealing with if he or she expects to be an effective manager.

§ 5-3. Insurance.

A financial manager must find out the types of insurance coverage that exist in the institution. The financial manager must be aware of the types of insurance coverage the student-athlete must have before the school will allow the student to participate in intercollegiate athletics.

A. *Basic Health Plan.*

Basic health coverage is provided by the University Health Services. The Health Center is funded by a mandatory student fee paid by all undergraduate and graduate students. The Health Center provides medical, mental health, dental and health-education services to students when they are on campus, protecting the community health through detection and treatment of communicable diseases.

B. *Supplemental Health Plan.*

The Department of Athletics requires that student-athletes have comprehensive medical insurance coverage before they may participate in the athletic program. Since the University's basic health plan does not provide total coverage for athletic injuries, the student-athlete must have additional medical coverage. The additional medical insurance requirement may be satisfied by subscribing to either the University Supplemental Health Benefits Plan, or the student-athlete's own (family) health insurance plan, e.g., Blue Cross/Blue Shield.

If the student chooses not to purchase the University's optional supplemental health plan, the department requires that the student complete the student health insurance affidavit.

Many athletic departments purchase injury medical coverage for all athletes, thus eliminating the concern for supplemental health plans. One is available through the National Association of Collegiate Directors of Athletics (NACDA). The underwriter is the Continental Agency Company.

At the University of Massachusetts/Amherst (UMA) the broad-based intercollegiate athletic program, including 28 varsity sports, makes it impossible for the Athletic Department to provide medical insurance coverage for almost 1,000 student-athletes. However, for full scholarship athletes, the department does purchase the UMA supplemental health plan.

C. *Travel Insurance.*

Most athletic departments provide travel insurance for intercollegiate teams. The NACDA Insurance Administrative Office also provides travel insurance for intercollegiate teams. This includes coverage for "bodily injury caused by accident . . .

> While in a conveyance and being transported in a group to or from a practice session, provided that a group is under the supervision and personal direction of a coach, manager, or other duly authorized representative of the insured person's institution or team; or
>
> While on a trip to or from an intercollegiate athletic contest in which he is participating other than as a spectator; or
>
> While on a trip authorized by the insured person's institution for the purpose of furthering the business of the organization authorizing the trip." (NACDA Student-Athletes Travel Accident Insurance).

The cost for this type of coverage varies according to student-athlete's gender and whether the participant is of varsity or junior varsity status.

It should be noted that most commercial carriers do provide substantial travel insurance for their passengers. *When you secure transportation for team travel, require that the vendor have adequate insurance coverage.* Minimum coverage that will be accepted should be established.

D. *Liability Insurance.*

In a day of unprecedented sports litigation, it is essential that members of the athletic department be protected by liability insurance. Many institutions provide liability coverage for all employees. If the institution does not provide adequate coverage, management should make certain that staff obtain necessary coverage. This is frequently accomplished by the addition of relatively inexpensive riders on existing policies. In some instances a $1,000,000 umbrella coverage with a $300,000 deductible provision can be secured for less than $150 per year.

§ 5-4. Inventory of Equipment and Supplies.

It is important to keep detailed records of all equipment and supplies. Information should include quantity on hand, date and source of purchase, and a yearly update of all capital equipment that was purchased or discarded.

This is a detailed and time-consuming task for which many departments have turned to computers.

Inventory records are important for the following reasons:

1. To justify the purchase of new equipment and uniforms by knowing the age, purchase date, conditions and holdings in inventory;
2. Use inventory control to keep stock at a minimum thereby reducing risk of loss through theft; and
3. A good inventory control system will assist the financial manager in determining what type of equipment and supply purchases can be delayed or omitted in the upcoming fiscal year.

§ 5-5. Purchasing.

During the course of a year most financial managers have to purchase a large dollar value of sports equipment, supplies, and capital equipment. Needless to say, it is extremely important to purchase these items at the lowest possible cost.

A central purchasing department facilitates purchasing procedures. Costs are reduced through volume purchasing and practices systematized. In one state the restrictions and assists are as follows:

1. All items costing $500 or more must be put out on competitive bid.
2. Unless there are extenuating circumstances, all purchases of $250 or more must be put out to competitive bid.
3. In the case of emergency situations direct purchases may be made without a competitive bid being obtained with the approval of the purchasing office.
4. In a tie bid, the contract must go to the in-state vendor.
5. Bids received after the closing date are not considered. In fact, they are not even supposed to be opened.
6. All bids are public information and must be shown to any bidder upon request. This happens frequently, as many vendors want to know who they are bidding against and the competition's pricing strategy.
7. Sometimes a vendor will submit a bid on a substitute (different brand) item. If the substitute bid is the lowest and the department does not want to accept it, then a written justification must accompany the purchase order, indicating why the low bid is unacceptable. It is good practice to require the coach or equipment manager to prepare the justification, as these individuals usually submit the equipment recommendations.
8. All purchases must be made using university purchase orders.
9. Except for extenuating circumstances, confirming purchase orders are not permitted. This policy is designed to eliminate the chance of duplicate orders being made either via the telephone or via a formal purchase order.
10. Regarding affirmative action goals, all departments are to purchase from small business and minority vendors, whenever possible.

Coaches should be given an opportunity to review equipment bids for their sport, particularly the uniforms. Once a coach approves an equipment or uniform item for purchase, the coach cannot question actions if he is not satisfied with the merchandise. The best example of the protection the practice provides took place several years ago when new University of Massachusetts/Amherst men's basketball uniforms were selected by the head coach. The results were disastrous, however, everyone suffered in silence because the coach had worked very closely with the salesperson in selecting the uniform specifications.

The financial manager's major role in purchasing is really twofold. One is to ensure that all items are purchased according to state and university policies. The second is to ensure that the purchases are within the set budget limitations. Many institutions do not have strict purchasing procedures. If they do not exist, formulation and institution of sound policies and specific procedures is a must.

§ 5-6. Team Travel.

Fifteen years ago the Athletic Department at the University of Massachusetts/Amherst (UMA) used rental station wagons and charter buses as the most widely used forms of team travel. Today at UMA, department vans, rental vans, charter buses and regularly scheduled airline flights are the normal modes of team travel.

In light of the high cost of rental vehicles and charter buses the department's five 15-seat passenger vans are scheduled as frequently as possible. In the 1960's, teams in baseball, field hockey, soccer, softball and similar sports were transported to contests in charter buses. However, today, unless trips involve more than two hours of travel time each way, the teams use the departmental vans. Additional sports such as cross country, golf, gymnastics, ski, swimming and tennis, all use department vans. This policy results in very significant savings, which allows the department to improve other programs.

Additionally, vans are used for spring-break training trips by baseball, men's and women's lacrosse and softball every year. The destination of these trips varies from Long Island to South Carolina.

Vans are popular with the coaches, particularly during championships or tournaments that are two or three days in length. Coaches find it much more convenient to have access to two vans rather than depend on a charter bus for local transportation once the teams arrive at the championship site. The introduction of the use of vans has greatly reduced the need to charter buses.

There are times, however, when charter bus transportation is either necessary or a more sensible kind of transportation. These times include busy weekends when all the vans are in use, bad weather, some long trips or when the cost of renting vans as well as the inconvenience of picking them up and returning them does not make it worth the department's time.

Since van travel is becoming more common in intercollegiate athletics, policies are needed to ensure that the most productive practices will be followed.

1. Some coaches prefer to drive. If a coach does not want to drive, student drivers are hired to drive the entire trip or some part of it.
2. Regular maintenance is a must for the vans and is most often performed at the University's garage.
3. If there is ever a question about the safety of a tire or any other part, it is replaced immediately, as safety is of the utmost importance.
4. When purchasing vans the dealer representative is asked to recommend equipment in terms of expected use; e.g., size of engine, heavy-duty shock absorbers, two 20-gallon tanks, front and rear heaters, among other choices.
5. During a national college athletic business managers meeting, the business manager from Louisiana State University mentioned that he always purchased vans stripped on the inside. A stripped van is without rugs, floormats or side paneling. Declining these options saves about $1,000 per vehicle plus it allows for easy cleaning. You can drive the van up on a curb and use a hose to wash out the inside of the entire vehicle.
6. Experimentation has shown that it is best to trade the vehicle in every three years or at approximately 60,000 miles. By trading in at this point, the maintenance costs and the chance of having vans break down — things which seem to occur more often after this point will be reduced. Additionally, the trade value is greatly improved. Coaches are also more receptive to using vans that are reliable.
7. The following are formal, standard operating procedures that should be followed in order for any program utilizing vans to be safe and organized:
   a. When a department van leaves the lot, the head coach is responsible for all vans assigned to the team, even if a student driver is also assigned to the trip.
   b. Safety requirements — if a coach or driver notices anything unsafe or any part that should be repaired, the situation should be reported *in writing* to the financial manager's office. *At no time should a coach or driver use any vehicle that is unsafe to transport student-athletes.*
   c. Department policy prohibits the use or transportation of alcoholic beverages in department vans.
   d. No tape or other material may be attached to van windows.
   e. Vans should be returned with at least three-quarters of a tank of gas. If it is impossible to fill up that day, then the vans should be filled up the next morning.
   f. Vans must be left clean after each use.
   g. Parking vans at individuals' homes is *prohibited* unless there is an unusual circumstance and permission is granted by the financial manager of athletics.

Adhering to the aforementioned policies is a significant part of every employee's job responsibility.

Air travel is becoming more prevalent. This is particularly so in the sport of men's and women's basketball. Arrangements are not easily made and virtually impossible to accomplish effectively if needs are handled through more than one office. The rule with air travel is to find a reliable agent and place all business in that office.

Instead of centralizing travel arrangements through the business manager's office the responsibility can be passed to coaches, particularly in the cases of football and basketball. Since these sports involve a great deal of compromising, as far as travel arrangements are concerned, and they have adequate manpower, it is usually better for all concerned if the staff for these sports make their own travel arrangements. Choices are made available to coaches following the receipt of bids from various companies. Proposed arrangements are approved by the business manager.

Occasionally, in the sport of football it becomes necessary to charter an aircraft. At UMA, our head football coach does not mind using regularly scheduled flights for travel to the opposing school. However, our coach wants to return to campus Saturday evening after the game rather than spend half of Sunday travelling home, when he could be reviewing game films. In this situation we very often have to charter a flight. In fact this was the situation in the Fall of 1983 when we played at Toledo in the evening. With no late night flights scheduled to land in the Hartford/Springfield airport, we were faced with having to charter a flight out of Toledo for our team. Sports Travel Inc. of Pittsburgh, Pennsylvania was contacted. Sports Travel is an agency that specializes in football charters and attempts to reduce costs by arranging for back-to-back charters, thus reducing the number of "dead-head" travel miles.

The following is an example that almost worked for a UMA/Toledo game. The situation was that Cincinnati was to play at Penn State Saturday afternoon, while UMA was playing at Toledo Saturday evening. The proposed charter arrangements required that the plane pick up UMA at the Hartford/Springfield airport Friday morning and transport the team to Toledo, Ohio. From there the plane would proceed to Cincinnati, Ohio to pick their team up and fly them to State College, Pennsylvania. The charter would stay in State College until after the Penn State-University of Cincinnati game was over from which it would then take the Cincinnati team home. The plane would then proceed to Toledo Saturday evening where it would pick up the UMA team and return it to Hartford/Springfield. Although the University of Cincinnati declined to participate in this joint charter, situations like this are arranged and produce significant savings.

§ 5-7. Budget Preparation (An Example).

Before an intercollegiate budget plan can be formulated, the athletic director or the athletic administration, including the individual responsible for managing the funds, the financial manager, must determine the departmental goals for the coming fiscal year. Examples of planned departmental goals would include: personnel needs, such as an academic counselor for all student-athletes; total program needs, such as a desired increase in the meal allowance for away contests; and individual program needs, such as the renovation of the basketball facilities.

Once the department's goals have been established, the financial manager's next step is to determine the department's total planned personnel cost.

The following items must be included in this determination:

1. What is the current salary cost of existing personnel?
2. What are the estimated salary costs of newly created positions?
3. What, if any, is the planned across-the-board cost-of-living increase? What is the effective date of this increase? Are there different percentage amounts planned for faculty, professional or maintenance staff?
4. What are the merit salary increase projections? What categories of employees are eligible for merit salary increases?
5. If faculty union or classified employee contracts are being negotiated during the budget preparation period, what salary increases or benefit changes do the institution's personnel office expect to be included in the new contract?
6. What are the projected changes in the cost of fringe benefits?
7. What are the potential personnel changes?

Many budget officers tend to focus only on projected salary increases. They should also be aware of changes in fringe benefit costs. A good example of a fringe benefit cost that was recently instituted at UMA for retiring professional staff employees is the payment to the employee of an amount equal to 20% of unused sick leave. Since retiring employees have normally accumulated a large amount of sick leave credits, the lump-sum payment of 1/5th of the unused sick leave can be very costly, and thus the financial manager must budget appropriately.

In the world of intercollegiate athletics unfortunately, because of the lack of program success, coaches are fired. In some cases a program's entire coaching staff (this could involve up to 10 coaches in football or 3 in basketball) may be terminated. However, while new staff are employed, already existing financial contracts must also be honored. Since coaches and professional staff at UMA are eligible for multi-year contracts based on the number of years of satisfactory service, (a policy referred to earlier in the chapter), the department's administration has to be very careful before issuing multi-year contracts. Thus, the budget officer must be kept informed of any possible terminations that may take place during the fiscal year in question.

It is impossible to emphasize enough the importance of proper personnel planning. An error or oversight in this major cost area could put the budget in a deficit position or at least reduce the budget reserves to the point where there is no flexibility to cover unforeseen situations. Personnel planning requires a great deal of research and communication between the athletic administration, the personnel office, and other appropriate parties.

Once the department's goals have been established and the estimated personnel costs have been determined, a program budget for each sport can be constructed.

It should be noted that the intercollegiate sport schedules have a major impact on the total program budget. The number of contests and distances traveled directly affect costs.

At UMA all intercollegiate scheduling rests with the Assistant Athletic Director/Business Manager. The arrangement permits planning in terms of budget and how much missed class time might be involved. If the budget officer is not involved in scheduling then he should work closely with the scheduling office to ensure that the department can afford the proposed schedule.

The best way to describe what is involved in the construction of an intercollegiate sports budget is to develop one by using hypothetical UMA varsity and J.V. football schedules.

The step is to cost-out the schedules (Appendix 1 at the end of this chapter.) which includes budgeting for officials, game operations, lodging, transportation, meals and guarantees.

1. *Officials.* — Each official receives $200 per game plus per diem and mileage.

Per diem equals $25 per official
Estimated mileage = 400 miles @ $.20/mile = $80.00
Per game cost = 6 officials x ($200 + $25 + $80) = $1,830.00
                          + clock operator @ $50.00
                          Approximate cost $1,880.00
          Rounded up to $1,900.00 per game.

2. *Game Operations* — Costs include security, ticket sellers, ticket takers, program sellers, ushers, overtime for equipment personnel, press box attendants, P.A. announcer and medical personnel.

3. *Lodging* — When estimating the cost of lodging, the same room rates are used for all sports unless the location of the event is in a high-cost area. Additionally, the cost of lodging is controlled by each sport travel squad, (as referred to earlier when discussing travel policy).

4. *Transportation* — When estimating transportation costs, use uniform bus and van costs for each destination regardless of sport. The following cost sheets were used by the UMA Business Manager in 1983/84.

BUS CHARTER COSTS

Destination*	Size of Bus 41	Overnight 41	Size of Bus 47	Overnight 47
Boston Area	$390	$560	$420	$590
Bradley Field	200	X	210	X
U. Connecticut	265	X	280	X
Dartmouth	500	X	530	X
U. Maine	X	1275	1350	X
Penn State U.	X	1650	1700	X
Philadelphia Area	X	1120	1175	X
U. Rhode Island	500	670	530	700
Rutgers U.	X	920	X	970
Worcester, MA	210	X	220	X

*by school name or city

TOLL AND GAS CHARGES

(per van from Amherst)

Destination	
Boston Area	$35
Bradley Field	20
Connecticut	25
Dartmouth	35
Penn State Univ.	125
Philadelphia Area	100
Univ. Rhode Island	40
Rutgers Univ.	70
Worcester, Mass.	30

Special situations do arise in which it is necessary to budget for charter flights. It should be noted here that when taking a plane, ground transportation costs must also be budgeted for.

5. *Meals* — At UMA the per diem meal allowance is $13.00 per day broken down into $3.00 for breakfast, $3.00 for lunch and $7.00 for dinner. Alternative allocation is an estimate of what it would cost to eat at the opposing team's dining commons. This gives the coach a choice to either make meal arrangements on campus and have the Athletic Department billed or have the cash handed out as a meal per diem. The only variations from this policy are department funded pre-game meals for men's and women's basketball and football, post weigh-in meals for members of the wrestling team, and a sit-down post-game meal for football, if the contest took place more than two driving hours away from campus.

6. *Guarantees* — On the 1-AA football level in New England for home and home series, guarantees normally involve just enough money to cover transportation, meals and lodging costs. If the game is scheduled with no return commitment, the guarantee normally covers transportation, meals, and lodging costs, plus a sum of money to compensate for the lack of a reciprocal date and the accompanying revenue it would bring to the institution.

Once the cost-out for the schedule has been completed, the next step is to transfer the totals to the summary page of the budget form. Once accomplished, cost estimates for items A to L on the summary page of the budget form can be calculated.

1. *Recruiting, scouting, etc.* — In the case of income sports, head coaches are asked to estimate how much money will be needed to meet recruiting and scouting goals. The request is to include the number of staff person-days on the road, the number of on-campus visitations, mailing, printing, telephone and other miscellaneous costs. If at all possible, the entire request is funded, but the expectancy is that the coaches will operate within the budget. As far as non-income sports are concerned, the same amount is budgeted for all these sports. The amount varies from year to year depending on the funds available. However, every effort is made to increase these budgets in order to keep pace with the competition and inflation.

2. *Dues* — At UMA the department pays for coaches' membership dues in National and Regional coaches' associations.

3. *Equipment* — After equipment and uniform needs are determined, the following format is used to summarize costs:

SPORT _____ 19___
BUDGET ALLOTMENT _____

Quantity	Brand & Catalog Number	Description	Previous Vendor	Unit Price	Total Cost
				$	

4. *Entry fees* — Entry fees are most common in the sports of golf, tennis, track and volleyball. These costs vary according to the type of event. They are estimated and placed on the schedule section of the budget form.

5. *Films.* — At UMA, all sports use videotape, except for football. A conservative football film budget is the 1983 estimate:

Spring Practice (April, May 1983):	
5 sessions - 2,465 feet @ $.33	$813.45
Intrasquad game April 30, 1983 — 985 feet @ $.279	274.82
Preseason (August, September 1983):	
4 sessions — total footage approx. 2,000 feet @ $.33	660.00
Regular Season (Sept., Oct., Nov., 1983):	
11 games edited to offense, defense, kicks.	
1,220 feet each game (2.95/ft), $359.90 per game	3,958.90
11 dupes, 1,220 ft. each (.192/ft), $234.24 per game	2,576.64
Two games in color (entire game from overhead plus 1/3 more footage roving sideline camera slow motion) 1,700 ft. each game including processing and 2 cameramen, $595.00 per game	1,190.00
Editing of color games into highlight films, $170.00 per game	340.00
11 Wednesday night practice sessions, total footage approx. 5,000 ft. @ $.33	1,650.00
Post season highlight film: editing of 11 black and white films (including checking and repair damages of original film)	280.00
Miscellaneous:	
Car mileage: approx. 2,590 miles @ $.21	543.90
Lodging at Toledo, Delaware, Lehigh	135.00
Meals	58.00
102 400 ft. color-coded plastic cans @ $.96	97.92
102 400 ft. solid-back plastic reels @ $.87	88.74
Contingency: (extra film game copy of special practices, etc.)	332.63
Total	$13,000.00

6. *Facility rental* — This category includes greens fees, indoor tennis courts and ski lift tickets. These costs will vary according to the facilities you have.

7. *Lodging and meals* — These costs involve the following categories:

   1. Team travel lodging (see the schedule section of the football budget form).

2. Pre- and post-game meals (see the schedule section of the football budget form).

3. Intersession meals and lodging — Many institutions have a long break between their first and second semesters.

   At UMA there is a five week break which puts a large financial burden on winter sports programs. In the case of revenue sports the Department pays for the meals and lodging of these athletes during the entire period. Currently, for nonrevenue sports, the Department is only able to fund meals for a two-week period. The allocation is calculated by using the travel squad x 14 days x a per diem amount. Charges for the men's basketball intersession meals and lodging costs totalled approximately $5,700, while costs for the track team's meals totalled $3,840.

4. Pre-season meals and lodging — At many institutions the department of athletics is charged for pre-season lodging and meal costs for its fall programs. At UMA the Department provides total support for football and one week of meal support for all other fall programs. The following was UMA's 1983 football pre-season lodging and meals budget:

Pre-Season Lodging:

Full nights August 18 - September 8	=	22 nights
90 persons x $5.50/night x 22 nights	=	$10,890.00
+ 20 freshmen x $5.50/night x 1 night extra	=	110.00
Total		$11,000.00

Pre-Season Meals:

90 persons x $10.00/day x 22 days	=	$19,800.00
+ 20 freshmen x $4.50 for one extra meal	=	90.00
Total		$19,890.00

It should be called to attention that the date of the first football game each fall has a significant effect on preseason lodging and meal costs.

8. *Personnel costs —*

   a. Coaching salaries — included are part-time coaching salaries in the individual sports budgets.

   b. Game operations — (see the schedule section on the football-budget form).

   c. Officials — (see the schedule section on the football budget form).

9. *Physicals* — At UMA preseason physical exams for all student-athletes are provided by the Health Services. However, the department is charged for the physical exam costs.

10. *Travel —*

   a. Bus/Van (see the schedule section of the football-budget form).

   b. Spring trip — At UMA the department funds a portion of the spring trip costs for the following sports: baseball, men's and women's lacrosse and softball. The allocation for each sport based on the following formula: travel squad x 9 days (spring break) x a per diem amount.

   c. Professional improvement — The following department policy state-
      ment applies to all full time professional staff:
         1. Full-time professional staff. Program head, head coach on nine-
            month or twelve-month contract may apply for an amount not to
            exceed $350 annually for travel expenses for professional im-
            provement (clinics, conferences, conventions and seminars);
            other full-time professional staff may apply for an amount not to
            exceed $200.
         2. Staff assigned by the Head, Department of Athletics, to represent
            the University on business is reimbursed in full for travel
            expenses.
         3. Unused professional improvement funds cannot be carried forward
            to subsequent fiscal years.
         4. Staff members may not borrow against future professional im-
            provement funds, e.g., may not use FY 85 funds in FY 84.

After many years of trying to determine the appropriate funding level for
coaches to attend various national coaching meetings, NCAA playoffs and
other events, the department initiated the aforementioned policy in order to
ensure that each staff member is treated equally. Besides providing order to
the area of professional staff development, this policy allows the financial
manager to prepare an accurate professional improvement budget.

   11. *Contingent miscellaneous* — This may include oranges, gifts to an
international team, soft drinks.

   12. *Guarantees* — Once budgets for the 28 intercollegiate sports have been
completed, the next need is to establish general administrative expenses.
These expenses are not charged to the specific sports' budgets, but rather are
budgeted for in central administrative accounts. The following are the major
budget categories under the heading of general administrative expenses:
   1. *Athletic Injury Care:*
      a. Physician coverage for contests
      b. Medical supplies
      c. Student trainer salaries
      d. Professional improvement allocation for full time trainers
   2. *Administrative Operating Budget:*
      a. Payroll
         i. Full time salaries and fringe benefits
         ii. Overtime
         iii. Consulting fees
         iv. Student employment
      b. Advertising for vacant positions
      c. Awards
      d. Clothing — t-shirts, shorts, socks, towels, etc.
      e. Dues-for department
      f. Printing
      g. Field marking materials
      h. Office supplies
      i. Postage

  j. Reconditioning equipment

  k. Rentals — e.g., portable bathrooms

  l. Telephone equipment costs for department and administrative toll calls

 3. *Capital Outlay:*

  a. Blocking sleds

  b. Gymnastic spring floor

  c. Scoreboards for basketball and softball

  d. starting blocks for swim team

  e. Two travel vans

 4. *Contingency Budget:*

  a. Championship Travel

  b. Funding for Unforeseen Circumstances

 5. *Sports Information and Ticket Office:*

  a. Photography

  b. Printing

  c. Student labor

  d. Telephone toll calls

  e. Travel — to contests and professional improvements

 6. *Facilities (Alumni Stadium at UMA):*

  a. Facilities bond payment

  b. Utilities

  c. Repair and maintenance

  d. Labor

  e. Custodial supplies

  f. Telephone

 7. *Travel:*

  a. Administrative travel

  b. Gas for all department vehicles

  c. Job interview expenses

  d. New employee moving expenses

  e. Department vehicle maintenance

  f. Van rentals

After all the administrative and sports budgets are constructed, the budget for the entire intercollegiate program is stated in the format shown in Figure 1. For purposes of comparison, the previous year's budget is included and the amount of increase or decrease for each Sub-Account indicated.

FIGURE 1

INTERCOLLEGIATE ATHLETIC BUDGET

1983-84

Sub-Accounts	1982-83	1983-84	Increase (Decrease)
Baseball	$ 21,000	$ 30,000	$ 9,000
Basketball (Men's)	78,000	95,000	17,000
Basketball (Women's)	45,000	64,000	19,000
Cross Country (Men's)	6,000	8,000	2,000
Cross Country (Women's)	6,000	8,000	2,000
Field Hockey	13,000	18,000	5,000

Sub-Accounts	1982-83	1983-84	Increase (Decrease)
Football	133,000	164,000	31,000
Golf (Men's)	6,000	7,000	1,000
Golf (Women's)	6,000	7,000	1,000
Gymnastics (Men's)	15,000	18,000	3,000
Gymnastics (Women's)	15,000	18,000	3,000
Lacrosse (Men's)	20,000	24,000	4,000
Lacrosse (Women's)	20,000	24,000	4,000
Ski (Men's)	9,000	10,000	1,000
Ski (Women's)	9,000	10,000	1,000
Soccer (Men's)	14,000	16,000	2,000
Soccer (Women's)	14,000	16,000	2,000
Softball	17,000	18,000	1,000
Swimming (Men's)	11,000	11,000	
Swimming (Women's)	11,000	11,000	
Tennis (Men's)	9,000	8,000	(1,000)
Tennis (Women's)	9,000	8,000	(1,000)
Track (Men's)	24,000	25,000	1,000
Track (Women's)	24,000	25,000	1,000
Volleyball	10,000	11,000	1,000
Wrestling	12,000	13,000	1,000
Athletic Injury Care	25,000	27,000	2,000
Capital Outlay	20,000	25,000	5,000
Band/Cheerleaders	1,000	1,000	
Contingent & Post-Season Play	30,000	35,000	5,000
Administrative Operating Expense	330,000	350,000	20,000
Sports Information & Tickets	26,000	28,000	2,000
Stadium	129,000	132,000	3,000
Travel	32,000	35,000	3,000
Totals	$1,150,000	$1,300,000	$150,000

§ 5-8. Control of Funds — A Major Responsibility.

An extremely important function of the financial manager is the responsibility to control funds. In the business world this responsibility would rest with the corporation's comptroller. The financial manager must make sure that the funds are spent in a manner that was originally intended. The financial manager must also ensure that funds are dispersed in accordance with state, university, NCAA, and conference regulations. In order to accomplish this, the following measures should be taken.

1. The financial manager must be aware of all department actions which involve expenditures of department funds. At UMA all department expenditures, including all personnel actions, are approved by the business manager.
2. School of Physical Education policy (Athletics/Intramurals is one of four departments comprising the School of Physical Education at UMA) requires that the dean's office also approve all department expenditures. This policy serves as a valuable control tool which further ensures that department expenditures conform to all appropriate regulations.
3. Regarding the control of recruiting and scouting funds, the department administrator who is responsible for monitoring NCAA regulations

reviews all recruiting and scouting invoices prior to action on the part of the business manager. Another requirement is that the head coach of the sport involved initial his or her approval on recruiting and scouting invoices. These requirements assist the department in preventing recruiting and scouting violations, as well as making the head coach fully responsible for the recruiting and scouting actions that took place.

4. It is recommended that periodically budget reports be distributed to appropriate coaches and staff. The nature of the reports can vary; however, they should include the original budget amount by category, funds spent to date, and the remaining balance by budget category as well as the total budget.

5. Review department procedures in order to ensure that they adhere both to internal and external audit recommendations.

If the financial manager follows the above guidelines, all expenditures will conform to the budget plan as well as to the prevailing regulations.

§ 5-9. Qualifications Needed by a Business Manager.

As is the case in other aspects of the intercollegiate athletic operation, effectiveness of the business office will be determined by its personnel. The critical appointment is that of the business manager. Unless he possesses certain competencies, the office shall always operate at a disadvantage. The resultant inadequacy shall not be without considerable impact upon all of the intercollegiate programs. The first consideration is our effort to protect against such loss in the appointment to the business manager's position. Qualifications needed by the appointee include:

1. Working knowledge of the management of an intercollegiate athletic program.
2. Considerable administrative and supervisory ability.
3. Ability to plan, organize and supervise the work of subordinates performing a variety of functions.
4. Ability to establish and maintain harmonious relationships with staff, students and the public.
5. Ability to exercise judgment and discretion in interpreting and applying policies and procedures.
6. Experience in wage and salary administration.
7. Ability to prepare statistical, financial and other appropriate reports.
8. Considerable knowledge of ticket sale procedures and accountability.
9. Considerable knowledge of intercollegiate athletic medical needs (physicians, athletic trainers and insurance coverage).
10. Working knowledge of bid specifications and procurement practices.
11. Ability to prepare travel arrangements for large groups.
12. Ability to serve on administrative committees.
13. Considerable knowledge of state and university rules, regulations and procedures.

Above all, the most important qualification is an ability to work well with people (human relations). As stated previously, a budget is only a financial plan and therefore there will always be changes and unforeseen circumstances which will require negotiations with coaches and staff. The financial manager must be capable of and willing to adjust to new situations.

The office of business manager is critical and pivotal but it is not the reason for the existence of the athletic department.

§ 5-10. Summary/Conclusion.

Administration of the budget can be accomplished with greater ease and fewer conflicts if care and attention are given to preparation of the budget. Planning should include careful analysis of those things that impact upon costs. It is a serious mistake to simply increase the budget by a certain percentage and to assume that growth in costs will be uniform. A new state law, a collective bargaining agreement or an act of the trustees could easily add tremendous costs that hadn't been expected.

Projections must be long-range. A minimum requirement is the number of years in the employment contracts for coaches and others within each unit. Budgets would be even more effective instruments if planning also included long-range scheduling for contests and shifts in the status of various sports or units. If a sport is to be upgraded from Division II to Division I or one is to be dropped to club status this long-range information must be included in planning undertaken by the business manager.

Finally, it is extremely important for the financial manager to treat all coaches and programs in the fairest possible manner. If the financial manager is viewed as someone who is fair to everyone while acting to serve the best interests of the total program, decisions will be readily accepted and the office viewed as a critical part of the athletic operation.

Appendix

BUDGET PLANNING FORM

YEAR 19_____ -19_____

SPORT _____ TRAVEL SQUAD _____ BUDGET CODE _____ Page _____ of _____

Opponent	H/A	Officials	Game Operation	Lodging	Transport	Meals	Entry Fee	Misc.
				___ Nights		B — L — D — B — L — D — $		
				___ Nights		B — L — D — B — L — D — $		
				___ Nights		B — L — D — B — L — D — $		
				___ Nights		B — L — D — B — L — D — $		
				___ Nights		B — L — D — B — L — D — $		
				___ Nights		B — L — D — B — L — D — $		
				___ Nights		B — L — D — B — L — D — $		

SUBTOTAL $_____ $_____ $_____ $_____ $_____ $_____

GRAND TOTAL $_____ $_____ $_____ $_____ $_____ $_____

Chapter 6

EQUIPMENT CONTROL

By

David Morelli

§ 6-1. Introduction.

It is important that all sport managers understand the basic elements of equipment management. An understanding of the basics will enable the sport manager to make informed decisions. This can be achieved by looking through the eyes of the person who deals directly with equipment control. The person(s) assigned this responsibility often views the task as a cycle that encompasses storing equipment, assessing needs, inventorying, maintaining inventory, issuing, and retrieving those items in inventory. The cycle may have to be altered to meet particular needs, but if the basics of it are understood, the equipment management process should be more efficient, require less manpower, and be easier for the person(s) directly controlling equipment.

§ 6-2. Selecting and Organizing the Storage Area.

The first step in controlling equipment is the selection of a proper storage area. Certain criteria must be considered when choosing or designing the equipment storage area. The location of the room should be as close to the athletes' dressing area and playing facilities as possible. It should be situated on the ground floor with accessibility for delivery vehicles. This type of location makes the process of receiving and issuing equipment more efficient.

To increase efficiency, the external design of the equipment room should be modeled after a mini-warehouse, with areas designated for receiving as well as issuing equipment. Doors in the receiving area should be extensive enough to accommodate substantial quantities and large pieces of equipment. This area should possess ramps to facilitate the use of hand trucks, equipment or laundry carts. The area utilized for issuing equipment should have one main window or counter-top closest to the athletes' dressing room. Also, near this window small issue-lockers should be installed. These lockers should be open in the back of the interior of the equipment room with individually locking fronts open to the athlete. This "post-office box" effect can save time because it eliminates the need for "ever-present" and by demand service throughout the day, in that an equipment assistant can accomplish the job as a "single-service" task. Of course, there need not be a way to issue equipment without the assistant if there is no way to return equipment without this person's presence. To remedy this problem, install a small dirty-laundry or used-equipment door situated off the floor for a bin to catch the used equipment turned in during the day. The door should be just big enough to serve its purpose but not so big that it endangers equipment room security.

§ 6-3. Security Considerations.

While considering the equipment room's design, plan for the security of the storage area. The area should be in a sturdy dwelling with secure locks on all doors and windows. The keys to the equipment room should be distributed only to persons who have a direct need for them and admittance to the equipment room should be restricted to people who have business there. Since this room often contains the largest, most valuable inventory in the athletic complex, burglar alarms should be a security consideration. The issue lockers should also be designed for security. If these lockers are not deep enough or do not have a removable backing, athletes may reach through their own lockers and reach into adjacent lockers to retrieve equipment that belongs to someone else. No matter what type athletic equipment is stored, its controllers must remember that the commodity being dealt with is appealing to thieves and souvenir hunters. Spending extra money for security will save money and headaches caused by mass equipment loss.

In designing the equipment storage area, consider its interior arrangement next. Since receiving and issuing areas are fixed by external design, it is necessary to make those areas efficient. In the issue area there should be separate pigeonhole-type lockers to accommodate each athlete that will use equipment on a daily basis. Individual pigeonholes should be numbered to correspond to the number assigned each athlete when he is issued equipment and should be used to store equipment that will be used frequently. The size of these lockers will depend upon the particular athlete's needs (for instance, one for football equipment would be much larger than one for baseball). If there are laundry facilities in the equipment room, they should be located in the issue area since laundry items will be reissued frequently. If heavy laundry equipment is used, proper fire-prevention measures, such as fire-activated sprinklers, should be installed.

When considering internal design the equipment room should be practical without neglecting security. In the receiving area, there should be ample shelving to store the necessary inventory in an organized manner. The size of shelves and total space involved depends upon the needs of a particular organization. Security in this storage area is increased by using cabinets with locks instead of open shelves. If possible, there should also be a special room where expensive equipment is stored. The place should contain a small, locked room of shelves within the equipment room. (This is a good area to keep game uniforms, expensive items held for sale or any item that is difficult to replace at a moment's notice.) Other particulars for the equipment area's design can be determined by visiting equipment rooms in similar facilities and observing operations.

After the design and location of the equipment storage area has been selected, the equipment must be arranged in an organized manner. By organizing equipment first, the equipment-control process will be smoother and easier to operate. Basically, when equipment is arranged in a neat, orderly fashion that works best for its controller, the result will be an efficient equipment operation. Some decisions about how to arrange equipment are dictated by available shelf space. Items that are issued frequently, however, should be stored near the issue area. Also, similar equipment should be stored in the same area whenever possible. This is especially advantageous when large quantities of equipment are handled. This facilitates finding items quickly and improves the inventory process.

§ 6-4. Inventorying Equipment.

Once equipment has been prepared in an organized manner, it is ready to be counted and inventoried. When counting equipment, records of the item counted and its quantity by size and brand should be retained each time the inventory is conducted. These records are valuable to the equipment manager in long-range planning, as well as day-to-day operations. When inventorying equipment, include equipment that is outside the equipment room, but is still the manager's responsibility. Such equipment includes items in players' lockers, field equipment, or court accessories. Forms, such as the one shown in Appendix 1 and Appendix 2 at the end of this chapter, can be helpful when inspecting an athlete's locker and these forms can also be used to obtain the players' current equipment sizes. Conduct an overall equipment inventory annually and check players' lockers at least twice a year.

After completing the overall inventory, equipment needs can be determined. This process begins by assessing the equipment needs of individuals who must be properly fitted for equipment they will use on the playing field. Sizes may be obtained by maintaining a file of the locker inventory sheets and by supplying athletes with sizing questionnaires that require information pertinent to the equipment controller's needs. With both of these methods, it will still be necessary for the controller to visually confirm that the sizes are correct. This size check is most important when dealing with protective equipment.

Equipment managers must take time to understand and learn the mechanics of the equipment so that they can effectively fit and size it for the individuals who will use it. This information can be obtained by consulting authorities such as equipment manufacturers or representatives, other equipment managers, equipment catalogs and magazines, information provided with the product, clinics and seminars, professional tailors and even the athletes. With proper information athletes can be sized correctly and these sizes will be retained on file for future use. (See Appendix 2 at the end of this chapter.)

When determining equipment needs, a variety of possibilities must be explored. Equipment needs for athletic fields and playing facilities equipment may be assessed by investigating applicable rules and regulations. Coaches' evaluations are the primary consideration in decisions about equipment and facilities. Administrators, physicians, and athletic trainers who are involved in the sports program should be consulted for equipment suggestions. It is important to plan for quantities beyond basic needs as well as replacement parts for equipment that requires frequent repair. This facilitates replacement or repair of inventory items damaged by wear and tear. As a general rule, the more physical contact involved in a sport, the greater the need for periodic replacement or repair.

§ 6-5. Budgeting.

Equipment-management personnel are becoming aware of the items that will be necessary to ensure a successful operation. When managers match the ideal amount of required items with the cost of the items, it is possible to accurately formulate a budget. Since most sports organizations operate within budget constraints, equipment managers must be prepared to formulate and submit a proposed dollar amount necessary to meet the needs of the program.

The budget process begins with the gathering of cost information of the predetermined items essential to the inventory. This information can be obtained by sending a list of items and quantities wanted to several sporting goods suppliers for price quotations. The lowest price should be used for budget purposes and a record of the price bids retained. Other resources for gathering dollar values include old equipment records, business-department files of old invoices or equipment catalogs.

Examine budget priorities before continuing the budget process. Policies may be determined by administrators rather than equipment managers, but no matter who decides, emphasis should be on protective and safety equipment. If faced with the need to cut back on budget requests, the cost area devoted to the athlete's safety should not be reduced for ethical as well as legal liability reasons. The remaining budget categories will be based on the manager's observations of the operational needs.

§ 6-6. Purchasing.

Once equipment appropriations are approved, the orders should be placed. The price bids used in formulating budget costs can now be used when deciding which items to purchase from the dealer. (These bids are often guaranteed for only 30 days and time becomes a factor.) When selecting sporting-goods suppliers, prices are not the only consideration. Service is a very important factor. If an equipment supplier with lower prices is unreliable in delivering goods or servicing the account, the more expensive alternative may be the best buy.

Consider questions of when and how to order equipment. Target dates for ordering depend on the time of year the equipment is needed and how much lead-time is necessary to produce the equipment. As a general rule, order equipment for a particular sport as soon as the season has ended. However, this will depend on the scheduling of the sport as well as the manufacturers' production schedule. The "how to's" of purchasing is often dictated by the organization's requisitioning policies and the seller's requirements in extending credit. Many organizations require equipment managers to complete purchasing requisitions which are then approved by business office personnel, who complete purchase orders before passing the requests to the dealer. These purchase orders contractually bind the dealer to prices and quantities agreed upon which prevent arguments over mispriced and mistakenly shipped items. Descriptions shown on purchase orders must be precise and complete to prevent problems of receiving incorrect items.

After placing the equipment order, the equipment controller should make periodic checks to see that new equipment is obtained by agreed upon receiving dates by contacting suppliers frequently. Maintain a file of phone numbers and addresses of suppliers. Keep a running tally of money spent out of the equipment budget to help the equipment manager stay within budget guidelines established for purchasing needs.

§ 6-7. Receiving Equipment.

After inventorying and inspecting deliveries, create records for items received with dates of arrival. The file is helpful in determining orders outstanding, further verifying lead times, evaluating the suppliers' service responsibility and gathering information for business office reports (in the form of receiving reports). Arrange new equipment in the orderly manner for which the equipment room was designed. If equipment areas need further rearranging, the time to do it is before shelving new equipment. If circumstances necessitate moving large portions of new equipment to another storage facility, do not store the equipment on shelves, just count, inspect and return it to the shipping container until it meets its final destination.

§ 6-8. Issuing Equipment.

With new equipment stored, the equipment manager prepares to issue equipment. The first task in this process is the creation of an enumeration system for issuing the equipment to the athletes. A number should be assigned each athlete and the number should correspond to the dressing locker and issue lockers. All items issued to the athlete must be recognized by the identifying numeral that is etched in permanent ink. This system of enumeration will facilitate the equipment controller's needs for separating the athlete's equipment when it is to be retrieved. Above all, establish a system with order.

Before the athletes' needs for equipment arise, certain items can be prepared for the upcoming issues. Since sizes are determined earlier in the equipment process, the proper items can be moved into issue lockers. Cloth goods and any item with standardized sizing can be numbered for identification before the athlete is present. The use of numbered mesh laundry bags or shelves with wire baskets can be used as an efficient means for controlling these everyday cloth wares.

The fitting of protective devices and items which vary greatly in design and sizing (such as helmets, shoulder pads or shoes) must be checked while the athlete is present for proper sizing. The importance of this process is greater if the equipment manager is servicing a younger age group because natural body growth causes a significant change in the athlete's size. While fitting protective equipment and special devices, the equipment controller must offer instruction for proper wearing techniques so the athlete uses equipment *correctly*. In addition, players' special protective needs should be explored while they are available for questions in this area (feedback from examining doctors and trainers is also important).

After issuing equipment, the athletes should become aware of equipment rules and regulations as well as the cooperation expected from them by the equipment manager. These policies should be in writing with important areas highlighted verbally in team meetings. Equipment procedures should address such things as the items available for the athletes' use; the system the equipment manager uses to issue and retrieve equipment and the rule that players must adopt to cooperate with the equipment manager. Procedures for laundering equipment should be carefully explained because laundered items are issued and returned daily. If a participant is uncertain about what to return, when to turn it in or how and where it is to be returned, confusion may result.

Once the necessary items are issued and explained, equipment controllers must consider how the equipment is to be maintained. Primary maintenance considerations involve keeping equipment clean, sanitary and in good repair. If the athletes' equipment is to be laundered daily, there are several ways this can be accomplished. If the equipment storage area does not have laundry facilities, an outside launderer must be utilized. The launderer chosen should be large enough for the organization's needs, reliable and located close to the equipment facility. Equipment managers with laundry facilities are in a more desirable situation since time is saved and security increased because laundry does not have to be transferred to another location. Also, having laundry equipment results in cost efficiency. If the initial costs of installing washers and dryers is affordable, the operation pays for itself by reducing daily costs of laundry (the more equipment laundered daily the faster savings are realized). A lack of laundry facilities may create additional equipment needs because lead time required by outside launderers dictates an additional set of everyday equipment for each athlete. Two sets of practice gear are necessary for situations where laundry facilities are internal (one set is being cleaned while the other set is being used), three sets may be necessary when external facilities are used.

Methods for laundering equipment must be decided upon when equipment personnel are responsible for this task. These methods can be formulated by reading labels on potential laundry items and consulting equipment manufacturers for suggestions. Also, professional launderers and reputable laundry detergent dealers are helpful when considering special stain removal needs. Further ideas may be gathered from equipment controllers in similar situations.

Equipment maintenance doesn't end with laundered items. All items under the care of the equipment manager must be checked periodically for maintenance needs. The number of times inspections are made depends upon the durability of the equipment being inspected and the frequency of use. During a seasonal sports program, inspect protective and special equipment as often as possible. After the season is over, all items should be inspected for repair needs and, if necessary, sent to qualified equipment reconditioners. When equipment personnel become well-acquainted with equipment construction, many of the repairs can be made in-house, lessening the need for outside repair. However, care should be taken not to incorrectly alter protective equipment for safety and legal reasons. If repairmen other than the equipment manager are needed, they should be qualified and dependable. For example, if a washer or dryer breaks down at a time laundry needs are extensive, the repairmen must be readily accessible. The equipment manager should become proficient in equipment maintenance by learning as much as possible about the equipment.

§ 6-9. Retrieving Equipment.

When it becomes time to retrieve equipment from the athlete, equipment managers must depend on records created while issuing equipment as well as being a good judge of human nature. No matter what the program's issue policies, records of items and quantities of equipment passed on to the athletes are absolutely necessary to facilitate the retrieval process. Typical methods that will assist in gathering equipment are to have the athlete sign a form attesting to the equipment check-out, keeping unattested issue records or issuing basically the same items to all athletes. Whatever technique the equipment manager uses, equipment retrieval is essential to the total program.

The equipment manager can require the mandatory payment of a deposit prior to issuing or hold awards until equipment is returned. Another technique is to withhold grades or restrict the athlete's use of clean laundry. A policy must be formulated regarding excuses, dealing with equipment loss and consequences of lost equipment.

Once equipment has been retrieved, the equipment cycle begins once again starting with the inventory stage. By retaining records throughout the different phases of the cycle, the process will become more familiar and easier to process. Note areas that cause problems for the organization throughout the equipment process and work on trouble spots before they arise again. In short, when dealing with equipment areas, be organized with facilities, inventories and records; follow your own natural equipment cycle, be informed about all aspects of the equipment responsibilities and protect the athletes like they were family members.

§ 6-10. Summary/Conclusion.

The sport manager should give attention and understand the basic process of equipment management so that informed decisions can be made in the control of equipment. The areas of importance regarding equipment control begins with the selection, design and location of the equipment room. The room must be organized efficiently, and securely to achieve a smooth and efficient operation. Retention of inventories and records is essential to operation of the program.

It is expedient to utilize the services of administrators, physicians, coaches and athletic trainers for consultation regarding equipment needs. While budget constraints dictate the purchase of equipment, the emphasis should always be on protective and safety factors. Ethical as well as legal guidelines affect the purchase of sports equipment.

A system of requisitions and records, inspection of deliveries, and maintenance of equipment all ensure effective equipment management. The correct fitting of equipment must be provided and periodic inspection is required. Special plans should be made in the process of retrieving equipment or costs for missing equipment will escalate and create financial problems.

The management of equipment is often overlooked by the sports manager but, in reality, may be one of the most important duties in the overall management process.

Appendix 1

EQUIPMENT RECORD

Date:

Locker #	Bag		Turtle Neck	Sweat		Pants		Jersey		S. Pads		Thigh Pads	Knee Pads	Hip Pads	Helmet	Shoes
	B	G		T	B	1	2	1	2	C	R					

Appendix 2

EQUIPMENT CHECK

Name	Locker #	Bag	Sweat	P. Pant	G. Pant	Chest	Jersey	Helmet	Face Mask	Hip Pads	S. Pads	Shirt	Shoes

Chapter 7

SPORTS MEDICINE SERVICES

By

Jerald Hawkins

§ 7-1. Introduction.

Of the various services provided by a sports organization to its clientele, none is more important than medical care. Whether such care takes the form of first aid, as in the case of an injured or ill spectator, or complete injury-care and rehabilitation, as with the competitive athlete, it is the responsibility of every organization to provide quality medical care for spectators and participants. The purpose of this chapter is to identify the methods which may be utilized in providing such medical care. Because of the diversity of medical-care needs of nonparticipants (spectators, employees, etc.) and active participants, it is necessary to consider two distinct aspects of medical care services: first aid and emergency care, and sports injury management.

§ 7-2. First Aid and Emergency Care.

The primary component of an organization's medical care system is that of first-aid care in the event of sudden illness or injury to one of its clients or employees. First aid is generally described as that process by which nonmedical personnel perform simple care procedures designed to alleviate the immediate threat of further injury. In the case of life-threatening injury or illness, this description may be extended to include life-saving procedures such as rescue breathing or cardiopulmonary resuscitation.

To adequately provide such services, careful planning and the development and utilization of available resources must be accomplished in the specific areas of training existing personnel to render first-aid services, providing first-aid supplies which are easily accessible and establishing a system of emergency medical care.

Every employee in the sport-related organization should be certified in both first aid and cardiopulmonary resuscitation (CPR). This is especially true for those whose daily responsibilities include direct contact with spectators and/or participants. First-aid and/or CPR instruction is available in most communities through the American Red Cross, the American Heart Association and other voluntary health agencies. It is often possible to schedule group instruction for an entire staff, thus making it possible for certification to be obtained with minimal inconvenience to the employees. With the skills acquired through first-aid and CPR instruction, all staff members will be prepared to render first aid and emergency care whenever and wherever the need arises.

Most first-aid and emergency medical-care procedures require some form of specialized supplies. The nature of such supplies may range from cotton-tipped applicators for cleaning superficial wounds to inflatable air-splints for use in immobilizing suspected fractures and dislocations. In order for first-aid supplies to be used effectively, they must be stored in a location which allows easy access. The most efficient method of providing first-aid supplies in a sport-related facility is to assemble several "first-aid kits" and place them in a variety of locations throughout the facility. The number and specific locations of such kits will depend upon the size of the facility and the types of programs it supports. A list of the recommended contents of a first-aid kit for recreational-sports facilities may be found below.

Contents of a First Aid Kit for a Recreational Sports Facility

Adhesive compresses (Band-Aids) — Assorted sizes
Adhesive tape — Assorted widths
Alcohol (70%) — one bottle per kit
Antiseptic solution (merthiolate, betadine, etc.) — one bottle per kit
Burn ointment — one or more tubes per kit
Cotton-tipped applicators
Elastic wraps (Ace bandages) — Assorted widths
Emergency contact card — one per kit
Eye pads (sterile) — Several per kit
Gauze pads (sterile) — Assorted sizes
Gauze rolls — Assorted widths
Insect sting kit — one per kit
Manual detailing current first aid procedures
Petroleum jelly — one tube per kit
Scissors (bandage or tape style) — one pair per kit
Soap (liquid or aerosol)

Other supplies which should be stored in a central location which is easily accessible to all employees:

Blankets (preferably wool) — two or more
Litters (military type) — two or more
Splints (inflatable air style or padded wood) — Assorted lengths
Triangular bandages — one dozen or more

The third basic aspect of an effective first-aid and emergency care program is that of developing and implementing a formal, policy-based approach to first aid and emergency medical care. When a participant or spectator is injured or becomes ill, it is important that he receives care that is promptly and correctly administered. To accomplish this, it is necessary that each employee not only be trained in first-aid procedures, but also be assigned a specific role to be carried out in the event of an injury or illness in his work area. For example, ushers or pages in a spectator sport facility should be trained in basic first aid prior to being placed on the job. With this training complete, each usher or page should be assigned a specific duty within the emergency care program. Among these role assignments should be: someone to administer primary first-aid care (usually two people); someone to maintain order and decorum among the other spectators or participants who are in the immediate area; and someone to summon assistance from either on-site medical personnel or from a nearby medical facility or ambulance service. While this approach may appear somewhat simplistic and even unnecessary, the delivery of first aid to an injured spectator is too often hampered by the confusion of the moment.

To adequately prepare for effective emergency medical care, the manager of a sport-related facility must establish a positive working relationship with those agencies which will be expected to provide support services in the event of a medical emergency. In most communities, this will include the local law enforcement agency, emergency medical services, area hospital(s) and one or more physicians who may be contacted in time of need. The manager should meet with representatives of each of these support agencies to exchange information with respect to the specific role that each will play in the event of a medical emergency. At this time, the agency representative should be given the opportunity to identify the "normal procedures" of the agency while the facility manager should provide information regarding the program's first-aid and emergency-care protocol. Based on this exchange of information, an agreement should be established which will govern the relationship between the facility and support agency with respect to the specific role of each during a medical emergency. Although the specific nature of this agreement will vary according to the needs and capabilities of both parties, one basic policy should be established. During any spectator event (game, concert, etc.), emergency medical personnel should be on-site to facilitate the immediate handling of any medical emergency. It is also recommended that a physician be present at all events although this may not always be possible.

A simple, yet very important step in providing effective emergency care involves placing "emergency-contact cards" in all first-aid kits and beside all business telephones. An "emergency-contact card" is simply a small index card which contains telephone numbers which are needed in a time of medical emergency.

EMERGENCY CONTACT CARD

Ambulance: Triad Ambulance Service 555-1234
Metro EMS Service 555-5678

Physician: Dr. John Smith (O)555-1357
(H)555-2468

or
Dr. Mary Brown (O)555-1470
(H)555-0369

Hospital: County General 555-1111

In communities where a single emergency code number has been established (e.g., 911), the "emergency contact card" may be simplified to contain only the emergency number and the names and numbers of physicians who may be contacted.

It is virtually impossible to eliminate the risk of sudden illness or injury to spectators and participants. However, it is possible to maximize the quality of emergency care provided through careful planning and the development of a systematic emergency-care plan based on the following recommendations:

1. Require all employees, especially those who work directly with program clientele, to be trained and certified in first aid and cardiopulmonary resuscitation (CPR).
2. Assemble and maintain a complete inventory of first-aid and emergency medical supplies and make these supplies easily accessible to all employees.
3. Establish an "in-house" system for providing first-aid and emergency medical care to program clientele and employees and thoroughly orient all employees with respect to this system and the specific role that each is expected to play.
4. Schedule and conduct emergency-care drills during which all employees are provided the opportunity to practice specific emergency-care procedures.
5. Develop, in cooperation with local medical-support agencies and personnel, a systematic plan for emergency care which meets the specific needs of the facility and its programs.

In addition to a standard system of first-aid and emergency medical care, an organization must develop a plan for providing emergency medical care during events at which large crowds will be present. Because of the unique and complex nature of such emergency medical preparedness, this concept will be discussed in detail in a separate chapter.

§ 7-3. Sport Injury Management.

Organizations such as schools, colleges, and professional and amateur sports teams are expected to provide comprehensive medical and health care services for their athletes. The American Medical Association (AMA) stated in its "Bill of Rights for the School and College Athlete" that, while participation in sports is a privilege, it also involves some basic rights on the part of the athlete. According to the AMA, these fundamental rights include the "right to good health," supervision, a thorough preseason history and medical examination, a physician present at all contests and readily available at all practice sessions and medical control of the health aspects of athletics. Don H. O'Donoghue, *Treatment of Injuries to Athletes* (4th ed. W.B. Saunders Co., 1984, preface).

Until recently, the responsibility of a school or college to provide adequate medical and health care for its athletes was essentially viewed as a moral or ethical issue. However, the issue of medical and health care for the school or college athlete is now finding its way into the American court room as evidenced by the case of *Gillespie v. Southern Utah State College,* 669 P.2d 861 (Utah, 1983). In this case a college basketball player brought suit against a college, its basketball coach and trainer as the result of an injury he received while playing college basketball and subsequent complications resulting in the loss of a foot. The athlete claimed that the severe-injury complications were a direct result of inadequate sports-medicine care but the jury found that the athlete "was 100% negligent and such negligence was the proximate cause of his injuries." This is merely one example of the increasing frequency of sports medicine litigation and, though no definitive legal precedent has yet been established, it is apparent that schools and colleges do have some legal obligation to their athletes with respect to the availability of quality medical and health care.

Regardless of an organization's legal responsibility to its athletes, there also exists a moral and ethical obligation to provide for the health and well-being of those who represent a school, college or organization on the athletic field. This obligation not only involves the availability of qualified, on-site medical and health care personnel, but also the provision of adequate health care facilities, quality supervision and instruction, and playing conditions which promote safe participation. In short, every sports participant should be afforded the opportunity to take part in the activity of his choice with the knowledge that everything possible has been done to assure that his participation will be safe as well as enjoyable and that, in the event of an injury, he will receive immediate and effective care.

Recognition of the responsibility to provide adequate medical and health care is only the first step toward making such services available. Too often, this aspect of the total program is viewed as a "frill" or luxury. Therefore, there may be little or no planning with respect to such critical issues as the identification and utilization of qualified personnel, formal program organization and the design and utilization of adequate medical and health care facilities.

§ 7-4. Personnel — "The Team Approach".

It has often been said that "everybody's business is nobody's business." Unfortunately, this statement accurately describes the manner in which many organizations approach the issue of providing qualified medical and health-care personnel within the total sport program. The high school or college coach may be required to not only perform his coaching duties, but also to care for the injuries sustained by his (and frequently other) athletes. Quite often, the responsibility for injury care is shared by the entire coaching staff and the issue suddenly becomes "everybody's business." In situations where personnel organization is allowed to develop according to the dictates of day-to-day needs, there is likely to be a serious lack of quality medical and health care for the participants. Even in those programs in which there is a "team physician" or "school physician" available, the absence of qualified on-site personnel (e.g., a certified athletic trainer) and the lack of a formal organizational plan for the delivery of medical and health care services will usually result in less than optimal medical and health care.

Medical and health care for sport participants may be most effectively rendered when there is a "team" of qualified professionals functioning cooperatively with the health and well-being of the participants as their common goal. While the specific composition of the "sports medicine team" may vary according to the unique needs of the organization and its programs, three specific persons are considered essential if effective sports medicine services are to be delivered: an administrative coordinator (athletic director, sports medicine coordinator, etc.), a qualified on-site athletic trainer, and a program physician.

The administrative coordinator of a sports-injury management program is basically responsible for such administrative functions as program planning and supervision, budget development and implementation and personnel management. This role may be assumed by any one of a variety of people, depending upon the size and functional nature of the organization. In the small school or college setting, the administrative duties may be effectively handled by either the chief athletic administrator (usually the athletic director) or the head trainer. In the larger, more diverse program, it may be desirable to place administrative responsibilities in the hands of a "sports medicine coordinator," thus relieving the chief athletic administrator and head trainer of these duties. It is recommended that such a coordinator function within the purview of the chief athletic administrator and possess expertise in the areas of program administration and athletic training.

Every sports injury management program should have at least one qualified athletic trainer. This person is generally assigned the title of "Head Trainer" and assumes the primary responsibility for on-site program direction including primary injury care and rehabilitation, day-to-day administrative details and the training and supervision of student assistants. Although not essential, it is strongly recommended (and in some states required) that the head trainer be certified by the National Athletic Trainers Association (NATA) since such certification is considered the standard of professional recognition in the field of athletic training. Criteria for certification may be obtained by contacting the National Athletic Trainers Association, Greenville, North Carolina.

The third member of the "sports medicine team" is the program physician. The "team doctor," as this person is often called, functions cooperatively with the administrative coordinator and head trainer to provide such primary medical services as performing preseason medical examinations, providing consultation and recommendations relative to extended injury care and rehabilitation, providing primary medical treatment for injured athletes, and attending home athletic contests for the purpose of offering on-site injury care and supervision. Needless to say, the program physician must possess an interest in sports medicine and the desire to work, often without compensation, with injured athletes. It would obviously be desirable for the program physician to be a specialist in an area which is related to sports (e.g., orthopedics). However, the most essential qualification for a program physician is a sincere interest and desire to be a member of the "sports medicine team."

The program physician is the only member of the "sports medicine team" who is not generally an employee of the school or organization. Therefore, locating and recruiting an appropriate program physician often proves difficult. The most common method of locating a potential program physician is by identifying those physicians who already have some form of relationship with the organization. The relationship may be geographic (i.e., a physician who lives and practices in the local community), professional (i.e., a physician who is a school or organization board member), or personal (i.e., a physician with friend or family ties to the school or organization).

Once appropriate candidates have been identified, securing the services of a physician for the sports-medicine program will often depend upon the compensatory nature of the position and the duties which the physician will be expected to perform. The issue of compensation for the services of a program physician may be resolved in one of three basic ways. If the organization's budget will allow, the physician may receive monetary compensation for services rendered, usually in the form of a retainer in an amount agreed upon by all parties and specified in a contract. If financial remuneration is not possible, many states will allow institutions to provide a physician with a "gift-in-kind" statement which may be used by the physician as verification of charitable contribution in the form of donated services to the institution. If neither of these forms of compensation are appropriate, the program physician will simply serve as a "volunteer" member of the sports-medicine team.

The duties or expectations of a program physician will vary, depending upon the unique needs of each program. However, the program physician is generally expected to provide the following services:

1. Compile and maintain a medical history of each program participant.
2. Conduct preparticipation physician examinations.
3. Attend all games or contests and as many practices as feasible.
4. Supervise and provide instruction to sports medicine personnel.
5. Be available to see injured program participants during regular office hours and provide treatment or referral as deemed appropriate.
6. Be "on call" for the emergency care of injured program participants at times other than during office hours.
7. Make decisions relative to the return to action of injured program participants.
8. Work closely with the other members of the "sports medicine team" in establishing policy and coordinating program activities.

When a program physician has been secured, it is imperative that his relationship with the program be spelled out in an agreement which specifically describes his duties and the form of compensation (if any) which he will receive. A sample agreement appears as Appendix 1 at the end of this chapter.

As programs and needs expand, it may prove desirable to add additional members to the basic "sports medicine team." With the recommendation of the program physician, medical specialists (e.g., orthopedist, dentist, ophthalmologist, etc.) may be included in the "sports medicine team," thus enhancing the specific services which may be provided.

§ 7-5. Organization.

All successful sports medicine programs share one common characteristic — they are well organized. Unfortunately, effective organization is not something that "just happens," but rather is the result of diligent planning and a commitment to excellence.

Several factors influence organizational success. Three factors which are critical, yet often overlooked are: the development and utilization of a formal organizational model; the establishment of policies within which the program will function; and the implementation of a system of record-keeping which will facilitate and document communication among the members of the "sports medicine team," players, coaches, and others with whom formal communication is carried on.

A formal organizational model or chart delineates the relative relationship among the various persons within the sports medicine program. The specific pattern or organization will depend upon the precise needs of the organization itself. A "Sample Organizational Model" for a small college is presented as Appendix 2 at the end of this chapter.

Without a formal organizational plan, the sports medicine program will not function as effectively as desired. At best, it will become a group of individuals, each performing the duties that he deems appropriate, inevitably resulting in a duplication in some services and a complete absence of others.

As with any organization, the sports medicine program should function according to preestablished policies. Such policies should be developed as the result of cooperative planning by the "sports medicine team," and should reflect the specific functional needs of the program. Policies should be written and implemented with respect to standard injury care and physician referral procedures, the transportation of injured athletes to and from hospitals and other medical facilities, the operation of the training room, the processing of insurance claims and other records and the specific responsibilities of staff members. These policies should be compiled and placed in a policy manual or handbook, and made available to every person involved in the program.

§ 7-6. Record-Keeping.

One of the most vital concepts in program organization is that of record-keeping and its influence on organizational communication. Communication is often classified as "formal," the exchange of important information or ideas that require written documentation and "informal," the exchange of less important information which requires no written documentation. Most of the communication within the sports medicine program is sufficiently important to be considered "formal" in nature, yet too often is carried out verbally. For example, an athlete or student trainer carries verbal messages from the head trainer to a physician or coach, often resulting in misunderstanding. If left unresolved, such misunderstanding may jeopardize the relationship which is essential among administrators, trainers, physicians, players and coaches. Effective record-keeping will help to alleviate many of the problems which may result from poor organizational communication.

Record forms are highly personalized communication vehicles. Therefore, it is necessary to design forms which reflect the unique needs of each program. Some typical forms are described below but it should be noted that these are presented merely for the purpose of illustration.

An essential instrument is the injury-report form (see Appendix 3 at the end of this chapter). The purpose of the injury-report form is to maximize the exchange of information among all of the parties involved in the injury-management process. While a form of this type may be printed as a single sheet of paper, it is highly recommended that it be a multicopy (carbon or carbonless) instrument so that each person in the injury management process may retain a copy of the form for future reference. For example, if the form is prepared in four parts, it may be used in the following manner. After completing and signing the top portion of the form, the athlete would be given the top three copies to take with him to the attending physician. The back copy would be retained in the training room as verification that the form had been sent with the athlete to the physician. The physician would then be asked to complete the lower portion of the form based upon his evaluation of the injury and to retain the back copy for his records. The athlete would then return the two remaining copies of the form to the training room where one would be filed and the other included with any insurance claim which might be submitted.

Some of the features of this specific form which enhance its effectiveness are the multiple-copy nature of the form which provides written verification for all principal parties, the athlete's signature verifying the circumstances under which the injury occurred and the immediate care provided, and the physician's written evaluation and recommendation relative to the severity of the injury, appropriate rehabilitation and post-injury return to activity. This information may then be shared with the appropriate coach.

Since communication between the sports medicine program and the members of the coaching staff is critical to the success of both programs, the final form presented here is one designed specifically to facilitate trainer-coach communication. The injury-care recommendation form may be used to provide a written record for the coach, the sports medicine staff, and the athlete's injury file concerning any injury which will require the athlete to discontinue or alter his normal practice or same routine. Constructed as a three-part form approximately the size of a small index card, this form contains information relative to the precise nature of the injury in question, recommended procedures for caring for that injury, and the athlete's status relative to return to activity. (See Appendix 4 at the end of this chapter.) When the form has been completed and signed by the head trainer, the back copy would be given directly to the appropriate coach, providing him with a concise, written statement which answers three important questions; "What is the injury?", "How will it be cared for?" and "When and under what conditions can the athlete return to play?" The second copy of the form may be posted in the training room as a written guide for staff members in caring for the injury. The original copy of the form may be placed in the athlete's injury file for future reference. A form of this nature not only enhances communication between members of the sports medicine staff and members of the coaching staff, but also provides written documentation of staff and/or physician recommendation should future questions arise.

Although effective record-keeping requires a significant amount of time and effort, the benefits of improved program communication are well worth the time and effort invested. However, to reap these benefits, the "sports medicine team" must analyze the needs of the program and design and utilize record-keeping systems which will best meet those needs.

§ 7-7. Facilities.

To a great extent, the quality of medical and health care that an organization may provide its athletes is determined by the quality of facilities utilized for this purpose. As with previous factors which have been discussed, the specific size and type of injury care facilities will depend upon the nature and scope of the programs it is expected to serve. It is not the purpose of this chapter to present a detailed discussion of facility and equipment specifications since such information is readily available in several sports medicine texts. However, it should be emphasized that all facility planning should include the direct input of all members of the "sports medicine team."

§ 7-8. Summary/Conclusion.

The manager in a sport-related organization, whether it be a spectator entertainment facility, a community recreation center, or a high school or college athletic department, assumes the direct responsibility for the health and well-being of his clientele. Therefore, every effort should be made to develop and maintain a program of medical services which will ensure the health and well-being of those he serves.

Appendix 1

PHYSICIAN'S AGREEMENT

STATE OF ...   )
)   PHYSICIAN'S AGREEMENT
CITY/COUNTY   )
OF ....   )

THIS AGREEMENT made and entered into the .. day of ......, 1982, by and between ......, a college having its principal place of business in ......, (hereinafter referred to as "College"), and Dr. ......, a citizen and resident of ...... (hereinafter referred to as "Physician").

WITNESSETH:

WHEREAS, College is desirous obtaining the services of Physician in connection with its ...... program, and

WHEREAS, Physician is skilled in the practice of orthopedic medicine (or other specialty) and is willing to assist College with its orthopedic (or other medical) problems in its ...... program,

NOW, THEREFORE, in consideration of the covenants and promises contained herein, the parties hereto agree as follows:

1. College hereby retains and Physician agrees to be retained by College as College's orthopedic (or general medical) consultant in College's ...... program for the school year 19..-...

2. Physician will act as a consultant with the College's coaches, trainers, athletes and other personnel with regard to orthopedic (or other) medical problems incurred by athletes in the College's ...... program. Physician's consulting services shall include the attendance of all of College's games, a schedule of which is attached hereto and incorporated herein by reference, and shall also attend all scrimmages as scheduled from time to time by College, notice of which shall be given to Physician not less than 48 hours prior to such scrimmage. Physician shall also attend all/none of College's other practice sessions, excluding scrimmages, during the term of this agreement.

3. Physician shall make recommendations to the coaching staff, trainers, and other personnel as to the handling of all orthopedic (or other medical) matters with regard to the athletes in College's ...... program. Such recommendations shall include prescribing treatment for injuries and other orthopedic (or medical) problems, and recommendations for surgical and other hospital procedures when necessary. All physician charges for such surgery and other hospital procedures are not covered under the terms of this agreement.

4. As compensation for all consulting services rendered hereunder, College agrees to pay to Physician the sum of $...... to be paid upon the execution of this agreement.

5. It is understood and agreed that Physician is an independent contractor with regard to all consulting services to be rendered hereunder, and is not acting as College's agent, employee or servant. [*Optional:* It is also understood that Physician is not an insurer of results in any medical treatment rendered under the terms of this agreement.]

6. This agreement is to be construed under and governed by the laws of the State of ....

IN WITNESS WHEREOF, the parties hereto have executed this agreement in duplicate originals on the day and year first above written.

```
...... College
By: _____
Dr. ..................................................................
By: _____
```

Appendix 2

SAMPLE ORGANIZATIONAL MODEL

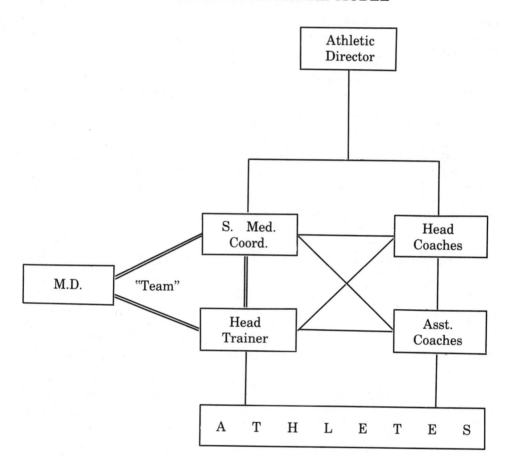

Appendix 3

INJURY REPORT

INJURY REPORT FROM ATHLETIC TRAINER TO PHYSICIAN
Name:　　　　　　　　Sport:　　　　　　　School:
Date of Report:　　　　　　　Date of Injury:
Person Completing Report:
　　　　　　　　　(Athletic Trainer)　　　　(Title)　　　(Phone)
Body Part Injured:

Mechanism of Injury (How? What Happened?):

Physical Findings:
Tentative Diagnosis:
Immediate Care:
Comments:

Follow Up:　　　☐ Physician Visit And/Or X-Rays Recommended
　　　　　　　☐ Physician Visit Not Recommended

_____　　　　　_____
　　(Athlete's Signature)　　　　　　　　(Trainer's Signature)

INJURY REPORT FROM PHYSICIAN TO ATHLETIC TRAINER
Name:　　　　　　Sport:　　　　　　School:
Diagnosis:
Treatment/Rehabilitation Program:

Copy of Specific Program Enclosed:　　Yes ☐　　No ☐
Estimated Time Loss:
Follow Up:　　☐ Must see me/another physician prior to return to practice and/or competition.
　　　　　☐ May be checked by athletic trainer in lieu of visit to a physician.
　　　　　☐ May return to practice and/or competition upon successful *completion* of the treatment/rehabilitation program specified above.
　　　　　☐ May return to practice and/or competition immediately with the following modifications:

Comments:

_____　_____　_____
　(Physician's Signature)　　　　　(Date)　　　　　　　(Phone)

Note: Keep pink copy for your records and return all other copies with the athlete.

Appendix 4

INJURY CARE RECOMMENDATION

INJURY CARE RECOMMENDATION

Name: Sport:
Date: Injury:
Recommended Care:

☐   May continue regular activity
☐   Should modify activity as follows:

☐   Must see me prior to return to activity:
☐   Other:

_____

(Doctor's signature)

Chapter 8

EMERGENCY MEDICAL SERVICES FOR LARGE CROWDS

By

Chester Lloyd

§ 8-1. Introduction.

As the football crowd grows anxious during the end of the second half of the season's last game, a middle-aged spectator clutches his chest, moans and falls backward into his seat. His wife and friends attempt to revive him, but he doesn't respond — heartbeat and breathing have ceased. If he is to have a chance at surviving the heart attack trained help must arrive shortly.

When incidents such as this occur at home, we pick up the phone and dial our local emergency medical service. But when life-threatening emergencies occur in a crowd, the public is often at the mercy of the facility for providing a planned, organized and rapid response to its emergency medical needs.

§ 8-2. Duty to Provide an Emergency Medical Capability.

Numerous studies have shown that medical emergencies occur with some frequency at large gatherings. One such study reviewed injury and illness data collected over four football seasons at a stadium with a capacity of 75,000. (Ref. 1) The results showed that an average of 5.23 patients (2.83-8.00 patient range) where seen by stadium emergency medical teams per 10,000 spectators during a four-hour game. Using this data, the facility could foresee from 21-60 medical or traumatic incidents per game. In addition, the stadium or arena environment may foster more medical emergencies than those expected in the general population, because many spectators gulp down "tailgate dinners," imbibe alcoholic beverages and then rush up 100 steps to their seats. For some, this type of activity is the ultimate stress test which increases the risk for cardiac problems.

Facility managers have a legal duty to protect and warn spectators of foreseeable hazards and harms. If medical emergencies and injuries which are foreseen in large crowd situations are not handled properly through an organized emergency medical response system, the spectator may suffer additional harm. Harm results from improper emergency management causing aggravation of the acute illness or injury.

§ 8-3. Standards and Guidelines Specify the Scope of Treatments.

The American Heart Association (AHA) sponsored a conference in 1979 to update standards for emergency cardiac care that were originally developed in 1973 by the AHA and the National Academy of Sciences — National Research

Council. Based upon medical research and reports during the 1970's, special recommendations were made for facilities where large crowds are regularly present or can reasonably be anticipated. In such facilities, the recommendations call for a basic cardiac life support capability to be available in 60 seconds or less and an advanced cardiac life support capability within ten minutes, preferably less. (Ref. 2)

Basic cardiac life support prevents circulatory and respiratory arrest via prompt recognition and intervention in cardiac and respiratory emergencies. This level of emergency cardiac care also provides for mouth-to-mouth breathing and chest compression (Cardiopulmonary Resuscitation — (CPR)) should breathing and heart stop. This procedure keeps the vital organs alive since the rescuer acts as the victim's heart and lungs. This procedure can be learned in 4 to 12 hours.

Advanced cardiac life support includes basic life support and elements of cardiac care that require more specialized training. Doctors, nurses and paramedics may provide this type of care which consists of administration of lifesaving drugs and defibrillation of the heart in an attempt to stimulate the heart back into action.

When basic cardiac care is initiated and followed quickly by advanced cardiac care, 80% of those spectators who suffer respiratory and circulatory arrest (sudden death) may survive. This is the basis for the special recommendations. If CPR is not provided to a pulseless and non-breathing patient, after four minutes, irreversible brain death starts to occur. When CPR is provided rapidly but advanced cardiac care is delayed, survivability will be low. The 1979 American Heart Association Standards and Guidelines go on to state that "failure of a facility to provide such a readily achievable lifesaving capability (following the special recommendations) may be found to represent legally actionable negligence." It is known that standards distributed by professional societies, such as the American Heart Association, are likely to be viewed as evidence of the accepted standard of medical care by the courts.

During the AHA conference, much attention was given to "cardiac care." While fractures and other acute injuries and illnesses are important, heart disease is the number one killer in this country. More than half of these deaths occur outside the hospital and many could be prevented through a rapid emergency medical response. If the facility can respond appropriately to a "sudden cardiac death" emergency, other emergencies, many of them not as urgent, will be handled effectively as well. It is important to note that those capable of specialized training in advanced cardiac care usually have the capability to treat other medical and trauma emergencies.

§ 8-4. Other Facilities and State Laws May Dictate Level of Care.

Many facilities which attract large crowds have programs that provide emergency medical systems. Other facilities may be judged by the standards set by such facilities.

Some states have laws relating to emergency medical care at mass gatherings. These laws address numbers of personnel, training, length and type of the event, equipment, and crowd size. Some laws seem impractical because they do not ensure basic and advanced cardiac care according to Heart Association Standards. For example, Connecticut law requires that any gathering of 3,000 persons or more lasting for 18 consecutive hours must provide one physician per 1,000 people. (Ref. 3) In addition, stadiums, athletic fields, arenas, auditoriums, coliseums or other permanently established places of assembly are exempt from this law. The law is probably never used with the exception of a state fair or outdoor music festival. On the rare occasion the law is applied, the physician requirement is not practical and is expensive.

It is important to note that whether a state law addresses emergency medical responses or not, a facility may still be held to other standards of medical care. These standards include the Heart Association's standards and those set by other large-capacity facilities nationally.

§ 8-5. The Emergency Medical System in Action.

Returning to the football game, the following scenario will suggest how a fictitious large-capacity stadium would likely handle medical emergencies.

After the victim's wife shook him with no response, she had to summon aid. She remembered reading the notice which came with her season ticket and which was announced over the loudspeaker at each event. "In case of medical emergency, please notify the nearest usher, police officer or emergency medical team." She had her friend run to the nearest usher to request medical aid.

The usher's orange vest made him clearly visible to the crowd. In addition, he was trained to concentrate on the crowd and not the game. When notified of the emergency, he knew how to react. His facility's emergency medical system had provided him with CPR training, written guidelines and practice in approaching medical emergencies.

On his portable radio, he notified the central communications center of a medical emergency in section L, row 25. He approached the victim and after a quick assessment notified the communications booth that he had a spectator who was not breathing and had no pulse. As he had learned from frequent drills, he positioned the victim across the bench with the help of another usher and provided CPR.

Central communications immediately dispatched a team of emergency medical technicians (EMT's) covering that sector of the crowd. The technicians had taken an 80 to 120 hour course covering the management of medical and trauma emergencies which was used as the ambulance training program for the state. This facility provided experienced EMT's to stabilize and then evacuate victims of medical trauma emergencies from the spectator area.

The communications center also notified the physician and both nurses in the emergency life-support station closest to that area of the stadium. While one nurse readied the station for receiving the patient, the physician and other nurse responded to the incident with advanced cardiac care equipment via a golf cart modified to serve as a "mini" ambulance.

Through the communications center other ushers and public safety personnel (police, security, etc.) were alerted for crowd control. Since all radio messages were coordinated through one central point, all facility public-safety and medical personnel were notified of the emergency and acted as per a planned, clear and concise protocol. Some responded to the incident, others filled in areas left vacant by those responding to the victim and the remaining public safety staff were alerted that resources for a particular area were busy and to be prepared to provide coverage to other areas as well as their own. The emergency medical-system coordinator, the security chief, the head usher and other administrative personnel were present in the center to help coordinate the response.

Shortly after the ushers started CPR, the team of two EMT's arrived with oxygen and a special patient litter to facilitate safe evacuation. The team continued CPR but provided ventilation to the victim now using the much-needed oxygen. The team prepared the victim for transportation to the waiting golf cart just outside the section L entrance.

In order for the patient to receive advanced cardiac care as soon as possible, the physician and nurse, both proficient in emergency medicine, met the EMT's with the cart and administered the initial steps of advanced cardiac care. Basic cardiac care, now supplemented by advanced cardiac care, was continued enroute to the life support station.

At the station, which offered a more controlled environment and an additional complement of life-saving drugs and equipment, the patient's heart resumed beating after a few rounds of treatment. The physician-in-charge relayed the details of the patient's condition and treatment to the local hospital via the telephone so they could prepare to receive the patient. After the victim's condition stabilized, he was transferred to the local hospital by one of the three ambulances stationed at the stadium. One ambulance was on the playing field solely for the participants, the other two were parked outside the life-support units on each side of the stadium for spectator emergencies. By having an ambulance near a station, the risk of hitting spectators on crowded walks and drives was lessened considerably.

The entire incident, from the initial call for help to hospital admission, was thoroughly documented by written reports. The EMT's, being licensed and responsible for basic cardiac care, documented their treatment which also specified that ushers were doing resuscitation. This report and the physician's documentation of advanced care were kept on file for legal purposes and follow-up evaluation.

In summary, a heart-attack victim was given a second chance at life because the facility's emergency medical system was planned and organized around the goal of rapid basic (within 60 seconds) and advanced (in less than 10 minutes) cardiac care. Coordination through experienced leadership and interagency cooperation was responsible for meeting this goal.

§ 8-6. Planning for Emergency Medical Response.

Plan an on-site, emergency medical-response system, by structuring the system around the following elements:

A. *Public Access to Emergency Medical Aid.*

1. Provide and train public safety officers, ushers, vendors and other facility personnel who know how to promptly summon medical aid.
2. Place emergency medical teams strategically throughout the crowd (coverage in parking areas before/after events).
3. Clearly mark emergency life support units (medical aid stations) and place them in highly visible locations.
4. Use printed programs and season-ticket package inserts to identify locations of emergency life-support units (so those with minor ailments know where to seek aid) and briefly describe how to summon help (for medical and trauma emergencies requiring evacuation by emergency medical teams).
5. Use public address announcements such as: "In the case of emergency, notify your nearest usher, police officer or emergency medical team."
6. Install public emergency phones or video monitors on exit ramps, stairways or other hard-to-monitor areas of the facility.
7. Provide emergency signs, done professionally, and targeted to the facility and crowd characteristics.

B. *Personnel and Training.*

1. Provide all non-medical personnel with guidelines on how to react in medical emergencies.
2. Train non-medical personnel (ushers and security) in basic cardiac life support (CPR).
3. Staff emergency medical teams with emergency medical technicians.
4. Staff emergency life support units with personnel capable of providing advanced cardiac life support (paramedics, nurses or physicians).
5. Provide an adequate number of public safety personnel based upon the size of the crowd, crowd make-up, facility lay-out, environment, event-type, general vs. reserved admission and past injury and illness experience.
6. Arrange for ambulance transportation by a competent service after patient stabilization in the emergency life-support unit; if outside ambulance service provides on-site ambulances, get proof that personnel are properly trained.
7. Utilize periodic drills to test the effectiveness of the emergency medical system and update the skills of facility personnel.

C. *Central Communications Center.*

1. Coordinate all public-safety communications (medical, security, crowd control, etc.) through a central post allowing for rapid relay of emergency messages.
2. Link emergency medical teams to each other and a central post via portable radios or other means.
3. Develop the capability of non-medical personnel to notify the central post (via radio, intercom or phone) to request emergency medical assistance.

4. Place supervisory public safety and administrative personnel in center to troubleshoot problems.
5. Locate the center preferably in press box or other location which allows view of as much of the facility as possible.

D. *Written Protocols and Guidelines.*

1. Make certain that all non-medical personnel understand written guidelines defining their specific roles in medical emergencies (i.e., who to call or what actions to take before medical teams arrive).
2. Provide the medical staff with written treatment protocols signed by the physician medical director covering all phases of patient treatment in the facility.
3. Develop plans that address actions to be taken when heavy patient load or simultaneous emergencies occur.
4. Coordinate mutual aid agreements and disaster plans with outside public safety agencies in case of heavy patient load or catastrophe.
5. Provide written protocols to demonstrate that the facility and its staff are prepared for medical and trauma emergencies should litigation arise.

E. *Record-Keeping.*

1. Document all emergency treatment rendered at the facility in writing.
2. Include in the record: The patient's name, sex, age, address, next-of-kin; nature of the illness or injuries and a description or the mechanism of how the injuries occurred; location and how the patient was found (i.e., lying face down, sitting, etc.); the chief complaint or signs and symptoms displayed by the patient; vital signs; patient's past medical history, current medications and known allergies to any medications; all treatment rendered by facility personnel (treatment rendered by other persons prior to medical team arrival should be noted, too); how the victim was transported to the emergency life support unit (stretcher, walked, etc.); disposition of the patient (to hospital via ambulance, referred to private physician, etc.); and data such as time call received, date, names of team members and who made the initial call for help.
3. If possible, obtain a signed refusal of medical treatment from any sick or injured person refusing medical assistance.
4. At the emergency life support station keep a log of all patients seen by name, injury or illness complaint and time.
5. Utilize complete records to prevent or defend charges of negligence.
6. Review records retrospectively to prevent future injuries by identifying hazards as well as crowds and events at high risk for problems.
7. Review records to assess emergency medical program effectiveness.

F. *Equipment.*

1. Provide adequate communications devices which permit clear signal reception in all areas of the facility.

2. Equip emergency medical teams (comprised of EMT's) with oxygen and other "tools of their trade."
3. Provide specialized patient litters for safe evacuation from the spectator area and provide a wheeled cart or other device for transport to the emergency life support unit.
4. Provide emergency life support units with state-of-the-art equipment for advanced cardiac life support and other medical and trauma emergencies.
5. Provide on-site ambulances properly equipped as per state and local laws.

G. *Physician Medical Director.*

1. Responsible for all medical treatment given by a facility's emergency medical personnel.
2. Experienced in emergency medicine.

H. *Administrative Coordinator.*

1. Responsible for the overall operation and management of the emergency medical response system.
2. Prepares written protocols and guidelines with the medical director as well as mutual aid and disaster plans with outside public safety agencies.
3. Experienced in emergency medical operations.
4. Probably the most important person in determining the success and cost-effectiveness of the facility's emergency medical program.

These eight elements are guidelines that will help assess present methods for handling medical emergencies or in constructing a new emergency medical system. Pay particular attention to items G and H. The coordinator and medical director should oversee the entire program. Specifically, the coordinator serves as the link between all agencies and should be available during events in the communications center. Whether the coordinator's position is full-time, part-time or assigned to an existing staff member depends on the facility size and event traffic.

A consultant knowledgeable in emergency medical operations at large gatherings may be used to evaluate and prepare an emergency medical system for a facility. In preparing a system, the consultant may identify community resources (personnel, equipment, etc.), evaluate local and state laws, develop training programs, review facility insurance coverage (relating to the emergency medical program), and give advice on crowd management and facility safety. A consultant can also instruct a facility manager in emergency medical-program maintenance and can be available for future planning. Using a consultant to develop a program to fit a facility may save time and reduces the chance for costly error.

A coordinator or consultant should select a physician medical director with knowledge of emergency medical response. This physician should underwrite all medical protocol and treatment given by the facility medical staff. To illustrate, a facility may request a physician from the local medical center's emergency department to serve as the director. If he agrees, for a stipend or as a service of the medical center, he and the coordinator would draw up treatment procedures addressing the scope of medical care provided in the facility. Only treatment provided for in writing, signed by this physician, may be given. Even if aspirins are dispensed by facility nurses, written protocol, signed by the physician should specifically define under what conditions and to whom aspirin should be provided. Whether the medical director attends each event or not, all medical treatment is carried out under his initial written protocol. The medical director, in cooperation with the coordinator, will want to certify that all medical personnel are competent. Should litigation arise, treatment protocol shows the courts that medical treatment provided at the facility followed the accepted standard of medical care and was given under the direction of the facility's physician medical director.

In planning a system, facility managers should use caution if they depend on outside agencies for on-site emergency medical needs. In a true account, while city ambulances and paramedics sped away from a stadium of 50,000 spectators to respond to a serious auto accident, a spectator with a medical emergency was without transportation to the hospital. Finally, a station-wagon-type vehicle was used because no ambulances would be available for some time. Fortunately, the facility had an on-site emergency medical system which attended to the victim. In this case, it would have been prudent for the facility to require that the ambulance contractor commit the ambulances to the facility from one hour before to one hour after the game.

If hospitals or ambulances are next door, the emergency medical response system should still be planned as if the facility were across town. Remember that the rescue vehicles may be out on other calls and a hospital's emergency-department staff usually is not available to come to the facility. Consider too that ambulance crews stationed outside the entrance may have long response times trying to get through the crowds. Only with the emergency medical personnel and the emergency life-support station(s) placed strategically throughout the crowd and the facility, along with other facility personnel knowing their roles in emergencies, can the public be assured of rapid access to emergency medical help. The days of the simple first-aid station are gone. Today, having enough people on-hand under one roof or in a confined area to populate a small city is quite a responsibility.

Liability insurance covering the facility should be reviewed when implementing the emergency medical program. Since the type of coverage depends upon the individual facility and insurance company, facility administrators should seek advice from their insurer or consultant.

Emergency medical technicians, paramedics, nurses and physicians are all state-licensed health professionals. Even though they may have liability insurance, a facility should have its own liability insurance policy. Ushers, security and other ancillary personnel who are trained in CPR or first aid will usually be covered under the facility's general-liability policy which may include an incidental malpractice clause covering personnel in the event they assist the medical teams with CPR or other basic procedure. Since it is not their specific duty to provide medical treatment at the facility, and provided they are not licensed health professionals, they do not need medical malpractice insurance.

In regard to outside ambulance companies contracted to provide transportation to the hospital or additional personnel, the facility should be named as an additional insured on the ambulance company's insurance policies. The facility should also check on the limits of such policies. All ambulance staff and vehicles should be checked to make sure they comply with state and local laws.

The argument has been made that having personnel with little or no training may be "safer" than having licensed professionals. This is not a valid argument because in court the facility with the documented and functioning emergency medical system in place will be better able to defend charges of negligence. The only loss may be that of the lawyer's fees. But without an emergency medical program, loss in the form of claims may be more because of damage done to a victim by inexperienced and untrained rescuers in an environment that called for trained professionals. Even the "Good Samaritan laws" are being challenged because victims need protection too.

In summary, plan your program around the eight guidelines to achieve a "tiered" emergency medical response; provide basic cardiac care initially using ushers or security personnel and continue with teams of emergency medical technicians who transfer the patient to an on-site life support station where advanced cardiac care may be provided under the direction of a physician.

§ 8-7. Program Complexity.

Every facility, large or small, should have a plan of action for medical emergencies and the capability of rendering basic cardiac care. The question of program complexity deals primarily with the provision of advanced cardiac care. The responsibility to provide advanced cardiac care is not clear-cut when dealing with facilities which attract moderate-sized crowds (1-10,000 spectators). Whether advanced care should be provided at these facilities or events may depend upon: event length and type (rock concert vs. musical), crowd type (age, emotion, etc.), a facility's or event's past illness and injury record, weather (i.e., warm weather often results in more medical incidents), and medical (personnel, equipment, etc.) and financial resources.

The special recommendations from the Heart Association do not define an absolute crowd size when dealing with the provision of advanced cardiac care for a "large gathering." If a facility attracts 40,000 per event, advanced cardiac care should be made available without reservation. But in planning a system for a facility with 7,000 (for example) in regular attendance, the decision to provide advanced care on-site may weigh on a facility audit addressing the factors listed above and other considerations which may surface during the investigation.

To illustrate, New York State's Mass Gathering Law requires a physician-on-site at any public function with 25,000 or more in attendance. If a facility in New York was expecting 7,000 "60-and-over folks" for a "senior olympics," a reasonable and prudent facility manager would do well to exceed the law and provide advanced cardiac care. If a person suffered a heart attack and was unable to be revived with basic cardiac care alone, considering the event and the type of crowd, a lawyer might argue that medical emergencies were foreseeable and the facility should have followed the Heart Association's recommendations.

As a distant alternative to on-site advanced care personnel in small facilities, a "life-support kit" carrying some essential resuscitation equipment may be kept and maintained at the facility in the event that physicians in the crowd are willing to help. The kit would have to be checked and restocked periodically with a physician's order. Facilities should take care and make sure those who offer to provide treatment with the kit are licensed physicians.

§ 8-8. Summary/Conclusion — Program Benefits.

Although there is initial expense for such a program, costs can be kept low depending upon existing facility and community resources. At a university, volunteer student EMT's may supplement a paid local staff. Equipment may be borrowed from university agencies or local service groups, such as the Red Cross or the local disaster agency. Having all agencies sit down after events to critique and improve public safety is not expensive. A facility's emergency response capabilities can be improved greatly through education, coordination and interagency cooperation.

At facilities hosting sporting events, a spectator emergency medical system will benefit athletes by making available to them the most up-to-date emergency treatment procedures. In certain facilities across the nation, spectators receive much more advanced emergency treatment than athletes simply because the athletic field is often the trainers' and coaches' domain and, except in extreme situations, off-limits to facility emergency medical teams. An experienced emergency medical technician or emergency physician should serve not to replace the trainer or team physician, but could offer valuable advice in handling emergencies on the field. After witnessing players being removed from the playing fields with unstable fractures which did not receive immobilization, or upon reading about a marathoner who was unable to find emergency medical aid when suffering heat exhaustion during her 20th mile, it is evident that athletes would gain advantages in spectator emergency medical plans.

Through rapid detection and prompt intervention of medical emergencies, the emergency medical system helps manage crowd confusion and promotes good public relations. In addition, facility safety hazards may be decreased by thorough review of well-documented injury reports. Most important, state-of-the-art emergency medical treatment, delivered by a trained staff, in a well-organized and controlled emergency medical system, will save lives and reduce risk and the chances for liability.

REFERENCES

1. T. Demetri Vacalis, Ph.D., & J. Blewett, M.D., "An Advanced Emergency Medical Care System at the University of Texas Football Stadium," 30 *Journal of the American College Health Association* 145-47 (December 1981).

2. 1979 National Conference on Cardiopulmonary Resuscitation and Emergency Cardiac Care, "Standards and Guidelines for Cardiopulmonary Resuscitation (CPR) and Emergency Cardiac Care (ECC)," 244 *Journal of the American Medical Association* No. 5 at 453-509 (August 1, 1980).

3. Connecticut Public Health Code (1980) § 19-549, Mass Gathering Law.

Part 3

MARKETING MANAGEMENT

Chapter 9

CHARACTERISTICS OF SPORT MARKETING

By

Bernard Mullin

§ 9-1. Introduction.

Sport marketing is probably the most exciting and dynamic area in sports management because it encompasses promotion, advertising, selling and public relations. It is the management function where the product meets the consumer, and as rapidly as consumer tastes change, so must marketing strategies. Given the recent explosion in interest in sport marketing, it is hard to imagine why so little attention has been given to the marketing of sport for so much of its history. Nowhere is this more evident than the aggressive effort put forth by the Los Angeles Olympic Organizing Committee (LAOOC) for the 1984 Summer games, contrasted with the marketing efforts of earlier games. The LAOOC, for the first time in the history of the Olympic Games, made a profit and presented games which will not cost the taxpayers of the host city dearly for many years to come. The LAOOC effort, and in particular the efforts of Peter Ueberroth, come on the heels of 20 years of build-up in the activity level of sport marketers and an ever-increasing involvement in the promotion and sponsorship of sport by corporations from business and industry. In this same time period, the print and broadcast media have markedly increased their coverage of sport, and the electronic media has provided sport organizations with multi-million dollar broadcast contracts that swamp revenue from operating income. Landmark legal cases involving franchise movement and the control of rights to broadcast sports events have totally changed normal business practices. Concurrently less publicized and seemingly less traumatic events have been occurring in the participant sport segments of the sport industry. New sports may have come and gone, but participant-sport consumers have totally changed their desires, and competition for the sport consumer's dollar has intensified to a level never experienced before.

As more attention has been placed on the management and marketing of sport by the general public and by the mass media, new approaches to marketing sport have become necessary (Ref. 1). As a result a new breed of professionals have entered the field, and a new discipline called sports marketing has begun to emerge.

§ 9-2. Sport Marketing Defined.

The term "sports marketing" was coined by the *Advertising Age* in 1978 to describe the activities of consumer and industrial product and service marketers who were increasingly using sport as a promotional vehicle (Ref. 2). Since that time the term has gained wide acceptance. Unfortunately, the media has tended to perpetuate its association with just one small portion of sport marketing activities, marketing, using sport as a promotional vehicle.

Not only is the current conception of the term extremely limited, it is totally inappropriate because it fails to recognize the dominant portion of sport marketing, which is the marketing of sport products/events and services. A further less than desirable factor is that the use of sports (plural) rather than sport (singular) reinforces the view of the sport industry as a diverse and uncoordinated series of segments which have little commonality. There is little doubt that each segment of the sport industry does currently operate independently and with minimal sharing of managerial practice. However, if standardized management and marketing practice is ever to come to the sport industry then the industry segments need to be treated as a homogeneous entity. Use of sport (singular) is important therefore in communicating this concept when associated with the terms sport marketing and sport management.

In an earlier work, the author defined sport marketing using an accepted definition of marketing as a basis:

> "Sport marketing consists of all activities designed to meet the needs and wants of sport consumers primary, secondary and tertiary participants and primary, secondary and tertiary spectators through exchange processes. Sport marketing therefore has developed two major thrusts:
> a. the marketing of sport products and services to consumers of sport; and
> b. marketing using sport as a promotional vehicle for consumer and industrial products and services" (Ref. 3).

Primary participants are those playing the sport; secondary participants are officials, umpires, etc.; and tertiary participants are such persons as broadcasters, P.A. announcers, etc. or possibly individuals gambling on the event. Primary spectators are those watching the event in person; secondary spectators are those consuming the event via the media, (television, radio, newspaper, magazine, etc.), and tertiary spectators are those who experience the sport product indirectly (for example, verbally from primary or secondary spectators or participants). It would also include indirect association with a sport or sport franchise, such as purchasing sport merchandise and souvenirs.

Given the overall focus of this text as a guide for practitioners marketing sport, this chapter will concentrate on the primary thrust of marketing sport products and services, rather than marketing using sport. First, the unique aspects of sport marketing that warrant a distinct approach from regular consumer/industrial product and service marketing are analyzed. Second, through illustrations from diverse segments of the sport industry, a case is made for treating the industry as a single, homogeneous entity requiring essentially similar marketing treatment for each segment. Such a concept should not be that difficult to accept. Simply stated it contends that whether the goal is to fill a stadium (this has been rather crudely but effectively summarized as "putting meat in the seats"), or getting more members to join a sport club or more people to use a ski resort (the author has termed this, "getting feet on the streets"), the factors which set each aside from general business are present, yet there is enough consistency to warrant a common approach.

Finally, but of greatest practical value, this chapter outlines the often forgotten elements of marketing (market research and the marketing information system) which must be considered by sport marketers before making any of the marketing mix decisions (product, price, promotion and distribution (place)). These factors provide the critical foundation in the development of any marketing strategy. In this respect both the needs of individuals possessing little or no background in marketing as well as those who have considerable sport marketing expertise should be satisfied. For the former, the chapter should serve as a "road map" for a new and uncharted trip. For the latter group it should serve as a "reference manual," reminding practitioners of the foundational stages of the marketing process and reinforcing the logic used in sound decision-making.

§ 9-3. The Development of Sport Marketing.

The majority of the factors which make sport marketing unique may not appear to be that significant when taken individually. Yet when the complete list is viewed, it is apparent that the sport product is markedly different from any other product or service. When this fact is coupled with some of the unique structural elements present in most sport organizations and the unique marketing environment in which sport marketers are required to operate, the need for a unique field of sport marketing becomes evident. Sport marketers actually face a challenge which, on the surface appears to many people to be less demanding than most other industries, but is in fact invariably much more challenging. In the light of such a challenge, it is doubly puzzling why until recently sport organizations have placed so little emphasis on hiring marketing professionals. A look at the most recent media guides of the major professional-sport leagues (Ref. 4), identifies surprisingly few marketing positions. In many cases the incumbents are former athletes/coaches operating in predominantly public relations capacities. Reviewing most sport industry segments reveals the same phenomenon. Few organizations perform any market analysis. Even fewer have market-information systems in place, or in-house advertising professionals on their staff who analyze promotional effectiveness.

§ 9-4. Why Sport Organizations Have Neglected Sport Marketing.

It is understandable that professional sport teams and high-visibility intercollegiate athletic programs have used the media's desire to give sport extensive coverage as an easy way out of spending marketing dollars. However, there is simply no excuse for the avoidance of professional marketing approaches in so many segments of the sport industry. Too much evidence exists that professional marketing techniques are critical to financial survival and too many people close to sport have called into question the old opinion that "winning is everything" in terms of attendance (Ref. 5).

One survey taken in the northeastern section of the United States revealed that aside from sales personnel, former athletes/coaches acting as community relations personnel, and the public relations staff (who are invariably former news reporters or journalism majors, not marketers), less than 25% of sport organizations surveyed had anyone working in a marketing capacity (Ref. 6). Of even greater concern was the revelation that less than 3% of those surveyed had anyone performing the central and most critical marketing functions (market research, the development and maintenance of a marketing information system, and hard analysis of promotional effectiveness). In the last four to five years these same progressive organizations (who not by coincidence also happen to be generally the ones with higher attendance or participation levels), have begun to hire individuals to fill the role of promotions director. The only exception occurs in the National Football League (NFL) where the majority of franchises are close to full-attendance capacity and apparently believe that they do not need such positions.

When we look at industry segments that cannot rely so heavily on media exposure, we find that professionalization in marketing improves. Approximately 20% of court and health clubs have hired specialized marketing personnel and have begun to train full-time sales personnel. Managers of sport programs at resorts such as Hilton Head in South Carolina and administrators of stadia, arenas and auditoriums have followed a similar pattern in recruiting sport marketing professionals to help them reach capacity, to attract conventions and to broaden their event mix. But, here again, such actions are often taken in a vacuum. Those being hired are invariably strong in sales and promotions rather than the careful preparation of scientifically collected market research, or the analysis of advertising effectiveness. One sport marketing executive with responsibility for both a major indoor facility and a professional hockey team recently said about his promotional efforts, "You have to just try things, maybe something outrageous, and then see what works for you!" It is hard to imagine how long such a cavalier attitude would be tolerated in general business and industry. The question remains, why has it been tolerated for so long in sport?

A major area of shortfall in the practice of sport marketing today is the lack of data collection. Why do sport organizations fail to collect, or worse yet, ignore the valuable information which is often generated as part of the normal functioning of the business? A classic example of this is the failure to retain the names and addresses of persons purchasing tickets with a check, or the returning of checks submitted by unsuccessful play-off ticket applicants without recording their names and addresses in a prospect file. Such information can readily be merged into a Marketing Information System (MIS) and be used effectively for direct mailings, rather than resorting to expensive mass media advertising campaigns.

In participant-sport marketing, similar fundamental errors are also being made, but here the question shifts to sales techniques. "Why do the majority of court and health clubs (tennis, racquetball, fitness and health centers), still have the tendency to hire part-time students as control desk personnel who then double as sales staff?" Surely club owners realize that the destiny (and financial stability) of the club is in inexperienced hands? In all but a few clubs, desk personnel comprise the primary consumer contact (on the phone, at the front desk, and for walk-in prospects). It seems incomprehensible that in a business subject to such high customer turnover, and one which is so susceptible to fads and trends, that the most critical marketing function for survival is held in such low regard. Yet it clearly has been overlooked in the past because of absentee ownership and in part because untrained managers have been hired from former participants and coaches. The major reasons they survived in the past was that demand was strong and the competition was no more sophisticated. However, once competition increased and demand dropped off it became a question of survival of the fittest. Needless to say the motivation to adopt professional marketing techniques has risen rapidly for court and health clubs in the last five years.

In the high-visibility segments of the sport industry (professional and intercollegiate sport), sport sponsorship and huge broadcast contracts have diminished the need to market. Yet with continued increases in the competition for the sport consumer's dollar, even in these industry segments, the organizations employing more sophisticated marketing approaches are much more likely to prosper. If a reminder is needed that no segment of the industry is in an impregnable position, a look at the current happenings in professional football should provide a stark warning. The once sacred "golden goose" of the NFL which has provided owners with a safe and consistent flow of "golden eggs," may soon be seriously threatened by the upstart United States Football League (USFL), and internal strife. Today the leagues are engaged in a player talent war, with the USFL apparently winning many of the early rounds. If the TV ratings and attendance figures reflect a significant shift, (the NFL statistics for the 1983 season were disappointing and the USFL figures for the 1984 season were quite good), then the structure of what has long been the most stable and profitable segment of the sport industry would be clearly shaken. No doubt the NFL will soon begin to reassert itself as the history of Commissioner Pete Rozelle's highly successful reign would project that it will. A major part of such resurgence must be an increase in the sophistication of marketing techniques at the franchise level. Only when all of the critical functions of marketing are performed can franchises expect to maintain high attendance in the face of diluted player talent and increased competition.

The reasons why sport organizations have not adopted a comprehensive marketing approach in the past are numerous, yet they are worth reviewing because they provide considerable insight into the future of sport marketing. An examination of these factors is critical both to the goal of providing justification for the existence of sport marketing as a distinct discipline, and to communicating to the sport marketer the need for understanding sport marketing concepts as a basis for marketing success. Reliance on totally intuitive judgments has never been sufficient, but in the future it will no longer be enough to get by. Simply stated, throughout the 1970's and 1980's every aspect of sport marketing underwent permanent changes. The market for the sport product, the competition, the marketing mix (product decisions, pricing decisions, promotional decisions and distribution decisions) and the marketing environment all have become more complex as the sport consumer market has become more complex.

The primary reasons why sport marketing has been a neglected science in the past are, perhaps not surprisingly, also the major factors which make sport marketing unique. For the most part the impact which each factor has on making the sport marketer's role unique is on the increase; therefore, there exists a strong need for a new breed of sport marketing thought. First, the stage is set for this "new thought" and then the milestones of this "thought-process," called the Marketing Planning Process (MPP) are outlined.

§ 9-5. The Unique Aspects of Sport Marketing.

Almost every element of marketing requires significantly different approaches when the product being marketed is sport. Predictably the critical differences lie in the unique aspects of the sport product, and the unusual market conditions facing sport marketers. The author outlined the various unique elements of sport marketing in an earlier work (Ref. 7). Each factor is identified under the relevant marketing topic heading, as follows:

A. *The Market for Sport Products and Services.*

   1. *Sport organizations simultaneously compete and cooperate.*

No sport organization can exist in isolation. Professional and intercollegiate sports require other franchises and schools in order to have meaningful competition. Without a partner a game of tennis cannot be played. If there is only one summer sleep-away camp in a market area, camp directors experience greater difficulty recruiting campers. If Johnny's best friend decides to spend his summer at home instead of going to camp, then Johnny does not want to go away to his camp.

   2. *Partly due to the unpredictability of sport, and partly due to the strong personal identification sport consumers experience, sport consumers often consider themselves experts.*

Few decisions in sport go without notice or comment by the media or by consumers. Every decision is second guessed, and can affect the lives (even if insignificantly) of many people. In 1983 Drew Sheinman, Director of Promotions for MLB's Baltimore Orioles, replaced the Oriole fan's favorite seventh-inning-stretch song, "Country Boy" with the song "That Magic Feeling." The fans booed him, but sport-management-trained, Sheinman was smart enough to learn from his consumers. He started a competition to see which song they preferred. Many of his promotional ideas led to the Orioles drawing two million fans and his winning "The Baseball Marketer of the Year Award." Sheinman capped the year by having John Denver appear personally to sing "Country Boy" at the 1983 World Series in Baltimore. Sport marketers and managers operate in a gold-fish bowl, which on occasion can impact negatively on marketing decision making.

To reinforce this fact, consider the findings of the Miller Lite Report on American's Attitude Toward Sports, (which was designed to be representative of the U.S. population as a whole), published in 1983 (Ref. 8). When asked, "Do you think you could play for a professional team if you practiced?" 52% of respondents said Yes. To the question "Do you think that you could do a better job of officiating than most officials?" 74% said Yes. To the question "Do you think that you could do a better job of coaching than the average coach?" — again the majority (51%) said Yes! No other business is viewed so simplistically and with such personal identification as sport is viewed by it's consumers.

B. *The Sport Product.*

1. *The sport product is invariably intangible and subjective.*

What each sport consumer sees in a sport is quite subjective. Few products are open to such a wide array of interpretation by the consumer. This phenomenon makes it extremely difficult for the sport marketer to ensure a high probability of consumer satisfaction. In a scenario of three fans attending the same event together, we might expect quite different views of the event. One fan may have loved the game, the second may have thought it was just o.k., but the third fan may have hated it. Amazingly enough, all three attended the same game!

2. *The sport product is inconsistent and unpredictable.*

Spectator and participant-sport events are equally unpredictable. A baseball game played today is different from next week's game even if the same starting line-ups and pitchers play. There are numerous intangibles such as weather, injuries to players, momentum, the reaction of the crowd and the records and standings of the two teams at the time they play. All of these factors impact on the outcome of the game, and consequently the excitement and satisfaction experienced by the fan. Participant sport is no different. Even two friends who play each other at the same tennis club at the same time every week, experience totally different games each time they play.

Consumer-product marketers market consistency. Sport products by contrast, market the excitement of unpredictability! If the sport marketer had to rely on consumer satisfaction from the event alone, there would be a lot fewer repeat consumers. Fortunately there are product extensions (the facility's amenities, clean restrooms, good-quality concessions at reasonable prices, half-time shows, scoreboards, etc.) to ensure consistency and provide a baseline of satisfaction.

In actual fact it is because the outcome of a sport event is not predictable that sport has so much charm as well as so much frustration.

3. *A greater percentage of the marketing emphasis must be placed on the product extensions rather than the core product.*

All consumer and industrial products and services stake their reputation on providing consistent product quality and service. Holiday Inns Incorporated advertises that there will be "no surprise" for guests. Every Inn worldwide will offer the same standard of service. Sport operates in sharp contrast to this, because no marketer can control how well his team will play, or, for example, how much the weather impacts on ski conditions. In sport, the marketing emphasis must be placed on the product extensions where consistency can be achieved.

This dilemma has often been referred to as the "Do you sell the steak or the sizzle?" controversy. The answer is not a simple one. For some consumers only the quality of the steak is important, for others the style and the atmosphere of the restaurant is the critical factor (the sizzle). For the majority, both are critical. In sport, given that we cannot guarantee the quality of the steak, we must sell both. But we emphasize that there will always be the "sizzle"!

There have been a few cases where sport marketers have overlooked this component of sport marketing philosophy. Perhaps most notable was the New York Mets abortive 1981 season campaign theme "The Magic is Back!" The theme attracted fans who reminisced about the 1969 "Miracle Mets" when they won the World Series of Baseball. After initially attracting considerable attention and interest, the campaign which was developed by the well-respected DELLA-FEMINA Advertising Agency of New York, backlashed on the Mets organization. When on-field performances failed to live up to the promotional promise the magic faded. So did the fans! By season's end the attendance levels were far below the prior season's already low levels. The sport marketer, guided by an ad agency had made a classic faux-pas — promising something he could not deliver! The long term negative impact was still being felt by the Mets at the gate in the 1984 season despite a highly successful record and exciting pennant race. The significant problem left for the Mets marketing department to solve was what could they do for an encore. The credibility of future promotional themes became seriously questioned.

4. *The sport product is a perishable commodity; it has to be pre-sold.*

Sport products are developed in anticipation of demand and are produced and consumed simultaneously. (Except for some spectator sports which are videotaped for tape-delayed broadcast). No marketer can save a seat for yesterday's game, or yesterday's lift ticket, or the 10:00 p.m. time slot on court No. 1 from last night, and sell it at a later time. The majority of sport products are perishable commodities, requiring preselling.

5. *Sport is generally publicly consumed, and consumer satisfaction is invariably affected by social facilitation.*

The loneliness of the long distance runner notwithstanding, almost all sport products are consumed in a public setting, and in the company of others. Further, the enjoyment of the activity is frequently dependent upon the enjoyment of others, or at least is a function of interaction with other people. One study showed that less than two percent of those attending collegiate and professional sport events attend by themselves (Ref. 9). Only a few sports (predominantly the ecological sports) can be undertaken by a single person. Consequently sport marketers need to recognize the role which social facilitation plays. Special programs and promotional plans need to be developed which maximize the enjoyment and satisfaction of the group, with different promotions aimed at the different demographic groups which make up the group. For example, more adult or "swinging-singles" promotions will occur in the 1980's and less and less promotions aimed at children.

6. *The sport marketer often has little or no control over the composition of the core-product and frequently has only limited control over some of the key ingredients of the product extensions.*

Most consumer and industrial product marketers have a major say in the composition of their organizations' product mix. The industrial marketer performs consumer research and then sets about to establish a product line which satisfies needs. In spectator sport marketing, this accepted marketing practice does not take place. The coaching staff and/or the general manager are in charge of recruiting, player drafting, trades and acquisitions. Players with major drawing appeal may be traded without consultation with the marketing staff. One of the more ignominious actions in this respect occurred in the National Hockey League (NHL), where the Boston Bruins traded away superstar and fan idol Bobby Orr. The nose-dive in Bruins attendance in the early 1970's after the trade stood in stark contrast to the decade of sell-outs which preceded it. Yet the innocent marketer was held accountable for filling the empty seats!

The other critical element of the core-product of a spectator sport organization, besides the playing staff, is the schedule. Most colleges are able to impact on their own schedules with the exception of conference and playoff games. However, all professional sport schedules are developed by the league office with limited input from the team's marketing staff. Often games are scheduled on impossible days to promote. To a lesser degree some participant sports experience a similar problem. Ski resorts, golf clubs, outdoor tennis and country clubs have no control over the weather which is the most critical factor in determining demand for their products.

    7. *Sport is both a consumer and an industrial product.*

Marketing theory classifies products into two categories. Those products consumed by an end-user are called consumer goods. Those products used by a manufacturer in the production of another product are called industrial goods. Sport is produced as an end product for mass consumer appeal for both spectators and participants (a consumer good). Spectator and participant sports are also used by business and industry who sponsor events and sport broadcasts and advertise in conjunction with sport events and sport organizations as a means of reaching their own consumers. Business also uses sport figures to represent, endorse and promote their products, and many businesses also purchase tickets and private boxes at sport events, in order that they may entertain their clients (an industrial good).

    8. *No product evokes such a strong personal identification and such an*
       emotional attachment as sport.

Fans of professional and collegiate sport often view themselves as being part of the team, and view their involvement in sport as a major thrust in their lives. The Miller Lite study previously quoted revealed the pervasiveness of sport in American society. Of those surveyed 95% said that they were affected by sport on a daily basis [In this study "affected by sport" was defined as playing, watching (in person or on television), listening to, reading or talking about sport]. What fan does not say, "We won!" when the team he supports wins? One study of soccer fans in Brazil (Ref. 10) revealed a remarkable association between productivity and fan morale dependent upon the fortunes of the national team. World wars have even been fought over sport, and if we are to believe the popular press, numerous divorces are the result of preoccupation with sport. The sport fan, and to a lesser yet more critical extent, the sport participant feels that the sport product belongs to him or her, and for many it is a critical component of their lifestyle. The positive side of such an emotional bond also carries a negative side. A strong backlash occurs when fan favorites are traded or when teams are moved, (Oh, those Brooklyn Dodgers!), and when product modifications are made. Once again this factor applied to participant sport to a much lesser degree. Many tennis players have a favorite playing surface which best complements their game and get most upset if they have to play on a different playing surface.

9. *Sport has an almost universal appeal and pervades all elements of life.* There are several ways in which sport can be viewed as having universal appeal:

   a. Geographically — sport is evident in every nation on the earth and has been an important part of most civilizations since the advent of man. (Interestingly, in a sport such as soccer which is played in an organized form by more than 120 countries, the national personality is often evident in the style of play.)

   b. Demographically — sport appeals to all demographic segments (young, old; male, female; blue collar, white collar). Sport has sometimes been referred to as the great "leveller" of people from different social classes.

   c. Socio-culturally — sport is associated with every element of leisure and recreational activity, along with many of mankind's more basal activities, motivations and needs. In this respect sport has been said to be a mirror of society.

Sport is associated with:

   a. *Relaxation and entertainment.* (It is theater, and melodrama; it is a play and according to catharsis theory it is a relief from stress).

   b. *Exercise.* (For participants it becomes a major part of some individuals' lifestyles. Few spectators gain any exercise value, except for "12 oz. armcurls.")

   c. *Eating.* (Spectators invariably eat while spectating. Participants often eat after exercising in the facility where they exercised.)

   d. *Drinking alcohol.* (Consumption of alcohol is often associated with viewing of sport. Many participants drink after playing sport.)

   e. *Sex.* (Sport has often been associated with sexual connotations. Women wanting to watch men in shorts showing their physical prowess, and men watching women in leotards in form-sports such as ice-skating and gymnastics. While these traditional sexual stereotypes are breaking down, many traditions continue. Cheerleaders, sport team groupies, taking dates to sport events and "seeing and being seen" at high school and college sport events, are no less popular activities today than they were twenty-five years ago.)

   f. *Gambling.* (Whether legal or illegal, dependent upon the state or the sport, gambling has a strong association with sport. In particular, a significant part of the popularity of NFL football is said to be attributable to the heavy betting on beating the point spread.)

   g. *Drugs.* (With stronger crowd security, the drug association in sport is primarily concerned with athletes' use of drugs.)

   h. *Physical violence.* (Both on the field, off the field and between participants, spectators and even officials.)

   i. *Social identification.* (Association with a particular group, institution or community.)

j. *Vicarious gratification.* (Basking in the reflective glory of a team's victory.)

k. *Economic/legal environment.* (Salary inflation, contract disputes, strikes, court battles in sport often parallel similar economic and legal undercurrents occurring in society as a whole.)

l. *Religion.* (According to renowned sport philosopher Michael Novak (Ref. 11), sport has many quasi-religious properties.)

m. *Business and industry.* (Apart from the direct association [sponsorship, endorsement, etc.] already discussed, much of the language, culture and mythology of business is associated with sport. "At XYZ Incorporated we have got to put a winning team together." "When in doubt, punt!" " John will be quarterbacking this project for us."

C. *The Price of Sport.*

1. *The price of the sport product itself is invariably quite small in comparison to the total cost paid by the consumer when consuming sport products.*

One estimate of spending by fans attending Pittsburgh Pirates baseball games indicated that just one third of the total cost paid by Bucs fans to watch Pirates games actually went to the Pirates organization (Ref. 12). The remaining two thirds went in transportation and entertainment costs and related expenditures to unaffiliated organizations. There is little that most organizations can do to impact on this relationship, except to ensure that they have full control over parking and concessions rights and to offer stadium clubs, etc., whenever possible. As a result most organizations accept this relationship as a fact of life. However, some significant trends have begun to evolve. At many ballparks a wider food menu is being offered. Some clubs have stopped using outside ticket agencies such as Ticketron, because of the surcharge (usually about $.50 to $1.00) and the commission fee (usually about 3 to 5%) which are levied. Instead they are becoming their own ticket agents once again.

This problem is particularly acute in downhill ski resorts, which have undergone some marked changes in the last decade. A hypothetical situation perhaps might illustrate this point best. For a skier from St. Louis, Missouri who wishes to fly to the Colorado Rockies for a skiing-weekend, the total tab might easily exceed $500 (with only limited equipment purchases). As little as $50 might be spent on lift tickets and perhaps $50 in food, drink and ski shop purchases at the ski resort. In this example at best only 20% of the total revenue generated by this resort's ability to attract a skier would end up in the pocket of the resort owners. Obviously any price discounts in weekend lift tickets contemplated by the resort operators would have a minimal impact in enticing this individual to ski more often. As a result many resorts have undertaken horizontal integration and now own the hotels, bars and stores in the towns surrounding their resorts. Twentieth-Century Fox Incorporated, the movie and entertainment company, purchased the ski resort of Vail, Colorado in the 1970's. In order to fully capitalize on their investment, they also purchased a good percentage of the retail businesses in the town.

2. *Indirect revenues are frequently greater than direct operating revenues.*

Each year professional and collegiate sports receive television contracts offering more and more dollars from local and national media to broadcast their games. U.S. television rights to the 1988 Winter and Summer Olympic games were recently sold for 400% of the previous fee. Each NFL team is guaranteed a $14m share per annum of the national television contract which is at least 200% of potential gate receipts for the largest of stadia in the league, even if it were sold out for the entire season. Concessions, parking, souvenirs and merchandising, program advertising, signage, sponsorship agreements, joint promotions, trade-outs and tie-ins all increase the organizations' non-operating revenue. Even in commercial health and fitness clubs, the indirect revenues in multi-sport clubs are beginning to rival direct membership dues and court usage fees as the predominant source of income. By way of illustration the most recent industry survey places indirect revenues in multi-concept clubs at just over 50% of gross receipts (Ref. 13).

3. *Sport programs have rarely been required to operate on a for-profit basis.*

As stated in point 2 above, many sport organizations can rely on significant revenue from non-operating sources. At almost every level of sport, outside financial support exists. Parks and recreation departments underwrite youth sport from tax-payer's dollars. The same dollars go to support the local school sport programs and college alumni are asked to bankroll athletic departments. One estimate (Ref. 14) indicated that just 60 of the more than 1000 colleges offering football programs actually broke even on football. Yet football continues to be referred to as a revenue sport, as if it were profit-making. Professional teams play in publicly subsidized arenas often at ridiculously low rates and in some leagues, ownership changes every five years once the tax-shelter advantages have been used up.

Over the years this "open checkbook" approach led to an atmosphere in which many segments of the sport industry did not need to operate with regard to the "bottom-line." Even the media helped support this state of affairs by providing free publicity. (Public organizations receive free coverage because of the commitment to public service; and the highly visible college and professional teams receive coverage because of widespread interest). As a result the professionalism in sport management suffered severely.

D. *The Promotion of Sport.*

1. *The widespread exposure given by the mass media to sport has resulted in a lowered emphasis on sport marketing.*

For the reasons outlined above, sport has not been forced to place an emphasis on marketing and promotion to the same degree as organizations in other industries. Sport has been able to rely upon publicity as its major promotional tool. Every newspaper has a sport section, in some cases it is the largest single section. The major papers have special supplements devoted to sport. The broadcast media devotes large blocks of time to sport coverage and approximately 20% of news time to sport. The reason why this happens is simply the widespread interest in sport! As cited earlier, the Miller Lite Study showed that 95% of Americans felt that their lives were affected by sport on a daily basis!

2. *Because of the visibility which sport enjoys, many businesses wish to associate with sport.*

The exposure granted sport by the media has not gone unnoticed by consumer and industrial product marketers. Sport provides a promotional vehicle where the audience (exposure) is often sizeable and the make-up of a sport audience for any given sport can be predicted comparatively accurately in advance. In addition the quality of the audience (the demographics) is generally good. Each sport attracts a different audience, consequently sponsorship of an event allows a corporate sponsor to segment its audience quite successfully when using different sports. Sport audiences and participants are usually higher income, up-scale groups who provide prime targets for product marketers. In addition, the association with sport places the company's product in a favorable light, and exposes the product at a time when the audience is invariably in a positive frame of mind. Consequently the natural resistance processes of the consumer are "let-down." The increasing use of athletes as product spokespersons is in large part due to the ability of the athlete to get the attention of the audience, thereby cutting through the "advertising noise." Not only does the athlete get attention, many are given considerable "source-credibility" by the sport fan consumer.

Once again, sport's ability to have its promotional expenditures underwritten by corporate partners through sponsorship, tie-ins (joint advertising or promotion), or trade-outs ("quid pro quo" — reciprocal trading or bartering of services without direct payment), is unequalled in any segment of the economy. The negative side is that such support leads to a reduction in the need, and consequently the motivation, to analyze advertising effectiveness. If you are not paying for it, why bother to see if it's well spent! Despite the "bottom-line" approach adopted by most organizations in their regular business practice, when it comes to associations with sport, there has been very limited hard analysis of the effectiveness of sport sponsorship. A recent survey of eight major corporations sponsoring sport events revealed that just two companies surveyed, Manufacturers Hanover Trust of New York and Anheuser Busch, Inc. of St. Louis, Missouri (Ref. 15) performed any direct analysis of return on investment, cost per exposure or any of the standard advertising response calculations. Simply stated, the other six were content to rely on anecdotal data, and the few isolated cases where market share increases can be linked to association with sport.

Hard empirical data on the effectiveness of tying into sport has been generally limited to athlete endorsements, with little being published on the effectiveness of sport promotion (Ref. 16). For example, the Miller Brewing Company (Ref. 17), Ford Motor Company (Ref. 18) and the Hertz Automobile Rental Corporation (Ref. 19) have all noted significant increases in market share from the use of athletes or former athletes. John Riggins of the NFL Washington Redskins spoke for Ford, O.J. Simpson, former NFL superstar with the Buffalo Bills and San Francisco Forty-Niners, spoke for Hertz, and Miller has used numerous former athletes and coaches, an owner and two officials to speak for their Lite Beer brand.

The net impact of the increasing interest in sport sponsorship is good for sport in every respect except one. Sport sponsorship provides less incentive for the sport marketer to stand on his or her own two feet and adopt a comprehensive approach to sport marketing.

E. *The Sport Distribution System and the Sport Facility.*

Most sport products are consumed in the location where they are produced. With the exception of the sporting goods industry and sport events which are broadcast, sport produces its product at the same location where it is consumed. Apart from the entertainment, food service and hospitality industries, there is no other industry which operates in this manner.

Traditional marketing spends much of its time and effort on the physical distribution channels and networks needed to get the product from manufacturer to consumer. However, sport does not physically distribute its product. The viewing rights to the product are physically distributed via broadcast networks and ticket distribution networks, which frequently lie outside of the direct control of the sport organization, consequently this realm of marketing which deals with physical movement of a product through distribution channels holds limited relevance to sport.

The above list of the unique aspects of sport marketing sets the backdrop for the market conditions in which sport marketers are required to operate. While none by itself is overwhelming, and some factors are not totally unique, the combination of all these aspects does provide a unique challenge for sport marketers which demands a significantly different approach.

In a nutshell, a sport marketer is asked to market a product which is entirely unpredictable, inconsistent and open to subjective interpretation. This task is undertaken in a highly competitive marketplace for most industry segments with a much lower promotional budget than similarly sized organizations in other industries. Finally, the sport marketer must do all of this with only limited direct control over his product mix. On the bright side, the media is anxious to give wide exposure to almost every move the sport organization makes, and many opportunities exist for revenue-generating associations with business and industry.

We now have an idea of what sport marketing is, and yet so little has been written on the subject. Almost no theory has been published in sport marketing and the few successful experiences which have been documented in professional journals rarely detail any fundamental concept or principles which are behind the successful application. As a result the novice is left with little more than guesswork when transplanting the ideas of the industry's "gurus" from one market situation to their own market conditions. Only the more astute marketer can selectively modify the ideas of Don Canham, who as the Athletic Director at the University of Michigan devised the marketing plans which resulted in the sellouts of their 104,000 seat football stadium for longer than anyone can remember. In marketing terms, Slippery Rock State College, Pennsylvania is a lot further than 500 miles from Ann Arbor, Michigan. What works for a Division I program in the midwest may not even work at another Division I program across the same state let alone for smaller schools. Not to demean the words of Don Canham, who is clearly a very insightful and successful sport marketer, the warning being sounded here is that marketers must realize that such words are unlikely to bear fruit unless the individual hearing the ideas and concepts for the first time has a frame of reference or a theory base upon which to hang the information. In the absence of prior experience, or a framework for taking an idea and modifying it to a given market situation, the chances for marketing success are indeed slim. It is hoped that the major benefit of this article will be to help provide such a framework for marketing decision-making. Let us now take a closer look at marketing and the steps in the process of developing, implementing and evaluating marketing strategy.

§ 9-6. What Is Marketing?

The student new to the study of marketing can be excused for naively believing that marketing is nothing more than sales. Two articles by sport industry analysis previously cited (Refs. 20, 21) would indicate that many sport organizations are equally naive about their marketing practices. To many of them, marketing is synonymous with sales and promotional gimmickry. Such an approach is almost understandable given the focus of many articles written by practitioners who laud their peers to "Promote or Perish" (Ref. 22). There is nothing wrong with sport marketers using the desire on the part of the media to provide free exposure to the sport product as a major promotional tool. Within certain limits there is nothing wrong with gimmicky promotions (especially when their cost is totally underwritten by a sponsor). There is nothing wrong with promotions and giveaways, as long as they do not detract from the sport itself. However, there are numerous questions which go begging a response in such a simplistic approach to sport marketing.

The first and most critical stage in marketing involves the development of a comprehensive Marketing Information System (MIS). In the MIS data is generated, collected and retrieved in a form which enables the decision-maker to make sound judgments about the product, the price of the product, the facility where the product will be sold, how the product will be distributed (if at all) and how it will be promoted. In the absence of hard data on marketing research and performance, much decision-making is necessarily heuristic (rule of thumb) in nature. The danger in such an approach was pointed out by Philip Kotler, considered to be perhaps the most influential writer in marketing. Kotler said that marketing information is the key to successful marketing strategy. In an earlier work the author reinforced this view: "making marketing decisions without market research data is like taking a trip without a road map" (Ref. 23). When it's an unknown trip, smart people simply don't do it! An MIS provides a system for performing market research, and providing continual analysis of the market for the product or service. Further it allows for the monitoring of competitive activity, along with an evaluation of the consumer's response to marketing strategies. With an effective MIS in place the sophisticated sport marketer would demand data on such questions as —

"What days/time-slots/opponents/programs should we promote using special inducements?"

"What is the impact on total attendance or participation levels when a particular night/event is promoted over another?"

"Which opponent or program offers the greatest elasticity of demand in response to a promotion or price discount?"
To illustrate why this data is important, let us look at an example.

"Should a National Basketball Association (NBA) franchise use a promotion which has major drawing power such as the San Diego Chicken or a Jacket Give-Away Nite when the opponent is the Los Angeles Lakers or when the San Diego Clippers come to town?"
Such analysis is not complex for an individual trained in marketing, yet currently this type of analysis is not being undertaken except in the more successful sport organizations. To expand on this question, and make it slightly more complex we might ask, "How is this decision affected if the schedule calls for the Lakers to play on a Friday night and the Clippers on a Sunday afternoon?" No sport organization known to the author is performing research at this level. Yet the output is critical in maximizing promotional effectiveness. Without solid analysis in an industry, myths are perpetuated *ad infinitum*.

It is evident that the bulk of professional and collegiate sport promotions are geared toward marketing the least attractive event-days on a schedule. These events are known in the industry as the "dogs." [The expression "dog" is used here in the same manner as it has come to be used in the popular vernacular of sport practitioners. "Dog" refers to an event that is almost impossible to sell out, such as a game against the team with the worst record in the league or an opponent without any stars. In a court and health club, it might refer to the 2 p.m. to 4 p.m. time slot Monday through Friday or Sunday evening.] One study of the promotions used by the Boston Celtics of the NBA seriously questioned the advisability of such a strategy, in terms of total draw and "bottom-line" gate receipts (Ref. 24). In fact, the more attractive event-day opponents offer greater elasticity of demand (as long as the projected attendance level without a promotion is not too close to the facility's capacity limit). Therefore, promoting the better teams invariably has a more positive impact on total season attendance and hence total revenues. In almost ten years of observation and involvement as a consultant in the sport industry by the author, the effectiveness of certain promotions which are in common use was questioned. In fact many traditional promotions such as bat day, jacket day, etc., often do not increase total attendance in real terms, rather they merely redistribute the attendance pattern of fans. Joe Fan, who lives 90 miles from a ballpark and brings his family of four regularly to two games per year, simply chooses to attend the two games which offer the greatest benefits (the free hat, jacket, poster or rock group playing between the ends of a doubleheader). In economic terms, Joe Fan simply maximizes his family's satisfaction for his sport-consumer dollar! Such consumer strategy is called "cherry-picking" and has no positive benefit to the marketer, even when the cost of the promotion is totally underwritten by a sponsor. The same concern is evident in participant sports. Promotions are only effective if they increase attendance frequency by new consumers, or if they induce the existing consumer to attend more often in the future. It takes time and continual evaluation to determine whether or not a promotion is truly effective.

Consideration of the above questions, and many more issues prior to the onset of any marketing strategy is critical to the success of the sport-marketing effort. Practitioners are only likely to consider such questions, and indeed find the answers to their questions, when such thinking is guided by a comprehensive framework of analysis. The Marketing Planning Process (MPP) outlined by Kotler offers exactly such a framework (Ref. 25). More than a framework for decision-making, the MPP is a flow-chart of the logical progression in marketing thought. Consequently, it forms an ideal topic outline for any discussion on sport marketing.

§ 9-7. The Marketing Planning Process (MPP): The Only Sure Way to Meet the Sport Marketing Challenge of the Future.

Kotler identified the MPP as the central thread to effective marketing. He not only used the process as a prescriptive guide to marketing decision-making, he also advised that its elements should become the major stage in the marketing audit. In the marketing audit all marketing functions and activities are reviewed at least annually to determine their effectiveness. Not only does the MPP provide the backbone of marketing, it communicates the interdependencies of each element of marketing. It also warns of the futility of making decisions in a vacuum. Perhaps more than most models of a process, use of the MPP forces the practitioner to "think each marketing decision through" before it is made.

Other chapters in this text deal with the sales and promotional aspects of sport marketing found in the marketing mix. Consequently, to understand how sport organizations should use the MPP (see the Appendix at the end of this chapter) to respond to the marketing challenges they face, this chapter will focus only on the elements of marketing which precede the core of marketing decision-making (the marketing mix). Not by chance, the elements of the MPP are listed in priority order of progression for marketing decision-making. Conveniently therefore, the MPP can be viewed as a "road map" for the development of sport marketing strategy.

To support the proposition that it is critical to consider every element of the foundational factors of the MPP before making a decision, extensive illustration from the world of sport is provided. Not by coincidence these applications also provide strong support for the consideration of sport marketing as a distinct field of study.

Relevant issues in each of the foundational elements of marketing as they apply to sport are now addressed for the most part in the order in which they appeared in the Marketing Planning Process:

A. *The Market.*

Any analysis of marketing must start quite naturally with consideration of the marketplace for the product or service, specifically an evaluation of the structure of the market, and the needs of potential consumers. One might easily ask at this stage, "How do you know what your market is unless you know what your product is?" The fact is that you do not know. Consequently, the first step for the marketer is to establish a preliminary idea of what the product or program concept or unique product position is. Once the market has been analyzed it may be found that the concept is not viable and needs to be amended; such modification would take place under the marketing-mix function, entitled "The Product." Given that the "position" occupied by the product in the market is evaluated in depth again under that section, it becomes evident that there are some iterative cycles to the MPP. There is no way around this duplication, you must know what your product concept is before you know what the potential market is likely to be! Fortunately such overlap and iterations are kept to a minimum.

B. *The Product Concept or Position.*

In defining the product concept it might appear that the optimal approach would be to identify a very tightly defined market segment to which a very specific product is targeted. This is the case in some markets, and is invariably the case for a new product attempting to penetrate an established market. However, many organizations have realized the benefits of defining their product concept broadly, and offering more than one product option in order to appeal to several market segments. General Motors realized many years ago that it was not simply in the automobile market, but rather that it was in the transportation business. This realization allowed GM to diversify into many other markets, which have proven extremely profitable. In a similar fashion spectator-sport organizations widened their appeal considerably once they realized they were in the entertainment business. Rather than simply selling their sport, they opened up their market to anyone interested in being entertained by offering pre-game, half-time and post-game shows, bands, cheerleaders, etc. Not surprisingly, the same metamorphosis has hit other sport industry segments. Most single-purpose tennis and racquetball clubs in the last five years have undergone a renaissance. For the most part, the clubs which have survived the shake-down period are the ones which broadened their concepts.

Dependent upon the market, and the competition, room does exist for specialized product positions. This is particularly evident in the soda and fast-food industries. The Kentucky Fried Chicken (KFC) chain, in response to intense competition from its giant competitors, the McDonalds and Burger King chains who started to offer chicken items, responded with a specialized product concept. KFC says, "We Do One Thing and We Do It Right!" Even the distant Wendy's chain with their highly touted, "Where's the Beef?" commercial attacks on the industry giants, developed a singular product position. The fast-food market is big enough and stable enough to support KFC's and Wendy's specialized strategies. However, most sport industry segments are often not as substantial, nor are they as stable. Athletes Foot, a national franchise chain entered into the highly competitive and saturated retail sporting goods market by specializing in athletic footwear. Their timing was excellent, as they anticipated the mid-1970's boom in the running shoe market. Once this boom peaked, they were wise to quickly diversify into the so-called "software" items of the sporting goods industry, namely T-shirts, athletic clothing, athletic bags, etc., or else they would probably have gone out of business, in spite of the fact that athletic shoes usually count for approximately 65% of sales revenues in the small/medium sized sports stores.

Reliance on a single profit-center is rarely a wise long-term strategy for any business, yet there has to be a central function to an organization's existence. For example, it is vital that sport marketers in an MLB franchise appreciate the raison d'etre of the game. As "America's pastime," baseball is inexpensive family entertainment. It is the "All-American game" and as such the afficionados of the sport feel that it must exemplify tradition and high morality. Baseball's commissioner handed down severe penalties to players on the Kansas City Royals who were convicted only of trying to obtain drugs, (although their use of drugs was admitted). Both the courts and baseball made an example of the players because of sports association with all segments of society, particularly its youth. This incident confirmed that baseball clearly wants to maintain its "home-grown image." While this image has a strongly positive side, the emphasis on tradition has sometimes been negative. In the past baseball's marketing strategies were too old fashioned and predictable. Baseball felt that it had to offer something for each family member at a price which families could afford. While there is nothing inherently wrong with that concept, there have been many sharp changes in the composition of the market which make such a strategy invalid.

In the modern family, Mom now works. Many families are headed by a woman. Young people are not marrying as early as they used to. There are fewer children in the average family and more and more senior citizens. With the current changes in the market for professional sport, the traditional promotional strategies aimed at children's needs to be re-thought. Promotional giveaways need to be targeted less at children. There has to be a de-emphasis of the bat days, helmet days, etc., and more of an emphasis toward young adults (beach towels, beer mugs and halter tops, etc.). The sport marketer needs to sell to Mom as head of the household to bring her children to the ballpark, and she has to be encouraged to come with a friend and her family. If necessary, the ballpark may need to have a child-care center! If senior citizens are to be attracted, the sport franchise must provide transportation and easy access to the ballpark. Senior citizens have special needs, namely ground-level entrances (no stairways), seats should have backs and cushions and need to be located in the shade, more day games need to be scheduled, and concessionaires need to frequently roam in the senior citizen section. All of these changes call for a rethinking of current marketing strategy. Interestingly enough, the attendance leaders in baseball, the Los Angeles Dodgers, the Philadelphia Phillies and in 1983 the Baltimore Orioles have already awakened to these facts.

C. *The Sport Consumer (Spectator and Participant).*

Perhaps one of the key factors that a sport marketer must recognize is that the sport spectator and participant market has never been more volatile than it is currently. At the same time, the competition for the sport consumers dollar has rarely been more intense. Not only are consumer preferences changing, but perhaps more importantly the essential structure and composition of the market is changing. People are showing less interest in spectating and more interest in participating, as evidenced by several independent studies. These are the Miller Lite Study (Ref. 26); the Perrier Study (Ref. 27); and, perhaps the most valuable of all the demographic studies, is the annual survey conducted by the Simmons Market Research Bureau of New York (Ref. 28). The sports which consumers wish to participate in most are no longer the team sports requiring heavy capital equipment, groomed diamonds or expensive goalposts. Rather they are the life sports of golf, tennis, jogging and the fitness activities such as aerobic dancing, swimming and nautilus/weight training. The ecological sports such as rock climbing, canoeing and camping are also strong. In each case, the equipment needs and the facility demands are generally lower than those demanded in the past. For the jogger it is the open road, for the walker, backpacker or mountaineer it is the countryside and for the aerobic dancer it is a tape recorder or video tape machine (VCR). All of these trends serve to make it harder for the spectator sport marketer to put "meat in the seats" unless he or she taps the trend. While it is becoming easier for the participant sport marketer to get the "feet on the streets," the competition as to the form which the exercise/sport will take has risen astronomically.

As if these sport market changes were not enough, even greater forces have concurrently come into play. A prolonged downturn in the economy through-out the 1970's and early 1980's which has only recently begun to turn around has depressed consumer spending at a time when public financial support for sport programs has been cut drastically. The effect is felt in every segment of the sport industry, not just in the high school and college athletic program cuts. There has also been reduced support for public stadia used by professional teams and of course severe reduction in institutional spending on sporting goods equipment.

While these overt changes have taken place, a more subtle but potentially more impacting long-term change has occurred. The comparative demographics of the United States population has slowly but inexorably changed. There are fewer children and more "swinging singles in their twenties." People have been postponing getting married until they are older. There are more divorces, and as a result more female heads of households. Family size has decreased steadily for the last ten years, and the largest growth segment in the U.S. population is the over-60's age group. When these demographic changes are combined with lifestyle (psychographic) changes, the picture is complicated even further. Children have moved away from participation in the more traditional American sports, the so-called "Big Three" (football, basketball, and baseball). They have instead moved into life-time sports which tend to be individual sports, and those team sports requiring much less outlay in equipment, facilities, coaching and officiating. Soccer is one of the few team sports to have benefited from these market changes, while ice-hockey, football and baseball in that order have been the biggest team-sport losers.

The sport marketer can only keep abreast of these changes if he/she is constantly accumulating data on consumer preferences and needs. More than this, the marketer needs to adopt an information perspective which goes beyond his/her own segment of the sport industry, and even beyond the industry to the economy and societal changes as a whole. Who cares where you borrow an idea from as long as it's a good one and you modify it to meet the special circumstances of your sport and your market? The real estate business got a huge boost in the late 1970's when it borrowed the concept of "time-sharing" from the computer industry, and successfully used it to boost sales of condominiums and resort properties. The lesson is to look within your own industry and beyond for answers to the questions you must ask regularly about the needs of your market.

Many of the specific questions which a sport marketer needs to know are listed in Chapter 16, dealing with the development and operation of an effective marketing information system. The marketing information system provides the framework for the regular collection, storage, retrieval and analysis of market data. A cautionary note is probably apropos here. Even with the most effective of systems designed to analyze market trends, not all of these market changes could have been predicted in advance. However, once these changes began to occur, a sophisticated system would have picked them up in sufficient time for appropriate action to be taken.

§ 9-8. Summary/Conclusion.

Sport marketers clearly face many unique challenges and demands. Not all of these demands are best met with decisive and aggressive marketing action. Many require considerable thought and a well-planned response. Yet the majority of demands do have comparatively simple solutions once all of the data is put together. In the 1980's and beyond, sport will continue to be quite unique but it will follow one principle experienced in all industries, without any modification. Those sport organizations most likely to succeed will be the ones who have the best handle on the marketplace. Such a handle only comes with the development, maintenance and continual analysis of every function of marketing. The structure for establishing such a comprehensive sport marketing function is the Marketing Planning Process. The element within the Marketing Planning Process which houses the self-evaluation and analysis of marketing functions is the Marketing Information System which is the subject of Chapter 16. Consequently the MIS becomes the cornerstone of effective marketing.

Simply put, the best sport marketers are the ones who have adopted an information-based approach to marketing. They have a better handle on the complexity of marketing sport products, because they know their markets better!

REFERENCES

1. C. Rees, "Does Sports Marketing Need a New Offense?" *Marketing and Media Decisions* 66-67, 126-32 (February 1981).

2. L. Kesler, "Man Created Ads in Sport's Own Image," *Advertising Age* 5-8 (August 27, 1979).

3. B. J. Mullin, "Sport Marketing, Promotion and Public Relations" 266-323 (unpublished manuscript) (Amherst, MA: University of Massachusetts, Department of Sport Studies 1983).

4. *National Football Guide, 1983; Pro and Amateur Hockey Guide, 1983; and NBA Guide, 1983* (St. Louis, MO: The Sporting News).

5. R. Kennedy, "More Victories Equals More Profits Right? Wrong, Wrong, Wrong!" 52 *Sports Illustrated* 34-41 (April 28, 1980).

6. B. J. Mullin, "A Survey of the Management Training Needs of Selected Professional Sport Franchises in the Northeastern United States," (unpublished paper) (Amherst, MA: Department of Sport Studies, University of Massachusetts 1979).

7. B. J. Mullin, "How Does the Selling of Sport Fit Into Sport Marketing?" (unpublished paper) (Amherst, MA: Department of Sport Studies, University of Massachusetts).

8. Research & Forecasts, Inc., *Miller Lite Report on American Attitudes Toward Sports, 1983,* at 71-117 (Milwaukee, Wisconsin: Miller Brewing Co. 1983).

9. "An Economic Impact Study of Pittsburgh Pirates Baseball on the City of Pittsburgh, PA" 34 (Pittsburgh, PA: Department of Economics, University of Pittsburgh 1979).

10. J. Laver, "Soccer: Opium of the Brazilian People," *Transaction* (Dec. 1969).

11. M. Novak, *The Joy of Sport* (New York, NY: Basic Books, Inc., Publishers 1976).

12. An Economic Impact Study of Pittsburgh Pirates Baseball on the City of Pittsburgh, PA, *supra* Ref. 9, at 27.

13. Panel, Kerr & Foster, *The Court and Health Club Industry: Facts and Figures Survey, 1983* (Boston, Mass.: Feb. 1984).

14. S. J. Eddy, A Comparison of Athletic Fund-Raising Methods of NCAA Athletic Departments, (unpublished paper) (Amherst, MA: Department of Sport Studies, University of Massachusetts April 1980).

15. N. Bolger, Sport Sponsorship: Is It Really Worth It? (unpublished paper) (Amherst, MA: Department of Sport Studies, University of Massachusetts 1984).

16. P. Sloan, "Who Gets Endorsements and Why," *Professional Sports Journal,* 21-23, 48 (July 1979).

17. C.P. Coate, "Using Sport to Change the Beer Drinking Habits of America: Miller Lite the Champagne of TV Ads," *Professional Sports Journal* 29 (August 1979).

18. J. Holmes, "Athletes as Pitchmen: When Riggins, Theisman and Palmer Talk, The Public Listens," *Washington Post* 1B-3B (January 4, 1984).

19. J. Lawson, "Minority Celebrities Reach Beyond Target Market," *Advertising Age* S-4 (July 30, 1979).

20. C. Rees, *supra* Ref. 1.

21. R. Kennedy, *supra* Ref. 5, at 36.

22. P.E. Hartman, "Promote or Perish," *Athletic Purchasing and Facilities,* 20-24 (April, 1980).

23. P. Kotler, *Marketing Management: Analysis, Planning and Control* 146 (3d ed.), (Englewood Cliffs, NJ: Prentice-Hall, Inc. 1976).

24. R. Leve, "An Analysis of Boston Celtics Promotional Strategy" (unpublished paper) (Amherst, MA: Department of Sport Studies, University of Massachusetts 1979).

25. P. Kotler, *supra* Ref. 23.

26. Research & Forecasts, Inc., *supra* Ref. 8.

27. Louis Harris, Inc., *The Perrier Study on Sport and Fitness in the USA* (New York, NY: Louis Harris, Inc., 1981).

28. Simmons Market Research Bureau Reports, 10 *Sports and Leisure,* (New York, NY: Simmons Market Research Bureau, 1982).

Appendix

THE MARKETING PLANNING PROCESS

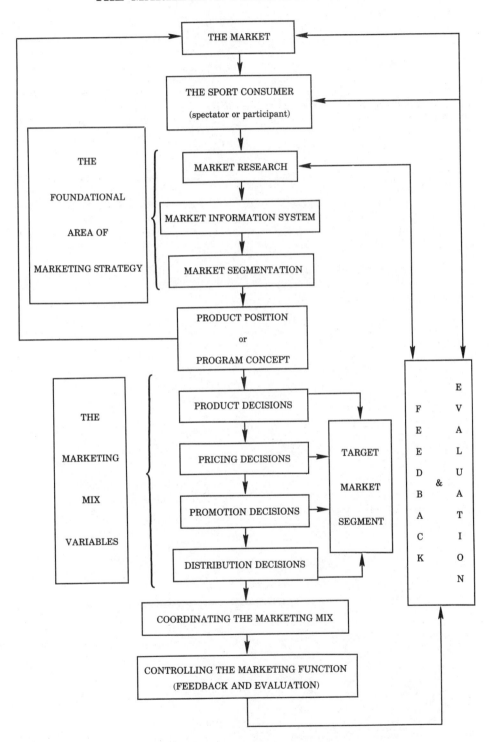

Chapter 10

MARKETING EVENTS AND SERVICES FOR SPECTATORS

By

Frank Russo

§ 10-1. Introduction.

The sport manager is accountable for achieving a set of desired objectives and results, whatever type of facility he operates. Whether he reports to a city council, a university board of regents, a corporate board of directors or any other form of hierarchy, his professional well-being depends upon his ability to satisfy the expectations of superiors.

In most cases, however, striving to accomplish the primary objectives set for his facility is not necessarily compatible with the ever-increasing pressure to balance the budget. To come as close as possible requires considerable marketing expertise. The facility manager must know how to market a variety of services to tenants and public in a manner which produces maximum profit and results in an ever-increasing level of repeat business. This chapter is designed to help the sport manager better understand the marketing aspects of various in-house services such as scheduling, advertising, box office, concessions, merchandising (e.g., sale of programs, novelties, T-shirts, etc.), parking and television.

§ 10-2. Importance of the Event Calendar.

Most sport managers are encouraged to book a well-rounded schedule of events geared to satisfy the desires of the market. Since rental income is such a major portion of annual operating revenue, this is an extremely important process — especially considering the tremendous level of competition for quality arena events.

If the facility has a sports franchise, its home game dates will form the skeleton of the annual schedule. Basketball and hockey teams, for example, usually hold their dates at least one year in advance. Also serving as part of the skeleton will be major family show attractions (e.g., circuses and ice shows). Once these dates are confirmed, the process of booking "fillers" or "one-nighters" begins in earnest.

§ 10-3. Fundamentals of Booking Events.

To book a successful schedule of events, a good first impression must be made on tenants and the ticket-buying public. The facility should be clean, well-maintained, well-lit and environmentally comfortable. The staff should be friendly, courteous and professional in the delivery of box office, parking, concession, merchandising and other services.

Another factor that plays an important role in securing events for the facility is the level of confidence others have in the quality of services. Trust on the part of the promoter and the ticket-buying public in the professional-ism of the facility manager and staff results in far more sales and repeat business than any other factor. The key element in the generation of trust is the record of attainment.

Advertising the facility in various trade publications such as *Amusement Business, Variety* and *Performance* is also an important aspect of the booking process. Let potential tenants know that the facility is available, competitive in its rent and pricing structure, and eager for their business.

There are certain extremely busy times of the year when many facilities wish they had more than one arena to take advantage of the availability of a number of attractions. Here it is critical that the operations and changeover staff be skilled in making it possible to schedule multiple events on any given day of the week. For example, if the basketball team, due to television requirements, plays a 4:00 game on Saturday afternoon which goes into triple overtime, can the staff prepare the facility in time for a 7:30 hockey game that evening? Or, would it be better to play it safe by simply not scheduling the basketball game? The answers should be obvious. Knowledge of what is physically possible in the facility by the staff is critical.

Complete and updated knowledge of the facility's financial status is also a key element in booking a successful schedule of events. If there is pressure to make a profit, do not book events that are marginal or likely to result in a loss. Require the financial staff to provide constantly updated profit and loss reports by specific event(s) and by general event categories so that it is possible to evaluate which competing demands for various dates on the schedule will have the greatest profit potential, not only in terms of rental income but also concessions and merchandising sales and other related revenue.

The basic day-to-day of the booking process should clearly be the responsi-bility of the facility manager or one designated representative who maintains the actual schedule book. Care should be taken to make sure there are no double bookings; highlights of any potential conflict due to moving-in or moving-out requirements of other shows must be recorded. The process of scheduling events also requires preparation of contracts and follow-up to make sure the contracts are executed and returned with the necessary deposits and certificates of insurance.

The schedule of events is the foundation of marketing efforts. It governs virtually everything that takes place in the facility. A weak event-schedule, or one that does not appeal to the ticket-buying public, will reduce returns from the efforts to market event-related services.

§ 10-4. Advertising.

Once an event is scheduled, it then becomes necessary to make the public aware of it by providing the necessary ticket-buying information.

Advertising strategy varies from show to show depending on the nature of the attraction and the anticipated audience. Where to place an ad is not always an easy decision. Event advertising and promotion budgets are usually underfunded. So, whether handling advertising in-house or through an outside agency there is a responsibility to be familiar with the local media (i.e., radio and print media as well as television) so that the ads placed for an event are most likely to reach potential ticket buyers, rather than those who might be marginally interested in the event, or not interested at all.

If there is an in-house agency an advantage is gained in that the facility can either keep the normal 15% ad placement commission as a revenue source or use it to purchase additional advertising for the same show.

It is possible to increase the advertising schedule for an event on a noncash basis if the attraction and manager are willing to allow a radio station (or, less commonly, a newspaper or T.V. station) to be the show's official media sponsor. For example, a concert artist whose music is in popular demand by a radio station's listening audience would make that station eager to become associated with the show. In return for some complimentary tickets which the station can give away through various contests as well as for the opportunity to have one of its disc jockey's as the show's emcee, the station is likely to provide two or three times the value of the complimentary tickets in additional advertising and promotional spots, which not only are designed to increase ticket sales for the show, but also to increase listenership for the radio station.

Never allow a media sponsorship to be construed as a sponsorship exclusive. Offer the media sponsor a promotional exclusive, but clearly retain the right to advertise anywhere else it is appropriate. Other radio stations and newspapers and very rarely television will accept tickets as noncash trade for advertising.

Media sponsorship should also not preclude an overall show sponsorship deal. For example, offer a member of the corporate community an opportunity to become involved as the official show sponsor. The Executive Director of the Hartford Civic Center secured the sponsorship for the Heublein Corporation for a Christmas concert that featured Tony Bennett and the Hartford Symphony Pops Orchestra. These two attractions, either alone or together, would not normally play a 16,000-seat arena. The funding of $15,000 provided by the sponsor was used to offset the show's advertising and promotional costs and offered Heublein the following returns:

1. Total name identification on all advertising as well as on the tickets, posters, display cards and on the Civic Center's own message center and outdoor marquee.
2. Fifty complimentary seats at cabaret tables on the arena floor.
3. A $2.00 group discount for all Heublein employees.
4. A cocktail party with Tony Bennett backstage after the event.
5. A Heublein banner in the arena as well as a program distributed to all patrons and tent cards on each table (Heublein paid for these items separately).
6. A rebate to Heublein of $1.00 per ticket sold, which Heublein in turn gave as a tax deductible donation to the Bushnell Park (restoration) Foundation. Because of this no-risk fund-raising opportunity, Foundation volunteers helped the show by working hard to sell tickets.

This sponsorship technique and variations on it may make an event possible that might not otherwise be economically feasible.

Another aspect of advertising is that which involves making potential tenants aware of your facility. Make every effort to budget funds each year for advertisements in various publications such as *Amusement Business, Variety Magazine, Aud-Arena, Billboard Magazine* and *Performance Magazine.* These national publications are read by people who make decisions to rent facilities such as yours for their events.

Budget funds each year to advertise the schedule of events in local newspapers in a format which people can clip out and retain on a month-to-month basis. Many facilities also publish a monthly in-house newsletter which is used as a direct-mail piece as well as a handout at the arena, the box office and other high-traffic locations.

If unable to maintain an in-house agency, it is advisable to interview and select a local agency to serve the facility and any tenant that needs such help. Ad agencies to some managers represent 85% confusion at a charge of 15%. If an outside agency is engaged the performance must be constantly monitored in order that more than simple ad placement is accomplished. The agency should advise the facility manager and tenants of the most appropriate advertising media plan for a given event and it should have a good sense of promotion and public relations.

Depending on policy, advertising can be sold in a variety of mediums throughout the facility. The possibilities include a scoreboard system, concourse display cases, Zamboni (ice resurfacing machine), in-house publications, message centers, outdoor marquees, upcoming event display cases, ticket envelopes, ticket backs and concession product containers (e.g., soda cups, beer cups, popcorn boxes, napkins). There are a number of potential advertisers for these items within the corporate community. Concession product vendors are willing to advertise their names and products on concession containers. This coupled with discount sale promotions will increase food and beverage sales for the facility as well as its vendors.

§ 10-5. Box Office.

Booking outstanding events does not guarantee high-volume ticket sales. The key to selling tickets is good information and easy access for the ticket-buying public. How these objectives can be accomplished was the focus of a manual written by Larry Karasz for Ticket Craft, *A Complete Guide to Box Office Management* (1982).

Two basic elements of an event are the performers and the audience. The mission of the box office is to facilitate the selection of audiences. This task is accomplished by providing tickets to patrons. As a result of the service, audience and performer are brought together, with the dollars generated from the sale of tickets held by the box office until distribution of monies between those responsible for providing services (performer, promoter, agent, sponsor and facility) is determined. The box office operation also serves a public relations function, in that its personnel frequently provide the only contact between patron and facility.

A considerable amount of planning and preparation is required before the box office opens for business. The primary product of the box office is the ticket. Selection of the type of tickets and the method by which they will be sold require careful study. A number of factors must be considered, including the physical characteristics of the facility, its seating plans and the type of ticket system, pricing structure and sales incentive plans utilized.

Reserved seating is the preferred method. It assures a customer a specific seat location at the time the ticket is purchased, well in advance of the event. This will encourage early reservations and sales and the convenience of having seats together for couples or groups.

More and more facilities are introducing computerized ticket systems as a substitute for the traditional hard ticket approach. Using computerized tickets improves service to the public by providing a number of remote ticket outlets throughout the market area, usually in popular retail outlets. These outlets increase customer awareness of the facility and bring people from greater distances than normal to see events.

Many facilities have further expanded service to the public with the addition of a telephone credit-card service whereby customers simply call a special box office number and charge tickets to MasterCard, VISA, and occasionally American Express. This brings the box office into people's homes. With a "chargeline" system it is essential that each transaction be validated. Allow adequate time to process the order, pull the tickets and either mail them or leave them in the "will call" window so they can be picked up prior to show time. Such a service if properly advertised and managed can account for 20% or more of your annual gross box office sales. Consider imposing a service charge of $1.50 to $2.00 per order. This charge is *not* part of the box office settlement with the tenant and can produce a substantial amount of net revenue each year for the facility.

The group sales department generates volume purchases by making advance tickets available at discounted prices. It is very important that all group tickets be paid for in advance since groups have a tendency to reserve more tickets than they are able to sell and may try to return them at the last minute. This may not only result in a significant drop in the number of tickets sold, but also cause "large holes" in arena seating. This can be avoided if arrangements include either advance payment or the return of tickets in time to permit resale. Group sales account for as much as 30% of the total ticket sales for a multi-performance family show.

The box office also produces substantial revenue for the facility. Generation of monies over and above that shared by facility and promoter is accomplished by:

1. Charging on a cost plus basis for season ticketing services.
2. Charging a flat fee versus a percentage of gross ticket sales (whichever is greater) for each event. It is not uncommon for facilities to charge approximately $500 to $1,000 minimum versus three to four percent of gross ticket sales. Normally included for this fee are the box office sales staff, ticket printing charges, the group sales campaign, staffing and telephone and bank charges for your credit card service.
3. Imposing a per order service charge for all credit card purchases.
4. Reimbursement from tenants for direct printing and mailing costs for group sales material.

5. Charging a special handling fee for all mail orders. This fee is totally retained by the facility and is not part of the financial settlement with the tenant.

The amount of success realized by the box office operation is directly related to the degree that it is visible and convenient to the ticket-buying public. Box office personnel must be well-trained, courteous, friendly, knowledgeable and interested in the special needs and desires of the ticket-buying public.

§ 10-6. Concessions.

Don Meyers, Manager of the Memorial Coliseum in Ft. Wayne, Indiana, effectively spoke of the significance of the concession operations when he offered: "A well-operated concession department is more often than not the determining factor in the financial success of an auditorium or an arena. Rarely is an auditorium successful without a sound concession operation. It is an accepted fact that good food and drink go hand in hand with recreation and sports." Over a decade later, Don Jewell, author of *Public Assembly Facilities: Planning and Management,* made a similar observation when he stated that:

> The importance of good concessions operation to the average arena or stadium cannot be overemphasized. The role of the concessions department drops proportionately with the size of the facility to the point that it may be of only slight concern in many performing art centers. Rarely is an arena, auditorium or stadium financially successful without an efficient concession operation. If the public decides that its entertainment and recreational needs are being properly served, it will return time and time again. The total experience, however, must be consistently satisfactory. Percentages vary, but all arenas report concessions revenue as an important and vital part of total volume.

The Hartford Civic Center is an example of the revenue potential from concessions. Concession revenue amounted to $2,130,000 or 36% of its operating revenue in 1981-82.

A fundamental matter facing all event managers is how concessions should be handled. The basic choices are in-house operation or leasing the operation to a private contractor.

In-house operations offer the following advantages:

1. Management has complete control of concessions. This permits immediate response to needs that arise.
2. Management controls pricing. A fair market price can be maintained thereby avoiding customer complaints of "ripoff" or "price gouging."
3. The quality of the product can be controlled.
4. There is greater potential for generating revenue.

The Hartford Civic Center realized a net profit that was at least 15% greater than the return that any concessionaire was able to guarantee.

Concessionaires stress the following advantages of a lease arrangement:

1. Volume purchasing enables the vendor to provide quality products at reduced prices.
2. Sales will be expanded beyond anything that could be generated with an in-house system. The concessionaire can return to the facility more revenue than would be possible with an in-house operation due to its supervisory experience, efficiency, expertise and capacity.

3. Capital outlays for equipment are avoided.
4. Management, staff, purchasing, maintenance, inventory, storage, and vendor relations are eliminated.

Before making a decision regarding arrangements for concessions, information must be gathered. A survey of facilities of comparable size and profile is essential. The analysis should include such categories as profitability, purchasing and product costs, personnel and labor costs, the ability to maximize sales, accounting and controls, facility management's involvement and right of approval and capital investment. Other sources of information are national headquarters of both the International Association of Auditorium Managers and the National Association of Concessionaires. This will be one of the most important deals ever negotiated for the facility.

Information gathering is also a must if physical design problems are to be avoided. Steve Rogers called attention to the requirement in an article entitled "Avoiding Concession Design Problems," *Managing the Leisure Facility* (November/December, 1980). Rogers listed as the major shortcomings:

1. not enough concession stands to serve the number of seats;
2. inadequate kitchen location and space;
3. no installation of floor drains in kitchen and stand areas;
4. no provision for a commissary for hawking (vending) operations;
5. service elevators on the opposite side of the building from storage areas;
6. no provision for exhaust (which causes a severe limitation in ability to present an attractive menu, especially with fried foods);
7. loading docks and storerooms on different floors than needed;
8. inadequate ventilation;
9. insufficient energy and water availability; and
10. lack of wide concourse areas to facilitate traffic flow.

Geoff Older, formerly with the Volume Services Division of the Interstate United Corporation of Chicago, stated that, "You can have stands that are functionally perfect, but located in an improper position." Invariably, architects give more attention to toilets, which so often are located where the concessions stands should be. Bert Pailey, also of Volume Services, states that, "Toilets do not generate revenue and people have a way of finding them. Those prime locations should be for concession stands."

Don Jewell in *Public Assembly Facilities Planning and Management* points out that to be effective, stands should be conveniently located to all seats. The patron should be able to reach the nearest stand in 40 to 60 seconds. Stands should be well-organized with clear indications of where the patrons should line up for service. Equipment, food and cash registers should be conveniently located so that items can be quickly served by a single person in each selling station. This will help to minimize confusion and interference among the stand workers and also expedite one-stop service to patrons.

Concession stands should also be bright, colorful, well-lit and decorated with attractive pictures of the food and beverage being served. Menu boards should be installed clearly indicating the products and prices. The ability to generate the aroma of food such as popcorn into the concourse will also do a great deal to stimulate concession sales.

In 1982 the National Association of Concessionaires (NAC) in conjunction with Coca-Cola USA and Cornell University published a study for NAC members entitled, "Creating and Handling Buying Fever," which discussed the basic elements of a successful concession operations marketing plan such as the menu, realizing profit potential, merchandising, promotions and cutting service delay time.

The study acknowledges that concession revenue often determines whether the facility operates profit or loss. This can only be accomplished with the right products and the right packaging at the right prices provided the location is easily accessible. In order to be successful a concession stand must influence the customer to purchase on impulse. The NAC study states that "human beings experience the world through five senses: sight, smell, touch, taste, and sound. A sensation that has a positive effect on any one or a combination of the senses creates a favorable response in a person's mind. It's when that response is translated into action that the sale is made. The impulse purchase."

The smell of a hot dog cooking on a grill is often all it takes to trigger a purchase. Attractive photographs of a soft drink or popcorn will also influence a patron to buy something before finding a seat. To create *buying fever* the snack bar has to be an "attention grabber." The more senses positively affected, the better.

One of the first items noticed by a potential customer is the menu. An impulse can be destroyed if it is overcome by resistance to high prices. The pricing structure should be reasonable for the products being offered. Brand name products are easily recognized by customers thereby eliminating questions about the quality of the merchandise. The menu should include items that require minimal preparation time and have a low average unit cost. This will cut labor expenses and increase profitability while permitting reasonable prices. It is advisable for the facility manager to sample the products being offered and periodically conduct a comparative price check with competing facilities.

The NAC report stressed the value of cleanliness and employee training. People are turned off by employees that look dirty or concession stands that look unclean and poorly maintained.

In 1981 concession sales surpassed $3.5 billion in the United States. Stan Briggs, in another NAC report entitled "Concession Employee Training" published in INSITE '82, points out that the industry needs a manual which can be a real working tool and a blueprint for training employees and managing successful concession operations. Employee training is a critical aspect of a successful concession operation. Briggs maintains that management has a responsibility to train its employees. The industry is heavily dependent on young people who are starting their first jobs. This increases the importance of a training program. Employee training is also a key ingredient in merchandising concession products. Train employees to suggestively sell. For example, one out of three customers orders a soft drink in a small size. Suggestive selling is a proven technique for getting that trade up. Have your employees take the initiative by *asking* if they want a large size. The employee must act to convince the customer that all items are reasonably priced and that buying larger sizes actually results in saving money. The menu board is the main vehicle to communicate values to the customers.

Promotions and marketing are also key elements of a successful concession operation. The Hartford Civic Center introduced these elements as factors in the bid criteria for the purchase of certain resale items. For example, in the award of the hot dog contract the successful bidder was Grote & Weigel, which not only had the quality product, but also committed up to $40,000 in advertising. The basic theme of their campaign was that Grote & Weigel franks were the official franks of the Whalers (Hartford's Home NHL Hockey Franchise) sold at the Hartford Civic Center. This had a significant impact on sales. Grote & Weigel and other suppliers enhanced the appearance of menu boards and product displays. They also purchased advertising space on the scoreboard and in concourse display cases.

In general, today's suppliers are in a position and often very eager to offer the facilities promotional devices, ideas and other information to move their products. In this manner, they actually become partners in the concession operation. They will provide promotional ideas, devices and, especially with a new product, colorful promotional posters and displays which can be extremely helpful in catching the customer's eye.

The key points of the NAC's "Buying Fever Check List" are listed as follows:

1. Review merchandising and menu boards for clarity. Communicate and make it easier to order.
2. Cut down on inquiry time through effective menu board layout.
3. Use combinations of menu items to reduce the number of customer decisions.
4. Keep your equipment in good repair. Perform preventative maintenance checks regularly.
5. Locate equipment and supplies for soft drinks and popcorn adjacent to the dispensers.
6. Place the menu board so that it is easily visible to all customers.
7. Ensure that employees check supplies during slack time and that additional supplies are easily accessible.
8. Make lettering on the menu boards large enough so that it is easily readable for all customers. List all brands of soft drinks carried in their logo script and all the names of sizes and prices for all items.
9. Provide containers or boxes for customers to carry large orders.
10. If you don't have a cash register, place an adding machine or table of prices for popular combinations for the employees to use.
11. Design your stand with promotions in mind. Build in space to handle premiums such as plastic cups and posters.

Many facilities do not capitalize on another highly profitable aspect of the concession operation — having "vendors" or "hawkers" take food and beverages to the people in the seating area who are reluctant to get up and risk missing part of the event. Another contribution made by "vendors" or "hawkers" is that they relieve the pressures placed upon permanent concession stands during intermission, when customers literally swarm the concession facilities.

§ 10-7. Merchandising.

The term "merchandising" describes the process of selling programs, novelties, T-shirts and other event-related souvenirs. This business has changed dramatically in the last two years, as T-shirts, jerseys and painter's caps commemorating each rock act's tour have become the fashion among concert-goers. Bands and acts, beginning with Billy Joel on July 11, 1980, are now routinely obtaining injunctions and seizure orders from federal courts to protect trade rights to their names, pictures and symbols. These rights were being exploited by unauthorized bootleggers at great loss to both the artists and the facilities in which they performed.

Because of the huge potential for the artist there is tremendous pressure on facility managers to both maximize sales and reduce the percentage rates they charge to the performers. Many managers are accused of charging exorbitant merchandising fees by representatives of the various attractions and supporting franchises. Herbie Herbert, Manager of the rock act "Journey" and Dale Morris, Manager of the country and western band "Alabama" are perhaps the most vocal crusaders against such high charges by facilities.

Merchandising seminars have proven to be the hottest topics on the agenda of various meetings and conferences of the International Association of Auditorium Managers. "Journey", for example, in 200 concerts in less than two years will gross an estimated $20 million in T-shirts and novelty sales. This is big business, and "Journey" and most other acts are looking more closely at percentages charged by facilities which usually average 35 to 40% of gross sales. While facility managers and rock artist representatives are battling one another over percentage rates, they unite to combat bootleggers. Bootleggers have a tremendous impact on merchandising sales for both the artist and the facility. The Hartford Civic Center coped with the problem in the following manner. On August 2, 1982, attorneys obtained from the United States District Court in Hartford a permanent injunction and an order of seizure permitting the restraining of the sale of counterfeit T-shirts, posters and other unauthorized merchandise at musical events at the Hartford Civic Center. The order, which was issued by the U.S. District Court Judge José A. Cabranes, was only the third such order ever issued in the United States. The other two were issued in Philadelphia and Cincinnati; however, the injunction in Hartford set a precedent since it imposed no geographical or time limitations.

The Hartford Civic Center was very active in obtaining temporary orders for most of its concerts prior to obtaining the permanent one. Concerts for which injunctions were obtained normally achieved merchandise sales of $3.31 per capita, while others only achieved $1.08 per capita. And, three major rock shows at the Hartford Civic Center since 1980 brought in average sales of $6.60 per capita. These included "The Rolling Stones" ($8.90), "AC/DC" ($5.63), and "Rush" ($5.11).

Prior to obtaining the permanent injunction, judges in Connecticut were issuing orders allowing the seizure of bootleg items sold at the Civic Center rock shows on a case-by-case basis. The new orders eliminated the need to go to court before each show thus saving a minimum of $2,300 per show in attorney's fees alone, which had been deducted off-the-top before the Civic Center split merchandising with the artist.

Because of the Hartford Civic Center's aggressive stand in obtaining the permanent injunction and because the permanent injunction resulted in significantly increased sales, there was less pressure to reduce the facility's standard 35 to 40% commission. Everyone made more money in this relatively unique approach to the merchandising wars.

Most facilities use an outside merchandising contractor rather than an in-house staff. The contractor is paid a percentage of gross sales — usually between 10 and 15% — and in turn provides and pays all sales staff, consigns over and inventories the merchandise from the artist and provides a full accounting of sales to both the artist and the facility. It is not uncommon for such contractors to invest up to $25,000 for attractive and permanent merchandise display stands in key areas in the facility's concourse.

Rock acts, as well as family attractions and sporting franchises, are looking more and more to merchandise revenue to balance their budgets. It is vital that the facility managers create and maintain an environment where merchandising can be maximized with a minimum of friction between the facility, its tenants and the merchandising contractor. The net effect is substantially increased revenue.

§ 10-8. Parking.

Parking is always a problem, but if handled properly it can also be a very lucrative source of revenue. Virtually everyone who attends an event arrives by car, but they do not necessarily have to park in the facility's lot. Parking operations in most cases, therefore, cannot be taken for granted. Careful attention must be given to creating an easy traffic flow so cars can enter and exit quickly. The lot must be well-paved, well-lit and secured, and management should have a graphic system that makes it easy for people to find their cars at the conclusion of events. An adequate number of cashiers and attendants will improve operations.

Additional parking revenue (at least $1.00 per space) can also be achieved by offering preferred or special parking for customers willing to pay the price to park closer to the building.

In many respects, parking is a very difficult operation to manage. Having good employees with qualities of honesty and trust is a lot easier when you have tight financial controls. John Root, Manager of the San Francisco Cow Palace, presented a paper entitled, "Parking — New Sources Of Revenue" to the 1980 National Conference of the International Association of Auditorium Managers. He shared the results of a survey conducted by the Cow Palace regarding different controls in effect at other facilities. They included the following:

1. Sensors or loops buried in each entrance line.
2. A single pass lane.
3. A cashier or checker watching the sellers and authorizing passes.
4. Spot checks on sellers.
5. Different colored tickets for different events, days or hours.

  6. Cash registers.
  7. T.V. monitors.
  8. Clean graphics and signs indicating special entrances.

The parking operation is second only to the box office in terms of direct contact between facility and patron. A well-designed and managed parking operation will ease crowd tension and allow for sufficient time for patrons to buy a snack and still get to their seats on time — and in a good frame of mind. There is no question that the ease of access and parking is a major factor in increased public acceptance and attendance at events.

§ 10-9. Televising Events.

Craig Vickers, Dantia Cork and Jim Milliot wrote an interesting article entitled, "Cable T.V. — A New Day Dawns for Facility Managers," which appeared in the April 1983 issue of *Auditorium News*. The authors offer "that pay television may one day lead to crowdless games played before a cameraman and technicians. Not only will there be no fans paying for tickets, there will be no fans to park, to eat refreshments or to buy (programs) or souvenirs."

More and more events, especially sporting events, are being televised either on cable, pay and/or network television. It is still too early to properly assess the impact that televising home games will have on actual attendance levels; however, there is a clear danger that if tenants are allowed relatively unrestricted ability to televise home games, some facilities may turn into little more than large broadcast studios.

Some in the industry, such as Joe Cohen of the Madison Square Garden's Cable Network, see cable television as an opportunity. This, of course, stems in part at least from the fact that the owners of Madison Square Garden Cable Network also own Madison Square Garden, as well as its two prime tenants, the New York Knickerbockers and the New York Rangers. In such cases, televising events can be controlled so that when the teams are playing poorly and attendance is down, revenue levels can be maintained by televising the product, whereas when the teams are playing well and there is a strong demand for tickets, television can be restricted.

Most facilities are not in such a powerful position. The owner of the facility and the owner of the sporting franchise become adversaries on the issue of whether or not to allow televising of a home game. One possible compromise is to negotiate a "make-whole" clause in the agreement with the franchise whereby the franchise agrees to reimburse the facility for any drop in attendance at televised home games. For example, assume that the Hartford Whalers played non-televised home games against the Minnesota North Stars in the 1982 and 1983 seasons and the average paid attendance was 9,000 per game. The Whalers were then offered a lucrative contract by a local television station to televise the 1984 game against Minnesota. The Hartford Civic Center granted permission and the game only drew 8,000 paid attendees. By virtue of the "make-whole" agreement, the Whalers would be responsible for paying the Civic Center for lost rent and concession revenue based on the following formula:

1. The average ticket price for the Whaler's 1982 and 1983 games was $9.50. This amount ($9.50) times the difference between the average attendance for 1982 and 1983 and the actual attendance for 1984 (i.e., 1,000) produces a revenue shortfall of $9,500 for the 1984 game, which, it is assumed, was due to the fact that this game was televised. The $9,500 shortfall in ticket sales times the Civic Center's rental charge (13%) equals $1,235 in "make-whole" rent payments to the Hartford Civic Center; and,

2. The Hartford Civic Center's actual concession sales for the 1982 and 1983 Whaler games average $2.50 per capita. Both the Whalers and the Civic Center agreed that the Civic Center achieved a 55% net profit on its concession operations. By virtue of the make-whole agreement, the $2.50 per capita figure would be multiplied by the difference in attendance (1,000). This equals $2,500. This figure would then be multiplied by the 55% net profit factor (so that the Whalers would not have to reimburse the Civic Center for overhead, staffing and product costs not actually incurred), thus requiring the Whalers to pay the Civic Center $1,375 in lost concession revenue.

The total formula would result in a reimbursement penalty to the Civic Center of $2,610. There are a number of variations to this formula, but the basic intent is to ensure that the facility does not suffer lost revenue as a result of franchise's desire to televise a home game(s). With such a "make-whole" provision it becomes less risky for a facility to allow its franchise to televise home games. And there may be certain intangible benefits derived by the facility and the franchise. For example, seeing a team play well and sensing the excitement in the arena may encourage more people to buy tickets and see the action live.

Once properly protected, it then becomes time to look more positively at the opportunities that television offers. For example, while tenants have the right to televise their product, they do not necessarily have the right to provide the "hookup" for the station(s) which has been granted the broadcast rights. The actual hookup contractor should be investigated. Contractors should be charged with installing permanent cabling/wiring in the facility to make hookups more efficient and economical. They should also be responsible for providing complete state-of-the-art television, AM/FM radio and closed-circuit television equipment (including uplink capacity), as well as the personnel and technicians required for the operation and maintenance of this equipment.

The television hookup contractor must also be able to clearly demonstrate the ability to reduce the cost of originating television transmissions from the facility while at the same time providing the facility with the greatest possible financial return. Without any investment or risk a net of $500 to $1,000 per hookup can be realized.

Knowing downside risks and having the spirit of cooperation with tenants the television industry can result in considerable benefit to the facility. There is no question that television will become an ever more dominant factor in the presentation of live events. Television revenue is too lucrative to pass up and many franchises need it just to break even. While facility managers should not stand in the way of such progress, they should first protect their own interests. *Be a partner — not a victim.*

§ 10-10. Summary/Conclusion.

The facility is, in the final analysis, a sales and marketing organization. Management's primary responsibility is to satisfy the tenants who rent the facility and customers who attend the events.

A strong sales and marketing capacity is critical to success. Once an event is confirmed, there is a limited amount of time to conduct the promotion, marketing and advertising campaigns, sell the tickets and actually produce the event. How the entire package of services and functions discussed in this chapter (i.e., scheduling, advertising, box office, concessions, merchandising, parking and television) is handled will determine the immediate and long-range success of the facility. Do not forget to be ever-conscious about providing a well-run, clean and safe environment. This will add to the enjoyment of those attending the events, and patrons in a good frame of mind will be more likely to purchase food, beverages and merchandising and return to other events at the facility. Take time to review the organization, inside and out, from a sales and marketing point of view. In fact, this should be a continuous process because management should never take tenants or the public for granted.

Chapter 11

FUND-RAISING STRATEGIES

By

Don Canham

§ 11-1. Introduction.

Virtually all minor and major organizations are constantly in need of funds. There are, of course, many reasons why effective fund-raising is essential, but in recent years the primary one is that inflation has out-stripped the ability of organizations to be self-sufficient with the normal or usual methods of acquiring budget money. Expanded programs, recessions and changing priorities also complicate stability where funding is concerned. The end result where fund-raising fails is, of course, the elimination of activities and various teams on both the high school and collegiate level.

§ 11-2. What Is Fund-Raising?

Fund-raising should be viewed as anything that increases revenue, including, but not limited to, concessions, merchandising, and grants.

§ 11-3. Guidelines for Fund-Raising.

It is important that the planning for any fund-raising campaign be shaped by the following factors. First, fund-raising must be program specific. For example, it is virtually impossible to raise money for general usage, while anything that directly benefits the student athlete, such as scholarship or equipment generates greater response from donors. Second, a prospect list from whom the funds will be raised must be established. Whether the organization will contact merchants, manufacturers, alumni, fans, the student body or professional people in the area are questions that must be addressed. Efforts will be more effective if contributors are able to claim gifts as tax deductions. In order for them to do so the project must meet IRS standards. Next, an *accounting* system must be established. Finally, an *acknowledgment* system has to be determined, with a complete follow-up on every dollar received. In short, a trail of paper must follow every gift. *Accurate accounting and acknowledgement must be a top priority in any kind of fund-raising.*

One of the biggest mistakes that novice fund-raisers make is to search for something new and different when, in actuality, it would be far better to adopt some program that has been successful at other institutions or other organizations. There are a multitude of events and projects that have been used successfully by others that can be adopted and used effectively regardless of the size and scope of the original undertaking. The challenge is not to originate activities but to be creative in the implementation of those things that have produced results elsewhere.

A definite *timetable* is a must requirement. There are programs that take as long as a year or more to complete, while others must be done in a very short period of time. The organization carrying out the plan must decide on a timetable to be followed. During the time of the project, constant progress reports must be filed by those involved in the fund-raising. In addition, the donors should be *updated periodically* as to the progress of the project. The reason for this is obvious. The people that have already given will give again especially if they are kept involved. The best prospects are persons who have a record of contributing to similar causes. Projects to fund athletes are a particular attraction for donors because the gift supports an enterprise that is highly visible.

In any fund-raising, the system of *checks* and *balances* must be utilized. An important caution is that all fund-raising be done through the department or the school rather than an outside booster club. One of the greatest mistakes in fund-raising is that rules of governing organizations are violated simply because outside groups are not cognizant of the myriad of rules under which school and collegiate sports are conducted.

Besides the tax exemption angle that can usually be applied when an educational institution is raising funds, we are constantly reading about outside fund-raisers who have operated out of their back pockets. Shortages and misuse of funds have occurred in every state in the union in this area. Therefore, whether one is having a pig roast, a raffle, Bingo-playing, an auction or a marathon, or whether one is attempting to sell tickets, the project must be under the *firm and absolute control of the educational institution*. Where fund-raising is done by organizations and not used for educational pursuits, it is absolutely essential that a legal binding contract be drawn and a board of directors meet periodically to monitor the funds.

Motivation of workers is essential to success. A system of rewards such as a trip to any football or basketball game, a dinner with a head coach, a free golf pass for a year, or a varsity-letter award can be used to satisfy the need.

§ 11-4. Cautions.

Regardless of what is going to be done, any fund-raising program has to evolve around *marketing* and *promotion*. The sum total of any successful program has always been the result of a good marketing program and one that dovetails with promotion. Probably the easiest way to understand the compatibility is to look at some of the things that have been done around the country. In every case, whether it is a swimathon, walkathon, celebrity auction or a flea market project, the idea has to be marketed not only *among the volunteers working the projects but also among the people you are soliciting from and, of course, it has to be promoted and publicized.*

We must always remember that one cannot fool the public. Whatever you market must be of value to the potential customer. A promotion that actually cheats the public will come back to haunt the promoter many times over, and fund-raising will fail.

§ 11-5. Fund-Raising Projects.

One project that is extremely successful at schools such as Michigan and Tennessee is the summer camp. In some cases this is a day camp or a live-in camp as at Michigan and Tennessee. Camps are usually well received on the campus because they keep the dorms busy during the summer months, and food service, janitorial and maintenance workers do not have to be laid off. Secondly, summer camps provide employment and supplementary salaries for the coaches. One institution in the country nets over $160,000 each summer with a gigantic summer camp using their vacant facilities as over 5,000 campers, both men and women, go through the summer program. Many schools, both elementary and secondary, now hold day camps for anything from sports to computer learning.

Celebrity golf tournaments run by athletic departments during the summer are not only a great way to maintain relationships with alumni and community, but also provide revenue as well. Oklahoma State runs one of the most successful celebrity golf tournaments for their former athletes, and well-known alumni return to play golf and pay money to play in a foursome with celebrities. To a greater or lesser degree, most of the colleges in the country do this and many are also doing the same on the high school level using local radio, television, political and athletic personalities as the celebrities.

Several high schools and colleges put on ox-roasts and pork days or chicken fries to raise athletic funds. In this plan the alumni can donate an ox, a pig or two, or chickens, or all could be purchased at a discount. The promotion revolves around the community where entire families come to have a picnic dinner at a reasonable cost with proceeds going to athletic or other support groups. Variations of the ox-roast theme are unlimited and can be carried out in different ways.

Gabriel Richard High School in Ann Arbor, Michigan has a raffle at a "hot dog" dinner that provides a tremendous amount of money each year to support its athletic programs. Many other schools across the country use a variation of a raffle. The Gabriel Richard plan is to sell 200 to 300 tickets at $100 each and then contact merchants around town for gifts or prizes that could be purchased at cost or below. Gabriel Richard has found that often the merchant will donate the item for a tax write-off to help the program. The school has a hot dog supper and the drawing provides a prize on every tenth ticket drawn. This spreads the excitement over the evening and allows many people to win something of value. It is culminated by a drawing for an automobile. The raffle ticket sales provide between $20,000 to $30,000, making the total income from the event sizable for the athletic program.

A weekly Bingo game benefiting the athletic program, band or other causes, if properly promoted, can support more than a few needs for funds. Other progressive schools rely on concerts and such events as Harlem Globetrotters or donkey baseball exhibitions to help finance their programs.

One area that is not explored by many schools located near professional teams or large universities is the stadium cleanup. High school teams clean the University of Michigan Football Stadium and the hockey and basketball arenas after each game.

In other areas, the concession stands are manned by various high schools and church groups. At the University of Michigan we man about 50 different booths with high school groups. There are hundreds of ways that energetic teams and ambitious coaches can ensure funds.

The prime concern at most institutions on both high school and collegiate levels is the attraction of fans to the stadium and there have been literally hundreds of things tried to increase the ticket sales. One thing that should be obvious is that a full stadium or a large crowd attracts people, and that is why schools have band days where up to 30,000 band members have been admitted to the stadium free. Not only do these *band days* create the feeling that everyone is following the team, but also the free ticket brings mothers and fathers to the stadium to see their children play, and they park their cars, buy hot dogs and souvenirs and get interested in the football game and return on another day. At Michigan we have long felt that the *spectacle* is what we sell.

We also approach the lady of the house because we feel that she controls the weekend. If we can have her tell her husband that it might be a good idea to see a football game and have a tailgate picnic, we are home free. The only thing we have to do now is to make sure that they have a good time because, as mentioned earlier, you cannot fool the public.

In Ann Arbor we have specialized in gigantic pre-game shows, half-time shows and post-game shows. At other institutions more flamboyant attractions have been held to get people in the stands to see the great spectacle of college football or a basketball game.

In an effort to increase attendance and thus funds, one cannot ignore group sales. Sales not only to manufacturing companies and other industries, but to churches, clubs, grade schools and high schools as well, certainly pay off. Discounted tickets are usually an attraction and when people get to the stadium, as mentioned above, they park cars, eat hot dogs and buy souvenirs. More important, if you have a show to put on you are making a fan. Cheerleading days, Boy Scout days, Girl Scout days and so forth with discounted or free tickets are now being instituted all over the country. Not only do these youngsters bring their parents who purchase full-price tickets, they all drink Coca-Cola. The special offer is almost limitless. One institution offers any student that has an "A" on their report card at either grade school or high school, a half-price ticket for a certain game. In addition to returns realized from public relations and product sampling, the half-price for an "A" promotion increased the sale of hot dogs and Cokes.

Prior to selling out the stadium on a season basis, the University of Michigan would allow a student to purchase a $2.00 ticket. In addition, we would allow an adult in free with every 5 to 10 youngsters. That way we figured the youngsters would have someone to drive the car bringing them to the game. We, of course, charge for parking. Before this practice was discontinued, we sold 72,000 discounted tickets in one year to these students. Now, 10 years later, these people are still our fans and are buying full-price tickets and no doubt one day will be bringing their own children to the Michigan football games.

One thing that was interesting in a survey Michigan once made was that weekly newspaper advertising was very cost effective. This is probably true because the paper is not thrown out each day; it is kept around the home until the next issue is delivered a week later. So, in fund-raising and promotion don't forget the weekly newspaper.

The University of Michigan is now promoting nonrevenue sports with the "Gold Key Card" where, for $25.00, an individual can purchase a card that will let him and a guest into every athletic contest on campus with the exception of football and basketball. When we sell 1,000 cards, it isn't hard to see that you are getting $25,000 for nonrevenue sports. When properly promoted by cheerleaders and athletes going door-to-door and merchant-to-merchant, the potential of the Gold Key Card is tremendous. In some situations, the "key" admission could include basketball and football. Everyone likes to think they have a pass and when the person walks up to the gate and flashes the card and walks in with his friend, without a ticket, I suppose it is assurance that he will buy again next year.

The most important factor in any fund-raising is the extent in which one gets others involved. It is extremely difficult for one individual, for instance, to raise money by phone contacts or letters, and it is virtually impossible for one person to raise any substantial amount of money for any project by personal contacts. If a letter campaign is going to be conducted, form letters simply will not do it. Personal letters directed to the individual, agency or corporation must be personalized and not mimeographed.

The same thing is true of trying to raise funds by sales of game tickets, cookies, T-shirts, coffee mugs and so forth. A group effort is essential. The most widely practiced method of involving people in a fund-raising project is by means of a team and league effort. Assume, for instance, that we are attempting to raise "x" dollars to send our band to the Rose Bowl Parade. After having decided what group and type of people we will attempt to get the funds from, we must determine what people we have available, in the largest possible numbers, to join our organization for this effort. If 30 people, for instance, are involved in raising our funds, then our major problem is motivating these individuals to develop their own enthusiasm. By dividing these 30 people into 5 six-man teams and naming each team with exotic names (Gophers, Bench-Warmers, the Green Hogs, etc.) we have our 5-team league established. A captain is appointed for each team and a regular weekly or monthly meeting is scheduled at the outset.

The competition between the teams to see which team can be the most successful is the first small step in motivating the individual fund-raiser, as no one enjoys losing. Further, something of value must be provided for virtually all of the fund-raisers. The establishment of a campaign-closing dinner takes care of that. Everyone who does any work will receive a free dinner for himself and spouse. Beyond that, awards for the teams and individuals are unlimited. In one outstanding fund-raising campaign a university received a donation of a trip to Hawaii for two from a local travel agent who happened to be an alumnus of the University. In another case, an automobile dealer provided a free car for a year. Prizes range from seats in the press box, to a trip on the team bus, to a seat on the bench at an important game in either basketball or football, to other things such as letter awards and plaques. There should be an award set up for the overall individual and team who raised the most money. There should be individual awards for each individual on the losing teams who did the best job, so everyone who has struggled and worked will be rewarded.

At some central point (the lobby of a bank or an office building or on the campus, etc.) a visible progress chart should be kept so that others become aware of the efforts of the individuals who are doing the hard work. In addition, the individuals on the various teams must receive weekly reports via the mail spurring them on with the success and failures of the various teams in the competition. One thing not to neglect if the fund-raising project is going to be continued for more than one year is the "booby prize" and the last prize. Often the individual who failed one year is a tremendous success the next. In addition, however, it reminds everyone if they failed to perform at all, they are going to be signaled out in a humorous way. However, the point is made of this lack of effort to everyone. In one case the "booby prize" winner one year became the leading performer in a later fund-raising project and won a vacation trip to Acapulco.

There are, like changing times, certain events that are successful in a given era. Recently, with the advent of the flea market, schools across the country have benefited handsomely from properly organized flea markets. There are high schools across the country where their stadiums are used for Sunday morning flea markets almost weekly during the summer with rental fees and some profits going to the high school athletic programs.

In Ann Arbor, Michigan, celebrity auctions have been successful. The celebrity auction is accomplished by the organizers securing one item from celebrities throughout the state as a gift. For instance, a governor's tie; a famous and well-known athlete's practice jersey; a book autographed by a famous author, and so forth. The auction can be tax-exempt, and because items made available by celebrities are contributions, the celebrity receives a great deal of publicity. Of course, in that connection, the gift auction has been existence for many years. In this operation the organizing committee of fund-raisers secures gifts from virtually everyone, and merchants, in general, are very generous with quality merchandise that simply hasn't moved off their shelves during the year. A general auction is held in the gymnasium or some such place and well-known auctioneers are secured to donate their time.

In the last few years in Ann Arbor, Michigan something similar has been extremely successful in that merchants hold a half-price sale extending over a two-day period. In this type of promotion, merchants are provided space in a huge indoor building and they run a big sale on merchandise that has not sold during the year. It is so successful that there is a waiting list for space on the part of merchants who are applying from various parts of the country as well as locally. It is an annual event and people know they will get tremendous bargains and the merchants know it is a way to clear nonmoving stock. The organizer makes his money in one of two ways. He can either rent the space to the merchant or can charge admission at the gate. In Ann Arbor we do both. This half-price sale has unlimited potential in small towns where it can be turned into an indoor county fair.

Many schools, of course, have used the celebrity roast and it is relatively easy to do because every school has a prominent person in town (mayor or a famous athlete). By using the local gymnasium or, in one case, a local restaurant on a Monday evening when it is normally closed, the overhead on the celebrity roast is virtually nonexistent. I think people have seen enough of them on television to understand how they are organized and run and the trick is to get the dinner donated either by the local women, the local bank, etc., and the funds from the dinner tickets sold would revert to the project.

§ 11-6. Grants as a Source of Funds.

Finally, too few schools and organizations are aware of the potential of foundations as funding sources. Virtually every town and every community have foundations of one kind or another; some individual, some corporate, some joint, and the local banks and libraries are sources to find these foundations and their purposes. Educational institutions, in particular, are the largest beneficiaries of foundation aid, and while the approach to a foundation remains a mystery with most fund-raising operations, it is one that should certainly be explored at the state and local level. National foundation aid is not as easy to come by as area aid, but to succeed in fund-raising one must try everything.

§ 11-7. Summary/Conclusion.

Responsible athletic administrators can no longer view their charge as simply one of overseeing an operation that is expanded or contracted according to the size of the budget made available. The requirement today is to generate funding sufficient to meet the needs of existing programs and to provide for the establishment of new programs. The requirement introduces new dimensions to sport management. It represents both challenges and opportunities.

The starting place for a successful fund-raising effort is planning. Uses for the funds raised must be identified. A major prerequisite is carefully worked-out organization, as is the careful selection of the project to be undertaken. Implementation of the project, monitoring of associated activities and careful follow-up will bring the project to a successful conclusion.

Chapter 12

TICKET SALES THROUGH PROMOTION

By

John Moore

§ 12-1. Introduction.

There are many ways to promote a sports program and sell tickets at the same time. Dr. Bernard Mullin, a professor in the Sport Studies Department at the University of Massachusetts, defines promotions in the marketing sense as: "A catch-all category for any one of numerous marketing efforts designed to stimulate consumer interest, awareness, and purchases of the product."

Mullin makes a case for a sport manager with marketing training who is equally effective in "filling seats, court time in a racquet sport club, selling athletic socks and attracting people to participate in sport activities in a resort."

This chapter will consider promotions that can sell tickets. Although the emphasis is on interscholastic and intercollegiate events, the promotional ideas apply to amateur and professional sports, all elements of commercial and public sports, recreational facilities, clubs, resorts, camps and service organizations. Marketing activities include promotional planning, effective handling of ticket sales, advertising, personal selling and sales promotion.

§ 12-2. Promotional Planning.

There are numerous ways to develop fan support and sell tickets, but careful planning is essential for the promotion to succeed. Promotional efforts must be organized four to six months prior to the actual event. It is important to prepare a budget for promotions, develop objectives, establish a time frame and target dates for the completion of various items.

It is good practice to incorporate the promotional plan into booklet form with individual responsibilities designated and deadlines set so each individual will realize that a delay can hold up the entire procedure. It is helpful to keep the booklet updated as the season progresses with notes on each event. If it is necessary to make changes in the project, records will help when planning for another season. Good planning will lead to successful promotion and help create a favorable image of the program and hopefully lead to increased revenue through ticket sales.

§ 12-3. Promotion Through Effective Ticket Handling.

There are more ways to promote ticket sales for revenue sports than there are promoters, but one sure way to attract fans is to make buying tickets as easy as possible. Ticket sales can be facilitated through ticket outlets, payroll deductions, toll free numbers, Visa/MasterCards, and the use of direct mail.

A. *Ticket Outlets.*

Some schools use a facsimile ticket program with large corporations. The University of Washington, in Seattle, works cooperatively with the Pay 'N Save Corporation with 50 ticket outlets located throughout the state. The Pay 'N Save stores are supplied with facsimile tickets for each home football game assuring the buyers that they can purchase the best seats available regardless of which Pay 'N Save outlet is used. The tickets are numbered by game with the section, row and seat number left blank. When a customer comes to the store the clerk calls the ticket office on a telephone line that is specifically installed for this program to reserve a preferred location. If there are no seats available in the preferred section, the best available seats are reported to the clerk and when the customer agrees to buy the seats, the clerk fills in the section, row and seat lines on a facsimile ticket. The ticket office at the University then "kills" the original ticket.

The Pay 'N Save Corporation receives a commission on ticket sales and has the advantage of extra traffic in its stores. The ticket outlets facilitate the purchase of tickets and the University benefits from the sale of tickets and the promotional advertising in the store.

Many small schools on both the scholastic and collegiate level may not have large corporations to set up ticket outlets on their behalf. These schools, however, can utilize banks, convenience stores or other businesses to display attractive ticket posters and order blanks. It is important when advertising season tickets to include the location of the season ticket order forms. Make the form easy to fill out and return and include a telephone number that is prominent on the envelope for persons who want to contact the ticket office with questions pertaining to certain game tickets. The order forms in the stores give daily advertisement for the sports program and convenience for ticket buyers while providing the stores or businesses the benefit of additional traffic and valuable exposure.

B. *Payroll Deduction.*

The University of Washington promotes sales with business and industry by allowing the employees to purchase tickets through payroll deduction plans. This allows the company the opportunity to give its employees an added fringe benefit while the University receives a specialized mailing list at the same time it markets its tickets.

Boeing Aircraft in Seattle, Washington is an example of a company that works cooperatively with a university to promote ticket sales. Boeing employs over 80,000 workers and the University of Washington offers them employee discounts on reserved tickets and family plans for selected games.

The University makes announcements during its games to show its appreciation to the employees of various companies that use this plan and at times its band salutes a particular company during its halftime show.

Some schools send computer cards to all the employees of a particular company and the order cards are returned to the school with mailing labels. When the school fills the order, the company sends a check to the school and collects the money through payroll deduction. The only work involved in the process for the ticket office is the task of putting tickets in envelopes, applying labels and mailing the tickets to the employees. Ticket sales cannot be handled any easier than this.

C. *Toll-free Number and Visa/MasterCards.*

Duke University, in an attempt to facilitate ticket sales, installed an 800 (toll-free) number for use within the State of North Carolina. At the same time it added to the convenience of its patrons by allowing use of Visa or MasterCards to charge tickets. The combination of the two was calculated to increase the sale of tickets and public response was so overwhelming that a second 800 number line was installed for year-round use instead of six months. Information regarding the toll-free and Visa/MasterCard use is sent to all Duke alumni within the State of North Carolina with a small, stick-on card that can be placed on the individual's telephone.

The 800 number is easy to obtain and can be installed and charged on a monthly basis or by the number of telephone calls that are received. This helps the ticket office monitor the number of calls received for tickets and gives an indication of the usefulness of the toll-free number.

The Visa/MasterCard charge program can be arranged through a local bank. In all of the promotional material, place the 800 number and Visa/MasterCard symbol in prominent places. Tickets to all home games can be obtained merely by calling the ticket office through the toll-free number and using Visa/MasterCard to pay for them. The tickets can be mailed to the purchaser or picked up at the ticket office on the day of the game.

Once again, every attempt is made to make the purchase of tickets as easy as possible, since ease and convenience will lead to increased sales and patron satisfaction.

D. *Direct Mail.*

Many schools and sports organizations in the sport industry use direct mail for all promotional campaigns since it is one of the best ways to reach the ticket-buying public. The cost of direct mail is relatively low when compared to the large number of people that are reached. Direct mail is flexible and can be targeted to a vast number of people or concentrated in a very small area.

Several suggestions that are helpful in planning the ticket order for direct mail:

1. *Mail third class.* Give ample time for the promotional piece and order blank to reach the public. By using the third class rate, substantial savings can be realized.
2. *Use color.* It is important that the promotional piece be colorful and attractive. The piece should be so designed that the patron will want to open and read it.
3. *Make it easy to read.* The secret in producing the promotional piece is the ease of reading. Keep the material simple, clear and concise and easy to read.
4. *Make it simple to order.* Be sure to make the order form simple so that the patron can understand the details and directions and enclose a check with the order form or call a toll-free number.

Target and direct mail to past ticket buyers of individual or season tickets. It is important to cultivate season ticket prospects by mailing pre-season publicity with comments from the athletes and coaches and information regarding outstanding performers and incoming standout-athletes. Highlight the dates of special events in the mailing.

In the spring or early summer, mail a personalized ticket order form that identifies the location of last year's seats and give the patrons the priority of retaining last year's seats. Later in the summer include the direct mail flyer to anyone who purchased a season ticket or tickets for individual games. Give previous season ticket holders as many opportunities as possible to order season tickets.

After the promotional flyer and ticket order have been mailed to past season ticket holders, members of the booster club, alumni within the state, those on the waiting list and others who for any reason have contacted the ticket office, decide who should receive the remaining flyers. Many schools mail the promotional flyer to every household in the county in which the school is located. This type of mailing list can be obtained from firms who specialize in such lists at a reasonable cost.

Coordinate the advertising campaign and other promotional plans around the direct mail flyer. Prepare the public for the direct mailing with advertisements in media, visible means such as billboards, posters and order forms placed in local businesses. The "blitz" type campaign keeps the school's sport program in front of the public and gets the public's attention toward the upcoming season and ticket sales. Two weeks after the "blitz" campaign place the direct mail flyer in the local newspaper as one final reminder.

The University of Michigan maintains sell-out crowds of over 100,000 for all home football games by using direct mail to reach over one million patrons each year. Michigan defers the cost of the direct mail flyer by advertising items sold in the University's school store. The list of items is included along with the ticket order. The public can order tickets (when available) but also purchase items bearing the school's logo from the school store. Don Canham, the Athletic Director at the University of Michigan, reports that the sale of coffee cups alone has paid for the direct mail campaign and furnishes additional revenue for the athletic program.

Code the mail order to monitor the returns. Some institutions use a system of dots to record where the returns come from. One dot is used for alumni, two dots represent former ticket holders, three dots indicate residents of certain areas while four dots signify those who respond to newspaper advertisements. This method enables the school to determine the value of the direct sales flyer to the various target groups. It may also provide an answer to the question of whether the first mailing is sufficient or if a second mailing is required. Utilize the ticket office staff to compile the location of the direct mail to make the marketing system work. This information will target potential ticket buyers for the following season and give directions for the use of funds to promote future ticket promotion.

§ 12-4. Advertising.

The goal of advertising is to develop interest in a particular sport program and use this interest to add revenue to operate the program. Effective communication is essential in addition to careful decision-making regarding which media to use in the advertising campaign.

It is necessary to develop an advertising budget to determine the amount of funding available for the promotional effort. Each of the media has sales representatives who will explain the types of advertising available and fee structures. After an amount is determined, divide the percentage of advertising to be used for the pre-season ticket campaign and individual game advertising. Include the amount of funds apportioned to radio, television, newspaper and billboard promotion.

Trade outs. One of the most economical ways to advertise is through a process known as trade outs. By this method a school offers a certain number of tickets or reciprocal advertising in its publications to the various media. In return, the media allocates advertising for the dollar amount of the tickets or advertising. The process is simple. For five individual tickets at eight dollars each or a total of $40 for the entire season ticket, the media allocates $40 in free advertising. It is possible to furnish $5,000 in tickets and add another $5,000 and receive $10,000 in valuable media publicity and guarantee a good advertising base. It is never a good policy to simply trade out advertisement without purchasing advertisements. Good public relations with the media dictate a balance in trade outs and paid advertisements. Trade outs make an excellent supplement and strengthen the advertising budget.

§ 12-5. Assistance From Business and Industry.

Business and industry can often provide valuable assistance in the promotion of ticket sales. Some of the more common ways it can help is through sponsorships, visits to shopping centers, group ticket sales at discount prices and help in promotional events at particular contests.

In planning for the sports year, remember that businesses often sponsor promotional items enabling a sport program to pay for the cost of a project or add revenue for the program.

Schedule cards are an important item to any sports program and this item can be sponsored by a business. Some organizations distribute over 100,000 schedule cards for their revenue sports and the cost is paid by a business that finds it a valuable means of exposure. The business usually puts its name on the card and through the distribution to large numbers of patrons receives tremendous publicity.

Other items that can be sponsored include posters, flyers and special days at games. Local businesses are often willing to assume the entire cost of promotional items and consider it an inexpensive venture that pays significant dividends. This is an economical way to reach the public and gives the organization and business an opportunity to reach many people and potential ticket buyers.

Elon College, a small liberal arts institution in North Carolina with an outstanding sport program, faces a perennial problem in its attempt to operate an intercollegiate sports program through revenue derived from ticket sales. While its athletic program is highly successful and nationally prominent, the college is located in an area in which spectator interest is centered around the Atlantic Coast Conference and particularly the Big Four (Duke, University of North Carolina, North Carolina State and Wake Forest).

Elon College's athletic director, Dr. Alan White, actively promotes the sport program through vigorous and often innovative ways. According to White: "We have tried about every type of promotional idea that we can think of, some have been successful, some not so successful." He points out that he tries various ways to promote the sale of tickets that include:

1. Season ticket sales for basketball and football;
2. All sports season tickets;
3. All sports family season tickets;
4. A family basketball plan; and
5. A family football plan.

Of the plans listed above, White reports that the family all sports plan and the season family football plan are the most successful.

The College utilizes other promotional plans that can be adopted by high schools, small colleges, large universities and other segments of the sport industry.

A. *Corporate Sponsorships.*

A corporation puts up front money for a particular event. A fast-food corporation, for example, sponsors a Friday and Saturday basketball tournament and distributes coupons that provide free admission to the games. In return the College gives radio advertisement to the corporation, provides advertisement in its program and features the corporation by putting up signs in the arena. The corporation receives tickets which it distributes through its restaurants. This sponsorship is offered to many other corporations in the area.

White notes that many corporations support his sport program in other ways that include:

> giving funds for advertisement, not only in the program, but also on the back of tickets with the usual coupon for a reduced price on various items. Tickets are sold to the corporation for the employees on a two-for-one basis or in some instances the employer makes the tickets available at a reduced rate. Some corporations give away items at half-time on a free drawing-type basis and provide sponsorship as well as the give-away prizes.

Many sport organizations encourage group sales at special discount prices to attract fans.

B. *Group Sales.*

Elon College invites junior and senior high school pep bands, marching bands and cheerleading groups to its sport contests. Many parents come with these groups and, in many instances, return if they like what they see.

The sports department works closely with the admissions office to promote tickets for high school students. The admissions office purchases a block of tickets for a particular sports event at a reduced price and invites prospective students and parents to visit the campus and attend the event.

C. *Shopping Centers (Mall) Visits.*

In most communities the majority of ticket buyers live in suburbs rather than in downtown areas. In like manner shopping is located in the suburban centers (malls). Malls are ideal locations to promote ticket sales. The businesses located in the malls are often eager to sponsor promotional visits from sport programs to increase attendance and sales.

One of the best ways to promote the sale of tickets is to get athletes and coaches into the community through special visits to the malls. Such visits give added support to the businesses in the malls who may also be supporting the sport program through advertisements or by being outlets for ticket sales. Duke University utilizes the shopping center visit to promote its program and sell tickets at the same time and recommends the following:

In communities with more than one shopping mall, plan several visits to the various malls. Visits can be scheduled by contacting the mall's manager who is usually interested in promoting events that attract people. It is preferable to schedule a Saturday afternoon in August for football or soccer or a week night for basketball or ice hockey. The week night activity should be scheduled at an hour that young children can attend.

The promotional visits should include cheerleaders to create a festive atmosphere and last for two to three hours. Many schools distribute general information about their institution and sports program and give out season ticket flyers, bumper stickers, pens, buttons and other promotional items. This is an excellent time to sell posters or yearbooks which the athletes and coaches can autograph for the purchasers.

During the mall visit, it is helpful to set up a game that will involve participation for the public with the athletes. This works very well in basketball and soccer. In basketball set up indoor goals, provided by a local sporting goods store, and sponsor a free-throw shooting contest with the athletes. The public is encouraged to kick a soccer ball into an indoor goal or participate in a dribbling demonstration with the members of the team. Small prizes are awarded the winners. Some schools receive a good response to sport clinics conducted by the athletes.

Encourage the athletes and coaches to wear game uniforms during the mall visits so the public can identify with uniform numbers as well as faces. Attempt to schedule the mall visits annually.

§ 12-6. External Promotional Events.

A. *Special Days.*

After plans are completed for promoting season tickets, look at each game on an individual basis and identify the games that will not sell out. Plan special day promotions to attract fans. These days can include helmet day, jersey day, parents day or celebrity day. The type of day will be influenced by the location of the school and particular interests of its fans.

B. *Autograph Day.*

One of the most successful promotions at many schools is an autograph session at the school where the public has the opportunity to personally meet the athletes and coaches. Many schools invite the public to their campus prior to the start of a particular season to meet the athletes and coaches dressed in game-day uniforms. Autograph days can be publicized through the media by featuring various athletes and coaches personally inviting the public to attend. The public is encouraged to bring cameras and take family pictures with the athletes and coaches. Some schools obtain soft drinks from the vendor who has the refreshment rights and provide them at no cost to the public. Autograph sessions are popular with the public and particularly children who love to meet athletes and coaches in the arena in which they play when they are dressed in game uniforms. Autograph days can be used for any sport.

C. *Youth Day.*

Youth Day is successful at many schools and a popular annual event. Several suggestions are as follows:

Select a day for Youth Day well in advance of the event and schedule it for a game that will have seats available. In football, for example, the day is scheduled in early spring. Avoid cold or inclement weather by choosing an early game. After a date is selected, contact various youth and church groups for names of the youth leaders and mailing lists. After the mailing lists are received, do an early mailing in May in the form of an announcement so youth groups can place the event on their calendars and plan to attend. The early mailing is very important for a good response.

Follow up the early mailing with another mailing in the fall after school has begun with final details of Youth Day. The details should include a time schedule for each event, name the speakers and provide directions to the sports arena. Enclose in the letter order cards for tickets to the game with special ticket discounts for youth and adults to encourage attendance at the game.

A typical Youth Day program format may include:

10:30 a.m.	Sing-A-Long (to give youth a chance to gather)
11:00 a.m.	Youth Day officially begins with a welcome from a school official (principal, president, or representative of the school). The welcome can be followed by several brief speeches by athletes, coaches, cheerleaders. Some schools feature an athlete or coach who can sing or play a musical instrument.
11:30 a.m.	Main Speaker. Select an inspirational speaker who relates to young people.
12:00 p.m.	Lunch on campus (opportunity to see campus).
1:30 p.m.	Football (Soccer) Game.

D. *Celebrity Day.*

Some schools have successful days when outstanding celebrities are invited to be honored or attend the game. In some instances, former athletes who have achieved special honors attract fans and alumni.

The Greensboro Hornets, a Class-A baseball team affiliated with the New York Yankees, experience sell-out crowds twice a season by featuring the San Diego "Chicken." The appearance of the San Diego "Chicken" is an annual affair and one that attracts tremendous fan support.

Many special days are possible. Boy Scout and Girl Scout Days are popular while Future Farmers of America Days are popular at schools with strong ties to agriculture. Some schools encourage statewide and regional meetings of youth groups and offer their facilities for displays. Discount rates on tickets encourage attendance by the youth groups, parents and friends.

The area of the country and the nature of the school dictates the type of special days that can be successful. Special days have an important place in the sport program's attempt to promote a favorable image and sell tickets.

Alan White, the Elon College Athletic Director, sums up promotions and its attempt to sell tickets when he says "We are constantly trying new things and it's more-or-less a hit and miss basis. We look at what major institutions are doing and try to adopt those things that are applicable to our situation. We also feel that we have created a few things on our own that tend to work for us."

§ 12-7. Summary/Conclusion.

There are more ways to promote the sale of tickets than there are promoters. Promotion is part of a marketing effort designed to develop interest in a program that results in the sale of tickets or product. Techniques that sell tickets on the interscholastic and intercollegiate sport level also are relevant for all elements of the sport industry.

Careful planning should precede any promotional effort and plans should begin early in the process. Incorporate the promotional plan in booklet form and use it as a guide and a future reference.

Effective ticket handling encourages the sale of tickets. Ticket sales can be promoted by the use of ticket outlets, payroll deductions, toll-free numbers, Visa/MasterCards and direct mail.

Advertising can effectively aid the sale of tickets and valuable media publicity can guarantee success in promoting the program.

Business and industry offer many ways to promote the sale of tickets. Sponsorship for various events can often attract fans. Group sales provide a means of promoting sales as does visits to shopping centers. Many sport organizations promote special days to attract fans. These include special days such as parents day, autograph day, youth day, and celebrity day. There is no sure way to promote ticket sales but each segment of the sport industry should try various promotions to find the ones that succeed for that particular sport program.

Chapter 13

INTERNAL MARKETING—A MORE EFFECTIVE WAY TO SELL SPORT

By

Bernard Mullin

§ 13-1. Introduction.

When launching a new sport product there is little choice but to attract first-time consumers. A common sport-marketing strategy in such situations is to focus a majority of the promotional effort on mass media advertising designed to attract a broad market base. However, when dealing with established products many sport marketers forget to change their tactics. They get locked into the "new-consumer" mentality. This mentality is prevalent whether the product is a professional or collegiate sport team attempting to attract new spectators, or a court and health club, or a ski resort attempting to attract new participants. Yet the data show that the more mature a sport organization is, the lower the impact of new consumers contributing to total attendance or total participation figures. This phenomenon occurs both in terms of the number of new consumers as a percentage of the number of existing consumers, and more significantly in terms of new consumers' total purchases as a percentage of total purchases by existing customers. Existing consumers usually consume at higher rates (they attend more games or visit a club or the slopes more often than new consumers). Simply put, existing consumers are more likely to be medium/heavy frequency users.

The "new consumer" myopia is understandable in those segments of the sport industry where demand is low and where there are high attrition rates, such as the high pressure sales approach used in some fitness clubs (European Health Spas, etc.). This phenomenon also applies to certain franchises of the National Basketball Association (NBA), the National Hockey League (NHL), and the North American Soccer League (NASL) in most of their markets. However, it is in these very sports (as demonstrated in the Pittsburgh Pirates data shown later), because of a high supply of the product (the NASL has 13 home dates, the NBA and NHL have more than 40 home dates, and Major League Baseball (MLB) has 81 home dates), that there is considerable room for increasing the attendance frequency of existing consumers. In fact, when increases in attendance/participation does occur, it is invariably due in large part to increased sales to existing customers. The same experience would be the case for virtually all segments of the sport industry.

Perhaps the only explanation for the widespread ignorance in sport marketing is that little if any market research is conducted by sport organizations. Any sport marketer who has collected data on attendance or participation frequency by his/her sport consumers realizes this phenomenon. The so-called 80-20 rule of marketing (where 80% of all goods consumed in a

157

particular product category are consumed by 20% of all persons consuming that product) does apply although the percentages are not equal across all sport segments. The impact of the so-called heavy, medium and light users will vary greatly from sport to sport, dependent upon the supply of events and the demand for the product. National Football League (NFL) franchises invariably have a much higher percentage of heavy users than MLB franchises, for example.

A few years ago at the MLB's winter meetings, attendance frequency data for a National League club was presented in a marketing seminar. Many marketing personnel from the major league clubs were not only surprised by the analysis made of the data, they were surprised that the data had ever been collected in this form. The data presented was taken from two studies. The earlier data came from the University of Pittsburgh study on the impact of baseball on the City of Pittsburgh (Ref. 1) and the later data came from a study commissioned by the Pittsburgh Chamber of Commerce (Ref. 2).

Table 1

ATTENDANCE FREQUENCY DISTRIBUTION AT PITTSBURGH PIRATES BASEBALL GAMES FOR THE 1978 AND 1980 SEASONS.

Attendance Frequency Category	No. of Fans in Category		% Change '78 - '80	Average No. of Games Attended		% Change '78 - '80	Total Attendance		% Change '78 - '80
	1980	1978		1978	1980		1978	1980	
Heavy Users (mostly season ticket holders)	11,000	10,000	+ 10	20	24	+ 20	200,000	264,000	+ 32
Medium Users	17,250	16,500	+ 4.5	13	16	+ 23	214,000	276,000	+ 28.7
Light Users	278,000	235,000	+ 18.2	2.5	3.75	+ 50	587,500	1,042,500	+ 77.4
TOTAL	306,250	261,500	+ 17.1	3.83	5.17	+ 35	1,002,000	1,582,500	+ 57.9

Source:
a) *An Economic Impact Study of Pittsburgh Pirates on the City of Pittsburgh, Pa.* 34-37 (Pittsburgh, Pa.: Department of Economics, University of Pittsburgh, 1979).
b) *Pittsburgh, Pa. Chamber of Commerce*, 1980.

The data provides a most dramatic illustration of the fallacy that new fans account for the majority of increases in attendance. For the Pittsburgh Pirates (known as the Bucs), a 17% overall increase in the number of fans attending games resulted in a 57% increase in total attendance, quite clearly because the average number of games attended by all fans increased 35%. In fact, a simple calculation (assuming all 1978 fans returned) indicates that just 200,000 of the 580,000 increase in attendance was attributable to new fans. Of course, it would be easy to assume that the team's success at the gate was largely due to victories on the field. While there is little doubt that it is a lot easier to market a winning team, winning simply is not the only thing, and it is not everything! Several people who have analyzed attendance (Refs. 3, 4, 5, 6) indicate that many other factors have an equal and sometimes bigger impact. They also warn against the adoption of a "winning is everything" attitude because it can easily become a convenient excuse for explaining away poor marketing performance. The New Jersey Nets of the NBA has been a prime example of a team which has drawn well despite poor on-court performance. While located in out-of-the-way Piscataway, N.J. the team topped the NBA in percentage growth in attendance despite having the worst on-the-court record over those two seasons.

§ 13-2. Internal Marketing — Getting Existing Customers to Buy More Is Easier and Much Cheaper Than Selling to New Customers.

Given that existing fans are usually already "sold" on the product, and that many of them are known by name and address, it would appear obvious that the simplest and cheapest method (direct mail to a high-response probability group) for increasing attendance or participation rates is to market to existing consumers. Marketing programs designed to target existing consumers to increase their frequency of usage and designed to get them to bring their friends has been called "internal marketing" (Ref. 7). Such marketing programs need to be organized systematically. "Sport Marketing, Promotion and Public Relations," a book produced by the author a few years ago for use by students enrolled in sport marketing classes at the University of Massachusetts/Amherst, proposed that a "stepping-stone approach" be used to target existing customers, where light, medium and heavy users would be targeted in sequence (Ref. 8). Shortly afterwards, in totally independent thought, Bill Giles (now owner of the Philadelphia Phillies) proposed what he called the "staircase approach" (Ref. 9), where the marketer would attempt to move fans up the stairs from being a light user to a medium user to the "ultimate" — a heavy user. Giles' analogy of the staircase seemed much more appropriate than a stepping-stone approach and it formed the germination of the concept presented in this chapter.

Figure 1

THE STAIRCASE APPROACH TO SPORT MARKETING

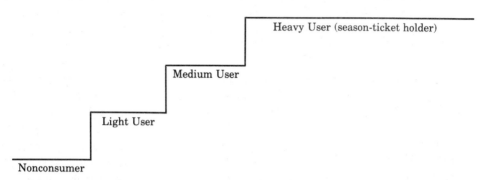

While the staircase analogy is an excellent foundation, it has limitations. First, it assumes that each step in the process involves a distinct and perhaps difficult movement. Second, it implies that all light users are on the same step. Observation of attendance-frequency distribution shows that this is not the case. Sport consumers are distributed in terms of their attendance or participation frequency across a continuum which runs from 1 through N, where N is the maximum number of events, contests or days that a consumer can consume. (N in professional sports varies greatly, the NFL has 10 home dates (8 regular season and 2 pre-season games); MLB has 81 home dates; the NBA has 40 dates; N for other sport industry segments also varies greatly from the 240 days that the Killington Ski Resort in Killington, Vermont was open in 1981 to the 360 days that a typical YMCA is open each year). In fact, the frequency distribution is better represented by an escalator, which has many steps, all of which appear to run into one another. The step between a heavy-light user and a light-medium user is just one extra game attended or just one more visit to a ski slope. When viewed in this manner, it becomes apparent that the marketer can make fluid the movement of a sport consumer up the frequency escalator.

§ 13-3. The Attendance/Participation Frequency Escalator.

In fact, the distribution of existing-consumers' attendance frequency is invariably a continual series of steps on an escalator which runs from 1 through N. However, before the consumer even gets into the ranks of the existing consumer, there are clearly several stages through which he or she passes. Bill Giles used the generic term "nonconsumer." But it would appear that there are several forms of nonconsumption. In one article discussing consumers it was suggested that as many as 50% of all people who consider themselves sport fans never attended a game (Ref. 10). In a survey of Boston Red Sox fans it was revealed that although almost 40% of all fans watching the Red Sox on TV were female, just a little over 20% of those attending games at Fenway Park were female. We can therefore construct three levels to the nonconsumer hierarchy.

Table 2

THE LEVELS OF NON-CONSUMER READINESS TO PURCHASE

Unaware nonconsumer —	this individual is unaware of the existence of the sport product, and consequently does not attend.
Aware nonconsumer —	this individual is aware of the sport product but for whatever the reason he/she does not choose to attend. Presumably the product does not offer the benefits this person is looking for, or this person has no need for this type of product, at least at this time.
Media consumer —	this individual is aware of the sport product and although they do not consume it directly, they do consume the product indirectly through the media. This is not limited to spectator sports but includes participant sports which receive media exposure.

Figure 2

THE FREQUENCY ESCALATOR FOR SPORT ATTENDANCE AND PARTICIPATION

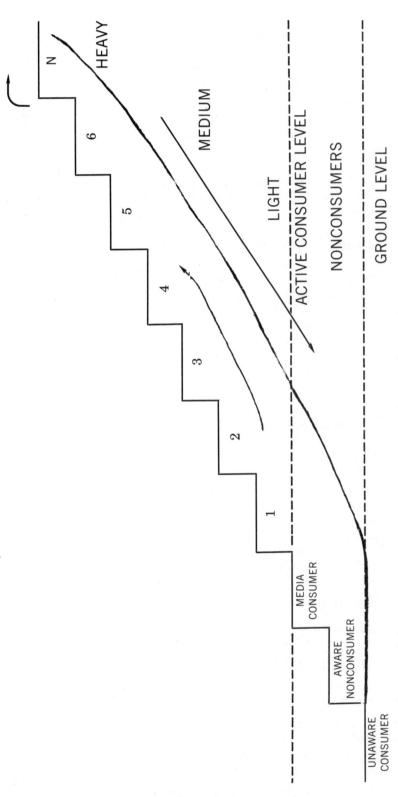

Note: Ground level of the escalator is the unaware nonconsumer. Because each step beyond this level represents a movement toward attending or participating in the sport product, it represents a progressive step *on* the escalator.

The promotional effort and expense required to move consumers up steps on the escalator is usually considerably less than that which is necessary to move consumers onto the escalator. But more importantly, unless the consumer is already satiated, the response to get an existing consumer to consume one extra game/event is likely to be considerably greater, cheaper and easier than it is to get an unaware or disinterested consumer to consume one game or event for the first time. Further support for the approach of targeting existing consumers first comes from the well-known fact that existing satisfied consumers are an organization's best salespeople. One estimate is that 70% of all consumers are referred by word of mouth from existing consumers. This "bottom-line" for repeat business is outlined in chapter 16, entitled "An Information-Based Approach To Marketing Sport." Using the multiplier effect it is shown that the total multiplied impact of word of mouth is 3.33 additional consumers from each existing member assuming that 70% of new consumers come from word-of-mouth referrals ($.7 + .7 \times .7 + .7 \times .7 \times .7$, etc.).

It is suggested therefore, that sport marketers who are in mature markets with a solid base of existing consumers focus their promotional efforts initially on attracting higher frequency of attendance and participation by existing consumers — not on attracting new customers. Once the response from these efforts has been assessed, then attention can be turned toward attracting new consumers. This strategy does not assume that the two efforts are mutually exclusive. It is clear that certain promotions and advertising efforts (such as direct-mail promotions to existing fans only) are mutually exclusive. It is clear that certain promotions and advertising efforts (such as bat days, Burger-King Nites, etc.) will reach both existing and potential consumers. It is also evident that organizations with adequate resources will be able to design promotional campaigns aimed at both groups which will be put into effect simultaneously. Most sport organizations, however, experience limited human and financial resources for marketing and consequently the following time-ordering recommendation is made. Given that the increase in frequency is most dramatic with the light users, and is probably the easiest to accomplish (assuming medium and heavy users are closer to their satiation point), the suggested program for starting a "one-way escalator ride" of increased consumption is outlined in order of priority to increasing total attendance frequency or total participation levels in a sport organization.

§ 13-4. Moving Consumers Up the Escalator — "The One-Way Escalator Ride!"

The programs outlined in this section include promotions used in sport settings which have been successful and some untried strategies which would appear to have considerable chance of success.

A. *Increasing Light-User Frequency.*

The light-user would *prima facie* appear to be the easiest of all consumers to "move on up" the escalator. Given that by definition they attend or participate in the sport product at the lowest frequency level, they would appear to have the greatest room for improvement. The experience of organizations who have applied "increased-frequency" programs has shown that this is in fact true for most light-users, although a hard core of consumers cannot be moved.

1. *Special Attractions and Give-Aways.*

The most common strategy used for decades is to offer special sales promotions such as *product give-aways* (hat day; bat day; halter-top day, etc.) or *quasi-price promotions* (2 for 1's, half-price days; ladies nights, etc.) or *special attractions* (the Great Wallenda; The San Diego Chicken; Rock Concerts or "Down With Disco").

The popularity and frequency of usage of the above methodology is testimony that these techniques do increase attendance. However, the lack of data on the true effectiveness of promotions is a great concern. In one study which analyzed the effect of promotional days on total attendance frequency at the Boston Celtics regular-season NBA games, it was shown that the increase in attendance at promotion nights was often at the expense of other dates. This phenomenon can be called "cherry-picking." Cherry-picking occurs when the fan merely redistributes his or her attendance preference away from one event day to the best nights (the cherries), and does not increase total attendance frequency. Several strategies which are designed to reduce cherry-picking are outlined in the section entitled "Theme Promotions." If the promotion cost is underwritten by a sponsor this may not be a major concern to the sport marketer. However, regular fan surveys are warranted to check that this is not occurring when promotions which result in expense to the sport organization are offered.

In court and health clubs, where a complete listing of members is readily available, and with the use of computer-based marketing information systems complete member-usage frequency tracking has become possible, significant improvements have been made in increasing light-user participation frequency. Special programs have been designed to meet light-user needs. In an excellent study (Ref. 11) performed by Weston Racquet Club Owner/Operator Dick Trandt, the former Harvard University MBA analyzed why light users either quit his club, or failed to play more often. First, he found out that there was a direct correlation between playing frequency and playing-skill level. Better players played more often, and players who could not improve their skill became frustrated and quit. Second, he found that the major resistance to increasing playing frequency was that the light users did not know of players with similar interest and skill who were available at compatible times. His response was to offer free clinics and lessons, and through his member-tracking program he was able to follow up personally on all members who did not increase their frequency. He also offered a game-arranging or match-making program which offered participants a guaranteed match with a comparably skilled opponent at mutually convenient times. The result has been court occupancy rates in excess of 90% for the last four years' 36-week winter season in his 14-court tennis club. This is by far the highest level attained in North America known to anyone in the court club business.

Similar approaches can be adopted by spectator sport organizations that maintain computerized records of ticket purchases, and season-ticket holders. Mike Huta, Director of Marketing for the Winnipeg Jets of the NHL became disenchanted with the high costs of using the Ticketron ticket-distribution network. He established his own distribution system in a market which has a dispersed population over a large geographic area. Retail stores would call the Jets office to obtain a seat location for a particular game. Upon a purchase the Jets office would then destroy the master-ticket for that seat location on that date to prevent duplicate sales and the remote ticket outlet (the local retail store) would hand write the details onto the ticket blank. The system worked well apart from some security problems. The solution suggested by the author to solve the security problem and to improve information flow was to have the ticket purchaser's name and address recorded along with seat and game number in the Jets ticket office computer. In this way, the legal ticket-user could be identified by a security guard if any ticket blank had been altered, and individual attendance-frequency could be tracked. A bonus was that a "hot name" could be added to the Jets mailing list!

2. *Theme Promotions.*

Theme promotions use a particular theme to attract consumers over a period of time. This strategy was first employed by Andy Dolich, who at the time was Executive Vice President and General Manager of the now-defunct Washington Diplomats of the NASL. He developed the theme "Year of the Uniform" where young fans would receive different parts of the "Dips"uniform depending upon the game they attended. (Shorts, shirt, socks, ball, etc.) The promotion was very successful for the youth-oriented soccer market. A similar approach was used by Dave Whaley, Director of Advertising for the Colorado Rockies of the NHL (now the New Jersey Devils) who modified the theme to meet their "swingles" (single, twenties to thirties) market. The Rockies' "Year of the Cowboy" theme featured coupons good for significant discounts on various aspects of western wear offered at a local store (boots, belt, buckle, jeans, etc.). Here again, market research revealed that the program was successful in increasing attendance frequency. In both cases it was academically trained sport managers who collected data first, and then developed the appropriate marketing strategy.

The theme promotions described above are what may be called "soft" approaches to frequency increase. A harder approach might be to modify the Rockies' discounts such that for each additional coupon collected, an added discount (a multiplier) would be available to induce higher attendance. Another example comes from Britain, where soccer clubs for years have always experienced a high percentage "walk-up" of cash admission on the day of the game. When games of special interest have occurred (local rivalries, or Football Association Challenge Cup (FA Cup) games) the games have often been made "all-ticket admission" with advance purchase required. Several clubs have successfully capitalized by selling the tickets only at the club's home stadium on the day of a prior home game, so that the fan would only need to make one trip to the stadium and be asked to line up on one occasion only. (Of course, they would also attend that day's game!) This latter technique is generically similar to using "coupon multiplier-discounts," and falls under the category of *contingent promotions.*

3. *Contingent Promotions.*

These are promotions which are tied to repeat purchases. Retail trades have used these very successfully for many years but to date they have received limited attention in sport. An ideal application of this technique would be to capitalize on what might currently be a deterrent to sales. Many sport organizations offer give-away promotions with the number of give-aways being limited (usually to the first 5,000 or 10,000 fans entering the stadium or arena). By offering rain-checks on the promotional item, redeemable at a later game, fans could be induced to return when they might otherwise not. Similarly contests and drawings where fans are asked to complete surveys or fill-in name and address blanks as entrants are disguised methods for obtaining basic demographic data, and provide valuable information for the mailing list. Completion of the form is tied to winning a prize having significant value (a car, color television, vacation, etc.). The drawing should always be held at a later game, and redeemable only if the person whose name is drawn is in attendance. This is a cheap way to increase frequency of attendance or participation.

B. *Increasing Medium-User Frequency.*

While many of the programs already outlined under light-user strategies may have a potential impact on medium users, there are some strategies which can be targeted specifically to medium users.

1. *Half-Season Plans.*

Many professional teams and some sport facilities (ski resorts and indoor tennis facilities, etc.) offer half-season plans designed to attract a light user who cannot afford a full-season plan, or whose time schedule does not fit the demands of a full season.

There exists ample evidence from several organizations that this approach works quite effectively in attracting the light user. However, the big fear of sport owners and managers is that there will be sales erosion from the full-season ticket plan (the heavy user). There can be no doubt that if the benefits of the half-season plan are too close to the benefits of the full-season plan, such erosion will occur. For example, the Boston Bruins offer first-half and second-half season plans. For many fans the first half of the NHL season prior to January is not that important because it is too early in a very long season (80 games running from October until May), and many people view hockey as a winter sport belonging in a time frame that comes after Christmas. In this situation, many season-ticket holders are tempted to give up the first-half plan. When introducing this plan it is evident that the sport marketer must collect data on the increase in revenue from light user "trade-up" and contrast this with the loss in revenue from "season-ticket holder erosion." If the balance is positive, then the overall increase in fan satisfaction is well worth the introduction of the plan.

2. Contract Time or "Pick-10," "Pick-20" Plans.

Many professional sports having a high number of home contests per season (baseball with 81; basketball with 40; and hockey with 40) have adopted this approach which has proven to be well-received. Under this plan consumers are given the choice of either buying a fixed portion of a schedule (booking courts every Thursday evening at 7:00 p.m.; or having every second home date; or seeing each opponent once in a season); or they are given a fixed/variable combination plan. Under the Pick 10 plan offered by the New Jersey Nets of the NBA, fans are given three contests against top-rated opponents; three contests against opponents with poor won-loss records and a choice of the balance of four contests. The Nets allowed total freedom of choice for their Pick 20 plan when their games were played at isolated Rutgers University Arena in Piscataway, N.J.

C. Maintaining Heavy-User Frequency — Rewarding Customer Loyalty.

By definition, the heavy user is at the pinnacle of the frequency escalator and it would appear impossible to move him or her any higher. The concern then becomes ensuring that the consumer does not "drop off" the escalator or move back down to a lower frequency of consumption. In fact, this concern is not limited just to heavy users. Data from court and health clubs (Ref. 12) indicates that nonrenewal rates are well distributed across all members, although it is usually highest in the light-user category because these members are not as committed, and there are many more of them as a percentage of total membership. While the distribution of light, medium and heavy users will vary greatly from sport organization to sport organization, it is likely that those industry segments having the highest supply of available event days open to the consumer will have a higher percentage of light users, and consequently a higher percentage of nonrenewing members. (This means that baseball with its 81 home dates per season will have a much higher percentage of its fans being light users in comparison to football with its 8 regular-season home dates, and college football with just six home dates having an even lower percentage of light-users).

§ 13-5. Preventing Defection and Reducing Attrition Rates.

The nonrenewing sport fan has been termed a "defector" by Matt Levine, a sport marketing consultant to professional sport teams (Ref. 13). The defector can be viewed as an individual who is going in the reverse direction on the escalator, or who has fallen off the escalator. This "reverse escalator" can be illustrated graphically, as a basis for identifying programs which would be effective at reversing the trend of defection.

Figure 3

THE DOWNSIDE OF THE FREQUENCY ESCALATOR FOR SPORT ATTENDANCE AND
PARTICIPATION

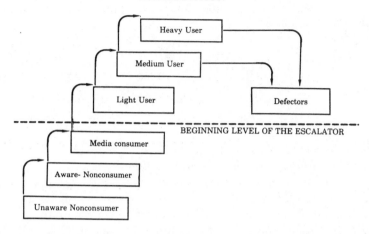

§ 13-6. Techniques for Reducing Attrition of Existing Consumers.

It is apparent that two broad categories of approach to anti-defection strategies can be developed. First, those programs designed to stop the consumer from defecting — preventative strategies. Second, those programs designed to get a defector to return to consuming the product — "Come Back to the Fold" strategies.

A. *Preventative Approaches.*

It has been said that you cannot please all of the people all of the time. There is little doubt that this is true. However, with good marketing and a good product, people who have been consuming the product on a regular basis should not defect unless something goes wrong or unless they naturally grow away from it (they get too old or leave the market area). Reducing membership defection on the front-end requires a good management information system, which may be somewhat unwieldy and very expensive for organizations with large number of consumers. For example the Philadelphia Phillies have over 500,000 different persons who have purchased tickets in the last three seasons, and an estimated additional 500,000 persons who call themselves fans because they "follow the team" via the media (Ref. 14). The Phillies have most of these fans identified by name in their computerized file. In court and health clubs, computerized information systems have been in place for the last few years and club managers have been able to track the frequency of participation by all club members and even guest and prospects. Just recently a new program was introduced for clubs which monitors frequency of attendance, and automatically prints a list of names of those members who constitute potential defectors. (Ref. 15). The program has three components:

Red Light —   Defector for more than three weeks

Yellow Light — Defector for two weeks or more

Green Light — Defector for a week

Club owners can choose a strategy for each group, but typically form letters are sent automatically via the word processing capacity of the computer. The essence of each is as follows:

Green Light — "We miss you, hope to see you soon"

Yellow Light — "We still miss you — have a free drink on us next time you visit (coupon enclosed)" and "let us know if anything we have done is keeping you away"

Red Light — A telephone call to find out "Where did we go wrong? What can we do to help you? How can we get you going again?"

As might be expected, the results have been very favorable. Members felt needed and were impressed with the club's efficiency and interest in them. Of course, a few members felt that their privacy was being intruded. On average, for ten clubs using the system in the first six months of its introduction, annual membership nonrenewal rates dropped from over.50% to just over 30%, resulting in an average increase in annual revenues of 18 to 25%. While such a system is more difficult to install in spectator sport marketing, it is possible to develop systems which do provide early warning of member defection.

B. *The "Come Back to the Fold" Approach.*

Sports Illustrated offers a personal letter from subscription director, Bob McCoach, in which he invites nonrenewing *S.I.* subscribers to immediately "put them back on *S.I.*'s active roster!" *Sports Illustrated* and all magazine companies have long realized that the sooner a defector can be identified and approached, the more likely that individual is to renew. Once again, much in the same manner as for preventative approaches, a solid market-information system is the key to any anti-defection efforts. Season ticket holders and members who are nonrenewing are readily identified once that have failed to meet the renewal deadline. An immediate telephone response is justified in such cases, followed by active efforts (letters, special offers, discounts, etc.) to encourage renewal or at least a trade-down to a medium-user plan. When all else fails a good rule of thumb is to keep the person on the active mailing list for 12 months (send them member's newsletters, fan information, special event information, etc.). After 12 months these individuals should receive renewal information and appeals for medium and light-user plans for the second year. After this time period they should be removed from the active list.

Where possible, the sport marketer should attempt to remove the "nonrenewal option" by programming an automatic renewal. Court and health clubs, perhaps because of their high nonrenewal rates, have been developing anti-defection programs much more rapidly than most other segments of the sport industry. Originally, most clubs offered a flat membership fee and per-court-hour usage payments. Under this schedule, members were actually discouraged from high frequency of play because of additional cost. Successful clubs soon switched to a flat initiation fee plus monthly dues; this encouraged high frequency of play because the fee was already paid. We might call this, "The All You Can Play Plan!" An offshoot of this approach was to have members pay by direct payment electronic fund transfer (EFT) transferred from their bank account to the club's bank account, and the natural extension was to remove the idea of a renewal date. Once a member, you were always a member, until you went out of your way to tell the club that you no longer wanted to be a member. Once a new season had started the member was locked-in to paying for a full season), and they usually kept active as members. Spectator-sport marketers could easily offer monthly time-payment plans where payment is guaranteed by EFT and renewal is in the contract as being automatic, unless the fan notifies the organization in advance of a certain date. Mike Huta at the Winnipeg Jets has even taken this strategy one step further. He has a local bank, Toronto Dominion, who provide loans for fans to buy their tickets so that the Jets get their cash-flow up front.

C. *Maintaining Fan/Member Loyalty.*

A major part of any anti-defection plan by a sport marketer must include concrete rewards to the consumer for being loyal to the sport organization. Unfortunately, sport organizations' loyalty to their fans has not been in the mainstream of management thought. There are many Dodgers fans whose lives are still affected by the Dodgers' move from Brooklyn, New York to Los Angeles, California; the move by the Oakland Raiders to Los Angeles and the Baltimore Colts to Indianapolis are two more recent relocations. If loyalty to a sport organization is to be expected, then loyalty to the fan/member by the sport organization is a prerequisite. There are many ways in which fans can be rewarded for loyalty:

1. *Season Ticket Holders or Full Membership Plan Consumers.*

1. Each year, full members or season-ticket holders should be given first choice at improving their seat location, or the contract time they have. Where possible, this choice should be in direct relationship to seniority as a ticket holder or member.
2. Certain milestones should be established, for example:
    (a) After one year's renewal, consumers could receive free programs at games, or free locker rental, or a discount on pro-shop/souvenir merchandise.
    (b) After five years, consumers could receive free membership in the stadium club, or free seat-backs, or free dinner specials, or a certain number of hours of free playing time, or even larger percentage discounts on pro-shop/souvenir items.
    (c) After ten years, consumers could receive free car parking at a location close to the stadium gate through which they enter, etc., or even larger discounts in the stadium club or on merchandise purchased.

2. *Medium Users.*

A similar set of rewards could be offered on a scaled-down basis for the loyal medium user.

C. *Light User.*

There are many light users who, for whatever reason (geographic distance, young children, lower incomes, etc.), cannot increase their attendance frequency. For these consumers some special efforts might also be appreciated to reward known loyalty.

1. Admission to a designated picnic area after a certain number of years on the club's active mailing list.
2. Special invitations to meet players when the "travelling caravan" visits their home town.

§ 13-7. Maintaining a Healthy Balance of Light, Medium and Heavy Users.

The balance between light, medium and heavy users is an important one. Unfortunately, sport organizations with inexperienced or untrained sport marketers have a tendency to go for as many heavy users as they can. This is a serious mistake; when an arena is filled only by heavy users many potential consumers are excluded from the product, and the long-term effect can be disastrous. In the late 1960's the Boston Bruins allowed their success at the gate to create a situation from which they are still suffering today. In the 1960's Boston Garden was sold out for years to only the season-ticket holders. However, once their superstar Bobby Orr left Boston, attendance declined rapidly and a whole generation of fans who might have received their initial exposure to the Bruins as light users was lost. Even though these fans watched their team via the media, many did not go to games at Boston Garden even though seats were now available because they were not in the habit of going, and because they did not conceive of being able to buy a ticket for home games. No ideal balance can be developed, because the dependence and the need for heavy, medium and light users varies widely across sport-industry segments. Given the lower number of home dates in the NFL, and the fact that most games are played on Sundays (apart from the very occasional Monday, Thursday or Thanksgiving game that an individual club may play), it is comparatively simple for a fan to attend all home games of an NFL team in a season. By contrast, the Pittsburgh Pirates data shows that less than one percent of baseball fans see every one of their team's home games.

Once the situation has arisen where a high percentage of fans are heavy users two problems occur. In tennis and racquetball clubs, all the prime-time hours are clogged up by just a few members. Discontentment occurs on a wide scale. In spectator sports, it becomes impossible to buy season tickets, and as in the case of the New York Giants of the NFL, a very long waiting list occurs. Ticket holders who die bequeath their tickets to descendants who rarely notify the club of change of ownership for fear of losing their tickets. In the late 1970's the Buffalo Sabres of the NHL had a 10,000-name waiting list, and were able to offer 400 nonrenewed tickets each year. Even when they offered half-season and quarter-season splits, few of their waiting list could be satisfied.

Although in the short term, a waiting list appears to be a nice headache to have, in the long term the over-demand problem may be as devastating to an organization as under-demand. Many tennis and racquetball clubs have gone out of business because they had reputations for being "clubs where you can never get a court!" The New York Giants of the NFL have recently tried to get control of their season tickets from scalpers (legal in New Jersey) who are getting 300% over face value. The Giants are offering to guarantee the current possessors of tickets bought from scalpers their own season tickets if they will just let the club know who the scalpers are. Such efforts are commendable and should be attempted by all organizations.

§ 13-8. The Added Benefit of Internal Marketing.

Once all the strategies aimed at increasing existing consumer attendance frequency have been exhausted, then it is time to turn toward attracting new consumers. Most sport organizations have adopted professional marketing techniques to accomplish this goal, but many have not fully capitalized on internal marketing strength. The common practices used by all segments of business and industry have been borrowed by sport organizations to generate leads and prospects, and professional sales-closing techniques have been employed. Spectator and participant sport marketers have moved away from using expensive mass-media advertising to direct mail and personal sales approaches which are now targeted at specific groups. It is not uncommon to find a professional team which has several sales personnel, each with a different specialty, having one doing corporate sales, one advertising sales, a third selling season tickets, a fourth selling to groups and a fifth involved in telephone sales to the general public. However, much of these sales efforts may be wasted by targeting toward one-time group attendees. The success of group sales, sales promotions and special events is entirely dependent upon two factors: first, how much did the promotion cost? If it was entirely underwritten by a sponsor, the long-term impact is of less concern. If it was an expensive promotion which the organization underwrote itself, then the long-term effect is of primary concern. Second, how many times did the consumers attracted into first-time attendance by the promotion attend for the balance of the season or year? If the answer is zero, then the effort probably was not worthwhile.

One informal study performed by one of the most professional sport marketers in the country, Andy Dolich, Executive Vice President of Marketing for the Oakland A's and a prime influencer behind the A's "Billy Ball" success of the early 1980's, revealed that the probability that a new attendee would become a loyal A's fan increased each time they came to the ballpark and had a positive experience. Dolich latched onto a magic number of three visits. When he was selling to groups for the NASL Washington Diplomats (now defunct) and when his current staff sells Oakland A's baseball, they attempt to get the group to visit three times in a season rather than once as most organizations attempt to do. As a result a higher percentage of group-fans, become loyal fans of their own volition. While no empirical data exists to support this contention, it is reasonable to assume that the impact of repeat trials of a product would follow a logarithmic formula, or an exponential (continually increasing) function. Namely, each time you come, the higher probability that you will come again. The author's research in sales-consulting for court and health clubs has led to the following findings. Each successive product trial which results in positive satisfaction (represented by a + sign below) will increase the repeat purchase probability logarithmically, and consequently a graph would show an exponential probability that a trial consumer will become a loyal consumer. For example, the repeat purchase probability which may hold true for group attendees who are drawn to attending or participating in a sport product is shown in Figure 4 below.

Figure 4

PROBABILITY OF REPEAT ATTENDANCE AFTER A POSITIVE EXPERIENCE

One trial	(+)	=	20%
Two trials	(+ +)	=	40%
Three trials	(+ + +)	=	70%

§ 13-9. Summary/Conclusion.

Sport marketing is continually advancing in terms of the techniques it is using. However it has been much slowed in its adoption of professional market research techniques. It is inconceivable that sport marketers can spend several thousands of dollars on mass media efforts without solid market information which supports the use of the media vehicle, or indicates the target market to which their message is aimed. As Matt Levine (whose work has received high acclaim, including a feature article in *Sports Illustrated*) exclaimed: "Professional baseball marketing is where consumer product marketing was in the 1930's, and that's just the good teams!" (Ref. 16).

This chapter made the case for gathering information on the attendance or participation frequency of sport consumers as a prerequisite to all marketing efforts. It has proposed that considerable room exists for increasing bottom-line attendance and participation figures purely by increasing the attendance frequency of existing consumers. The technique of focusing marketing efforts on existing customers first has been called "internal marketing." Internal marketing has been shown to be cheaper and more effective at increasing total attendance and/or participation levels. In turn, more satisfied existing consumers attract more nonconsumers so that internal marketing has added benefits.

While every director of an intramural program on a college campus would prefer to have five students, each participating in one sport, than one student participating in five sports, the bottom-line figure presented to the university administration is usually one and the same thing. In the long run, the heavy-user intramural participant should become a good product salesperson to increase the number of new consumers, 3.33 at a time for a much lower promotional dollar and less sales effort. The same phenomenon occurs in all segments of the sport industry when internal marketing techniques are employed. Internal marketing is cheaper, easier and more effective in the short and medium terms. Of course, long-term efforts are needed to attract new fans but incentives given to existing forms (such as free guest passes, reduced ticket/membership prices when friends are referred, etc.) invariably are more effective and are much cheaper than most mass media campaigns.

REFERENCES

1. "An Economic Impact Study of Pittsburgh Pirates Baseball on the City of Pittsburgh, PA" 34 (Pittsburgh, Pa.: Department of Economics, University of Pittsburgh 1979).

2. "Update: An Economic Impact Study of Pittsburgh Pirates Baseball on the City of Pittsburgh, PA" (Pittsburgh, Pa.: Chamber of Commerce 1980).

3. D. Canham, Speech given at the First Annual Sport Management Art and Science Conference (SMARTS I) (Amherst, Massachusetts, May 10, 1979).

4. B. Giles, "Special Efforts Needed to Attract New Fans," *Athletic Purchasing and Facilities* 16-19 (October 1980).

5. R. Kennedy, "More Victories Equals More Fans Equals More Profits, Right, Wrong, Wrong, Wrong!" 52 *Sports Illustrated* 34-41 (April 28, 1980).

6. B. J. Mullin, "Sport Marketing, Promotion and Public Relations," unpublished manuscript. (Amherst, Mass.: Department of Sport Studies, University of Massachusetts 1981).

7. *Id.* at 251-57.

8. *Id.* at 138-40.

9. B. Giles, *supra* Ref. 4, at 17.

10. C. Rees, "Does Sports Marketing Need a New Offense?" *Marketing and Media Decisions,* 66-67, 126-32 (February 1981).

11. D. Trandt, Unpublished study of participation frequency by members at the Weston Racquet Club, Waltham, Mass. (June 1982).

12. J. Bannon & P.E. Rose, "The Court Club Industry: A Nationwide Assessment" 36-39 (Champaign, Ill.: Department of Leisure Studies, University of Illinois January 1980).

13. M. Levine, 8 *Sport Marketing Review at* 3-4 (May 1978).

14. D. Montgomery, Personal conversation with B. Mullin held at the Winter Meetings of Major League Baseball, Dallas, TX. (December 10, 1980).

15. *COURT-SPIN, The Court Sport Information System,* National Sport Management, Inc., P.O. Box 911, Amherst, Massachusetts, 01004.

16. R. Kennedy, *supra* Ref. 5, at 38.

Part 4

MEDIA AND INFORMATION MANAGEMENT

Chapter 14

PUBLIC RELATIONS

By

Jeaneane Williams

§ 14-1. Introduction.

Public relations in sport management is an all-encompassing term. Taken in its simplest form, it means the positive relationship of the organization/institution and its *total* personnel complement with *all* of its public constituencies.

In many respects, the sports manager's role must be considered one in which public relations is a major key. Especially in service agencies and youth clubs, public relations may be the component third in importance to the sports program — behind actual participation and the recreational/physical fitness value. The reasons are obvious. In organizational sports (YMCAs, etc.), in amateur sports, or in high school or college sports, the program is often the best way to rally public constituencies to the institution or organization. Those most aware of this are probably high school coaches and principals or small-college athletic directors and presidents; the number of "booster" clubs across the country witness the fact.

In some sport management positions, the role of good public relations becomes less significant, but it is always, nevertheless, vital to the organization and its success because every operation's success depends on some part of the public for its existence. For the YMCA director, that may include every member of the city council. For the new health-spa owner, that may be the crotchety 85-year-old widow whose property adjoins the building. To the high school basketball coach, it may be the irate father of the best basketball player on your team (who has just flunked two exams). To the college athletic director, it may be the institution's largest benefactor who has a passion for football and has just found out that the board of trustees has voted to drop the football program. To the Boy Scouts sports camp director, it may be the neighbors across the lake who don't like the midnight "good, clean" (but noisy) fun that roused them out of a sound sleep. To the new local "farm" pro baseball manager, it may be the local media and the sports editor who "really doesn't like baseball all that much."

In many cases, it may seem that good public relations will be simply smiling and listening to complaints and trying to help. That's not all there is to it, however. The best key in good public relations is always going to be proactive PR. That means trying to cover all bases *before* something gets to be a problem, explaining and getting approval in advance, not *after* being called on the carpet by a City Councilman or an irate neighbor.

There are two important categories of public relations: internal and external. If you don't have the first, it is nearly impossible to have the latter.

§ 14-2. Internal Public Relations.

Good internal public relations means, at its simplest, communicating openly and often with personnel in the organization. The best promotion for an event can be negated if one of the employees gives a disgruntled response to a television reporter. The new members in the health club will be furious if they are not advised by the receptionist taking court reservations that the racquetball court is temporarily under water because of a plumbing leak. If students are taken out of an English class to make the extra practice that's just been called, count on losing credibility with at least the English teacher (and maybe with the student, the parent and the school board too).

§ 14-3. Regular Communication Essential.

Make it a habit to communicate with the staff and support personnel in weekly planned meetings. Sessions need take no more than 30 minutes, but they are essential, even if the total staff component equals two people. Pre-plan an agenda by jotting notes on a handy desk pad. This will ensure that even minor events with major implications for an employee will not be overlooked. It may be possible to lengthen one of the sessions every few months and use it to sketch out long-range plans for the organization. No one, from the janitor to the bookkeeper, likes to be surprised with the rewiring paraphernalia hanging from the front door on a Monday morning.

If your sports program is part of a large organization (college, school, etc.), make sure that communication with the other parts of the internal organization is maintained. If there is an internal newsletter, newspaper or even a central bulletin board, be sure to publicize changes that will affect other areas well ahead of time. Try to plan schedules that will not be a burden, not simply for the staff or players, but for others who must schedule other events.

§ 14-4. External Public Relations.

Communicate with the external public both directly and through the media. Be aware that these are two very different kinds of communications — yet they ultimately reach the same people.

§ 14-5. Communicating Directly With the Public.

A. *Negative Public Relations.*

Negative public relations is most often practiced unwittingly. Its result can be, in many instances, devastating and, even when the initial effect appears to be positive, one has to ask what the long-term effects might be. What effect, for example, have the widely publicized tiffs of Billy Martin had on his team's overall image to the public? For every fan out there who has applauded his spirit and his idiosyncrasies, how many fans have been turned off?

It is inevitable that a sports-related organization will have problems from a public-relations standpoint. The very nature of the work means someone is going to get hurt sometime and it is going to have an effect on the program. Don't try to avoid publicity about accidents; respond openly, quickly and honestly to their occurrence.

Accidents need not produce adverse publicity. In order to avoid it, planning is essential. If a player gets hurt, be sure your coaches and other employees react promptly, not simply by getting proper medical treatment taken care of, but by also advising those who saw the accident about its seriousness or its nature. Public address systems are often the best way to take care of such incidents. If the game is being announced, see that someone gets an accurate explanation to the announcer. If there is no PA system, ask school officials to help pass the word. If an injury occurs in a public facility such as a YWCA, be sure to ascertain the seriousness and cause of the accident. If equipment is at fault, know about it before the media descend or before the insurance claims-adjuster appears. For a stadium manager or a pro team manager, the first people to deal with are the media. Know the facts.

In most instances, the worst public relations words are "no comment." Use them only as an absolutely last resort. It's generally just as easy to say, "We are investigating the incident and we have already asked the staff to check this out, but we really don't know the exact details just now and will have to get back to you." Most often, that kind of response is really accurate and it shows greater concern for the interests of the television or newspaper reporter than "no comment."

In really serious instances, when something major has happened and it is certain that media will pick it up, don't wait for a call. Do the organization, public, and media a service by reacting *proactively*. "Control" of the media is impossible and should not be attempted. The worst thing that can happen following an accident is to refuse to see or talk with the media and leave them in the dilemma of trying to serve the public (i.e., readers, viewers) without proper information. If a reporter must resort to interviewing anyone available for on-the-spot comments, don't expect an accurate account to appear in the media.

B. *Written Communications.*

Written communications are some of the most essential proactive PR tools that can be used. They are a visible image of the program and the operation. They must be, first and foremost, accurate and clean, with correct spelling and grammar. They must be clear and carefully thought out. They must project a coordinated image of the operation.

Perhaps more than any other organization, sports programs seem to have a problem coordinating their image. In too many instances, the problem is related to their logo (or mascot or team emblem). While often passed off as a cute idea, too many sport organizations tie themselves irreparably to some insignia that will give them an inappropriate visibility for the remainder of their existences.

C. *Your Print Image.*

A great deal of care should be put into everything to appear in print about an organization — its letterhead stationery, its logo for banners, uniforms, activity buses, scoreboard, billboards, brochures — anything to be seen by the public. Every printed piece should have some continuity with the overall image.

If the organization can possibly afford it, hire a reputable design firm to provide a logo and guidelines for its use on your printed materials. If the organization has an established logo, make time immediately for some careful thought about it.

Questions that must be addressed are:

1. Is this the kind of image around which I want to structure my job?
2. Does this image meet the current and perceived future program offered?
3. Is this the kind of logo that will attract the clientele (customers, players, supporters, members, fans) we want? (Quality tends to attract quality. A "red neck" image can easily come across from a garish design and gaudy colors. A "trite" logo can detract from the quality of an organization. A "cute" logo can subtly belie the seriousness of a program.)
4. Does the logo do justice to the scope of the program? (If the sport program has broadened since the logo was designed, it may no longer be appropriate.)
5. Can the logo be used properly in a way that will produce the desired results within the framework of the budget? (If the logo was designed for color printing and you are stuck with a one-color brochure, problems will arise.)

All of those questions are important because the printed materials of the organization will reflect, to a great extent, on the quality of the job being done, as perceived by the public.

If a design professional cannot be hired, check the volunteer network. It is possible a parent, a supporter, or a member who is in the advertising or design business will be available. Ask for advice and help.

If the organization is of a size to afford someone to write and design publications on a full-time or part-time basis, choose that person carefully. Make sure that the organizational image being sought can be translated into printed pieces through the skills of the employee. Look at writing or design samples in detail; if unsure, ask a volunteer professional for advice.

If the budget is small and all of the work must be accomplished in-house, find a printer who can be relied on for design and formatting. It may be necessary to pay a little more for the total job with a full-service printer who has both typesetting, design and printing production facilities, but it will be worth it. And it will probably save time and money in the long run.

If the organization is one that requires fund-raising for its existence, your written communications take on even more importance. Studies show a direct correlation between the quality of a fund-raising brochure and the dollars it brings in. Even the texture of the paper in your brochure will subliminally affect the potential donor; a smooth-finish paper generates fewer dollars than a quality rough-texture; and off-white textured paper will generally produce more money than a stark-white sheet. Anything will produce more money than a poorly mimeographed or photocopied sheet. Ask your printer's advice, but do not always ask him to do the job in the least expensive way possible. It is not just *his* income flow that will be affected.

§ 14-6. Use of the Media to Communicate With the Public.

Good media relations can make or break an organization in many instances. Two cardinal rules stand out in the area of media relations:

1. Think carefully before you speak.
2. Honesty is the best — and only — policy.

Because of the national interest in sports and physical fitness, it is often relatively easy to attract local media attention to a winning team (or even a despairingly losing team), to an outstanding athlete, an unusual sports event, a special piece of sports equipment, a unique physical-fitness device, a record-breaking winner, an offbeat record-breaker.

A. *Newspapers.*

Especially in small towns, it may take nothing more than making a telephone call to the local newspaper to get good sports page coverage. Often, however, media coverage grows increasingly difficult as the size of the town or city (and the newspaper circulation) grows. The increase in size brings along the likelihood of similar competition within the area — an unusual feature is probably duplicated across town.

B. *Radio.*

Radio coverage and publicity have much in common with newspaper coverage — they depend on size. If the sports operation is in a small city with a locally owned AM radio station, audiences can be reached simply by providing station announcers with appropriate information. Written news releases, originally designed for print media, can be edited and shortened for radio stations. If the sports organization has its own information officer, it's possible to get much more publicity than simply reports of final scores on the radio with just a little creativity. The same is generally true for FM radio stations, although more of them have stricter programming formats and your coverage will therefore be less frequent.

C. *Media Realities.*

If the town or city has several radio stations or more than one newspaper, never try to play one medium against another. It's a losing game. Understand what is unique about each station or paper, and then play *to* that strength, but don't try to set up a competition.

For example, if one radio station plays contemporary or mainstream jazz, a look at the listener profile would likely indicate a middle-aged, moderate-income audience. Suggest or create a news feature that focuses on some aspect of the sport organization that will be of interest to listeners, and the station will probably use it. A predominantly country and western music station would not be interested in a feature on a comparison between ballet and football moves and a classical music station will not likely announce Boy Scout tournament scores.

Be realistic in efforts toward the media; do not offend them by treating them all alike and sending them mass-packaged material through the mail. A personal visit to the newspaper office or broadcasting station is not inappropriate on occasion, but do not do it too often. Make an appointment when planning to stop by with an idea or a news release; remember their time is valuable too. In many instances, business may be transacted over the telephone or through the mail, but be sure to keep up the personal one-on-one approach every once in a while.

One word about reporting sports scores for teams: it's amazing how often the newspaper or the radio will report them if the information is made available. School and college sports directors should recruit student assistants to be directly responsible for telephoning scores to the media immediately after a game. Coach the student in performing this task by giving him proper credentials, a title and seeing that he gets basic information clearly and concisely. It is surprising how much more visibility can be obtained on a regular basis.

D. *Television.*

Television is a medium in a place by itself. It is the least likely medium where regular coverage of events other than those staged by large university or major pro teams will occur.

The reasons are obvious: Programming is far more standardized, in stricter time segments, with less opportunity for local information. The most likely spots for media attention are the local early and late evening news segments or the community affairs programs (often morning or early afternoons only). Again, forethought in electronic media relations is important: do not waste their time with a point that is too complex for spot coverage — remember their time is in spoken segments measured in seconds, not column inches. And it is often newsworthy only if it makes a good picture. Do not be disdainful of what may appear to be a TV cameraman's excessive interest in some off-beat aspect of the sports program; media disdain is a habit too often practiced by those in public or media relations. The result is the same cameraman or reporter may be the one to cover the "really big event" — and give it less than his best because you have offended him earlier. Media personnel are just like everyone else: they respond to courtesy, to helpfulness, to friendliness. And they remember where they got them — and where they did not.

Do not overlook cable TV stations in your geographic area. Many of them are looking for features or ideas that will be of local interest.

E. *Media Aids.*

Do not be hesitant to contact newspaper, radio or TV reporters with an idea for a story or feature segment. Often they will ask to have it in writing (it's always good to have a brief outline already in hand), and be sure to give them plenty of planning time. Even in big city media operations, it is often impossible to assign on-the-spot coverage without several weeks' notice, and the talk show sequences are often planned several months in advance.

If part of a nonprofit organization, it will be less difficult to secure publicity for events. The media, perhaps even subconsciously to an extent, often seem to think in terms of revenue and advertising. Under current federal regulations some broadcast media still are required to provide "public service announcements" (PSAs) — many of which are subtle "advertisements" for nonprofit organizations. Offer ideas for PSAs, however, even if the organization is not-for-profit. Many stations automatically allot a certain number of hours or minutes each year to PSAs out of a spirit of community involvement. The PSA on physical fitness can as easily be filmed in a health spa as in a university athletic clinic.

F. *Media Relations Expertise Valuable.*

If possible, hire someone to handle media relations even if it is only on a part-time basis. The work is time consuming; sometimes the pay-offs are a long time in coming, but can be worth it. If the organization is small, consider asking for volunteer help. Often, the mother of a Girl Scout or a Boy Scout has some writing talent that can be capitalized on. In many cases, a parent may have an affiliation with one of the local media that can be very helpful to a nonprofit sports manager. Be careful not to overstep the ethics of the media profession, but seek advice and counsel from those who know the answers.

For instance, the father of one of the students on the high school's soccer team may be the arts editor of the local newspaper. Do not ask him to try to get the sports editor to write a feature about the Brazilian twins who have just moved to the school district and have joined the team. Consult him about the story idea instead; try to get him interested in helping to write the story idea which can be marketed to the sports editor. Ask the mother who is the television producer for advice on some community-affairs time for the team because it has managed to sell enough chocolate bars to buy its own uniforms, but don't ask her to intercede with the sports reporter. The mother can help with an outline, she can help you visualize the photographic aspects of the idea, but she may be unwilling to use her influence directly. If she can help with the strategy and the name of the person to contact, that may be all that is needed. Or she may be willing to "put in a word" — sometimes a word from the right person will suffice. But be properly grateful for it, and be sure to follow through.

It is important to a media relations effort to determine resources that are immediately available. Find out which students have parents who are journalism or other media professionals. Solicit the "pros" for help, advice and ideas for publicity. Managers of physical fitness centers or health spas should make it a practice to find out if any of the members are employed by the media — try out publicity ideas on them or ask them for advice about features. If affiliated with a YMCA or YWCA or other similar organization, check the board of directors for media professionals. In the case of a city recreation department, seek out any media-connected parents of the children who use the facilities. They may be able to help you directly with feature ideas.

§ 14-7. Summary/Conclusion.

The importance of public relations to an organization is often overlooked. Many people feel that good public relations is easy — that anybody can do it. And it *is* true that everyone within an organization does public relations — good or bad. From the receptionist who answers the phone to the trainer, the coach, the team doctor, the ticket taker, the activities coordinator, the star quarterback, the promoter, the mascot, the manager — the public is building an impression of your organization based in part on the people who work within it.

In Search of Excellence, one of the best-selling nonfiction books of all time, defines the qualities that make large companies excellent. One of the book's authors, Robert H. Waterman, Jr., in a recent speech, identified one of the common threads of all excellent companies. He defined it as simple courtesy. In its most basic format, public relations is courtesy — courtesy to all segments of the population or the constituency, both internal and external.

Some detractors of *In Search of Excellence* have complained that much of what it describes is obvious. The fact is, however, that authors Peters and Waterman were able to find only a few large companies that regularly practiced the obvious.

So it is with public relations. Everyone seems to know what it means; too few seem to practice it.

Public relations in sport management is not a luxury — it is a necessity! Its value can be measured in the success of the program and the way in which it is viewed by all its constituencies.

Chapter 15

TELEVISION AND SPORT

By

David Klatell

§ 15-1. Introduction.

For many sport executives an understanding of television and communications technologies industries is basic to the long term success of their organizations. Although the relationship between television and sport has undergone many alterations through the years, it has grown ever more central to effective financial management, indeed, the financial viability, of many sports enterprises. The most difficult aspect of this relationship may be its changeable nature, and the pace of that change has been greatly accelerated by technical and marketplace factors whose driving force may originate in fields far removed from sports, but whose impacts are directly felt by sports enterprises. The underlying message to sports executives and entrepreneurs remains one of change and impermanence: nothing remains the same in the television/sport relationship for very long, and few assumptions can wisely be made based on past performance of either party. Television contracts are to be approached with considerable caution. They are not, as some have unwisely claimed, the answer to everyone's problems.

§ 15-2. Risk/Benefit Assessments Must Be Considered.

Any assessment of a potential relationship with television must begin with a thoroughly honest (and sometimes painful) evaluation of both the risk/benefit ratio to television and sports organizations alike, and the real marketplace value of the rights-holder's property, when measured against the universe of such available properties. Simply put, what is valuable to the sport manager, his colleagues, fans or ticket-holders may be of greater, equal or lesser value to a television executive, and adjustments must be made by both parties to recognize that reality. Any and all discussions concerning a potential television contract must begin with the sport executive or entrepreneur looking at the proposition from the strictly parochial financial perspective of the television executive: what is in it for him? It is the perspective that will govern the relationship.

§ 15-3. Role of Sport in Programming in Earlier Age.

The television/sport marketplace (loosely defined) presents some interesting challenges to the potential entrant. These challenges can be separated into several distinct, but interrelated groups: those related to audience research, viewing habit and viewing preference as expressed by program schedules; those concerned with financial factors such as rights fees, advertising sales, subscriber penetration and production costs; those affected most by the

185

advance of technology, such as cable television, satellite delivery and regional networking; and those influenced by independent forces such as government regulation through antitrust, copyright and communications law. During the last several years the pace of change has accelerated in each of these areas, usually setting off a reactive change in each of the others. No sensible person lays claim to a certain vision of the future, and the twists and turns of various developments often seem to strain credulity (not to mention existing contracts), so sports executives must work harder than ever to keep up with the latest relevant news, and carefully evaluate its impact on their particular situation, rather than the television/sport industry as a whole.

A very simplified description of the increasingly complex world of television sports must incorporate an understanding of the breakdown of traditional, longstanding behaviors by television toward sport, and what that breakdown means in today's marketplace. The first thing to remember is that the traditional Big Three networks — ABC, CBS, and NBC — were never very enthusiastic about sports programming in the first place. They began carrying sports to fill dead spots in their weekly schedules at very low cost. In the 1950's and 1960's most sports rights-holders sold their events to television at prices, which, although they seemed high at the time, were still less than those of alternative programming under consideration by the networks. Advertisers were few, and they had to be convinced that sport was an efficient vehicle for delivering a male audience to their commercials. The national monopoly of the Big Three essentially squeezed out potential rivals on a regional basis, and concentrated all advertiser dollars in their reach. It was a stable, predictable, and somewhat noncompetitive arrangement. Viewers, advertisers, entrepreneurs, programmers and rights-holders had no viable options. The marketplace was essentially static, until it was turned topsy-turvy by the intertwined march of technology and regulation.

§ 15-4. Impact of Deregulation.

In the late 1960's and early 1970's newer, more efficient means of delivering and distributing television programs began to emerge. First there was "basic" cable, then with increasing rapidity, satellites, "pay" cable, pay-per-view programming, direct-broadcast satellites and related electronic offsprings. These technical marvels were facing great obstacles in their attempts to crack the existing system, and the government (usually, but not always through the Federal Communications Commission) swung away from its long-standing position in favor of the traditional system, and began deregulating television technologies to permit the new entrants greater access and viability when competing with the Big Three and other giant communications corporations such as RCA. The net effect of this change in regulatory philosophy and intent was to encourage the entry of many new corporations and competitors, the redivision of the existing marketplace, the redefinition of audience size and composition, the skyrocketing of rights fees, and not least of all, the straining of resources and finances well beyond the ability of many participants to sustain.

§ 15-5. Threat of Oversaturation.

What we now witness in the television/sport industries is a turbulent world of emerging (but not necessarily growth) companies struggling to establish and maintain a market niche in an ever-more competitive environment for rights, which makes their eventual success more costly and less likely over the long term. Mergers, leveraged buy-outs, and outright collapses are no longer uncommon in the television-sports world. The marketplace has been divided among so many national, regional, local, *ad hoc* and part-time sports programming options that, with few exceptions such as the National Football League (NFL), the marketplace may be too saturated with programming for the audience to sustain the financial support for any of them. This trend may be further accelerated by the deregulation of the National Collegiate Athletic Association's (NCAA's) and other group rights-holders' television contracts.

The United States Supreme Court upheld, on June 27, 1984, lower court rulings invalidating the NCAA's exclusive control of college football on television. In the months following the Supreme Court ruling, free-market forces, now relatively unfettered by regulatory constraint, burst forth, as literally dozens of proposed television packages were proposed or adopted. Conferences, associations, independent colleges and universities and coalitions of various description announced their interest in establishing new television packages (and garnering greater television income) from the deregulated marketplace. Unfortunately, the economics of this free and open marketplace are such that many participants are suffering growing doubts that the results have been worth the risks and whether, in fact, many original supporters of the challenge to the NCAA television contract had not brought about their own demise.

The Universities of Oklahoma and Georgia, for example, were the main litigants against the NCAA, and its exclusive control of television contracts. They assumed that a freer marketplace would allow them to maximize income potential by establishing regional football networks within their prime geographical areas, while at the same time making available more of their football games to national and multi-regional television networks and packagers. Early results, however, were very disappointing, as these universities (among many others) discovered that the economics of deregulated network television are insufficiently predictable to support a multitude of football packages. Supply and demand dictated that the increase in available packages would commensurately decrease the value of all but a very few. Negotiating leverage, which the universities had hoped would shift their way, as packagers avidly pursued rights-holders, swung dramatically in the other direction, as rights-holders were forced to compete with each other for access to air time.

By one estimate, some $42 million in potential college football television-rights fees were "left on the table" unspent, when negotiating leverage shifted towards the networks and programmers. Instead of a bonanza, many of the football rights-holders faced a diminution in anticipated revenues, a shortage of air time and its associated national visibility, and continuing welter of legal and regulatory barriers brought on by the overlapping nature of the numerous new television packages.

Many football rights-holders discovered to their chagrin the old television axiom that "no contract is less exclusive than the one you sign," and that their spanking new, "exclusive" contracts quickly came into conflict with those of competing rights-holders or program packagers. For example, who should own the rights to, pay the fees for, control the scheduling of, and keep the income from a televised game between a member institution of the College Football Association (CFA) — which is under contract to ABC and ESPN, and a member of the Big Ten or Pac-10 which are similarly committed to CBS television? What happens when Harvard (Ivy League team under contract to PBS) plays Boston College (represented by Katz Television)? The two teams are not only committed to mutually exclusive television contracts, but the Harvard/Ivy package is on noncommercial television.

Revenues for even some of the most prestigious football programs fell dramatically in the unregulated marketplace. It is estimated that the CFA had expected to receive a rights fee from network television in the $34 million range, but it only got $12 million from ABC and another $10 million from ABC-owned ESPN. The ABC contract brought each team appearing on a telecast approximately $300,000, compared to $700,000 under the NCAA contract. University of Pittsburgh officials estimate a reduction of television income from a predicted $2.1 million to about $1 million a year. Boston College, Miami, and many others suffered similarly.

The most troubling question regarding financial opportunities in this new atmosphere remains the attitude of the advertisers and pay-television subscribers towards the greatly increased choices now afforded them. Oversaturation of programing cannot fail to diminish the appeal of television sports, nor to spread too thin the available dollars and audience. Sport managers and entrepreneurs need ever-increasing competence in audience assessment and research to properly gauge the market niche available for their product on television. A highly competitive, deregulated marketplace environment places a premium on audience research. More fundamentally, it requires a clear understanding on the part of sports managers and entrepreneurs that by and large the audience is the advertisers.

§ 15-6. Audience Research Is Essential.

Everything in television revolves around audiences, and audience research. Without sufficient numbers of viewers, innovative programming will meet a swift and remorseless demise. Sports programming is no different, and sports rights-holders must examine the most basic questions about audience behavior and composition before advancing. Consider potential viewers: What kind of event(s)? How many, over what period of time? What season? What time and day of the week? Is something similar already available to them? What other sports options are available to them on television? What other non-sport television programming? What non-television activities such as sports participation, family activities, other entertainment or sleep? Until these questions are fully answered by factual data (usually obtained through a market survey or market consultant), no further discussion is warranted.

Sport executives must also understand that advertisers are no longer interested in strictly the size of audiences (in this regard, the term "mass media" may be archaic) — they are interested in the largest possible audience which is likely to purchase their particular product or service — and no one else. In addition, they are interested in reaching the most members of that select audience for the least money. Thus, efficiency, not simply size, becomes the prime consideration in evaluating whether to buy advertising time in a sports program. Can the advertiser reach as many thousands of potential consumers through your program as he can through other sports programs, other television programs, other media (radio, magazines, outdoor advertising, direct mail, trade publications, product tie-ins, etc.)? Can he accomplish this for less cost per 1,000 viewers than all other options? Can he afford the advertising rates on television, or the necessary production costs? Has he already committed the available budget to other advertising vehicles?

A second examination must be made by the rights-holder to determine the nature of the product's value to a potential rights-buyer, especially in light of the rapidity with which things are changing. For example, is the product really a local, regional or national event? Can this be demonstrated through past rating performances, market surveys or attendance records? Is the product capable of sustaining long-term (multi-year) interest among viewers, and thereby encouraging commensurate advertiser support? This is most important today, since the majority of television-rights contracts are net financial losers for the buyer through the first years of the contract, and only tend to become profitable in the "out" years, after inflation and ad rates rise sufficiently to overtake production costs. Does the product really appeal to enough advertisers at all, or might it be better suited for a subscriber-based system such as pay cable, in which viewers essentially behave as at-home ticket buyers? What is the depth of their financial and emotional commitment to you? Are there intense fans, many blasé fans, few intense fans, or few blasé ones? Can they afford the cable system and the pay channel? Do they even have cable available in their home town or city?

A third area which demands examination is the consideration of exactly what is expected by obtaining a television contract. Think here in terms of total value, rather than simply money. For many different rights-holders, value received may consist of very different components and rewards. Is the prime concern monetary return in the form of a rights payment? Or, is it monetary reward in the form of shared advertising revenue, or subscriber fees, or marketing opportunities, or ticket sales, or in the equity value of a transferable contract itself? If monetary reward is less important (or unattainable), one may receive more net value through exposure, promotion, the "big league" atmosphere of television, recruitment or other spin-offs.

There are negative values, too, which should be considered. Should the schedule be changed to accommodate television? Rebuild or re-equip the facility? Discomfort season ticket holders? Participate in production or promotion activities? Alter the dates, times, locations or rules of the event to fit television's schedule? Can the event be edited for broadcast? Will editorial control be retained and the story line portrayed? Will players or participants seek extra considerations for allowing their performance to be televised? Most television personnel prefer not to raise such problems, and they do not mean to interfere or dominate the decision-making process. They are simply compelled by the realities of their own budgets and schedules and pressures to demand such stipulations when necessary.

Assume after consultation with appropriate staff and colleagues the decision is made to seek a television contract. There are so many systems, technologies, companies and programmers out there, how is a meaningful assessment of their suitability, strengths and weaknesses to be accomplished? There are five major options.

§ 15-7. Five Major Options.

Broadcast networks still represent the royalty of the traditional order. They offer the advantage of national operations (with more than 200 affiliate stations that reach virtually every American home), large, efficient organizations capable of handling the most complex deals, outstanding, experienced production capabilities, very impressive financial resources and stability, established viewer habits, and proven track records with advertisers and audience researchers. They suffer, however, from some of the weaknesses their very size and scope create. They need to make much more money on any given contract to support their enormous overhead. They can be conservative, "hide-bound" and slow to react to opportunity. Sports programming is just one of many options available to them, and often suffers a lower priority than entertainment, specials and news. Since they are national in operation, it is harder to get affiliate acceptance (or "clearance") of many regional or local events such as ice hockey, tennis and auto racing. Their affiliated stations do not have to carry the networks' programs, and often choose to preempt such programs in favor of local ones, and this happens quite frequently with sports programs. The broadcast networks need to sustain reasonably high ratings to continue sports programs; their threshold for program continuation is much higher than that of smaller, leaner companies. Network viewership remains the highest in television, but it has begun slipping measurably in recent years. No one can predict where it will bottom out, or what impact this will have on their interest in, or ability to underwrite giant sports rights fees. In sum, the Big Three remain very much atop the television sports market. They display all the marketplace strengths and weaknesses of traditional dominant corporations in a rapidly changing world. They may be the last of the dreadnoughts, but they still pack one tremendous wallop, and will for many years.

Advertiser-supported cable programming is usually referred to as Basic Cable because it is made available to viewers for the basic monthly rate charged by local cable operators. There is no additional "pay" charge for such channels, and it is supported by advertisers, not subscribers. Entertainment and Sports Programming Network (ESPN), and USA Network are perhaps the best known representatives of this industry segment. Advertiser-supported cable companies are essentially hybrid, marrying the financial system of conventional broadcast systems to the technology of cable. They offer some advantages to the rights-holder, which include an enormous amount of air time to be filled (hence the demand for sports programming), a much smaller scale of operations and overhead (thus a much lower threshold for program continuation), the excitement and real growth of cable as an industry, more flexible program schedules, and the sort of eagerness to please which often characterizes new businesses. On the other hand, they do not reach millions of American homes (and never will) due to population patterns and the economics of cable installation and operation. They are, with very few exceptions, unprofitable. Their production crews and facilities are not equal to those of the broadcast networks. In many cases, they are not officially measured by the major national television ratings services, so providing accurate data to advertisers remains a problem. They cannot afford the large rights fees demanded by premium events, and often end up with program schedules which include a large dose of minor events, foreign sports, repeats and inexpensive talk shows. They offer the opportunity to get in on the ground floor of national television, but questions remain whether the rest of the building will ever be constructed.

National pay cable is typified by the hugely successful Home Box Office (HBO) which, significantly, places the programming emphasis on entertainment, not sport, this industry segment appeals not to advertisers, but to subscribers. It is able to offer certain prestige events of somewhat limited appeal (Wimbledon, boxing, etc.) because its monthly subscriber revenues permit selected-rights fee purchases; the program schedule for sport is predicated on the belief that every event should be a "special," not part of a season-long series. The events are not sold to subscribers on a pay-per-view basis, but as part of the overall quality of the monthly or annual program lineup. The sports department works within a fixed budget for program production and acquisition. Advantages include the demonstrated ability to reach a quality, "upscale" demographic audience, the promotion available to a "special event," and the freedom from having to make an instant profit on each event, as would be the case with pay-per-view.

Disadvantages include the relative unimportance of sport to the parent company, the fact that not all cable households buy the pay-system tier, and their relative indifference to the purchase of whole seasons of repeatable events, such as football, baseball, or basketball.

Regional cable systems vary tremendously in nearly every characteristic. However, they commonly display a mix of the attributes we have already discussed in national systems. Some are advertiser-based, some subscriber-based, and some a bit of both. PRISM, SportsChannel, SportsTime, Metrosports and a host of others have been established to service a local or regional market, on the assumption that fan loyalty is essentially local in nature, and that loyal fans will be willing to pay for cable to see their favorite team(s). The regional systems may offer sport on a full-time, part-time, or *ad hoc* basis, and may combine more than one team or sports property in the programming mix to attract and retain viewers. The advantages of such a system may include the fan loyalty already mentioned. There are many examples of fans being interested in particular local teams or events, rather than the sport itself. Production costs and facilities are much less than those required for national events. Marketing the product is easier, thanks to the natural constituency it enjoys. Rights fees may be garnered by the rights-holders in addition to those available from network contracts, or broadcasters. They may serve as a hedge against declining gate receipts, or a new way of reaching (and receiving income from) potential ticket buyers who cannot obtain a ticket to sold-out events. They may extend the "reach" of an event to fans who live some distance away, or who cannot attend for other reasons.

Regional cable services have, in many cases, developed an unenviable track record, because they face some formidable obstacles. Most common is the resistance of television viewers or fans to "pay" for what they used to get (or think they should get) for "free." Of course, no television is "free," it is just that broadcast television raises money indirectly through advertisers adding to the cost of their products, while "pay" television actually bills viewers directly. In any case, many people, including politicians who know a popular issue when they see one, seem to believe there exists a constitutional right to see sports on television, without direct charge. So fan and viewer loyalty is often tempered by their resistance to what is perceived as unholy commercial interference with the natural order of things.

A basic law of economics tends to make this problem worse. That is, to maintain or increase the value of a product, one generally needs to reduce supply, thus increasing demand or value. In the case of sports properties, this usually means reducing the number of events or games available on "free" television, to encourage enough people to pay for the events on television, so as to maximize income to the rights-holder and telecasting company. Fans and viewers of broadcast television never react well to the diminution or elimination of their accustomed sports-viewing habits and opportunities. However, since no one will pay for what he can get for free, some reduction of the available broadcast inventory is necessary.

Regional networks also suffer from several understandable problems. Defining the region of interested viewers is not so easy as it seems, and matching that region to an available delivery system is tricky. Also, many other sports rights-holders may inhabit the same region, and either compete for access to the delivery system, or take regulatory action (through the courts, league or conference rules or commissioners) to deny you access to all or part of the region. Ad hoc or part-time networks featuring one team or event run counter to the long history of viewer preference for continuous program scheduling, rather than the on-again, off-again problem presented by such networks. The solution to this problem often takes the form of assembling a multi-sport, multi-event sports channel, with several teams or rights-holders contributing events to the overall programming package, thus presenting much more continuous sport programming. A problem may develop even here, however, because dispute between rights-holders are not uncommon, usually concerning who gets the "better" air dates and times, and which rights-holders receive the greater rights fees. The natural rivalry for the total sport dollar in any given marketplace may place rights-holders in a tense cooperative agreement via cable, while still competing fiercely for the same fan support throughout the region.

Finally, the proliferation of regional/local packages portends the oversaturation of the marketplace which inevitably leads to the decline and fall of some programmers and rights-holders. Viewers already enjoy the offerings of broadcast networks, advertiser-supported national cable, local broadcast stations and national pay services. In addition, they commonly receive via cable at least two so-called "superstations" which feature sports. How much more sports can the viewer watch? At what price? Regional sports packages are tantalizing ventures which have swung between the extremes of great success and failure. They are for the rights-holder with excellent instincts, superb understanding of the market, a thick skin and the willingness to assume risks.

The superstations are local television stations (WTBS in Atlanta, WGN in Chicago) which make their local signal available to cable companies nationwide via satellite transmission. They enable the rights-holder to reach a very sizeable percentage of cable homes on an advertiser-supported basis. The superstations therefore resemble ESPN or USA in the sense that they are usually part of a local cable operator's basic package offered at no extra monthly charge to subscribers. They present a compelling opportunity to develop viewers and fans well beyond the natural local or regional area of the team or event, without having to make a deal with one of the national networks. The Atlanta Braves ("America's Team") are the prime example of this strategy. Advertisers can purchase time on a superstation for much less than they could on a national network, and still reach a large number of homes throughout the country. Disadvantages include a host of regulatory problems, including a tariff imposed on all cable systems receiving more than two such superstations, league and conference blackouts of "invading" signals to protect local franchises, and the inability of cable operators to amend or delete any of the strictly local commercials inserted in the city of origination (for example, an Atlanta car dealer who buys time in Braves games will be seen by all national viewers).

The choice of an appropriate delivery system remains one of the most challenging and significant decisions the sports manager or entrepreneur can make, and often reflects the sophistication of the professional advice available to him in such considerations. In general, however, the premise remains that each situation is different, and must be evaluated without regard to personal preference, emotion, or the track records of others.

§ 15-8. Factors Influencing Contractual Decisions.

What then does the programmer or network executive think when a rights-holder expresses interest in negotiating a contract? The first thing that should come to mind is not price or production, but "Do I need this program?" Indeed, does his company stand to benefit from this program more than any other option? Again, benefit may best be defined in terms of total value rather than monetary return alone. Does the program establish a reputation for quality sports programming that will be helpful in other negotiations? Does it build a comprehensive and popular sports programming line-up that appeals to viewers and advertisers? Does it allow for year-round or all-day continuity of programming? Does it preempt the competition from acquiring such programming? Does it throw off associated benefits such as the recruitment and retention of large audiences which will stay tuned to watch other programs during the course of the year, thus increasing their revenues, and earning a substantial (but indirect) profit? Does it provide outstanding opportunities for marketing and promotion? Will it encourage affiliates to carry your programming? It is not unusual for sports programs to be bought by television, despite their inability to generate an immediate and direct profit.

Property may even have considerable value to the television programmer who doesn't even know when or where he wants to air it. Magazine format shows such as "ABC's Wide World of Sports," "CBS Sports Spectacular" and "NBC Sportsworld" frequently purchase a number of small events which are kept on the shelf as inventory until an appropriate occasion or sudden change in programming (the rainout of a live event) requires insertion of different material with little notice. Some events in this category have value to programmers precisely because they can be videotaped, edited, and played back at some later date without causing any stir among the viewers. In fact, a whole mini-industry has developed around companies which stage, produce and make available to television "Made For TV" events ranging from tennis tournaments to refrigerator pulls. It is oddly logical that, because these events have no real fans, or home towns, or schedules, they make excellent filler material for television, and are much in demand.

A television programmer will also want to determine whether a particular sports program fits neatly into the programming schedule he is developing, and whether it builds on, rather than contradicts, the audiences attracted by other sports programs already on the air or under consideration. For example, no programmer worth his expense account would place bowling and tennis, baseball and golf, or other incongruous combinations together in a schedule, since they appeal to vastly different demographics.

The seasonality of television also enters the deliberations. It is generally agreed that the most effective television programming is live (with the rare exception of blockbuster miniseries), and sport is generally live and exciting. Therefore, one could presume that the best time for sports television would be when everything else consists of repeats. In fact, though, the summer is often a dead period even for sports, because the HUT levels (Homes Using Television) decline dramatically with the arrival of warm weather, and sport suffers as a result. During the winter months, when throughout much of the country people are at home watching television, sport has a difficult time cracking any programming slot outside the traditional weekend daytime "ghetto." During other periods of the year when all-important ratings "sweeps" are taken to set future advertising rates, most television companies eschew sport other than Super Bowls and World Series, to prevent damage to their overall ratings. It is for this reason, and this reason alone, that CBS pressured the NBA to move its entire schedule forward nearly a month, so the playoffs would not appear in, and subsequently damage the all-important May ratings book.

Rights-holders must also anticipate the programmer's interest in filling holes in existing program schedules, rather than in adding programming to the already-strong time slots or seasons. The United States Football League (USFL), whatever its weaknesses in terms of player quality or franchise stability, nonetheless successfully fulfilled ABC's need for a strictly seasonal package that could be bought for a low price, and sold to advertisers desiring to reach certain demographic segments at that time of the year. Remember too that advertisers have very specific seasonal plans for their products and their advertising campaigns, and these plans must play a major role in any calculation of receptivity towards a new television-sports venture. The same company may spend 500% more of its advertising budget in one quarter of the year than in another. Programs which meet the need to spend that seasonal budget efficiently have a much better chance of success, and sports managers must take the time to learn what the potential advertiser's seasonal spending pattern indicates about potential opportunities.

When both a rights-holder and a potential purchaser agree to negotiate a contract, it is of paramount importance that both sides, but particularly the rights-holder, clearly agree and understand exactly what is meant by the catch-all phrase, "rights." This refers, of course, to copyrighted material or performance. However, there is frequently considerable confusion regarding multiple interpretations of "rights," which as a term is used mistakenly only so often as the term "exclusive." In fact, both are misused constantly (or, at the very least, misinterpreted) and their combination is often a signal flag for trouble: "exclusive rights" can and does mean many different things to many different people.

Let's take the issue apart to examine the potential hazards to the unwary sports manager. Does the institution really own the rights to the event or events in question? Or are the rights held or shared with a conference, league or association? Do the participants or players assert a copyright claim for their performance? Does the institution hold the live performance rights, but not those relating to taped, filmed, or edited performance? Does it hold the rights in perpetuity, for a specified length of time? Who has the power to assign the rights to another person or institution? Who controls the rights to all aspects of the event: the ski slopes, the ski tour, as well as the individual tournament? If the institution is satisfied in this regard, the next step to ponder is what to do with those rights.

Should they be sold in separate packages (i.e., broadcast television, cable television, pay-per-view, syndication) or other arrangement, in which each purchaser gets "exclusive" rights — but only for limited purposes? Should portions of the rights be sold to multiple bidders within the same technology: overlapping NCAA football and basketball packages with NBC and CBS; NBA contracts with both ESPN and USA in cable; Wimbledon contracts with NBC and HBO. Should the package be split in terms of length, so that various components of it are up for renewal at different times, thus offering some safety from sudden withdrawal of all television? Are American, or the North American, or worldwide rights being offered? If it is taped programming under consideration, are first-run rights sold, or is there permission to air the same program several times? It is essential that this be clear, since many a mistake has been made that led to loss of control, and thereby lost income to the original rights-holder.

The issue of copyright control has been complicated by changes in television technology. If the program is broadcast on a local station or network, does it become their copyright or the institution's? If that broadcast is then "captured" from the air by a cable company, or transmitted via another technology, whose copyright is it then? What are the legal options to protect the value of the copyrighted performance as it travels through the maze of transmission technologies, and reaches a variety of audiences, who may not be paying for the privilege? The sport manager and his attorneys need to be quite specific from the earliest discussions with television programmers, because lack of specificity can damage only the rights-holder.

It may be beneficial to engage the services of an intermediary to help sort all this out. Consultants are available, but they range in experience, ability and scope of activities. Some specialize in communications law, others in sports television marketing and sales, others have production companies, and so on. When faced with the highly complex and technical nature of the questions at hand, maintaining a distance from the specific details of program packaging, sales and production will likely be an advantage. If a third partner is involved, the manager must be specific in assigning duties (and rights) to the representatives or intermediaries — has the sales/production company agreed to represent the rights-holder, or has it become a partial rights-holder itself? Make consulting contracts quite specific, with detailed tasks, budgets and deadlines. This is a prudent precaution that no legitimate consultant or representative will resent.

Does the organization wish to conduct much of the television business itself? This may be the best idea, provided there are expert personnel on hand or under contract. Another choice is to retain the available advertising inventory and sell it, thus retaining all the income. It is also possible to produce the events, either through a wholly owned production subsidiary formed for the purpose, or through a subcontracted production company. This will depend not only on the availability of trained personnel, but the expense of first-rate equipment and remote trucks, the suitability of the site(s) for color television production, the distances involved, travel schedules, the cost of telephone long-distance lines or satellite transponder space, the salaries of announcers, technicians, security and a host of related expenses. The warning is that unless programs look and sound as attractively professional as the networks at their best, credibility will be lost with the viewing audience, which will make the inevitable comparison. *Television remains an industry based on perception, not reality, and that holds true in sports production.* Viewers want all programs to offer the same multiple camera angles, instant replays, cleverly placed microphones and famous announcers, regardless of a limited budget or local technical crews. This has often emerged as a problem with local and regional broadcasters, and cable companies, and is sometimes a problem with rights-holders who, through ignorance or greed, wish to undertake all the production themselves, rather than surrender it (and part of the income) to professionals.

Successful television sports packages often come under attack for siphoning fans away from the arena and into their living rooms. This issue deserves discussion, as it illuminates one of the stickiest problems facing the sports manager or entrepreneur. To-wit: when is enough television exposure too much? Does keeping an event off television really increase gate receipts over the long term? Most studies indicate the answer is no, and point to the powerful marketing influence of television to recruit fans. But is an expanded television package the cause of diminished attendance, or the solution to it? Are the people watching at home former ticket-buyers who have given up, or additional fans, who never bought a ticket anyway? What games should be allowed to be telecast? Home or away? Weekend or weekday? Games in which there is a full house? Games in which your victory is expected thus dictating a schedule which shows less glamorous opponents, or games the fans want to see against the top competition, which may beat you consistently? Offer regular season games only, playoffs only, or a combination? If there is more than one sports rights-holder in the market, should head-to-head competition be avoided in programming (in home events or telecasts)? In short, the potential for television broadcasts to enhance or damage gate receipts may be influenced by everything from climate to the location of the arena; to the price of tickets relative to other entertainment options. In cases where an organization offers the dominant sports attraction in a marketplace, television will probably enhance that position. If, on the other hand, it is in a relatively weak position, it will be necessary to commission research which reveals the causes of public ambivalence, and then decide whether television will improve or worsen the situation. In general, however, it is better to be on television than not.

The entrepreneurial options and opportunities open to the astute sports manager have been discussed in some detail, with an eye towards the maximization of revenues available from television. Before abandoning the topic, however, it may be helpful to return to the concept of total value as the basis for a more philosophic argument — an argument for an adaptation of the theory of corporate responsibility. In this case, that theory may be construed to imply that under certain circumstances, it is preferable to restrain one's own accrual of benefits to bolster the competition; thereby creating a healthier overall environment for all participants. While it is surely possible in this increasingly free-market atmosphere for certain rights-holders to realize enormous additional revenues, if they proceed to do that to the exclusion of, or at the expense of, their sister organizations, then the competitive marketplace may collapse both on the playing field and in the boardroom.

A totally free market cannot be fair to all, or even most participants, unless that market has the ability to expand to accommodate demand, and all participants are free to seek their own niche by developing specialized products. Unfortunately, sport is not such a market, because many aspects of a rights-holder's behavior are constrained or stipulated by governing rules adopted by leagues, associations or conferences. In many instances, certain expenditures are mandated by these rules. To totally deregulate the revenue-raising mechanism of television one may incorrectly assume that all rights-holders will benefit from the deregulation. Is it good practice for a rights-holder to forego some potential revenues to support less fortunate colleagues? This kind of revenue sharing or pooled rights fees has been a cornerstone of the television industry for more than twenty years, and numerous franchises, leagues and associations could not exist without it.

What exactly do pooled rights fees accomplish? Some obvious things, such as the increased negotiating leverage enjoyed by a person representing multiple rights-holders working together; and some measure of equalized income for all members regardless of market size, bankbook or business acumen. But it also produces some less obvious results, such as the sense of corporate responsibility, and exerts strong influences upon the development and implementation of government rules and mechanisms. It has been said, for example, that the secret of NFL Commissioner Pete Rozelle's unquestioned position atop the sports industry is a direct result of his unparalleled success in maximizing (and controlling through his office) the television revenues of his league. Indeed, until Al Davis, managing general partner of the Los Angeles Raiders, came along with his various successful antitrust claims against the NFL and Rozelle, it was generally believed that the NFL Commissioner could depend on the support and agreement of the owners because he delivered so much television revenue to each club that it was simply not worth their while to challenge the system. Some analysts have even gone so far as to say that the best measure of any commissioner's power to truly fulfill his mandate of governance is to calculate the percentage of total revenues which pass through his office before distribution to the individual franchises or member institutions. The higher the percentage controlled by the central office, the more power and prestige accorded the commissioner. Those leagues, conferences or associations with a heavy emphasis on independent, unilateral revenue generation by members can be counted on to have weaker central authority and governance.

The question therefore remains: in a deregulated, free-market atmosphere, should rights-holders restrain themselves to forestall some of these impacts, and to reassert the primacy of corporate responsibility in sport?

It may be surprising, but true, to state that in the mid-1980's governance is controlled by television (through its economic impacts), rather than the reverse, which is surely not the way most people intended. A totally free market will inevitably lead to oversaturation and retrenchment by television programmers and sports managers alike, although the damage to both parties may be lasting. The economies of scale dictate that such a free market would divide the existing universe of advertiser and subscriber dollars among increasing numbers of participants, whose costs would not decline commensurately. The result will be scattered viewership and dispersed dollars — both very negative indicators in television sport.

A more cautious approach which recognizes the benefits of competition within a relatively stable marketplace (while observing the legal and regulatory guidelines describing appropriate efforts to achieve some stability) characterized by numerous moderately successful participants, may be more attractive in the sense of full value, than a free market characterized by a few hugely successful participants. The operative bywords are caution, restraint and enlightened self-interest. Consider their implications very carefully.

The issues, problems, opportunities and procedures outlined in this chapter may serve to thoroughly confuse the unenthusiastic or fainthearted reader, whose previous inclination was to avoid the complexities of television altogether, hoping somehow the problem of dealing with it would be handled by someone else. Certainly the knowledge and instincts required to take full advantage of the television opportunities that may exist are not commonly found among sports managers. However, the number of knowledgeable managers is growing, if only because the modern sports manager has realized the absolute necessity of understanding television.

It may be easier to contemplate the studious absorption of such knowledge if you think of television not as a monolithic, multifaceted business, but as many separate businesses which happen to cooperate and occupy the same corporate headquarters. Think of television as:

1. a sales organization;
2. a production company;
3. an audience research firm;
4. an entertainment manager;
5. a distributor of electronic hardware;
6. an advertising agency; and
7. a sports investor.

By disaggregating the broadcast sports industry into its component parts, the modern sports manager or entrepreneur will feel more comfortable in demystifying the people sitting across the bargaining table, or listening to a proposal. In fact, most television sports personnel are perfectly ordinary mortals, no smarter or tougher or less likeable than any other group. They are, however, operating under very different corporate guidelines than most executives, and must, at one time or another, approach their business as if they were representing only one of its aggregate parts. Be prepared for this, and for the resultant confusion when the same television sports executives appear to be wearing different corporate "hats" under different circumstances.

In the final analysis, sports managers need to understand that there exist no deep, dark secrets for success in television sports. There are no simple, magic solutions to complex situations. Television executives are not better prepared, except through repeated experience, to interpret past performance data and extrapolate a dependable prediction for the future of any particular sports concept. They depend on research, ratings performance, sales ability, promotion and a lot of faith. Sports managers have (or can surely develop) these abilities also, and can put them to good use in establishing an equitable and mutually satisfactory relationship with television.

§ 15-9. Summary/Conclusion.

The relationship between television and sport remains intimate, but like many such relationships, it may seem more exasperating and less predictable with each passing year. Sports managers and entrepreneurs certainly cannot be faulted for occasionally throwing up their hands and wistfully wishing for a return to the days before television dominated sport in the United States. Nor can they be blamed for coming to the realization that the "good old days" could never provide the revenues now necessary to operate a first-class sports program, and that television is the only game in town for many of them today. The astute sports manager and entrepreneur will then make it a priority to learn as much as possible about the television industry, with a necessary emphasis on the perspective of television executives and their corporate sponsors, so as to be able to compete in the competitive rights fee marketplace.

Sports managers and entrepreneurs must make exhaustive and exhaustively honest assessments of their television suitability, attractiveness, marketability, uniqueness, popularity and audience, and then realistically negotiate a total value for their televised product which will be supported by the marketplace, accepted by advertisers and subscribers, and will provide both sufficient revenues and growth to encourage continuation of the program concept.

Attention must be paid to the regulatory environment in television sport, and the dramatic impact any change may have on existing and future contracts and opportunities. Technological advances must be examined not only as offering the possibility of new and better technical television, but as a reflection of governmental regulatory policies which may favor the growth and development of one or more industry segments at the expense of others; hence offering competitive advantages to certain programming concepts and services over others.

Contractual decisions must be independently arrived at, and must accurately reflect the rights-holder's priorities, rather than simply an adaptation of other, seemingly similar contracts. Careful scrutiny must be given the interlocking, or overlapping nature of many modern television sports contracts, to ascertain exactly what provisions will be operative in cases of two or more seemingly exclusive contracts at loggerheads. All contract provisions have a value, although that total value may not be quantifiable at the outset, so rights-holders must decide before entering negotiations with television programmers what the rights-holders really regard as the bottom line for their sports program (profit, visibility, promotion, prestige, image-enhancement).

In the final analysis, the sports manager or entrepreneur will have to become a television sports specialist (or hire one) to successfully compete in this most competitive league. It must never be forgotten that television can get along without sport relatively better than the reverse, and that recent trends have accentuated the disparity. Therefore, the business of television and sport is much more concerned with television than sport, and managers must accept this reality if they wish to participate in the industry.

Chapter 16

AN INFORMATION-BASED APPROACH TO MARKETING SPORT

By

Bernard Mullin

§ 16-1. Introduction.

The case for the development of an information-based approach to marketing was made extensively in Chapter 9. In this chapter the elements of the data storage system [called a marketing information system (MIS)] are outlined. In addition, the types of data which a marketer needs to collect are discussed. The major contribution of the chapter is to highlight the use of the data in determining the most appropriate target segments which marketing strategy is later developed to reach.

An MIS can be as simple as a system of index cards, or it can be as complex as a fully integrated database, stored and retrieved on a mainframe computer. Obviously there are many alternatives in between these two polar extremes, and just where an organization chooses to make its stand depends upon the following factors:

1. The size and geographic dispersement of the market for the organizations product or service:
   The larger the market, and the more geographically dispersed the market, the larger and more complex the MIS.
2. The availability of data on consumers and potential consumers.
   The more data available, the larger the MIS.
3. The budget allocated to the development and maintenance of the MIS.
   The larger the budget, the more sophisticated the MIS.

Whether the index card system or a computerized system is chosen makes no difference in the type of data needed to be collected, nor to the analysis and manipulations to be performed with the data.

The difference between manual (paper) and computerized (electronic) systems is that electronic systems permit storage and analysis of much greater volumes of data, the data can be analyzed much more quickly and accurately, multiple departments in the organization can access the data at the same time, and data from various sources can be integrated. While the differences are significant and permit much more powerful marketing data to be generated in electronic-based systems and hence more sophisticated marketing strategy to be developed, the time taken to maintain a simple index card or paper file system is still worth the effort. Even for the sport entrepreneur working in the smallest of organizations the payback is considerable. The problem with manual systems is that they require long hours of tedious work, and this often deters all but the most ardent of sport managers. With the continual decline in the prices of mini computers and software programs, there appear to be electronic systems which fall into the price range of even the smallest of organizations (For example, the IBM Personal Computer (IBM-PC), with sufficient memory capacity to handle the records of 1,000 customers, and a printer costs around $4,000; for a capacity sufficient to handle tens of thousands of records it would cost under $7,000. An additional $500-$1,000 would be required for database and word-processing software, making the capital outlay a quickly cost-justified investment, particularly when the computer could be used for other management functions such as accounting, inventory control, etc.). It is relatively clear that in the next five years we can expect the overwhelming majority of sport organizations in all sectors of the industry to be employing computers to manage their MIS databases.

Below, the characteristics of an effective MIS are developed, along with some guidelines of how the system should be used, and the potential benefits which can accrue for those taking the time to develop and maintain an MIS.

§ 16-2. Characteristics of a Marketing Information System (MIS).

An MIS should have the following characteristics:

1. It must be centralized. An organization needs to have all of its data located in one centralized system.
2. The various data bases (consumer files, accounting records, sales records, etc.) need to be fully integrated so that, the data from one source can be contrasted and/or combined with data from another source.
3. The data must be retrievable in a form which the marketer can use for decision-making.

Only if *all* three of the above conditions are met, does an MIS reach its full potential. As a simple rule, the MIS must contain only the information that will be used by the marketer, yet it must contain *all* of the information that the marketer needs to make effective decisions. One caution needs to be offered at this time, many marketers fall into the trap of feeling that the only data which is relevant is that which they collect themselves about their market, and their own consumers (called primary data). In almost all industries there is a wealth of data which has already been published (called secondary data), which is invaluable to the marketer. Much of the secondary data used by marketers comes from federal, state or county government sources (such as population demographics); or from public sources (such as local chamber of commerce data), or from trade and industry associations and publications (industry averages, profiles and standards performance and cost ratios). Additional information from independent market research agencies such as the A.C. Nielson Co., Simmons Market Research Bureau, and Louis Harris, Inc., all of whom collect data on consumer preferences, viewing and participation habits, product purchases, etc., is extremely valuable but can be expensive. Data from all of the above primary and secondary sources should become part of the overall MIS, and should be updated at least once a year.

For many sport industry segments, external secondary-data sources provide the sole "yardstick" by which the organizations' own data can be contrasted.

For example, in 1981 a major New England college contacted the author to perform market research for them concerning their intercollegiate football program. The team had suffered significant and continual declines in paid attendance despite a steadily improving won-loss record. One of the most relevant pieces of information which the athletic administration had ignored was the fact that their attendance decline rate was significantly lower than comparative schools throughout New England, and far below the drop-off in interest being experienced at New England high school football games over the same time period. While this information did not solve their problem *per se,* it did provide a most critical backdrop in deciding which media alternatives should be employed to boost sagging attendance, and particularly in estimating the probability of favorable advertising response.

The author stated in an earlier article that "Marketing without a marketing information system (MIS) is like taking a trip without a road map!" (Ref. 1). Simply put, smart marketers do not do it! Every marketing decision should be made only after the impact on all of the key elements of marketing have been fully considered. A list of the major information needs of a marketer is given below, broken down under the headings of the key elements of marketing.

§ 16-3. Informational Needs of the Sport Marketer.

The first thing that a marketer needs to do is to define the extent of his market area. A concept which has been used in the retail industry is that of the "critical trading radius" (Ref. 2). The critical trading radius was initially conceived as a system of concentric circles of mileage using the facility location as the center and 5-, 7- and 10-mile radii as milestones. The concept has now been refined as a series of nonconcentric radii based upon consumer traveling time to the sport facility rather than straight mileage. The size of the critical trading area varies with each segment of the sport industry. Commercial recreation clubs (racquet sports and health clubs, etc.) would have a 20-minute driving time radius from the facility in which 80-85% of members and potential members would reside; retail sporting goods stores in urban and suburban areas would have a similar trading area to the health clubs. In rural areas, the radius naturally expands considerably. The trading radius increases as the degree of competition decreases, for professional sport teams; intercollegiate athletic events; and coliseum, stadium and arena events, 80% of the market resides within a one-hour driving or traveling time radius, (longer for weekend afternoon events). For small ski resorts near population areas, the radius will be an hour or less. For all destination resorts (the more popular ski resorts; sport resorts such as Hilton Head Island in South Carolina and Disneyworld, in Orlando, Florida) the trading area is almost unlimited. The concept of traveling time rather than straight mileage reflects more accurately the decision criteria of a consumer, and consequently is a more accurate predictor of potential demand.

The data which is critical to be kept on hand concerning the nature and extent of the market is as follows:

1. Size of the market (total number of individuals living within the critical trading area).

   This outlines whether or not the market has sufficient size to support the product.

2. The demographics of individuals residing in the critical trading radius. Specifically, the major factors are:

   a. Total population within trading radius (year round residents and commuters),

   b. Breakdown by age, sex and income relevant to the profile of target consumers.

   From these data, the marketer is able to make predictions on total market potential. When industry averages are available, it is possible to predict quite accurately the total demand for a particular product. For example, in the bowling business, it has long been an industry standard that one bowling lane is demanded per 10,000 population. More recently, similar "rules of thumb" have been used for court and health clubs which are based upon age, sex and income.

3. The purchase behavior and consumption patterns of those living and residing within the market.

   Where possible, data on the spending patterns of consumers are helpful in determining potential market demand. Marketers have found demographics to be extremely useful in determining the profile of potential consumers, and yet demographics have their limitations. For example, a 35-year-old college educated, white professional male living in Iowa is simply not the same "animal" to a marketer as the similarly-profiled individual residing in New York City. The major difference is life-style characteristics. Life-style characteristics are called psychographics and are usually captured through A.I.O. (activity, interest, and opinion studies (Ref. 3)). Psychographic studies tend to be expensive and they are difficult to undertake. Data take much more effort to solicit and respondents are not always forthcoming in offering opinions and attitudes. Consequently, many decisions are made in the absence of such research. When no hard demographic data are available, or when the data bear no relationship to the product being marketed, it is essential that at least a "quick and dirty" pulse-check of consumer attitudes be performed concerning key product attributes. Illustrations of this latter process might be a verbal sampling of opinion of participants in a road race as to certain aspects of the race's total organization, form and marketing. Or a more comprehensive study might be to ask individuals to complete surveys on their attitudes concerning running shoes, where several products are compared. The first series of questions would concern the product attributes which the individuals felt were more critical in their choice of shoe. The second would deal with their subjective ratings of each shoe on each of the attributes they identified.

From these data a strong idea of key product attributes can be developed which determine product choice. The strength of one's own product can also be "guesstimated," along with the areas of weakness according to consumer perception. Similarly, some general ideas about the competitors' strengths and weaknesses can also be developed.

4. The level of spectatorship and/or participation level by sport(s), broken down by demographic categories.

    This identifies the profile of the target consumer of any given sport. All promotional strategies and advertising media choices are then designed to reach this target market segment.

One leading expert in Sport Marketing, Matt Levine, once said that all of marketing boils down to how well you know the market (Ref. 4). There can be little doubt that knowledge of the market is critical to marketing success, even if there are other important factors impacting on success.

A. *The Consumer.*

The ideal situation for a marketer is to be able to identify all of his consumers by name, address and phone number, so that they can be communicated with directly. In private clubs, this is quite easily accomplished, and yet the author's research has revealed that the majority of sport clubs which have more than 1,000 members at any one time have only a superficial idea of their demographic breakdown of the membership, and often only a crude "guesstimate" of the total head count. Of course those with computerized membership databases are able to keep completely accurate information (assuming that the database is kept current!). Comprehensive consumer information is often collected by sport organizations as a regular business practice, but much of this data goes unused. Baseball franchises that make it to the play-offs often throw away the names and addresses of unfilled ticket applications, when these individuals clearly should be added to the mailing list. Retail sporting goods stores ask for customers' names and addresses when they fill out the sales receipts but these names and addresses are rarely recorded in an MIS for marketing use; instead they lie in an accounting or tax records file.

The data on existing customers which are most critical to be kept for marketing decision-making are as follows:

1. The name, address and phone number of consumers.

    Used for communication and correspondence, and for direct mailings.

2. Frequency of purchase/use of the product; type and quantity of product purchased/when purchased.

    Used for tracking usage frequency, targeting low-frequency users, and upgrading existing consumers from lower-priced products to higher-priced products.

3. Method of payment/location where purchased/purchase lead time.

    Used in determining price, distribution outlets and lead time in promoting events and ticket distribution.

4. The media read/viewed or listened to; which media/message led them to purchase the product?

   Used to determine promotional effectiveness and lead analysis.

5. The pattern of consumption — Does (s)he consume alone, with family, or friends? What does the consumer do before, during, and after consuming the sport?

   This information is extremely valuable in marketing planning, particularly in deciding such strategies as what promotional items to offer (is a particular event-day more likely to attract families, couples, business groups or friends?). What kind of concessions would be best? Is a post-event disco party likely to succeed? Should we promote more to the father, mother, single female, etc.?

In short, the major goal of a marketer in establishing an MIS should be to know the name, address, phone number, sex, occupation and income of all consumers, along with information about what product(s) they buy, when and in what quantities, and with whom they consume the product. If possible, additional information on what media they view, read or listen to is extremely valuable, as well as any information on which promotional message or media helped to attract the consumer.

B. *Competitors.*

The MIS should contain up-to-date information on competitors which would include complete price list(s), product line(s) offered, promotional strategies, sample advertisements, promotions strategy and special promotions, etc. Any organization offering a similar product or service whose critical trading radius overlaps more than 25% with your own trading radius is to be considered a competitor. Usually this means that the competitors' facility or retail outlet will be located within 30 minutes traveling time of your own facility.

One strategy which the author uses in sales-training seminars for court, health and fitness facilities is to require all sales staff to visit all competing facilities and to critique competitors' strengths and weaknesses.

C. *Future Trends.*

No organization can exist without strong consideration being given to the future. In sport the ability to project future trends may be even more critical than in other industries. Sport continues to operate in a highly volatile marketplace, with fads coming and going. With sport trends apparently running in seven-year cycles, the industry is not one which can be taken for granted. Perhaps the most vivid illustration in this regard is the court and health club business. The majority of facilities in this industry segment started in the eastern USA 20 years ago as indoor tennis clubs. New trends started in California and spread east as clubs added bars and lounges; weight rooms (later Nautilus centers); racquetball courts; aerobic dance studios; cardiovascular fitness centers; pools, saunas and jacuzzis; multi-purpose rooms; day-care centers and pro shops. The more sophisticated clubs now have moved into stress management, diet and nutrition education classes and cardiovascular-risk screening so that they are now really "Wellness Centers."

Few other industries have experienced such marked changes, in such a short period of time, and yet it is clear that evolutions in this segment of the sport industry still have some way to go! Other sport industry segments have not changed their concept quite as drastically; however, changes in the market for their product have been equally volatile.

§ 16-4. Integration of the Data Sources.

Invariably, the full value of an MIS is realized only when data from various sources are integrated into a common database. As discussed earlier, given the size and complexity of the information, this often requires a computer in order to manage the system. For example, a small, retail sporting-goods store as part of it's existing procedure collects the customer's name, address, item(s) purchased, the amount purchased and date of purchase. Currently this information is written onto the multi-copy sales slip (receipt) given to the customer at the time of the purchase. All that is required for the development of an effective MIS is to organize these receipts by alphabetical order, or better yet, to log them onto 5" x 7" index cards and the store owner now has an MIS!

When the sales slips, data from telephone inquiries and information on institutions/groups, etc., in the market area are all logged into the database, integration can then occur.

§ 16-5. Application of the MIS.

Even the smallest of sport organizations, such as a sporting goods retailer, can use a simple manual system quite effectively. Each customer record (an index card) would contain a customer's name and address and the marketer would log the purchase date, item(s) purchased and amount of purchase on the columns beneath. Sophisticated systems would maintain a running total of the amount purchased broken down by product categories. Perhaps a coding system would be used (football = 1, tennis = 2, swimming = 3, etc.). Cards would then be scanned at regular intervals. Prior to the fall football season, any card showing a check in the football column, indicating that the customer made a purchase of football equipment, would then be pulled out and that person's name would be placed on a mailing list to receive a football-equipment catalogue, or a flyer announcing a sale on football equipment. For those customers who spent say, more than fifty dollars in the store over the preceding six months, a personal invitation could be mailed to them for a special pre-sale evening at the store. These "heavy spenders" would have first choice of sale merchandise, would be allowed to invite a friend, and might be treated to a floor show of next-season's merchandise, hot hors d'oeuvres and champagne. Inviting a friend makes the consumer feel like a "bigshot," gives them greater satisfaction and, more importantly, attracts new customers.

A. *The Advantages of Electronic Systems.*

It is self-evident that any MIS is useless unless it is well-maintained, and readily accessible. If the maintenance of the system becomes too costly compared to the return, then marketers will not maintain it. Consequently, computers offer an alternative whose ease of maintenance is comparatively low and whose return is great. Better yet, the price of computers is constantly dropping into a range where no sport organization can afford to be without one. The most significant impact of computerized MIS, however, is their ability to integrate data from a variety of sources to provide the most telling and useful information. For example, a court and health club with a computerized MIS may be able to identify members who are available to play in the low-occupancy hours that the club is open, by analyzing the demographics of these members they can then tailor-make a program which appeals to this specific group. Such data has revealed at several locations tremendous demand in the early morning and at lunchtime for aerobic classes for working married women. The timing of such classes is critical because of the need or desire of the mothers to be home with younger children as soon as possible after the work day.

Although integrating and using the information for marketing purposes is more difficult without a computer, it is not impossible, though it is unlikely that any such integration on a manual system will be relatively simple. Inspecting index cards to select recent purchases and cross-tabulating this list by zip code to determine market penetration in an area not previously advertised to, is a simple but laborious task, yet the value of the effort can be immense. As one sport executive recently said, "Half of our advertising budget is totally wasted! If we ever knew which half, we could save a lot of money." Without an MIS it is almost impossible to identify just which dollars are being wasted. Perhaps the most telling factor is that organizations with a well-kept MIS invariably spend less of their promotional budget in advertising than their non-MIS counterparts.

B. *The Impact of MIS on Promotional Budget.*

The smallest of sport organizations allot four-figure budgets on advertising to attract individuals who are not currently consumers; the larger organizations allot six-figure budgets. A sport industry rule of thumb for the promotional budget is five percent of total annual expenses for an on-going organization and 10% of total annual expenses for a start-up organization, or one needing to increase its market share. While advertising is critical to attracting new consumers, all mature organizations can usually obtain a much better return by giving incentives to existing customers to purchase more of the product or to promote the product more to their friends. This latter strategy has been called "internal marketing" (Ref. 5). Internal marketing strategies can usually be achieved at much lower cost and with greater returns in sales volume than the majority of mass media campaigns designed to reach non-users. Consider the following questions: What do professional sport teams do to reward the loyalty of a season-ticket holder who has held a season ticket for several years? What does a tennis or country club do for the member who has been there ten years? Unfortunately the answer too often is, Very Little! Marketers have known for a long time that satisfied customers generally spread positive word of mouth and attract other customers. One estimate (Ref. 6) projected that 70% of all sales in many segments of the sport industry come from word of mouth from existing customers. For many sport industry segments the figure could be even higher. If we take this relationship to its logical extension, then we can see that the total positive impact of word of mouth from just one satisfied member/customer would be as follows:

Satisfied customer *A* refers .7 additional customers
Those .7 additional customers refer another .7 x .7 = .49 customers and those customers in turn refer .7 x .7 x .7 = .34 customers

The total impact of this relationship can be calculated using a simple geometric progression as .7 + (.7 x .7) + (.7 x .7 x .7) .... + N or more simply using the economic multiplier formula (6), below:

$$\text{total impact} = \frac{1}{1 - (\text{W.O.M.\%})}$$
$$\text{total impact} = 1 \div (1-.7) = 1\ (.3)$$

The *total impact* of 70% W.O.M. = 3.33 total persons referred by one person's positive word of mouth.

If the W.O.M.% is higher, then total impact is much higher. In fact, the relationship is a logarithmic function. For example, at 80% the multiplier is 5.0. The impact of the multiplier can be used as a most powerful tool for motivating personnel, particularly when sales staff realize that if they sell to one person, they will refer five others on average. Similarly, for service personnel they must be made to appreciate that, if they turn off one person at 80% W.O.M., the organization loses five customers.

Despite the power of this relationship, too many organizations ignore the importance of tracking the purchase frequency of existing customers. In this respect, two major relationships need to be tracked: first, the breakdown of low-, medium- and high-frequency users, in order that programs and promotions may be established to increase attendance frequency; and second, the tracking of consumers whose frequency of usage is dropping. This latter group is obviously getting ready to quit. As stated previously, many organizations do not even collect the names and addresses of customers when they have been "handed them on a plate." Such information is available on checks and letters. Valuable information can be easily obtained from credit cards, phone calls, and walk-ins. For example, it would be interesting to know how many collegiate athletic departments maintain files of the names of those purchasing student season tickets for football and basketball games. Of greater interest is how many of these schools stored that information in a retrievable form for later use? There is little doubt that students who bought tickets while in school comprise a high-probability response segment for alumni season ticket mailings, particularly when cross-tabulated by an address inside the critical trading radius. It would also provide a high probability response group for alumni fund-raising for athletics and cut down greatly on wasted mailings and phone calls to low probability individuals. There simply is no way to go back and recreate this information at a later time, you have to collect it right there and then!

In multi-purpose sport clubs for the last four years, the better-managed clubs have been tracking attendance of members on a member-by-member basis using software programs custom-designed for the industry (Ref. 7). The information obtained allows the club manager to develop special programs (tournaments, ladders, aerobics classes) and promotional ideas (free racquet-ball lessons for aerobic class participants, guaranteed game arranging with a compatible partner, etc.) designed to increase usage frequency or deter member attrition in the low-usage member. It also reduces overcrowding at peak-times by limiting the frequency of participation of heavy-users, (members cannot hold more than one court reservation at a time). Such computer-based MIS for clubs have helped reduce attrition rates from an industry average of approximately 35% of membership lost per year down to 20-25% per year. This translates, for an average-sized club, to maintaining $100,000 of revenue per annum which would otherwise be lost (based on an average-sized club having 2,000 members with average revenue per member of $250 per annum. Such a club would normally generate 50% of its revenue from membership dues and court-time fees (approximately $500,000) with anywhere from an additional $250,000 to $500,000 from product extensions such as bar and lounge, pro shop sales, lessons programs, aerobics classes, etc. For a $20,000 investment in a computer system, the club could expect a 400% first-year return on savings from the reduction in membership attrition alone). The benefit does not include the savings on promotion costs (advertising) and selling costs (commission, sales training, etc.) which would have been incurred to replacement membership. To say the least, a $20,000 computerized MIS justifies itself on that statistic alone.

C. *How MIS Fits Into the Marketing Process.*

The MIS provides the link between the market and the marketer, and it is therefore the lifeline of marketing. Perhaps the most critical factor of marketing success is the ability to collect accurate and timely information about the consumers and potential consumers, and to use this data in the formation of marketing plans which are specifically targeted to meet the needs of specific consumer groups (known as target-market segments). Marketing-mix decisions must be based upon accurate and comprehensive data on the market, the competition and how the market views the product, its pricing structure and the promotional messages transmitted about the product. Simply put, anything short of a complete MIS leaves the door open for competition to erode the organizations product position and to eat into its market share.

In reviewing the data generated in the MIS it becomes readily apparent to the marketer that not all consumers have the same wants or needs which they expect to have fulfilled by the sport product. The recognition that consumers have different aspirations, needs or wants, and the grouping together of consumers based upon certain characteristics common to a group is called market segmentation. The process of segmenting consumers into several target-market segments is a necessary pre-condition to any marketing-strategy development. In order to maximize consumer satisfaction and therefore maximize the chance of marketing success, a different marketing strategy (called a marketing mix) requiring a unique blending of product, price, promotion and even place (seat location, access to certain amenities) must be developed for each target segment. Without a doubt, identification of the key target-market segments is the single-most important output of the MIS.

§ 16-6. Market Segmentation — Targeting for the Marketing Mix.

There are four common bases upon which market segmentation (grouping by similar characteristics) are usually performed. They are:

1. *Demographics.* — Such characteristics of the consumer as sex, age, income, geographic location, occupation, etc.
2. *Psychographics.* — Lifestyle characteristics of the consumer such as activities they engage in, interests such as being sport-oriented, outgoing, healthy, etc., or opinions/attitudes they hold.
3. *Benefits.* — The specific benefit(s) the consumer is looking for. For example, weight-loss, relaxation, entertainment.
4. *Usage rate/frequency.* — The purchase frequency or frequency of product usage. This is usually broken down into heavy/medium and light users.

Most segmentation has traditionally employed demographics. There are several reasons for this. On the simplest level, demographics appear to tell us quite a lot about differences in purchase behavior. It is self-evident that men and women generally have different needs that they wish to have satisfied from a sport product. Also, the needs of young and old are invariably far apart. Demographics are generally readily accessible from government or other publications and most consumers do not mind giving out their demographic information (age and income are sometimes sensitive). However, demographics have their limits. Two individuals having identical demographics yet who have different lifestyles may differ widely in their purchase behavior.

As a result of the limitation of demographics, marketers became interested in psychographics which measure activities, interests and opinions, which would go beyond where demographics leave off. The reason psychographics are not used more extensively for segmentation is that they are not as readily available, and are therefore expensive to generate on an individual basis.

Benefit segmentation has increased in its usage in recent years because of its simple effectiveness. In fact, many sport marketers have practiced benefit segmentation for many years without recognizing the term. Examples of benefit-segmented sport products are corporate boxes, padded seats with backs and arms, stadium club membership, and court and health club membership plans such as the Gold Plan (total club usage), Silver Plan (Nautilus only) and Bronze Plan (wet-area amenities only).

The final basis for segmentation is product-purchase frequency or product-usage frequency. This method is widely used throughout almost every industry and has been used most effectively in sport. Examples are season ticket plans, mini-season plans, contract-time rates in court clubs, family season passes to ski resorts, etc.

In reading down the list of methods for performing segmentation, it no doubt became apparent to many readers that these bases were not mutually exclusive. In fact, combinations of demographics and benefits abound, along with the combination of usage frequency and benefits. The critical questions for the marketer in deciding whether or not to choose the market segment, whether employing single or multiple-segmentation bases are as follows:

1. Can the segment be identified? It is all well and good to say that the consumer of a product is "sport-oriented" but is it possible to identify sport-oriented people? For example, can you purchase a mailing list of *Sports Illustrated* readers? Is the *S.I.* reader likely to be a soccer fan anyway?
2. Can the segment be accessed by a particular media which the majority of the segment views, listens to or reads? If there is no way to reach the segment, then there is little point developing marketing messages targeted toward this group.
3. Is the market segment big enough in size and potential response (sales) to warrant spending time and money developing a targeted product and promotional strategy just for this group?

If the answer to each of the above questions is "Yes," then the marketer needs to identify significant clusters or groups among consumers and potential consumers for the product or service being marketed. This is done by reviewing the demographic, psychographic, benefit and usage-rate data available on consumers. Much of this data is already available in published form from secondary data sources such as government population data, industry publications and several excellent studies on sport consumers exist, namely the Perrier Study, the 1983 Miller Lite Study on American Attitudes Toward Sports, the A.C. Nielson data on viewership and the Simmons Market Research Bureau's statistics on demographics of sport participation, spectatorship and viewership, along with invaluable data on the media which each market segment views, reads or listens to.

Once the clusters/segments have been identified they should then be placed in priority order based upon size of potential response. Shrewd marketers identify just the top two or three untapped segments to be targeted at any one time. In mature sport-marketing departments, where there exists a strong existing base of consumers, it may well be possible to run marketing and promotional plans targeted at more than three distinct segments, but this is rare.

The days when consumer needs were satisfied by a single product are long gone. Henry Ford's insistence that the consumer could have a Model-T Ford in any color that he liked as long as it was black, simply would not hit the mark in today's marketplace. At the same time you cannot be all things to all people.

Not all of the segments identified in a market need to be targeted. Dependent upon the product concept as outlined in Chapter 9, it is perfectly possible to specialize in a single segment, at least in the initial introduction of a product. In the long term, more than one segment invariably must be targeted. For new products and mature products the early target segments are likely to be the opinion leaders among the larger, target segment groups. These opinion leaders would then spread word of mouth to other members of the group, thereby reducing the sales response time to the advertisements considerably. The marketing-mix for opinion leaders is likely to be a direct approach rather than a mass-appeal approach. An illustration of this technique would be a marketer of a new Major Indoor Soccer League (MISL) franchise who might first target opinion leaders in each of the ethnic groups traditionally playing soccer in the market area, along with targeting the coaches and officials of local soccer leagues at all levels. At the same time owners and managers of retail sporting-goods stores, radio stations and other media having influence on the target populations would be contacted with specialized appeals designed to raise the level of consciousness about the sport and the franchise. This strategy is particularly effective in sports where marketing staffs are small. Often these opinion leaders can be harnessed to help sell the sport product. In this way each opinion leader is given incentives to sell to their groups. The author has called this technique "positive pyramid selling" (Ref. 8).

§ 16-7. Summary/Conclusion.

The return on investment on the sport promotional dollar is directly proportional to the marketer's ability to accurately segment the market and target the appeal to that particular group. The ability to segment is directly related to the sophistication of the MIS. A distant second is the creativity of the message. Remember that Clara Peller's "Where's the Beef?" commercial for the Wendy's hamburger chains may have received lots of attention and creativity awards but the research showed that too few people remembered that it was a Wendy's commercial, and even fewer increased their consumption of Wendy's products.

Without an information-based approach to sport marketing, at least half of the promotional budget is likely to be wasted. The only problem is that without an MIS the sport marketer will never know which half is being wasted. With an MIS the marketer knows who the consumer is, what he or she needs, and if he or she has slowed down in consumption frequency. Promotional efforts can then be specifically targeted toward an "internal marketing" approach to selling sport which is the topic of Chapter 13. Internal marketing is a method of using existing consumers to sell on behalf of the organization and includes marketing strategies designed to increase consumption frequency and to reduce the attrition rate among existing consumers. This latter strategy is only possible with a sophisticated and up-to-date information system, with data collected now for immediate and long-term use. As the Fram Oil Filter television commercial says, "You can pay a little now (to build an MIS) or you can pay a lot more later (for expensive mass media advertising)."

REFERENCES

1. B.J. Mullin, "Sport Marketing, Promotion and Public Relations," unpublished manuscript (Amherst, Mass.: Department of Sport Studies, University of Massachusetts 1983).

2. M. Levine, "Increasing Attendance By Knowing Your Market Better," *Auditorium News* 8-10 (October 1977).

3. H.H. Kassarjian & T.S. Robertson, *Perspectives in Consumer Behavior* (Glenview, Ill.: Scott Foresman & Co. 1983).

4. M. Levine, *supra* Ref. 2.

5. B.J. Mullin, *supra* Ref. 1, at 180.

6. Pance, Kerr & Foster, "The Court and Health Club Industry: A Nationwide Assessment" (Boston, Mass.: International Racquet Sports Association 1983).

7. *Court-Spin-The Court Sport Information System* (Amherst, Mass.: National Sport Management, Inc. 1981).

8. B.J. Mullin, *supra* Ref. 1, at 198-201.

Chapter 17

COMPUTER APPLICATIONS IN SPORT

By

George Danziger

§ 17-1. Introduction.

Managers these days are being barraged with advertising and other literature aimed at convincing them that they are virtually criminals if they try to operate any sort of enterprise without the aid of a computer. A calm, rational assessment of the potential value and utility of a computer to a particular organization is most difficult when so much energy is going into creating an atmosphere of panic. Viewed historically, against the background of the slow and steady growth of scientific management, and in terms of the development of mechanized and then automated data-handling equipment over the last century, this sudden rush to computerize everything from phone lists to care of the family dog is nothing short of funny.

Any office today can, in fact, fruitfully employ a computer to perform many routine, and some nonroutine tasks. Given that wages, benefits, office space, and other considerations combined put a price tag of nearly $20,000 on the annual employment of even the most menial file clerk, any device or methodology which promises an increase in the productivity of expensive labor deserves a closer look. Costs and benefits remain the guidelines. If a $3,000 computer can increase the productivity of a $20,000 per annum employee by 20%, the machine apparently will pay for itself in less than a year. Considering training time, space and maintenance for the machine, cost of the software, insurance and other items, estimate of the useful life of the machine, the hypothetical example remains a solid investment. Since computers can be cost-effective, why is adoption by business less than complete?

§ 17-2. Computerization Is Avoided.

The most likely reason computerization is avoided is that the range of choices is overwhelming, and integrating the computer into the ongoing life of the office seems such a difficult task that it is hard to know where to begin. There are over 300 different computers on the market. They range in price from $100 to over $1,000,000, and the choices between minicomputers, mainframe computers, single-user, multi-user, floppys, hard disk, dot matrix, letter quality and on and on which makes it difficult to proceed with confidence. Then there are questions of the choice of tasks for the computer; who in the organization will actually use the machine; and how all of this will tie together.

While it may be obvious that an under-$600-complete system with a letter-quality printer is not really equivalent to an over $100,000 16-station multi-user mini-mainframe with laser jet and multiple-impact printers, the advertising, and the salespeople who handle the low end aren't likely to point out (or even know) when their alleged "full-featured" system is going to leave you back in manual mode doing by hand what you hoped to do on the computer. The vendors of systems at the upper end are also not likely to reveal that a system being considered will not only do everything required by one business, it also could handle 100 operations of similar size at the same time, and still have left-over capacity to handle the motor vehicle bureau for the State of Illinois.

Beyond the problem of vested interests, unreliable vendors, opportunists and the like, there are very concrete problems and explanations for the chaos in the marketplace. The first is that despite the nice, compact, smooth plastic housings for the computer, and not withstanding the utterly trivial applications to which most computer hardware is put, computers are among the most technically advanced and complex devices our civilization has yet produced. It takes many levels of engineers and programmers to make the power of the computer accessible to users. The system designers depend upon the chip designers; the systems programmers depend upon the people who write the interpreters and compilers; and all of these people are supporting the applications programmers who presumably are generating the kinds of programs that fill real needs. This is a long chain. It takes time for word about the users needing a particular kind of application to filter down to those who can put it together, and the translation between programmer and user lingo might not be perfect.

Learning to recognize that "a relational database with programming language interface and file compatibility (DIF) with DIF formats operating on control program/micro (CP/M) machines" is a must in order to set-up a job-bank matching system, for example, seems to be the only way to identify appropriate hardware and software. While some salespeople are willing and able to help the buyer distinguish between a job such as the one above and another in which a far less-expensive and less-complex list-manager will suffice, like a phone list, skilled assistance usually carries a high price tag. Decisions with regard to the best course to follow are difficult, in that choices today are numerous.

§ 17-3. Fundamental Understanding — Computer Is Only a Tool.

A computer is a tool, as pencil and paper are tools, to be applied by management to the solution of real-world problems. Furthermore, a computer once set up to perform a particular task will most likely go on performing that task economically for years and years. Regardless of newer, faster, shinier, better models, a running machine doing a useful job is still worth two on the shelf in the computer store. Finally, computers do not think; that remains a job for people, and the idea that a computer can accomplish a task which the users do not understand is an expectancy held only by the uninformed. Adding a computer will not correct or even improve a situation created by confused management.

§ 17-4. Five Rules of Computer Sanity.

What follows was called "horse sense" back in the days when horses were considered useful tools. Later, it became known as "common sense." Nowadays, it is so rare, that these following old adages can be passed off as brand-new ideas.

Rule 1. *If you don't know what you are doing, you can't do it.*

This rule seems trivial, but it is a corollary of the idea that there is nothing new under the sun. There is the widespread belief that people who cannot keep a set of books straight by hand, will be able to do so if the accounting is set up on a computer. Similarly, people imagine that they will know the meaning of the graphs and charts produced by an elaborate computer analysis of their operation, even if they haven't the foggiest notion of what it is they are looking for. There are some "expert systems," computer programs that are half instructional material and half operational procedure. Using such programs is the same thing as taking the time to understand a process before attempting to implement it. It is the person and the person's understanding which then makes it possible to implement the application, not the "smart" computer.

A more subtle interpretation of this rule lies in the application of the sociology of knowledge to mundane office situations. It is usually the boss, or the top management people purchasing a computer. What these people usually are not aware of is that their concept of the work of the office is generally quite distorted. They are not the front line workers, they are not in the trenches; they are actually the least likely people in any organization to know about the work-flow details that are required to intelligently buy a computer.

Management, in fact, survives because of the "biological" computers, the office staff, that are already up and running. Like all good computers, these workers know their programs, get their input and generate their output, all the while appearing to management like some "black box." That is manage- ment knows, hopefully knows anyway, what is going into the system, and what is coming out, but virtually never knows about the details of what goes on inside the box: filing systems, volume of paper, or the calculations and cross-filing of information that is part of the day-to-day work flow in any office. Management may lay out the big picture, even put in the numbers where the "colors" of the "paint by the numbers" big picture are supposed to go. But only rarely is it management that mixes the colors and fills in the details. Before specifying what a computer is to accomplish in any office, a thorough review of every file cabinet and its contents and every pile of paper on every worker's desk is required. Only then can management even begin to claim to understand what really keeps the enterprise on an even keel.

Rule 2. *Don't buy an unemployed computer.*

Management rarely hits upon the notion that simply hiring more employees will cause growth of an enterprise. For some reason, however, the idea that once a computer is in place, a use will be found for it does not seem to bother people very much. Without yielding to this backwards logic, it must be admitted that the cost of a rather powerful microcomputer is so low, less really than the first year's depreciation on a new car, that to simply buy one, bring it into the office and then find out what it can do, does make some kind of sense. In some ways this can be the cheapest and most efficient way to get a concrete sense of what computing is all about. Within that context, the manager who sets out on a fishing expedition into computing with nothing more than an open mind and an open checkbook just might come up a big winner.

The problem is that the ultimate use for such a machine must still await the hard work of detail analysis of *needs, requirements* and *applications.* What generally happens with fishing-expedition computers is that they get stuffed and mounted or, in a sense, set to work on the corner of some executive's desk where the machine has all the utility of a Rolodex but looks far more impressive. The executive, imagining that this computer "stuff" is all taken care of, never discovers what a powerhouse is lying right there at hand, and an opportunity to really move the enterprise ahead is lost. Ultimately, this kind of purchase is counterproductive to the genuine change computers can bring to an organization. The situation can become almost hilarious when other managers from the organization go fishing with the admonition to be sure that whatever they catch has to be compatible with the boss's system. The implication of course, is that they had better not be any more successful than the boss at coming to grips with the reality of computers.

Rule 3. *If it ain't broke, don't fix it.*

This old adage applies to computers in that after a review of potential applications for computerization, and bearing in mind that the applications selected should constitute real, concrete tasks that are well understood by management, the choice is often made to computerize the one or two things in the office that are already well under control on a manual system. Much more common is the decision to bring back a job that is running perfectly well at an outside service, payroll for example, and set it up as the first application for a new in-house computer.

Picking the first application in a new installation is a subtle and demanding job. True, it is better if the application is one that is well-understood, and true, it must be a useful task, one in which there are measurable gains to be anticipated. There are, however, one or two other guidelines to keep in mind. The first application should be a job that is not running well, or at all, in the current environment. For example, a mailing list application in which a combination of xeroxed labels, an old Addressograph machine, and long sessions at the typewriter are getting the job done, but there are measurable inefficiencies in the system.

Addressograph plates are not cheap, and alterations to the list are slow and noisy. Sorting of lists to take advantage of reduced bulk rate mailing regulations might not be possible. It is difficult to target a mailing to selected portions of a list using the older methods. Not only are extra pieces then sent out, but the impact of receiving mailings is diluted when not every piece received by parties on the list is directly relevant to them. They are more likely to drop the next mailing unopened into the "round file" if the last one received was about a part of the operation that is of no interest to them. Finally, a good computerized mailing list is a hot commodity. There is a lively trade in lists that are in machine readable (floppy disk) format, and additional leads can be purchased from a list broker on a part-exchange arrangement. Commercial services to handle bulk mailings are available, and the difference between their rates when names and addresses are supplied on disk versus typewritten on paper should be enough to convince the most hardheaded manager of the virtue of computerized mailing lists.

The ultimate reason to pick such an application as the first for a new computer lies in the office politics. Taking on a job that is not running well (or at all) is less threatening to the employees. Instead of resistance, open support will be met when the staff perceives that a "dog job" is being pulled off their backs. Employees are then excited about getting to try out the computer as it is not going to be used to set a benchmark for their own performance. Rather the arrival of the computer serves to confirm what they knew already: the mailing list job just could not be done right with the old equipment, so it was not their fault when problems were encountered. People can then get used to the machine in an environment that is nonthreatening (to jobs), nondisruptive (of running systems), and noncritical (to the overall operation). Another reason to choose an "out of the way" task is that if the computer does not work, at least it will not be involved in a critical function.

Rule 4. *The competition for a computer is a pencil.*

Walking into a computer store these days, one is confronted by rows of new machines, their screens showing smoothly running demonstrations of accounting, word processing, spreadsheet and financial-analysis packages. The salespeople will guide the buyer through comparisons of the features and capacities of each of the machines. The virtues of each type of hardware and software will be explained. Just a few details will be missing. *It takes no less than 40 hours for anyone, including experienced computerists, to become comfortable working at the keyboard of a new computer. Then it takes no less than 20 hours to become comfortable with the details of a particular program.*

What this means is that these time investments must be made, and then amortized over the life of the machine before it can be said that the machine is "saving time." Consider implementing a computer application that is well-understood within a small organization, for example, a general ledger and accounts receivable and payable. Now let us imagine that the bookkeeper of 30 years experience is retiring, and the decision has been made to buy a microcomputer to handle the job rather than to take the time to train a clerk to take over these vital tasks. The scenario appears to make sense, but consider: Is it possible that a clerk who doesn't understand bookkeeping will be able to keep books on the computer? Is time going to be saved in the training cycle? Is it even possible that management will be able to set up the chart of accounts, and get the program running without the aid of the soon-to-be-retired expert?

The first three rules of computer sanity illuminate the fourth. The rows upon rows of new computers lined up in the store are not competing among themselves for a slot in your office. The whole class of computers is competing with the manual methods embodied in the pencil. It takes longer to be trained to run a computer than to do the same job by hand, and just as much understanding of the task is required. Furthermore, these relationships hold true regardless of what type of computer is being considered. Ultimately, a job must be done by hand, or at least laid out and walked through using manual methods before it can be even considered for computerization. Then, only if long-term advantages in handling the complexity or the repetitive nature of a task are possible does it makes sense to move a job to the computer. Sometimes it turns out that having set a job up for a manual operation, the job turns out to be not bad at all, and certainly not something that requires a computer to be performed.

Rule 5. *The law of diminishing returns applies to computers.*

Review again the first four rules for computer sanity, and a pattern should begin to emerge. Each potential application must be reviewed and justified as an independent unit. Picking the first application for a new computer in an organization is not easy, and it is suggested that the application selected not be a central function to the operation of the office. It is better to start with a problem area, an important ancillary-support function. Success in handling that function can then be a springboard to further applications. These will of course be chosen from the more central and vital areas within the enterprise.

Most managers set out to install a computer with a wish list of applications in mind. Mulling over the software in the computer store, they see programs to handle not only accounting, but also word processing, electronic correspondence (EMAIL), office scheduling, mailing lists, and on and on. It is easy to imagine that once the system gets rolling, additional functions will just pour out as from a faucet. They assume that the staff using the computer will experience a rising training curve and become more facile and comfortable with the machine, making it easier to implement each additional program. Generally, this will prove to be the case.

Unanticipated problems start to pop up, however. Programs are not consistent as to their use of control keys, and operators switching from one application to another can become confused. Some computers run a mix of programs based on several different operating systems, and time for learning the personality of the different operating systems must be set aside. There will be disk format incompatibilities between these systems, and materials, programs, and operating times will have to be segregated. Scheduling time on the machine itself will start to be a problem. A moment will arise when it will be clear that the office can no longer function, for better or for worse without the computer, but not everything can get done at once. The computer itself has become part of the problem.

To illustrate this, consider this typical sequence. Imagine that 70% of the labor in a particular office is devoted to building and its attendant accounting and bookkeeping functions. A computer with software to handle order entry through accounts receivable is installed which also generates shipping labels and a mailing list. Prior to this installation, 15% of office labor was expended on maintenance of the mailing list, and sending out catalogs. Once these two jobs are absorbed, which formerly required 85% of the total labor for the whole office, the labor for the two areas is reduced to the same number of hours that billing and accounting alone previously required. Success is gathering momentum. It is decided to extend the use of the computer to handle purchasing and accounts payable, and this is implemented *despite the fact that our imaginary firm deals with very few vendors.* It appears that so little is now required to complete the general ledger function on the computer that these steps are added also.

Payroll seems a natural add-on for example, so another employee, who previously spent one day a week collecting and cross-checking payroll information and then a few hours doing the requisite calculations, and filling out of checks and stubs, is put through a training course. Now, instead of taking several hours to do the calculations, it takes only a few minutes. Right after the first stage of automation, the computer could be left running virtually all day with the order-entry program. Now there are several different operators standing in line to get their work done on the machine. It takes six trips from one part of the office to another to fit the payroll job into the flow of work on the computer, and time savings are being "dripped away." Rush orders have to wait for open computer time to be processed. Then, the computer breaks down, and everything grinds to a halt. Management decides the system is too crowded and fragile with only one machine, so a second computer is purchased and installed.

It is at this point that the cost/benefit analysis should be recalculated. Two machines, a lot of training, software, systems support have gone into the installation. In refiguring the numbers, it will become clear that each and every function that was added to the system, rather than helping to build a larger base for amortizing the investment, served only to decrease the overall system productivity, and to dilute the value of the investment. A deeper analysis of the situation will reveal that what is happening here is a form of having hardware-chasing users, the cart before the horse syndrome that follows hiring an unemployed computer.

In this case, the order entry and mailing label job was probably the right place to start despite its centrality to the whole operation. A list of priorities constructed before the machine was ever brought into the office should have had at its top: *Nothing is to get in the way of goods going out the door.* Based on that dictum, a second set of functions, in effect every other operation in the office, might have been grouped together and seen as justifying a second computer. A review of the potential applications might have led to selection of different hardware for the second computer. With these factors in mind, a machine could have been purchased for the order entry and mailing label function of a size and capacity for which it is economically justifiable to dedicate the computer to that single function. The same end result, two machines, with an ability to serve as mutual back-up in case of mechanical difficulty would have been reached anyway. The difference is a lower net cost in cash, confusion and intraoffice strife.

§ 17-5. How Computers and Computing Are Sold.

What one finds in the computer marketplace depends on where one looks. The market is highly fragmented, and there is simply no one source to which one can turn. A local computer store is not the place to look for a completely integrated package to meet the needs of a particular industry. Similarly, very few computer consultants are willing to train users to develop applications for themselves from off-the-shelf software. Vendors are quite naturally more concerned about selling what they have than in finding the very best solution to a particular cost/performance set of requirements and constraints. The internal networks among various sources for computers and computing are still poorly developed at this time. Even if a vendor of low-end small-business systems recognized that requirements for a particular business call for a larger multi-user minicomputer, for example, it is unlikely that the vendor would know where the appropriate equipment could be secured.

There are three distinct ways in which computers and computing can be acquired:

1. packaged systems for which a vendor guarantees the final product, *the usable output;*
2. hardware and application program packages for which the user has only to handle the initial system configuration by following the cookbook directions provided, and/or using advanced productivity tools such as VisiCalc, dBase, etc.; and
3. hardware and user written programs.

Beyond the lease, rent or purchase question (which is really a matter of financing), and cash flow, there are further options more relevant to the gist of this chapter. The questions that need to be considered are: In-house versus outside consultants for expertise; how much future growth to buy for now; and the role of the computer in the enterprise in general. Some organizations start up computer operations at the novice level, and after investing much time and expense, discover that it is possible to recoup the investment by selling to other firms the programs and expertise they have developed. As always, it is important to clearly state and understand your own goals before any project is undertaken.

There are three distinct levels of computers on the market. There are the personal computers (desktop and portable microcomputers), which operate as stand-alone machines on the principle of one user, one computer. At the extreme other end of the scale are mainframe and mini-mainframe computers which serve anywhere from 32 to hundreds of users at the same time, each of whom might either be working on some small part of the same application, as in a ticket-reservation system, or on wholly unrelated tasks as is the case with time-shared networks like Compuserve, the Source, and most university computer centers. In between are the larger micros, super-microcomputers, and minicomputers which handle from 3 to 16 users and have the ability to handle more than one application at the same time, but are more generally used to handle a set of closely related functions within a single organization which require multiple keyboards and printers in order to accommodate the volume of data.

There are three different ways to acquire software. There are vertically integrated packages of programs which have been customized to meet the needs of particular industry or type of enterprise. These packages sacrifice range of application for specificity so that a dental office package includes dental charts, and a health club package includes attendance recording. At the other extreme are the operating systems and programming languages, C-Basic, M-Basic, Cobol, running in MS-DOS, CP/M, USCD Pascal and on and on. Every computer has to have an operating system to operate, but it is possible to purchase a vertically integrated package, as described above, and never even know what the operating system of your computer is. Curiously enough, most first-time computer users imagine that they can buy a computer, sit down and write some BASIC programs and get running with whatever they need after only a few weeks work. Suffice it to say, there are no second-time users who suffer from this illusion. Occupying the middle ground between these extremes are two related, yet distinct classes of software products: generic application programs, and productivity tools.

Along the shelves in the computer store will be found a wide range of accounting, telecommunications, financial analysis, graphics and other programs which enable the user to open the box, insert the disk and get started on a particular application. Complete accounting systems, including payroll and tax packages are available to handle the needs of surprisingly large organizations on personal computers. The telecommunications programs convert personal computers into terminals which then can be connected via the phone lines to other, much larger computers. There are programs that enable the user to develop graphic presentations, perform statistical analysis, compose music, complete production tasks. The list seems endless.

Generic application programs have two characteristics which make them extremely useful and valuable. They attempt to provide in the package all the knowledge the user needs to make the computer perform the task selected, and by following the enclosed directions, they can be adapted to the exact manner in which the user wants to run the job. Accounting programs, for example, permit the user to enter a firm's chart of accounts, checkbook numbers, and other details so that the finished reports should be indistinguishable from those produced by a custom program written for that firm and that firm alone. These programs represent the fruits of hundreds upon hundreds of hours of development time, and given the effort that has gone into them, the prices are more than reasonable. A review of ready-to-run software should always precede any decision to write one's own programs; reinventing the wheel is never good business. These programs do, however, differ widely in their capacities and flexibility, and it is important before making any purchase to try out a program at the computer store to determine whether it will indeed be adaptable to your requirements.

Productivity tools differ from application programs in that each can be used to accomplish a wide range of tasks, a range that in some cases approaches that of programming languages like BASIC. At the same time, they provide the user with a format and set of commands and controls over the operation of the computer which are far more powerful than are available in programming languages. The concept of power as used in reference to computers is perhaps a bit odd. For example, in BASIC, it is possible to write a program to display a word on the screen vertically, horizontally, in highlighted (color-reversed) letters, and even to print it in reversed order. Recourse to assembly language routines is required, however, to print upside down or to actually turn the individual letters backwards. Using a productivity tool, it is not possible to do much but print the word on the screen, although some of the language-like productivity tools will handle highlighting.

In common parlance, the usage of the word "power" would rank the "power" of these different terms as follows: Assembly language, BASIC and productivity tools, which are exactly the opposite of what "power" means to a computerist. The number of different things that can be done with a system are defined as its "range." The ease, simplicity, and directness with which different operations are accomplished is defined as the "power of the system." Thus, when moving from assembler language through BASIC to a productivity tool like VisiCalc, the trade-off is between decreasing range in favor of increased power.

A typical productivity tool, like VisiCalc, requires only a single keystroke to tell the computer to accept some word from the keyboard, print it on the screen, and store it for later reference. In BASIC, the same steps could be accomplished with perhaps one line of a program, but most likely several would be required to get the details right. Assembly language routines for these same steps might run to 20 lines. VisiCalc is rigid, slow, and limited in range compared to assembler, but it is more powerful. Assembler can be used to wring the last little trick out of the computer, but programming in assembler is awkward, slow, painstaking and error-prone. VisiCalc is rigid, yes, but only if one wants to program a game. Assembler language programs run very fast, but assembler is fast only if one ignores the time it takes to write the program. If one wishes to generate a cash-flow analysis for example, VisiCalc can put the results in your hands in a matter of minutes, BASIC in days, and with assembler, well, the best bet is to use the assembler to write a program called VisiCalc, and then do the cash-flow analysis. That's what they did at VisiCorp, the publisher of VisiCalc.

Management must resolve the questions of the different classes of hardware, and the different methods by which software is developed and sold into a plan for acquiring and installing a computer system. The choices management faces are best viewed as lying along four independent dimensions: operating speed; system capacity; system flexibility; and development time. Each choice, as outlined above, offers a particular combination of these factors, and results in a particular set of hardware, software, and labor costs. These costs then can be further resolved into first costs and life costs. Buying a vertical package, if a suitable product can be found to meet your needs, will incur considerably higher first cost than would buying a computer and using the operating system and language that come with it to write your own applications programs. There is no doubt, however, that the time invested and programming labor, amortized over a single installation, would far exceed the purchase price of the vertical package.

Much harder to project is the overall cost involved in choosing a vertical package over generic-application software and productivity tools. In this case, the cost of labor to master the separate programs is hardly greater than the time it takes to learn to use the vertical package. Implementing each function stepwise, as it is developed using the productivity tools, gives an organization time to adapt to the computer. Conversely, there is no assurance that the system that evolves will work as intended, as is guaranteed with the big price tag for vertical packages. Turnkey systems, vertical packages, and service bureau-type operations come closest to mimicking the kind of deals that IBM used to make. Delivery of a complete running package, training, manuals, and machine all ready-to-go cuts development time to nearly zero. Service bureaus, which have gone out of favor over the last few years, offer a user the opportunity to have the benefits of a computer without the computer. Arrangements are made to transport raw data to a computer which is owned and operated by the service bureau. The printed reports come back to the user.

As with other parts of the market, a mixed environment is evolving in the turnkey area. Some vendors offer systems in which the bulk of routine processing is done on the user's computer which is supplied as part of a package by the turnkey vendor. More complex routines and analyses are handled by the vendor's computer which queries the user's computer, processes the data it finds, and transmits the requisite reports back to the user's computer which then prints out the results. Such arrangements are found in restaurant management packages, for example, where the day-to-day operations can be handled on a far smaller and cheaper computer than is required to handle menu analysis and inventory exception reports.

Regardless of how a computer may be acquired, there is a core set of functions for which business computers are used. Generally all of these functions are implemented at some point in one form or another as an installation matures and develops. Vertical packages usually include modules to perform each of these functions although the individual elements might be hard to isolate and identify. Users who assemble their own systems over time eventually acquire software for each of these functions, although they might find it hard to integrate the functions into a smoothly operating whole. A fair percentage of user-written software consists of small programs, called patches, which facilitate transfer of data between functions performed by commercially acquired applications programs.

To facilitate functional integration, especially for users of productivity tools, authors of these programs select data-storage methods, or file formats which permit the results of one program to be fed into another program more or less automatically. Thus, a publisher will offer a series of programs which accomplish a range of functions: filing, mathematical analysis, report generation, and graphing, for example, which can be performed on a single set of data, or body of information, in a stepwise fashion. Some publishers provide the ability within their products to read data files generated by other publishers' programs in addition to having full facilities with their own proprietary data format.

The latest trend in software is complete functional integration within a single program. Programs like Lotus 1,2,3, Windows, and operating systems such as Visi-ON, DES-Q, and the system in Apple's Lisa and MacIntosh computers offer what is in effect a whole new way of relating to the computer.

The user simply chooses the function which is to be performed next, and the computer then sets itself up to perform the requested function. Questions of file and data formats all are part of what the computer handles automatically. Much of the demand for accessibility and data interchangeability developed first among users of personal microcomputers, and at present writing this type of software is available only for these machines. This kind of integration is so useful and powerful, however, that there is a rush on among the manufacturers and publishers who serve the upscale minicomputer and mainframe markets to provide the same kind of facilities for their customers.

§ 17-6. Classes of Productivity Tools.

A. *Word Processing.*

The central function in any system is word processing. Most novice users imagine that the word-processing function is limited to correspondence. Indeed, the ability to type in text, review and correct it on screen, and have the final "letter perfect" copy come spitting out of a printer, has sold more personal computers than any other application. There is more to word processing than correspondence, however. Combined with a modest file-manager program, which is really no more than an electronic 3 x 5 card file, word processing becomes mailing-list processing. There are yet other word processing programs which have facilities to manipulate information as it is stored by the file manager program to produce tabulation-type summary reports, and virtually all word processing programs can be fed tables of information from productivity tools like VisiCalc which can then be included in the body of a report. Some operating systems and programming languages depend on a word processing program to enter and edit other programs.

Every computer system inevitably is equipped with word processing facilities. Although some initial resistance might be encountered among the office staff, a 30 to 50% increase in productivity can be expected with word processing over the use of typewriters by the same operators. Experience has shown that if the operators are encouraged and permitted to use the time liberated by word processing to work on other jobs instead of simply doing more pages of text per day, then the reception that word processing will receive will be positive. Experienced typists appreciate that the computer can accept text faster than the best typewriter, and that revisions, particularly rearrangements of text, can be accomplished in moments instead of requiring retyping. Spelling-checker programs, automatic centering, footers, headers, pagination, among other features, and one-key, user-defined glossaries further speed production of text. About the only thing the typewriter is used for in offices that employ word processing is to fill-in pre-printed forms, and even that can be done by word processing if there are enough repetitions of a particular form to justify the set-up time.

B. *File Management.*

Another function implemented in virtually every installation is list or file management. These terms cover a wide range of complexity and power. There are programs which can handle a list of phone numbers, and little else, and which offer the advantages over the same function implemented with pencil and paper of being able to sort alphabetically, to add, delete, and alter entries, and print out a fresh clean list after the alterations have been made. File managers differ from database managers (see below), and range upward in power to systems which can be used to create rather sophisticated accounting and record-keeping systems. A file-manager program can be used to enter, store and select information to be included in a statistical analysis, or to generate a list of data categories from a file of information which can then be fed into a word-processing program to generate form letters of the type that address the recipient by first name, and inquire by name and breed in the body of the letter about the health of the family dog.

C. *Database Management.*

True database management programs are virtually special purpose languages. Entire application systems can be developed using these "languages" and, in fact, the bulk of the vertically integrated packages on the market were written that way. Database management programs go beyond file managers by allowing classes of information from different files, i.e., employees in one file and job skill requirements in another, to be brought together into new relationships or files which themselves can then be reviewed and selected from. For example, finding all the people in a file who match a set of search criteria (two left feet, all-thumbs) is a file management job. Producing a listing of all the members of the "people" file matched with all the job opportunities in the "jobs" file for each type of person (jobs requiring one through two thumbs; three to five; five and over, etc.) is a task for a database management program. Because these programs are virtual languages, applications will generally have to be developed by experienced programmer/consultants. Conversely, file managers are intended to operate as user-defined systems and are much easier to work with to produce the desired result.

D. *Spreadsheets.*

The third class of productivity tool which turns up in virtually every installation is the spreadsheet program like VisiCalc. Even without the ability to both send and receive information from/to other programs, spreadsheet software runs a close second to word processing as a selling point for personal computers. These programs provide the user with a very large, if only imaginary, piece of paper which has been divided by rows and columns into individual cells. Into each cell, the user may enter text, numbers, or formulas. The formulas can refer to the numbers which have been entered into other cells. Any kind of numerical analysis which can be performed with pencil, paper and calculator can be done much faster with a spreadsheet program. Given the computer's ability to erase and reuse a cell allowing for corrections and/or revisions, the spreadsheet programs can be used to produce results not only more quickly, but more neatly than by manual means.

If some of the numbers on the input side of the formulas in the spreadsheet are changed, then at a touch of one key the values on the output side of the formulas will be recalculated and displayed in an instant. This kind of analysis is referred to as "what if" modeling, and testing. Preparation of a cash-flow analysis with the use of a spreadsheet program as a mental exercise will make apparent the utility of these programs. Changing the rental paid for office space, for example, alters the whole cash-flow projection. As a manual task, the results are a mess, or the job starts all over again. Using a spreadsheet means that the result of the change is viewed instantly. As the object of this sort of analysis is to explore the impact of various altered inputs on the output of the system, not only are spreadsheet programs ideal for the task, but it is difficult to imagine that anyone would persevere to perform a thorough job of such an analysis without the aid of a spreadsheet program.

The newest of the spreadsheet programs are edging toward full language status. The user can construct a model, fill it in, run it through various test situations, save the model, with or without the specific numbers used, for reuse at some other time, and print out on paper all or selected parts of the spreadsheet. The spreadsheet can be "programmed" to execute one function, i.e., add two numbers from the sheet, or use the value of $1.00 instead of the sum of the two numbers just mentioned, depending on the status of yet a third item of information. Additional functions are available to set a target value, and the computer will repeat a set of calculations until the target value is reached. It is also possible to give a name to part of the spreadsheet, naming the bottom line of a financial analysis "bottom line," and then the numbers found at "bottom line" can be reused elsewhere in a different context. Equipped as these programs are with loops, branch on condition, and assign functions, they are in effect very powerful, but limited-range languages. It is possible, using the latest of the spreadsheet programs, to develop functioning relational database and accounting applications in addition to "what if" models.

E. *Accounting Packages.*

Most organizations find it to be cost-effective to purchase a program or generic software package to handle their complete accounting system. As described above, these packages are designed to be adapted with a minimum of difficulty to the particulars of each enterprise. In operation, little more than ordinary care and diligence in data entry is required. Compared with the effort of keeping a set of books by hand, or of recording and transmitting the transactions to an outside accountant, these programs practically give back the ledgers, journals, balance sheets and statements for free. Except for the very cheapest and simplest of this class of software, budgeting, forecasting and charts of comparisons between budget and actual performance are included as standard features, along with the more usual year and quarter-to-date summations, and prior year comparisons.

One precaution that can not be overemphasized is the need to provide back-up disks for your records. The manual that comes with the package will inevitably include rather tiresome directions as to how to make back-up or spare copies of the disks on which to store the transaction information. For some reason, users refuse to believe that these precautions are worth the effort until they have been "burned" at least once. Disk drives are phenomenally reliable, and disk-based data storage is very efficient. But, faulty handling, stray static, electrical storms, and Murphy's Law all dictate that the little extra effort required to provide back-up is worth it, even if you actually use the back-up only once in a very long while. Failure to back-up data disks can lead to being forced to reenter as much as a whole year's transactions.

Although generic accounting packages are highly flexible, there are some types of organizations that will be unable to utilize these packages. There are, in addition to the general purpose packages, more specialized packages available. Law firms, accountants, consultants and others who bill by the hour and medical/dental offices in which billing is by the procedure find that each lawyer, accountant, and doctor is best treated as an independent profit center within the organization. Professional sport representatives and consultants can most likely adapt one of these time-accounting packages to their requirements with very little difficulty. Such packages are almost as common as the generic sort and usually cost only a bit more.

The requirements of accounting within college and university budgets, or for volunteer organizations are a bit more difficult to match. These organizations generally have no need for the profit-and-loss type of analysis, and can even dispense with the payroll function as this is usually handled at a higher level than the individual department. Much more important for such organizations are the budget function, which ties into fund-raising, forecasting cash requirements, and allocation of expenditures to budget categories. There are so-called "home accountant" programs which can be adapted to meet this need. These are cash-based as opposed to accrual-based systems, and handle anything from simple home budgets to large-scale sole proprietorships. By redefining the credit card and various check and savings account provisions of the programs to refer to available funds and debts incurred, a little mental gymnastics will then take the place of a lot of programming. If the accounting application required is so quirky that none of these tricks will work, then working up an application using a database manager or spreadsheet program is a better route than using BASIC.

F. *Financial Analysis and Solution Software.*

Without a doubt, the largest number of programs on the market fall into the category of solution software. These are programs that perform a single kind of narrowly defined task, such as "given these inputs (which the user then enters) the answer is ...." There are programs that do loan amortization, net present value, future value, depreciation, operating ratios, break-even, economic order quantities, and so on, through programs to figure how long shoe laces need to be when given shoe size and number of eyelets. One good thing about these programs is that they are usually sold by the disk-full, for something like a dollar a program. At their worst these programs are trivial. The exact algorithm, or mathematical procedure, being employed is not usually visible to the user and might yield results that should not be relied upon. For most of these applications, a user is better off taking formulas from a reliable textbook, and then working out the algorithm using a spreadsheet program.

This latter procedure is embodied in a series of products released by the same publishers that handle the spreadsheet programs themselves. Referred to as solvers, or tools, these products are part textbooks, part reference work and part template for the spreadsheet program. A template is a nearly complete, filled out spreadsheet which has blanks in it for the user to enter the relevant numbers for the actual case under analysis. In effect, solution software of this type converts the computer into an expert system. The actual expert is the person who developed the template, and the computer conveys that expertise to you in the form of a structured solution to your specific problem. A wide range of financial applications are available in this format as are templates for bridge design, electronic circuit analysis and on and on.

Falling into this same class of software are a multitude of nontrivial packages of which the statistical analysis programs are of the greatest interest. The better packages are well-documented so that it is possible to determine which procedures have been implemented and which of the recognized texts have been used as a basis for the implementation. This information is, of course, required if the results of the analysis are to be published.

G. *Graphics.*

One of the most dramatic tricks computers perform involves graphics ranging from simple plotting of numerical data to animations. The ability of a particular computer to produce pictures and the resolution of those pictures is limited by the available hardware. Briefly, each dot on the screen corresponds to a memory location. Every computer has some limited amount of memory available, and portions of it must be allocated to all the different functions the computer performs at one time. The resolution of the screen pictures is measured in "pixels," or the number of dots which the computer controls individually. If graphics are to play a part in the use you plan for your computer, then this factor should be high on your shopping list of requirements, as the hardware must be there for the graphics software to perform its magic.

Graphics programs are used for clarifying large bodies of data by producing charts and graphs. The old adage that "a picture is worth a thousand words" is particularly true when a program combines both graphic and statistical analysis to produce scatter plots of data and then a series of best fit lines and curves. Dot matrix "graphic" printers can produce usable-quality text and also permanent "hard" copies of the pictures, charts, and graphs. Full-color printers and plotters are coming on the market which, coupled with full-color graphics programs, permit the user to generate in a matter of minutes the kind of presentations that formerly required hours upon hours of nasty work with X-acto knife and ink pens.

H. *Communications.*

Communications programs require that the computer be equipped with a piece of additional hardware, called a modem, so that the internal signals which the computer uses can be sent and received over phone lines. Once that hardware is in place, there are all sorts of possibilities. First, there are a few technical notes to explain. When two computers are connected to each other, one of them is acting as the host, and the other computer acts like a terminal. It is possible for the computers to swap roles back and forth, but generally, only one of the computers is configured to behave like a terminal. The distinction seems a minor point, except that for some installations and applications, a terminal is all that is needed, and terminals are generally cheaper than computers. The difference is that a terminal lacks a processor, cannot load and run programs, and cannot control disk drives or other devices (peripherals) like printers, etc. When one works at a terminal, the computer one uses is elsewhere and it has control over the terminal. The terminology is, unfortunately, not all that exact, for the screen and keyboard of a personal computer can properly be called a terminal while the actual computer is elsewhere, inside the box, in this case.

Communications programs cause a computer to behave as if it were a terminal rather than a computer. The remote computer, if we restrict this discussion to telecommunications with remote computers, controls the display that is on the local computer's screen, and provides the prompts and reads the keyboard to gather input. To further confuse the situation, there are "dumb" terminals, whose operations are limited as described above, and "smart" terminals which retain some degree of control over the local peripherals. "Smart" terminals have a major advantage over "dumb" terminals in that they can use the disk drives of the local computer to store data that is to be sent to or has been received from the host remote computer. The cost components in telecommunications processes are the phone-line charges and the "connect time" charges. Users of the host computer are charged for access by the amount of time. "Smart" terminals can reduce the connect time by enabling the user to prepare data to be sent before connecting to the host computer, "off-line" as it is called, and, once connected, the data can be transmitted in a continuous stream. Similarly, data being received from the host can be stored on a disk, "spooled," for later review off-line. Virtually all the new communications software configures the local computer to behave like a smart terminal.

Any task that can be run on a stand-alone computer can be run at a terminal connected by a modem through phone lines to a remote computer. For most applications, however, the cost of the phone line and connect time would quickly pay for a fully functioning local computer to be used independently of the remote computer. There are a wide range of applications for which remote computers can perform tasks that are not practical locally. These typically involve huge amounts of data or require so much brute computer power (or both) that it simply is not economical to keep the operation idle between uses. By allowing large numbers of users to share the resources, the cost of a large-scale system can be distributed across a wide base. The best known of these systems are Compuserve and the Source, each of which numbers its subscribers in the many tens of thousands. These systems can not serve all their subscribers simultaneously any more than the phone company could accommodate every phone subscriber if they all tried to make a call at the same time. The more users that are "on-line" at one time, the more work the host computer has to perform. The "response time" is a measure of the time that it takes the host computer to receive and respond to a user's input, and this can become quite slow on some systems.

A major use for these network systems is in the access that they provide to databases of literature. Virtually every article in every journal and magazine, book, government publication, and newspaper published, at least over the last ten years, has been indexed by subject, author, and keywords in different computer files. Working back beyond that ten-year horizon the degree of completeness falls off; however, the number of publications that can be accessed through these services exceeds ten million individual entries. One can not begin to claim to have researched a topic without having combed through these databases. Unfortunately, there is not a single system through which to route all this information into; rather there are hundreds of individual databases maintained at both private and public expense and to which access is provided at varying rates. Typically they are organized by subject area: toxicology, water resources, career placement, etc. There are hundreds of individual databases and there has emerged, in response to all this information and the demand of users to access it, a new profession — the information broker. There is even a database of database experts who can serve as information brokers, and it currently lists some 10,000 individuals and firms nationwide who can help answer your questions.

On a day-to-day basis, a subscription to one of the major networks can provide access to news, weather, more up-to-date government statistics than can be found in print, airline schedules, and moment-to-moment flight delays at major airports. Access to the other databases can be had through the networks. Another useful aspect of the networks is EMAIL, in which text is transmitted to the central computer addressed to a particular subscriber. When that subscriber connects to the system, the "letter" is delivered. Using a "smart" terminal to reduce connect charges, the cost of EMAIL is quite reasonable, and there are local phone numbers to use in almost every location throughout the country to gain access to the network without having to pay long-distance charges regardless of where the "letter" is delivered. Small portable computers can travel with a team on the road, for example, and information could be exchanged with the home office at a fraction of the cost of voice or telegraph communications.

There are other uses for communications between computers. As described above under vertical packages, there are programs which require more capacity than is available to the local computer, but at the same time, the use of these programs is not frequent enough to justify purchase of the additional capacity. In such cases the data collected locally can be sent to a remote computer, "uploaded," for processing, and the results can be returned to the local computer, "downloaded," for printout. This process is quite common in research applications when statistical analysis calls for large data matrices to be manipulated in memory. Large computers, such as are commonly found at university computing centers, can handle these jobs, while it remains practical to handle the more routine collection and collation of data on a smaller local computer.

An interesting variation on this theme is the service offered by DRI Inc., through which a question can be put to their research staff in the form of a series of responses to a computer-controlled questionnaire. The answers come back in the form of a VisiCalc template downloaded a day or so later to the questioner's computer. Ask a question, for example, about the impact that a new sport facility has had on the pattern of recreational spending in a particular city and what impact might be projected for a similar facility in another city, and DRI will research the various economic and demographic databases and construct a model in VisiCalc format which will permit the questioner to explore all the factors in the equations. It is even possible to protect your ideas by withholding the name of the contemplated target city for your project. DRI will construct the model showing where the demographic details which would identify your target are to be entered into the template after it has been downloaded and you are off-line. This kind of semi-automated consulting is surprisingly inexpensive.

§ 17-7. Sizing Equipment to Applications.

Even though the cost of hardware has been sliding steadily downward, there is simply no reason to acquire a larger, more complex computer than is needed for the application. The factors to be considered are total file size, number of distinct files and the degree to which they must be integrated, number of tasks to be handled per unit time and the response time required from the system. All of these factors must be taken into consideration, along with questions of who within the organization is going to be the person with direct responsibility for day-to-day operation of the system. It should be recognized that personal computer systems are designed to be operated and cared for by just plain folks, while larger and more powerful systems will require that operators trained in the care and feeding of the system be available whenever the system is running.

A. *File Size.*

Information processed by the computer must be stored in files. While the exact calculation of file sizes is a complex matter, it is fairly simple to arrive at ballpark figures. Consideration of how the information is going to be used within the applications to be implemented can then lead to solid conclusions as to the size and type of file storage devices required. File sizes and capacities are part of the performance specifications for different computers which can be compared to the projected system requirements. In general, a single letter, number or character will require one byte of storage. Files can be compacted somewhat, but the full advertised capacity of the disk drives of any computer system is not really available to the user, so things balance out.

For example, a file is to be constructed on the children attending a summer camp. There are 200 children in the camp and the file will consist of 200 entries, or records as they are called, each of which will have space allocated to hold information in the following categories:

1) Last name   15 characters
2) First name, middle initial   12 characters
3) date of birth (mm/dd/yy)   8 characters

4) sex	1 character
5) home street address	20 characters
6) town, state	14 characters
7) zip code	5 characters
8) parent/guardian name	20 characters
9) number of years at camp	1 character
10) bunk assignment	2 characters

Total: 10 "fields" of information storing 98 characters

The file for the campers will require 98 x 200 = 19,600 characters which would require 20K of file space. As the smallest disk-drives in practical business computers hold 130K of user-defined information, there is no problem here with this file on any machine. Consider, however, the additional data that could be added to this file such as medical history, alternate address for parents and/or guardian if they are going to be traveling throughout the summer, names and addresses of other family members who could act in the parents' stead in the event of an emergency, school attended and grade, particular areas of skill, programs the camper would prefer to be part of if electives are offered at the camp, skill levels attained in swimming, riflery, and other sports, etc.

Adding this information could easily quadruple the size of the file. Add a few more campers and it starts to look like a bigger capacity disk drive will be called for. At this point it is important to review the information that is proposed for inclusion in the file. It is easy to see the utility of the information in the first 10 fields as listed. This information will be used over and over again in different contexts from attendance rosters to mailing labels. It will be used to determine the staff and facility requirements throughout the camp season. A similar argument might be made for skill levels and an activity history being included in each camper's record. On the other hand, alternate emergency names and addresses, medical history, and parents' traveling addresses are the kind of information one needs once, and hopefully not at all. Presumably, it is available in written form on the very documents from which it would be copied into the computer. All that would be accomplished by adding that information to the computer record would be to clog up the system and create a dangerous potential for error, i.e., incorrect emergency numbers. This information is best left in written form on the original documents.

Consider now the utility of entering information for each camper on the grade and school attended. Is this information in the category of best left on paper, or will it have some utility? A marketing application for the information is one possibility if the campers and their families would agree to act as referrals for potential new campers. One way to respond to inquiries would be to send, along with the usual brochures, the names and addresses of campers from the same school, class or nearby school as that of the potential new camper. An alternative technique is to match zip codes of the campers' home addresses and then cross-match by dates of birth using information that is already in the file. The question is which method is better, and is the school-based approach, if it is better, efficient enough to justify the labor of typing in the name and address of the school and the grade of each of 200 campers.

Imagine that the management of this camp decided that providing a fitness and skill analysis with a progress report on each camper would be an excellent means to convey to the campers and their parents the growth that has been attained during the season. To implement this plan, it would be necessary to set up tests and record and collate the results for each camper. Say the testing was to be administered in ten skill and performance areas once each week for the eight-week season, and that a two digit numeric code was used to record each result. Each camper would then have:

        10 tests x 8 weeks x 2 digit codes = 160 characters
        160 characters x 200 campers = 32,000 characters

to add to the file or an additional 32K of file space. The total file requirement of 52K will still fit nicely on one disk. Now consider what would happen if the camp was attended by 600 campers, not 200. A total of 98 plus 160 or 258 characters times 600 records or about 155K would be required to hold the file. It appears that the file size has exceeded the capacity of the disk drive.

B. *File Integration.*

The problem is a "straw man" however. Most file-manager programs permit the user to spread a file across several disks. A more important point is that a file of skill and performance levels need not contain the names of parents or guardians or the home address of the camper. The file for 600 campers containing only campers' names and test results will fit nicely on a disk, and the file of addresses can be maintained separately. Only information that is to be used together needs to be kept together. Even inexpensive personal computers can be equipped with disk drives that will handle 40 million bytes of data and while it is easy to get file sizes in the thousands, even 100,000-byte range, 40 megabytes (40,000,000 characters) as it is called, represents a lot more data than one is likely to key in during the course of a summer. Working a steady 40-hour week for an entire eight-week summer season, and based on an industry standard of keying in 12,000 characters per hour, a 40 megabyte disk would be only 10% full.

If a stadium manager wished to generate a mailing list of facility users, a modest concession might be offered to every patron who filled out a card giving name, address, occupation, and number of events attended each year at the facility. Assuming 25,000 seats three-quarters full and 70% compliance with the informational request, the data generated would look like this:

1) Last name	15 characters
2) First name, middle	12 characters
3) street address	20 characters
4) town, state	14 characters
5) zip	5 characters
6) occupation	10 characters
7) number of events	2 characters
8) event attended	1 character

Total 8 fields, 79 characters for 13,125 individuals = 1,036,875 bytes, which will require at least 86 hours to enter at the keyboard, in theory, while in fact no less than quadruple that time should be allocated for deciphering handwritten original data. Add to the job parameters that the gathering of data is going to be repeated three times in one week at different events, a basketball game, a concert, and an international gymnastics meet. Assume further that the same numbers of respondents, roughly 13,000, turn in data at each event. For maximum utility, repeats, that is the same names appearing on more than one list, are to be coded by the system to indicate that they have attended a particular combination of events. Now one last constraint — the total data entry job is to be done within 4 weeks of the start.

It appears that a file of at least 3,000,000 bytes will need to be constructed in four weeks. The condition of the original data indicates that nearly 770 hours of data entry will be required in four weeks; a full-time effort of five operators. A further complexity is that the entire file, apparently, must be constantly available to each operator as the work proceeds so that matches when they occur can result in a change-of-event code for that respondent rather than duplication of the individual in the file. Selecting hardware for this task follows from the file structure and the time frame imposed to generate a mailing list of almost 40,000 facility users. First, the system must handle the volume which dictates a hard disk drive. Second, the system must permit all the operators to access the file for comparison and entry at the same time. The term for this is multi-user. While preparing this mailing list, management might have some other jobs for the computer, like the payroll, keeping the books, etc. The computer must, therefore, be capable of multi-tasking, that is, of running more than one job at once.

Such a multi-tasking, multi-user hard disk computer is actually still quite a small machine. It is a microcomputer, not even a super-microcomputer. Its cost per work station will closely approximate that of personal computers, but its operating system will be far more complex. This means more advanced and extensive training will be required of at least one member of the office staff. A problem with this type of machine doing this kind of job is that even though it offers multiple work stations, it is still just one computer. When it breaks down in part, the whole system is generally down. If the common file-access problem in the job specification outlined above could be avoided, as it can be, then a group of personal computers working along side of, but independent of each other, could very well get the same job done. Another difficulty with a single machine serving multiple work stations is that confidential information, like pay scales, which have been entered into the system has to be protected from being reviewed (or even altered) by unauthorized persons. Passwords offer some degree of protection, and these are always incorporated into any multi-user system.

If the job above were handled by stand-alone personal computers, the individual disks being prepared by each operator could be "dumped" as they were filled up, into a single hard disk drive attached to one of the microcomputers. Part of the dump routine could be a check for prior entry of the same name. If a match were found, the event code could then be modified appropriately. There are applications for which periodic file consolidation will not provide adequate system performance, however. A system handling ticket sales and reservations must provide up-to-the-minute information. If the volume of data entry requires more than one work station, then inevitably the system must be of the multi-task and multi-user variety. If a seat is then reserved by one operator, another will not be able to resell the same seat because they will be working from the same file, in that they would be in effect pulling tickets out of the same bin. If a separate program is required to re-configure the seat availability chart based on the particular set-up used for an event, that program could then be run at the same time as the mail is being opened, and ticket sales from that source and phone-ins and walk-ins are also proceeding.

C. *Local Area Networks (LANs).*

There is an intermediate technology between the stand-alone computer and the multi-user, multi-tasking level of complexity. These are the LANs or local area networks which permit a group of computers, which can even be a mix of different brands and models, to be connected in a sort of daisy chain. Along the chain there can also be located printers, hard disk drives, modems and other hardware. Unlike the situation involved with a single computer supporting a group of work stations or terminals, the LAN structure permits each computer to continue to function independently of the others. Each node or computer in the LAN can access the peripherals in the network and send and receive data from other nodes. LANs are limited by the physical distance over which they can operate with the greatest distance being about one-quarter mile, large enough for almost any building. Beyond that distance, modems can be used to connect a series of LANs.

The obvious advantages of the LAN are that expensive peripherals like hard disks can be shared between machines, and that if a series of programs operate on the same data, then one file can be made accessible to each computer as it is needed. The accounting department and shipping department could share a customer file even though each is performing different but related tasks. This simplifies passing data between nodes as the disk can be used as an intermediary if the receiver computer is being used for an unrelated purpose when the sender is ready to transmit. New transactions processed by the shipping department computer, for example, can be stored until the accounting department computer is ready to update customer accounts. Programs stored on the hard disk can also be loaded and run by any of the computers in the LAN. This architecture appears to be an ideal compromise between the limitations of stand-alone personal computers as to the amount of data that can be physically entered per unit time at a single keyboard, and the vulnerability and complexity of multi-user, multi-tasking systems. One major problem remains to be solved however.

In the software used for multi-user systems, it is assumed that more than one user might be working with the data in a particular file at the same time. The programs are constructed with a set of protocols that in effect monitor the files to ensure that, if two users are working with the same record in the same file, they will be queued through so that whatever changes are made by one user are conveyed to the other before the second user works with the record. In the case of the LAN-connected personal computer, the software being run is the same as is used when the computer is being used as a stand-alone unit.

The protocols for multi-user access to the same file at the same time are not included in these programs. On the plus side, the programs used are much simpler, hence inherently more reliable, and the individual users are not constantly waiting for the central computer to respond to input. It can only be assumed that over the next few years, the multiple-access glitch will be worked out. LAN architecture offers advantages over the standard multi-user design in cost, flexibility, redundancy, back-up, and throughput, a measure of the amount of work that can be performed per unit time on the system as a whole.

D. *Mainframes and Super-microcomputers.*

Much of what has been said here about smaller computers also applies to the computers at the other end of the size scale. Organizations which require large computers for their operations are likely to have full-time computer professionals on staff. Briefly, there was a time when the trend in computer system design was toward increasing centralization and building ever larger and larger computers. A countervailing attitude, much like the parallel line of thought in management theory, held that each task should be accomplished *in toto* at the lowest possible level in the organization. Distributed data-processing theory argued that no purpose was served in transmitting data up to a central monster computer which then processed the data and returned the results to the lower level where those results were needed.

LANs, microcomputers, and modems, particularly the autoanswer-type modem which can be called into operation by a remote computer, have made it possible to have processing power where it is needed, and only the results of processes are transmitted to a central location for compilation. As the volume of data is reduced by processing at lower levels, top management levels, even in very large firms, are finding that modest-sized computers are adequate to meet their needs. Those remaining enterprises and organizations which require mainframe computers, no doubt, as stated above, have sufficient staff muscle and expertise to need no further advice here.

§ 17-8. Summary/Conclusion.

Finding the right combination of hardware and software for an organization is not an easy task. Clarity of purpose and a clear concept of who in the organization is going to operate the equipment and who is going to benefit from the information generated is important. In many ways, almost any choice of equipment, as long as it is of sufficient size and capacity, will do, as long as management is prepared to recognize and capitalize upon the far-reaching effects that computerization has upon the manner in which work gets done within an enterprise.

In planning an installation, the choices are to purchase a system such as:

Turnkey: complete software and hardware package from a single vendor who takes sole responsibility for the set-up, training, and installation of system;

Generic application and productivity tools: purchase of software and hardware which the purchaser then uses to develop "custom" applications; or

Hardware and programming language: lengthy and potentially very expensive programming of a system essentially from the ground up.

In general, the cost of one to three personal computers, and the kind of work they might be put to requires some in-house expertise for the successful specification of the system and its installation. The level of expertise required is not, however, that great, and can be readily acquired through reading and/or short courses available at local colleges and universities or through local vendors of computer systems. Taking a "computer literacy" course, and then purchasing a personal computer for use by management for the analysis of manually generated operating data is an excellent way for an organization to enter the world of computing.

Multi-user systems, in which either more than one user at a time will be connected to a single computer, or a number of independent personal computers will be tied together into a Local Area Network (LAN), require that one or more permanent members of the office staff be trained to a rather high degree to serve as resource people and system "managers." This is particularly critical if and when power failures or other emergency situations place the central files in jeopardy. Purchase of such systems is most commonly made through turnkey vendors. It is vital that an enterprise seek out the advice of an experienced consultant who has no interest in selling a particular system to the organization, and that the competing proposals of the turnkey vendors be reviewed with this consultant. On the one hand, a major investment in programming must be recouped by the vendor over a relatively small customer base which explains the high prices these vendors demand. On the other hand, shameless profiteering, "hype" and "flat-out bunk" are not unknown among vendors.

Custom programming for a particular system, as opposed to customizing an off-the-shelf application program (generic), or working up the specifics of an application using a productivity tool, is costly and frought with risk. Every avenue to seek out proven software, including contacting the manufacturer of the hardware, should be undertaken before setting out to write one's own programs. There are thousand upon thousands of published programs, and only if you are setting out to do something that's never been done before is it likely that you will be unable to buy the needed software someplace.

Purchase and operation of systems in the $30K-and-up range will require full-time in-house data-processing management personnel. The first step in acquiring such a system is to hire the manager who can then guide the organization through the purchase and installation of the system. Primary qualifications should be a knowledge of how business is done in your particular type of enterprise, and a proven track record in new installations. One danger in start-up systems is the failure of the managers to adequately document the new systems so that replacement personnel can take over and run the system in the future. Beware of empire builders, and provide economic incentives to the data processing manager which will encourage not only a well-run system, but a well documented one.

Lastly, the computer is put to different kinds of uses by different members of an organization:

Archive: recording and recalling operational information, the database function;

Analytical engine: modern management's all-purpose calculator figuring out everything from simple cashflow to alternative investment schemes; and

Document producer: word processing to full-color graphics, the computer can generate high-quality documents in a fraction of the time such activities formerly required.

The kind of equipment and personnel required to use the computer in these different ways are obviously different. More and more, managers are placing computers on their desks and using them in place of paper and pencil. Executive productivity is becoming an issue along with the productivity of the balance of the office personnel. There is a trend toward placing in the hands of management a tool which permits direct examination of the organization's data archive, incorporation of the data selected directly into an analytical schema, and direct production of presentation-quality documentation of the results of the analysis, all without calling upon the services of either skilled programmers or less-skilled filing clerks and typists. The goal of using this type of system is not only to increase the efficiency of management, but to also increase its sophistication by making it easy to do what was formerly time consuming and difficult.

GLOSSARY

The following glossary is offered as a convenience to readers of this chapter.

Application software: a program which, with its accompanying manuals, permits a user to start from scratch and bring an entire process under control by the computer. An example is a payroll package, or accounts receivable. Nothing beyond a basic knowledge of the operation of the particular computer being used should be required for the successful installation of a generic application program.

Computer: a machine which processes data into information.

Daisy wheel: printers that use the impact method of printing one character at a time just as a typewriter does. This produces what is commonly called "letter quality" print. These printers do not do graphics (pictures, charts) and are slower and more expensive than dot matrix types.

Data: the raw facts out of which information can be constructed.

Database management: a step up from file managers in which all the relevant facts in an organization are poured into the system by means of a variety of data entry forms or screens each designed to prompt and guide the user through the orderly entry of some part of the whole body of data. Once the data is entered, it can be flexible; rearranged into subfiles of various types of related (hence relational) data. From the subfiles information of all types can be constructed from the original data.

Disk drive: a device for storage and recall of data and programs. Moving data from the computer's memory to the disk drive is called "saving" and moving from disk drive to computer is called "loading." The disk spins inside the drive.

Dot matrix: printers that utilize a series of pins to form letters and/or pictures and graphs. The print quality can be very good with the better dot matrix printers, and they offer speed, flexibility, and moderate cost as advantages over other types.

Efficiency: a measure of utilization of systems resources by the program. Generally users should not concern themselves with efficiency unless a choice of one program or another leads to having to expand the system by adding memory or disk drives because the programs are not efficient.

File or list manager: a productivity tool which mimics the traditional file box. It allows for sorting, merging, and limited calculation based on the data found on the individual records (analagous to the individual cards in a card file). File managers also generate reports or lists based on the information in the file or varying degrees of sophistication.

Files: data is stored, generally on disk, in files. Some systems distinguish between stored programs and stored data calling only the latter files, and other systems simply refer to data files and program files.

Floppy disk: a diskette for use in a disk drive made of a bendable plastic (hence "floppy") coated with magnetic recording material much like that on cassette tape. Floppies are used for small through medium-sized files and come in $5^{1}/_{4}$ inch, the most common, and 8-inch diameters. Several new formats in 3- to 4-inch diameters are coming on the market.

Hard disk: a polished aluminum disk takes the place of the bendable plastic of the floppy design. The hard disk permits higher rotation speeds and greater storage density than is possible with floppy disks and so are used whenever large files must be made accessible at one time to the computer.

Hardware: the computer and associated printers, disk drives, the visible part of the system.

Information: the sense that a human being perceives when data is processed in some manner — like beauty, information is in the eye of the beholder.

Ink and laser jet: an emerging method of printing in which the print image is either literally squirted (ink jet) or burned (laser) onto the paper. The result is "letter quality" at dot matrix speed with full capability for graphics. One drawback is an inability to produce multiple copies at once (carbons), but this is definitely the coming thing.

LAN (Local area network): a form of hooking computers in a circle in which the resources of one machine then become accessible to all. Permits much of what can be done with a single large computer serving multiple users without either the expense or complexity of large mainframes.

Mainframe: traditional large-scale computers still distinguished by both sheer size but also large-size processors and internal data paths and storage which allow the machines to operate several orders of magnitude more quickly than minis or micros.

Microcomputer: a computer on a chip, the advent of which led to the development of the personal computer.

Minicomputer: formerly referred to the smallest computers, later to the mid-size multi-user and multitasking 16-bit computers and distinguished from 32-bit mainframes. Currently a term in transition as 32-bit microcomputers and multi-user micros come into being, and current minis use single chip microcomputers internally.

Modem: a device which converts the computer's internal electronic signals into audio signals (and vice-versa) which can then be sent and received over telephone lines. Permits the communication of data and programs between computers (and users) at remote locations and between dissimilar systems.

Multitasking: also called multi-programming — see multi-user below.

Multi-user: a computer which serves several users simultaneously. Numerous architectures are grouped under this term and it is applied both to a single machine performing one job with multiple users entering and extracting information and data at once, e.g., a ticket reservation system and to multiple users using one computer for different and perhaps unrelated tasks at the same time. This later is referred to as multitasking.

Personal computer: a single-user computer which generally can perform one task at a time at the command of the single user.

Plotter: a type of printer which uses moveable pens to literally draw the output from the computer onto paper. Plotters produce the best pictures and graphs and use multiple pens to give color output. They tend to be slow and expensive.

Power: the ease with which particular choices, once selected by the user (or programmer) are executed. A powerful program may be limited in range, but allow the user to accomplish much work in a short time because each action in itself is so productive.

Printer: a device for making printed output called "hardcopy" of the information generated by programs from data.

Productivity tool: a program which offers the user a very powerful problem-solving tool which operates over a more or less wide range. Thus a database, or spreadsheet program can be learned and employed for a wide range of applications which will get a lot of work done quickly because the time required to get the system working is very small compared to writing a program from scratch.

Program: an organized procedure which a computer can execute to process data into information.

Programming language: a method of constructing a series of instructions called a program. Languages share common characteristics when viewed in the abstract, but concretely differ widely in the skill required for their use, their range and power, and in the efficiency and speed of the final set of instructions they produce for the computer to execute called the machine language or object code. The most widely known language, BASIC, generally produces such slow execution times that its use in "real-life" business situations is very limited. Assembler language code, which is essentially machine language with some aids for the programmer, produces, in skilled hands, the fastest programs.

Range: the number of different options, operations, or choices that a system offers to the user (or programmer) at any one time. A trade-off is always present in the system between range and power.

Software: the programs, utilities and other instructions which the hardware executes (performs) or "runs."

Spreadsheet: a productivity tool which offers the user a large grid of cells into which may be entered words, numbers, and/or formulas. Any kind of task which can be worked out on paper can be done with spreadsheet programs.

Terminal: the user works at the terminal which accepts input from the user, traditionally from a keyboard although many alternatives are in use, and which displays results to the user either in print or on a monitor (video) display. The keyboard and monitor of a personal computer are together a terminal, although the term is generally restricted in use to refer to connection to a remote computer. Terminals can be dumb, simply accepting input and displaying output, or smart, i.e., having some local control over the disk drives and/or printer attached to the terminal remains in the hands of the user.

Throughput: a measure of the actual amount of work done by the system and the users per unit time. Throughput becomes an issue when users are found waiting for the system to do something rather than the other way around. Throughput can be adversely affected by poor program design and by having to wait for printed output, among other executions. Print buffers, "spooling" and other hardware and software tricks can improve throughput, as can good clean software design particularly when it comes to keying in of data (data entry).

Turnkey: hardware, software, training, and installation purchased together from a single vendor.

Word processing: the use of computers to handle text. Offers the ability to store the text in files, merge text with other files, and includes everything from mailing list processing to automated typesetting.

Part 5

FACILITY MANAGEMENT

Chapter 18

MANAGEMENT OF SPECTATOR FACILITIES OPERATED AS JOINT VENTURES OF UNIVERSITY AND COMMUNITY

By

James Oshust

§ 18-1. Introduction.

During the past several decades, college campuses have become the site for development of structures once considered primarily the province of cities and counties. These structures are more commonly referred to as public assembly facilities. A "public assembly facility" is any structure, building or complex of buildings used for the viewing of or participating in spectator-oriented events and activities. More simply put, it includes those facilities most often referred to as auditoriums, theatres, arenas, coliseums, exhibition halls and a myriad of other names which will be discussed later in this chapter.

The word "public" does not itself mean the facility is necessarily publicly owned or controlled by any particular governmental entity. It does define the structure in question as one which is open to public use, for rental, and promotional enterprise as compared to a school building used just for classwork, a church or the private auditorium of a fraternal organization used only for the benefit of that group's membership.

In the early 1960's, the University of Illinois, at Champaign-Urbana, constructed a 16,000-seat arena to house its basketball program and certain elements of its major college theater series each year. The University of Illinois recognized the need to provide a forum for the entire community. The Illinois "Assembly Center" was a forerunner in a development that resulted in the construction of public assembly facilities on college and university campuses across the country. It represented a dramatic departure from the past.

The purpose of this chapter is to describe the various strategies employed by colleges and universities to obtain spectator facilities. It should be remembered that, as with all situations, time quickly changes certain parameters and there is nothing within this chapter that should be considered without potential for measurable change unless it be the basic principles of sound management, fiscal reliability and consistency in operational practices.

§ 18-2. Reasons for Building Public Assembly Facilities on University Campuses.

There were three principal reasons for building public assembly facilities on campuses. First was the need to house those activities very much a part of the university or college schedule. They included the performing arts, various campus dramatic societies, and musical organizations. More often than not, they included athletic facilities for various team sports and in some parts of the northeast, even hockey was favored to the degree that it merited its own structure.

Secondly, schools felt there was a need to maintain a high degree of sensitivity to the academic community and a closeness of administration with the student body through the provision of spectator-event facilities on campus. In many cases, the campus was a captive community. At many universities, from 10,000-30,000 attendees could easily support the several dozen events held during a particular building's scholastic schedule year.

To some observers, possibly one of the greatest impetuses for such development was the ease of acquiring special grants, federal moneys, state and community subsidies. And there was always the alumni association coffers which seemed to prosper or decline according to the success of a particular athletic program each year. Money literally flowed from a number of sources and thus it was not difficult for universities or colleges, whether publicly or privately endowed, to raise the two to four or more millions of dollars necessary for a center for the performing arts, a large arena, or whatever other such facility fit the then-considered primary needs of the school. This was not true, however, in communities that bordered and often surrounded these campuses. In the tax-supported community, prices were rising, inflation was beginning its heinous upward spiral again, and "keeping the cost of government down" nearly sounded the death knell for many proposed public-assembly facility bond issues.

There were of course, those instances when federal grants, the famous, or to some, infamous "revenue sharing plan" or other such money exchange devices did provide needed seed money for funding one or more facilities or ancillary developments in a city.

Then the great surge of interest in professional sport franchises, particularly in the late sixties and early seventies, added fuel to the fire of competition for potential patron dollars. But mainly, it was academic institutions that had the initial ability to construct facilities for their own uses during those years.

§ 18-3. Funding Plans.

The methods of acquiring these collegiate facilities started, as do most community projects, with an approach to primary funding. In the case of state-controlled institutions it would be initiated in the state legislature as a seed-funding grant supported further by guarantees of revenue potential from alumni and athletic fan-support organizations. This, coupled with federal entitlement grants, arts foundation grants, and various other such funding sources would quickly fill the "war chest" necessary for a particular project and many such buildings were conceived, designed, constructed and implemented in far shorter time than it took to change a particular course of study or develop an academic field of endeavor at that same university or college.

During the mid-1970's colleges and universities found their funding sources drying up. Federal grants and "in kind" fundings had vastly diminished and in some cases, ceased to exist. Alumni, faced with their own personal and business financial problems, had to diminish their input into athletic department coffers. Universities were no longer able to put together funding packages for the construction of needed facilities. At the same time the demand for bigger and better arenas for athletics and other campus activities continued to increase. The answer to the problem was found in joint ownership. Academic institutions united with their home communities to subsidize the construction and operation of a large facility to be used in part by the university and for the revenue potential needed to sustain the facility, as a public assembly center for the entire area. Examples of this merging of interests can be found in the Tallahassee-Leon County Civic Center in Tallahassee, Florida; the University of Florida Facility in Gainesville, Florida; the Lexington Civic Center in Lexington, Kentucky, more commonly referred to as Rupp Arena, named after the legendary University of Kentucky coach Adolph Rupp; and the University of New Orleans arena in New Orleans, Louisiana. There are numerous others of course, but it is hoped that the examples mentioned here will provide the broadest spectrum of approach and involvement so as to reflect the best "average" situation faced by such ventures.

Management requirements for facilities constructed under the new arrangement are identical to those for any public assembly facility. Although the ownership, and thus the resultant control, was dictated by who has paid the price of construction and who has supplied the necessary funds for operation, it should be remembered that once the doors are opened to the public for whatever purposes, the facility must maintain a posture similar to that of others in the industry. The public must feel it will receive a consistent and sufficient mode of event operation. Regardless of the ownership of the facility in question, its methods of funding, administrative source or other such particulars, certain basic requirements must exist in developing an operational technique in keeping with industry needs and standards. Unless the facility conforms to established practices for the public-assembly facility industry it will be viewed as unstable. Such a label will result in an erosion of its capacity for conducting business.

§ 18-4. Elements of a Standard Operational Policy.

A standard operational policy concerning any public assembly facility, regardless of ownership, funding source or unique characteristics, should have a consistent schedule philosophy; a consistent event operational policy; a clear and monitored recognition of purpose; and active promotion of the facility and its services to those groups vital to the facility's success.

A. *Consistent Schedule Philosophy.*

Often a facility is designed and implemented with one set of highly publicized and vocally espoused schedule concepts. Unanimity of thought and an almost magnanimous attitude toward any and all in the community who would wish to make use of the facility becomes the basis for which the project is promoted and eventually comes to fruition. Nevertheless, once the facility is in operation, certain pressures begin to build. Certain factions form and there then develops the division as to who should use the facility, who should have prior right of domain, and in the most basic sense, "who actually runs the building?" Regrettably, this invariably leads to the demand by certain local groups that they, as part of the funding community or membership in the tax body that ostensibly supports the facility, should have use of the facility for little or no payment. If this agreement prevails, then no method of additional funding, rental charges or usage fees can ever truly provide a realistically valid financial picture.

In the case of athletic facilities, too often the athletic department, particularly through strong alumni-support activity, seems to hold sway. It is well-recognized that a basketball arena is of primary importance to the basketball team from late November to approximately the first weekend of March in each school year. Yet, there are facilities that have been literally taken out of the marketplace during that period by the insistence of a coach or athletic director that the facility during that same basketball season also serve as the practice floor for the team. With this in mind, there are many days that the facility goes unused because of the desire of the coach to keep the building sacrosanct to one and only one type of event.

In certain cases, the student government or student affairs office becomes very involved in the facility's operation and particularly that of scheduling. Contemporary music concerts are aimed toward the student body and thus, theirs might be the only sponsorship or involvement permitted.

When summer arrives, many schools or combination facilities feel the market period is over and it would be more economically viable to keep the facility closed. Ostensibly, some building administrations contend that this is the time for normal seasonal maintenance. Others feel that very little staff is available, and with the college or school out of session there is no potential audience. This may be true in some small communities. In the normal sense, however, it should be recognized that when students leave a campus there may be a number of other students in the overall trade area returning home from other distant campuses.

A consistent schedule philosophy must be developed in advance of the facility's completion. It should be administered and controlled by management personnel with professional expertise, and should not be countermanded at whim by other administrative officials unless there are definitive and eligible considerations that might preclude certain types of bookings. There is also a very shadowy legal question regarding the rental facilities and freedom of access.

Once a facility has been developed and put into operation to serve a multitude of public interests, both academic and community, the facility's ownership is under the legal obligation to provide a consistent access to the facility. If there are any precluded events, they should be addressed prior to a facility's opening. If there are activities which take preeminence over others, then they should become part of the predetermined schedule allocation. If there are inconsistencies in the schedule philosophy or there are those items which come within the academic and/or cooperative community that the administration feels are offensive or contradictive to the best interests of either group, then those items should be discussed fully and such action, if found to be legally allowable, can be taken to preclude such events. It should be emphasized time and time again that in any such discussions, there is no such thing as preclusion of liability under the first and fourteenth amendments to the Constitution. These amendments particularly refer to freedom of speech and due process.

The university or college, as with any governmental entity that comprises the community administration, cannot set themselves apart from those jurisdictional controls with which any private business would have to comply.

If a certain event is part of standard entertainment industry fare, it cannot be precluded if other such acts have been allowed to perform and there are no clear cut and constitutionally allowable prohibitions that can be exercised. Artistic judgment is not one of the criteria provided the owner of a facility in selecting which act shall perform and which shall not, so long as the facility is operated in a manner so as to entice, lure, invite and induce various spectator activities to use its facilities.

B. *Consistent Event Operational Policy.*

Just because a facility may be student-oriented in the tenor of a great number of its activities, when the general public enters the facilities to attend any event, they should expect a certain consistency in treatment. That includes trained event-staff, medical personnel, security, and administrative personnel. Even if a student activity is to be controlled by the students and thus they are responsible for staffing and other event-oriented services, the facility owner may have placed the professional requirements to meet public needs in the hands of those who are not trained to provide such services. Such students can provide a basic work force if they are guided by professional administration. In many cases, facilities on university campuses or in a cooperative academic/community arrangement can be excellent teaching tools for students and provide a certain sense of involvement heretofore unavailable in most campus/community activity formats.

The same is true with a system of maintenance for the facility and provision of certain vital services, including the access by the public for uses and attention to public inquiries, complaints, and so forth. To have one policy for one group and a different policy for another is, in most simple terms, discrimination. For example, the student government association wishes to have a concert with a certain contemporary music group. The student government will provide the ushers, security, set up the staging and do whatever else is supposedly requested by the act or group. They will guarantee the act or group and sign any and all contracts. The school realizes that the cost is as great or even more so than any revenue potential and in fact the concert is being "subsidized" by student fees or other such budget allocations.

Several weeks later an outside promoter or separate organization from off campus wishes to use the facilities for a similar activity, and within the scheduling philosophy this is allowed. Yet the rental figure is much higher, there is a requirement for certain amounts of staff, security, medical personnel, even to the extent of requiring certain unionized service groups such as stagehands (International Alliance of Theatrical and Stage Employees). When queried, the facility's management or administration states that the previous concert was "promoted" by and for the students. Not only will this affect the credibility of the facility but is totally indefensible if litigated within the context of overt selectivity without conscious regard for constitutionally required criteria for access of all similar groups.

Access to the facility by user groups and tenure of those groups in the facility, provision of services and supply of appropriate material must be the same for all parties concerned. True, there are differences in the level of needs and there may even be some differences in charges. Yet, if a facility in itself becomes actively engaged in presenting a spectator event and its rates and fees and provision for normally expansive services create an economic hardship for a competing community facility elsewhere in the area, another sensitive issue arises. Can one governmental entity — a state operated university for example — actively compete with a city-owned and operated public assembly facility or a privately owned facility in the same community? In some cases, both are governmental entities and enjoy their existence through a sustaining tax base; in the latter example of the private facility, an unfair competitive factor can be claimed.

C. *Recognition of Purpose.*

Although somewhat similar to Items A and B, this area is often more clearly articulated by complainants than are the first two factors. What appears to be criticism of certain scheduled events or complaints about inconsistency in event-operations policy could be better stated as a contention that the school or combined academic/community authority no longer recognizes the original purpose of the facility. Is the facility developed strictly for an on-campus and interdepartmental relationship and to provide services for a very restricted and predetermined user group? Or, was the structure built and is it operated to serve the overall community while at the same time filling certain needs of the school where it is located? The Rupp Arena situation in Lexington, Kentucky is an excellent example of where the needs of the University of Kentucky not only are fulfilled by providing the beautiful facility that now exists in the city of Lexington but also, they provide a certain financial base in an activity area that a lot of buildings do not enjoy. Yet, the purpose of the facility was and still is to provide a community and consumer trade area-wide forum for a multitude of activities.

Recognition of purpose is so important because it is an emotional issue at best. It is the very fiber of certain community and/or academic institutional concepts. The arts theater that is used by more groups off-campus than on-campus often created hard feelings among certain school officials, particularly those closely allied with the workings of the school's theater department. In retrospect, there are those avid alumni who, supporting their college athletic programs, will find that the intervention of a certain event, thus precluding their favorite team's constant access to a particular arena floor for practice, strikes at the very heart of the school's tradition and time-tested values in their personal viewpoint.

D. *Promotion to Those Groups Vital to the Facility's Success.*

This section is directed to the facility that particularly needs the community's involvement so as to make the building fiscally viable. Or, in those cases where the services to the community were a very necessary part of the original funding request, there continues to exist the need to direct the attention of that consuming public to the advantages and facilities available at the building in question. Alumni groups are very close-knit organizations that can be reached by direct mail. Often, many of them live in the trade area, or if not, are extremely attentive to each and every mailing, telephone call or public announcement concerning their alma mater. The university community itself is a close-knit entity due to the proximity of one person to another. Dormitory living, close in-campus housing, mutually attended classes, and the traditional atmosphere of the scholastic community make advertising and promotion of events and recognition of needs of a facility far simpler.

But there are those many thousands of individuals in the trade area who are not connected to the school in question. They may accept the school for what it is, and be happy with the advantages of having a particular academic institution in their community. They may even feel there is a benefit in having the number of individuals residing in town even if only for a nine-month period each year. Yet, it is to these people that a facility must direct certain promotional aspects. An ice show or noncollege-oriented activity in an 11,000-15,000 seat facility may require an audience factor made up of from 50-80% of nonschool people. Thus, if there has not been a consistent and strong approach to achieve rapport with this trading area even before the facility is finished, there can exist, as regrettably does in a number of communities, a greater gulf or separation between the school's efforts to promote the facility and the acceptance by the community that this is a structure and an activity schedule designed with all of them in mind.

The pronouns "I" and "us" must be couched in the more broader term of "we." The community should not be cut off from the operation of the facility either by access to the events or promotional mediums. Once a division of opinion concerning a facility appears then a chasm begins to form. It can take years to correct, and has in some situations, and there are certain situations where this division of opinion between the consumer area and the academic community in question has never healed properly. The separation of the two entities and the philosophic and emotional distance between these two groups is but the proverbial tip of the iceberg and could very often be merely a reflection of a deeper and greater split that may have existed long before the facility was ever constructed.

The unique quality of any spectator facility is its normal unsuitability for any other type of use other than that for which it was originally designed. An auditorium is an auditorium and a basketball arena still remains a large open space structure suited primarily for spectator usage even after the seats and playing court have been removed. In recent years, restorative techniques and architectural ingenuity have turned some abandoned department stores and other large retail sales facilities into fairly acceptable convention and exhibition areas. This ability to be transformed rests primarily in the structure's similarity to the standard exhibition hall or convention center configuration — that of a flat floor, four wall structure divided by movable partitions into meeting, exhibition and banquet space.

This is not the case with auditoriums, theaters and larger arena-type structures. Once a facility is constructed for these specific purposes it serves little good to attempt using it for any other purpose radically apart from that for which it was originally built. With this in mind, the owners and operators of such facilities must quickly determine the most practical and efficient method of operation within the building's basic design.

Size is not as important a factor in operational stratagem as one might think. The large, multi-thousand-seat facility has more area to be cleaned, more seats to be repaired, more lighting instruments to be replaced, and more space to be heated and air-conditioned. But on the other hand, it also produces a larger amount of revenue during most usages thus allowing for a greater allocation of support funds or event receipts to budgeted maintenance categories.

There is a strong operational similarity of any such structure to many small businesses. As with such businesses the product line is somewhat limited by the type and size of structure involved, the permanent staff is not overly large, and the level of specific activity costs are related directly to the size and type of event scheduled. Although the structure may appear unique, practical fiscal policies, efficient maintenance techniques and sound personnel practices coupled with innovative and aggressive promotional programs still form the basis of any successful facility operation.

§ 18-5. Importance of Organization, Cooperation and Discipline.

To operate with the highest degree of efficiency and productivity under existing circumstances any such facility, however large or small, must emphasize three basic tenets. They are organization, cooperation and discipline. The organization must be well-defined, simple, clear in its goals and objectives and yet flexible to meet changing times. State-of-the-art is an expression that has been coined for the modern day computer world. It should also be remembered when dealing with any organizational structure. New conditions, changes in market potential, fluctuations in the local as well as regional economy, and the increasing development of managerial techniques can all have bearing on the basic structure of any facility's management system.

Cooperation in any facility, regardless of size, is imperative. It begins with the desire of the owner-operator to provide a consistent and unfettered support of its management staff. That cooperation then must pervade all staff activities. It is carried forth into the community through a sincere desire to be of assistance in fulfilling not only what the owner-operator and management feel are community needs, but what the consuming public themselves feel the facility can do for them as potential users.

The last of the three-part concept, discipline, must be both individual and organizational. An unbending attitude is not a reflection of discipline but of an overly rigid management personality. An unquestioning obedience to every request, every demand and every desire for change by others is also not reflective of discipline, but rather of insecurity and insufficiency in the needed professional approach to the management responsibilities required in operating any public assembly facility.

If you have organization, cooperation and discipline in their appropriate forms and degree of sufficiency to meet normal management challenges, you then can safely assume you have "control" of your facility's operation. Control may be the most important element in any successful facility operational technique. By control we mean that the various aspects of facility operation are within the authorized domain of the facility management and its owner-operator. Any changes, additions, or deletions are developed by, implemented by, and the responsibility of that same management/owner-operator combination.

Every facility must control its own scheduling procedure and booking authority. Although there may be some scheduling limitations, particularly in the case of athletic facilities where practice time is provided, or community-oriented centers where certain traditional or periodic activities take precedence, once those limitations are recognized and parameters set, the scheduling must then remain within the province of the facility's management.

Extremely important is control of finances which includes accounting procedures, collection and payment of funds as well as management of any and all contracts that might deal with franchises such as leased concessions, labor service contractors and parking service operators among others.

Management of any facility requires control of all individuals who make up the facility's permanent and temporary staff. The selection procedure may necessitate involvement of a personnel department somewhere else in the overall organizational set up. There are, of course, numerous regulations, procedures, techniques and limitations for indiscriminate hiring and firing that are very much a part of current Affirmative Action programs, Equal Employment Opportunity and other state and federal regulations regarding the acquisition and disposition of personnel. But after the personnel forms are completed and the individual joins the facility's staff, he or she has come under the direct authority of the facility management and its authorized agents both in the performance of the individual's assigned responsibilities as well as application of appropriate personnel discipline and merit evaluation procedures.

§ 18-6. Public Relations.

"Public relations" means many things to many people. Most important to any spectator-oriented facility is the direct concern that the facility relates to its consuming public, their wants and their needs. Without direct involvement with such promotional and public relations programs, a facility management team has little or no control over its own merchandisable potential.

As in the case of any physical structure, preventative maintenance is the least expensive and most effective method of ensuring continued physical plant operation at peak efficiency with a minimum of continuing deterioration in both structure and plant equipment. Preventative maintenance, repair procedures and equipment replacement are essential parts of every annual budget consideration. They are the direct responsibility of the management team and thus, that same management team must have full control over these appropriate measures necessary to successfully carry on an effective maintenance program in the facility.

On the horizon or in the "tomorrow" of spectator facilities are some fascinating and challenging new concepts that may in time totally revamp the entire image of public assembly and spectator facilities so long considered impervious to change. Those new features just coming into view include renovation of facilities for multi-use where once they were considered suitable for only a limited type of activity. These renovations can encompass collapsible seating, electrically operated folding walls and partitions to divide floor space into smaller use areas, special floor coverings to provide additional styles of court services for such activities as indoor tennis and soccer, along with increasing seating capacity or in some cases, reducing cavernous buildings to more intimate, energy-efficient and operationally functional structures.

A combination of operational styles with the merging of community with academic institutions, various departments of the same government, quasi-private authority and governmental involvement have created a myriad of management structures and funding approaches that dazzle even the most veteran facility observer.

§ 18-7. Private Management Arrangements.

With this introduction of innovative funding and operational combinations has come the element of private management. Numerous facilities throughout the United States are now operating under what is generally referred to as private management contracts even though the facilities themselves may have been originally designed, funded, constructed and operated by governmental entities before entering into an agreement with a private management firm. Many advantages appear available through this type of management contract, not the least of which is the elimination of the traditional political squabbling and controversy that has plagued many city, county and state-operated facilities as well as the internecine institutional politics that even affects some academic institutional facilities. The subject of private management versus public ownership and operation, as further augmented by variations on the same theme, is a subject far too complex and broad to be covered in this chapter. The reader may wish to contact the International Association of Auditorium Managers, 500 North Michigan Avenue, Suite 1400, Chicago, Illinois 60611, whose membership includes a diversified group of ownership and operational combinations. A list of their membership would be a starting point for examination of the multitude of "operational arrangements" as currently exist.

§ 18-8. Trends.

Automation is an expression perhaps ill thought of in certain industries where it may have meant a decrease in the number of individuals utilized for certain functions. But in the spectator facility industry, automation in plant operations as well as the management and administrative services field may be the answer to what is the constant spectre of large overhead costs during a budget year that features a fluctuating and often capricious schedule potential and activity level.

In the plant operational field, computerized heating, ventilating and air conditioning controls, as well as devices for the shedding of excess energy demands and the conservation of fuel supplies has become an inevitable consideration during every building's annual budget review. Most recent has been the introduction of management programming, schedule consolidation, financial "spread sheets" and operational planning guides provided through the magic of "in-house" computer systems. These systems, whether several terminal units with limited data base or the more expansive and all encompassing "mainframe" configurations, present management personnel with far greater access to operational and financial data than ever enjoyed before.

This, coupled with the proliferation of automated or "computerized" ticketing systems allows a facility to literally and figuratively reach out to the consuming public with their most visible product identification — the event ticket. Where once the use of hard tickets to an event limited the number of agencies or "outlets" that might provide distant customers access to an activity, today a number of buildings have either developed their own system or are part of national computer ticket chains that can provide almost instantaneously tickets to a popular event hundreds of miles away from the facility in question. In addition, existing software provides quick retrieval of sales data as to where, when and how often tickets are sold. This is an invaluable tool for the advertising and promotion sections of any facility but even more importantly, to management itself. It is this type of recorded customer demand that indicates scheduling possibilities for future events.

§ 18-9. Summary/Conclusion.

The development, design, construction and eventual operation of a public assembly facility can and often has been the most dramatic and at times traumatic experiences ever undergone by any community. Whether the structure was built and is operated by the city in question, or is county owned, or privately built and operated, or part of the neighboring academic institution servicing that community, or the facility is a part of the total community recreational system, it is important to recognize that man is a gregarious creature. Man has gathered in urban conclaves for centuries, and will continue to seek the company of his fellow man; in doing so he will desire to be entertained, edified, educated, inspired and more directly stated — emotionally fulfilled by the presentation of events and involvement in activities at structures and facilities designed for these specific purposes.

Chapter 19

EVENT MANAGEMENT

By

Frank Russo

§ 19-1. Introduction.

There is a phenomenon that causes managers of public event facilities to recognize the importance and specialized nature of the role of the event manager. Each event must be managed; if not, it will assuredly mismanage itself. At one time the event manager simply coordinated activities prior to, during and following an event to ensure that equipment, physical setups and personnel were provided to meet all contractual requirements. Now, however, the event manager must become involved in many, if not all, of the following important tasks:

1. Scheduling and directing event, admission and crowd control staff, including ushers, ticket takers, security guards, private-duty policemen, firemen, and emergency medical service personnel;
2. Ensuring that tenants understand and comply with house policies and rules and regulations;
3. Making tenants fully aware of all that is involved in staging an event in the facility to avoid surprises, hidden costs and arguments. This is usually best handled at a production meeting with the tenant;
4. Developing, implementing and monitoring emergency operations and evacuation procedures; and
5. Ensuring compliance by all tenants of federal, state and local fire, building, and life safety codes.

During an event many things occur simultaneously that must be coordinated and managed. The box office, which is often the only contact many patrons will have with a facility, is open and in full operation. The concessions department sells food, beverage and merchandise. Security concerns itself with admission and crowd control and the ushering of people quickly and safely to their seats. The facility crew puts the final touches on the event setup and keeps all public areas free of debris, trash and obstructions. The engineering department makes sure that the Heating, Ventilation and Air Conditioning (HVAC) system is working properly so that everyone is comfortable, monitors the life-safety systems and also responds to such mundane tasks as repairing a plugged toilet or leaking faucet. Meanwhile, stagehands and other technical crew members are tending to a variety of details necessary to successfully stage the event.

Since the coordination and management of a facility is complex, a clearly established liaison between the tenant, the public and building management is critical. This responsibility often falls on the event manager.

257

The event manager is responsible for the protection of the performers as well as the physical plant and, most importantly, the well-being of the attending public. The balance of this chapter is an attempt to provide practical information for developing a comprehensive plan that will cover all these areas of responsibility. The emphasis will be on how to manage events rather than constantly reacting to one crisis after another.

§ 19-2. Radio Communication — A Critical Tool of the Trade.

A key to successful event management is a properly functioning radio communications system since total and instant communication, in certain situations, may mean the difference between life and death.

If a radio system is not available, it is advisable to contact local police, fire or civil preparedness department for guidance.

In an operational radio system, there are basic radio usage rules that should be followed:

1. Radios and pagers should be for business use only.
2. Since the number of radios and pagers being used by various personnel places limitations on air time, transmissions should be concise and any unnecessary conversation should not be tolerated.
3. Because Federal Communications Commission (FCC) regulations govern all language on the air, use of profane and/or obscene language and derogatory remarks should be strictly forbidden.
4. Because they are very costly to replace or repair, radios should be placed in holsters and not carried by hand. Microphones connected to the radio make this easy and very convenient. Also, earphones make it possible to hear even during a loud concert.
5. A code system to communicate critical information should be developed and all security personnel should be required to memorize and use it. Such a code system should be developed for the following types of situations:

   Fire (specify location)
   Bomb Threat (discussed in more detail later in this Chapter under Security and Emergency Procedures Manual)
   Medical Emergency (specify location)
   Engineering Emergency (specify kind and give location)
   Elevator Emergency
   Telephone Fire Department
   Telephone Police Department (specify need, i.e., police or ambulance)
   Accident (specify location)
   Disturbance and/or Breach of Peace (specify location)
   Assistance Needed (specify location)
   Return to Headquarters
   Telephone Headquarters or Other (specify)
   Try to Locate (usually a person)
   Assignment to a Certain Area or Check of a Certain Area
   Discovery of Something of a Suspicious Nature (specify location)

Stand by for an Announcement (emergency pending)
Resume Normal Activity
Sign on the Air
Sign off the Air (give location)
Testing Radio Equipment
Break

§ 19-3. Architectural and Physical Considerations.

Thomas Minter, currently the Manager of the Lexington, Kentucky, Civic Center, stated to the International Association of Auditorium Managers that "security begins on the drawing board." He observed that many problems can be avoided by proper design and planning of public facilities. This notion is supported by Don Jewell in his book, *Public Assembly Facilities: Planning and Management* 124 (New York: John Wiley and Sons, 1978), when he states that "safety begins with good architectural planning." Jewell correctly points out that while such considerations are well covered by governmental building and fire codes, to some extent management's need to guard the entrances and exists to restricted or ticketed areas may be in conflict with rapid evacuation in emergency circumstances. Careful planning by the architect in cooperation with your management team and state and local fire officials as well as the facility's insurance representative (risk manager) will do much to prevent serious operational and public safety problems. But, the process does not end here.

Because you are morally — and legally — responsible for public safety, ensuring public safety is an ongoing process which requires constant inspections of the physical plant to make sure that all hazards and potential hazards are eliminated before the public arrives.

Another architectural/physical consideration is Thomas Minter's recommendation that a facility be zoned into "activity areas" as follows:

1. The "public area" is where the public may move about freely and have access to all public facilities, concession areas, first-aid services, restrooms, drinking fountains, facilities for the disabled and public telephones. These public accommodations should be available without requiring access by the public into other zones within the facility. They must also be provided in sufficient number so as to discourage public demand to exit and return through admission areas.

2. The "performance area" includes backstage and dressing facilities. These areas require separation from the audience and service areas as much as possible. Such physical separation greatly enhances the ability to provide privacy and security for the performers or athletes. The use of backstage passes for those persons necessary or desired in the back-of-the-house is mandatory if effective control is to be maintained.

3. The "service area" includes workshops, custodial and concessions supply rooms, the shipping and receiving entrance, utility rooms, and equipment storage areas. The service area can most effectively be secured when performer and public access is restricted. Employee

theft can best be reduced and general order and inventory control maintained if this area is further restricted to only those persons actively employed by your facility.

4. "Support personnel areas" include police and security offices and the first-aid station. These areas should be adjacent to public areas but have access to the back-of-the-house entrance in order that those persons who serve the public may enter and leave without public surveillance, as well as allowing for removal from the facility of those who require medical attention or police detention.

§ 19-4. Admission and Building Access Control.

Only persons who have purchased a ticket or have been given authorized passes should gain entry to the facility.

Admissions control actually begins in the box office with the ticket itself. Tickets must be clearly printed on a type of safety stock to prevent counterfeiting. The ticket must allow the staff to quickly check the event, date and performance time, as well as the section, row and seat number(s). Admissions-control personnel should be trained to spot strange-looking tickets. Tickets should obviously be printed by a reputable and bonded ticketing company that ships them with the audited manifest directly to the box office to be counted, racked and distributed under direct control. An alternative to this, of course, is computerized ticketing, which may offer even greater control.

Most admission-type events fall into two basic categories: "general admission" which permits a person to sit in any available seat on a first-come, first-serve basis, and "reserved seating" which provides patrons with a specific seating location.

It is advisable to open the doors to the facility approximately one hour and fifteen minutes prior to the scheduled starting time. This will allow patrons adequate time to find their seating location, go to the restroom, purchase a snack, socialize, and get settled before the event begins.

It is important to constantly monitor the size and mood of a crowd in the lobby and outside the facility before the doors are opened. Have an adequate number of ticket takers and turnstiles to allow the crowd to enter in a quick and orderly fashion. Prior to opening the doors, however, the event manager should conduct a radio check to ensure that the performers and the house staff are ready for the public. The ticket takers should be supported by a supervisor, a "customer relations representative" to handle problems, and adequate numbers of security guards and policemen to handle trouble and/or to supervise a search and seizure operation. The duties and responsibilities of the admission control staff are discussed in more detail later in this Chapter.

There should be a system for admitting people to the facility that do not have tickets. Many facilities use a photo I.D. system which provides one of the best means of identifying persons with legitimate business. Employees, show personnel, and service contractors do not have an inherent right to be at an event. A system of I.D.'s and backstage passes designed to restrict entry is absolutely critical to building security and safety.

§ 19-5. Crowd Management.

In any crowd situation a risk to public safety is inherent and cannot be totally eliminated. While no facility can anticipate all the situations which might lead to disorder, cooperation between the facility management staff and promoters, agents, performers, admissions control staff, security, police, fire and government officials will do a great deal to minimize risks.

Crowd management requires *always* being prepared for the worst. The worst happened at Cincinnati's Riverfront Coliseum on December 3, 1979. Thousands of patrons were awaiting admission to a concert to be played by the "Who," a very popular rock group. General admission with festival seating had been established for the event. The anxious crowd (which was held outside the building until just before the concert was to begin) mistook the sounds of musicians warming-up as the opening of the concert and rushed the door. Eleven people died and eleven more were injured. The situation was not riotous or out of control and the deaths were senseless. But this, more than any other occurrence in recent memory, graphically shows the need for advance planning, precautions and sensitivity to people who buy tickets for events. Regardless of the size of the crowd, proper management is essential to minimizing and hopefully preventing unsafe situations. The tragedy promoted a careful study by the City of Cincinnati. Recommendations presented in *The Report of the Task Force on Crowd Control and Safety* are given below.

1. There should be clearly defined and published house policies which should be followed for each event. The facility management staff should be clearly in charge and ensure compliance with all laws, house rules and regulations, health standards and common sense practices.
2. Carefully evaluate the effects of the sale of alcohol. If necessary, place a security person, or preferably a uniformed policeman, at the sales outlet.
3. Clearly define the chain of command and the duties and responsibilities for the event manager, as well as all policemen, security guards, ushers and usherettes, ticket takers and first-aid personnel. Be sure they are constantly trained on how to properly react in an emergency situation.
4. Encourage patrons to report dangerous and threatening situations.
5. Avoid general admission ticketing and seating if at all possible.
6. Carefully plan the sale of tickets, especially when the demand will greatly exceed the supply. Develop a fair and equitable distribution system. Control your lines. Treat the crowds well and courteously. Do not allow line cutting. A wristband ID system works well here. And if necessary to ensure fairness, establish a maximum number of tickets each customer may purchase. And if it appears that some people in line will not reach the box office before the event is sold out, let them know as soon as possible and do not allow any more people to stand in line.
7. Conduct search and seizure to confiscate bottles, cans and other items which may be used to injure others.

8. Establish legal attendance capacities for each event setup, and obtain the written approval of the fire marshal and building inspector. Also, designate handicap wheelchair-locations in a manner least likely to cause them to serve as obstructions in case of an emergency evacuation.

9. Pay close attention to the architectural plans and designs of your facility. Do not allow illegal and dangerous obstructions. Be careful where you place your turnstiles. Make sure your graphics system works to your advantage and to the crowd's advantage by helping them get to their seats and other conveniences and exits as quickly and safely as possible.

10. Develop an emergency evacuation plan.

Some other comments and observations by the Cincinnati Task Force worth noting here are:

1. A clean, well-maintained building and a hassle-free atmosphere will do much to reduce crowd tension.

2. Be in control of the stage and the attraction. Do not allow the attraction to overly or dangerously excite a crowd.

3. Before and after an event and during intermission, play soft, soothing music.

4. Do not turn the lights off completely. Allow at least three footcandles of light to illuminate aisles and emergency exits.

5. Keep people without floor tickets off the floor.

6. Keep aisles clear.

7. Make sure the public address system works and that its volume and clarity are adequate.

The International Association of Auditorium Managers (IAAM) recently established the IAAM Foundation. The first major project to be undertaken by the Foundation will be a crowd management study. The project is an outgrowth of years of behind-the-scenes planning and research on the part of Dr. Robert Sigholtz, the Foundation's first Chairman, and Dr. Irving Goldaber, an internationally known sociologist, specializing in the study of social violence.

The first phase of the project calls for a comprehensive review of crowd control literature, supplemented by the combined field experience of facility managers within the IAAM.

Goldaber recently stated that:

Crowd management encompasses all that is undertaken by professional personnel in the public assembly field to facilitate the comfort and safety and lawful nature of crowd gatherings so that those in attendance may have satisfying experiences. Crowd management activity occurs in both the inner administrative office and the outer public parking lot. It focuses, for example, on aspects of executive decision-making, managerial expertise, supervisory responsibility, public relations, patron services, traffic regulations and safety and security. It includes among its concerns such matters as architecture and interior design, food and other items either provided or vended to those present, and the sociological capability to read "the mood of the crowd." An effective crowd management approach begins with the first blueprint for the event or assemblage and ends when the last patron has vacated the area. For this reason, crowd management deals with planning, preparing, conducting and taking remedial action. It is the sum of all that is undertaken to obviate the need for crowd control action involving forceable restraint.

§ 19-6. Crowd Violence.

A growing problem in facilities throughout the United States is that of crowd or spectator violence, especially at rock concerts which attract large numbers of young people. Often there is a metamorphosis that occurs when certain fans go through the turnstiles. They virtually abandon the constraints normally placed upon them by society and feel totally free to act in an uninhibited manner, including the physical destruction of property, physical threats and other antisocial behavior.

Contributing factors to crowd violence, according to Goldaber, involve a number of low-level sources of tension including close and involuntary contact with strangers, abnormal physical discomfort, and competition for space, goods, services and information. These tend to frustrate fans and make them more irritable and belligerent than they are when they are alone or in smaller groups. Crowds also provide a degree of anonymity which encourages troublemakers to act more irresponsibly than they might in situations where they can easily be identified and punished.

Everything possible should be done to make the facility hassle free and comfortable. A fact of life is that large public assembly facilities — and sport facilities in particular — when compared to those offered to other crowds, are often somewhat inefficiently designed, uncomfortable and unattractive. This atmosphere and the fast and easy flow of such basic emotions as elation, anger, panic and vengeance are contagious within a crowd and may create so-called mass hysteria. Moreover, sporting events regularly draw the largest crowds of any public event.

People lose control when they identify so fully with an athlete or a team that they begin feeling physically aggressive. Crowds at sporting events regularly respond by cheering, booing, hissing, stamping their feet, waving their fists, screaming, and threatening and yelling at officials.

One problem in particular offers facilities a serious dilemma. Because competition for events is becoming greater and facilities are forced to offer overly competitive rent deals, the facilities must exploit their concessions and other ancillary sources of income in order to make a profit. The sale of alcoholic beverages unquestionably contributes to fan violence and crowd disorders. Yet, beer, wine and cocktails are perhaps the most profitable items a facility sells. The facility manager must therefore exercise close and constant care in the monitoring of the alcoholic beverages sales and be prepared to call them to a halt when necessary — even if it means giving up an extremely lucrative source of revenue.

Another problem which complicates your ability to manage a crowd is violence on the part of professional athletes. Richard B. Horrow, Executive Director, Miami Sports and Exhibition Authority, is the author of *Sports Violence — The Interaction Between Private Law-Making and The Criminal*

Law (1980, Carrollton Press, Inc.), in which Horrow emphasizes the alarming trend toward excessive violence in all professional sport. The well-known comedian, Rodney Dangerfield once quipped that he "went to a fight the other night and saw a hockey game break out." As athletes become more competitive and as the pressures to succeed become stronger, the possibility of violent conduct during a game increases, and this causes a spontaneous reaction with the crowd. Athletes are taught to be aggressive and to be tough because one of the skills of sport is violence. The fans expect and demand violence, and the players themselves accept the fact that many less talented players must be more violent to compensate for inferior talent.

If violence erupts on the playing surface, the security team should be prepared to respond. For instance, they should be watching the crowd and not the event. They should be polite but firm with any troublemakers who, if uncooperative, must be ejected.

One way to effectively manage a crowd and contain violence is to conduct an advanced assessment of the anticipated audience. This will help decide on the necessary level of security staffing. The event manager must bear in mind that security requirements are not the same for all events. Each event has its own particular personality and should be considered separately from all others. Obtain as much advance information as possible about the audience and the performers and then plan and be prepared. Good sources of information are counterparts at other facilities where the event was already held. They can describe the nature of the crowd and how it reacted during the event. The box office is also a good source of such information, since it has already had contact with part of the crowd during the ticket-buying process. The local police department should also check with its counterpart in other cities to determine what type of criminal activities and disorders occurred.

§ 19-7. Security and Emergency Procedures Manual.

There is no substitute for well-trained security staff. The most basic training tool for security personnel is a written manual covering as many pertinent topics as possible in plain and simple language. Use the manual to welcome and indoctrinate your security personnel. Emphasize that they are there to provide professional service on behalf of the facility. The manual can provide security personnel with guidelines and help them be alert and safety conscious.

The manual should contain a clear written outline of the chain of command in your facility. Moreover, it should describe what is expected of the security staff. For example, security officers should:

1. Be able to handle any normal situation which they may encounter and know how or where to get help if required.
2. Be alert at all times while on duty. Always be on the watch for activities, conditions or hazards which could result in injury or damage to persons or property.
3. Have an attitude that reflects proper human and public relations.
4. Be helpful. When fans arrive at an event they are usually confused. The location is unfamiliar and they are often late and do not know where to go or what to do.

5. Be courteous but firm at all times.
6. Properly obey and execute all orders given by superiors.
7. Take pride in their duties and maintain a keen interest in their job. This will show in the manner in which they perform their duties and will be recognized by all who come in contact with them.
8. Act without haste or undue emotion. Do not argue with visitors, fellow employees, or supervisors. Present a calm friendly bearing.
9. Remember that courtesy earns respect, knowledge gets results, patience receives cooperation, service increases good will, and the total application of these qualities gets the job done well.

Written procedures are one thing, but if they are not read, understood and carried out by the people on the front line they are meaningless. Such service will be exemplified on their part by the use of tact, friendliness and courtesy while maintaining a professional attitude in the performance of their duties. Let them also know that they are important members of your professional crowd management team.

Given these general expectations, the manual should also contain a section on the specific duties and responsibilities of each job classification:

A. *Usher Supervisor.*

The usher supervisor should supervise, not usher. This means that he or she will be free to respond to problem areas. Each event should have an appropriate number of supervisors assigned according to the total number of ushers being used and the anticipated size of the crowd. Supervisors should be alert for any problems or unusual difficulties encountered by any usher under his or her supervision and offer assistance and advice if needed.

B. *Usher.*

An usher, on the other hand, has the primary responsibility for making certain the patron is assisted to the proper seat. In addition, an usher should:

1. Be certain that each patron is properly greeted.
2. Check each ticket completely for event, date, performance time, as well as section, row and seat.
3. Offer clear directions to seating locations and service accommodations.
4. Act on customer complaints. If necessary, refer complaints to the Usher Supervisor.
5. Keep aisles clear at all times.
6. Ask patrons to surrender any bottles or cans in their possession. If necessary, refer such a problem to the Usher Supervisor or a policeman.
7. Try to anticipate problems and act before they become serious.
8. Enforce house policies such as "no smoking."
9. Use a flashlight to assist patrons to their seats when the lights are down.
10. Be sensitive to the needs of mobility-impaired people such as senior citizens and handicapped persons.

C. *Event Security Officer.*

The event security officer is a key figure in the safety of each facility. He or she is a figure representing authority and safety to the various patrons and visitors of your facility. Their professionalism and courteous attitude will make your patrons feel they are in good hands. By an officer's presence alone, potential trouble situations may be avoided. Specifically, the security officer is responsible for the following:

    1. Reporting on time and ready to work.
    2. Wearing the proper and complete uniform.
    3. Following instructions by reading and memorizing post orders.
    4. Remaining at an assigned post until relieved.
    5. Exhibiting proper courtesy at all times.
    6. Not eating, drinking or smoking while on duty.
    7. Being alert to minors possessing alcoholic beverages.

Another key element of the manual is the section on emergency procedures. For this portion of the manual you should solicit the input and written approval of the state and local fire marshal, police and civil preparedness departments, and your contractual medical and ambulance services.

The most common form of emergency is the bomb threat. The manual should, therefore, describe the role of employees, as well as the overall emergency evacuation procedure. Employees should be instructed to cover assigned areas carefully when requested to make a search, noting any unusual package or item. If one is found, they should be instructed not to touch it, but to notify the supervisor immediately.

In case of the necessity to evacuate the facility, event security officers should follow any instructions given very carefully. They should always remain calm and in command of their area, never using any panic-producing language such as "bomb," "fire," or "explosion." Many lives may depend on their calm and efficient actions.

Many facilities use the Phase Coding System which was designed as a safe method of conveying to event personnel the type of problem, location and action to be taken without alarming any members of the general public that happen to overhear radio transmissions, phone conversations, or person-to-person communication. The purpose of this coding is to prevent the greatest of all threats — panic.

The Phase System is an escalating and compartmentalized plan to help prevent another great threat — overreaction, while simultaneously informing all necessary personnel of the type, location and current status of the problem.

Phase 1A indicates smoke, water, a small crowd disturbance, or an equipment or lighting failure. Descriptive information should be provided on the location, size, seriousness and nature of the problem. Security should clear the immediate area until the problem has been controlled.

Phase 1B indicates a bomb threat has been received and all staff should immediately conduct a search for an explosive device. Notification should be given when the search is completed.

Phase 2A indicates a serious fire, flood, crowd disturbance, equipment failure or other problem. Security should be posted at the location of the problem and control access to the area.

Phase 2B indicates that a suspicious package or device has been located. The fire department and police bomb squad should be dispatched to investigate and decide whether or not a full or limited evacuation is necessary. Ambulances should be called for standby.

Phase 3A indicates the need for an orderly evacuation due to failure of the regular power system. This will most likely result in the cancellation of the performance. An appropriate pre-recorded message should be activated over the public address system and ambulances should be called for standby.

Phase 3B indicates the need for an immediate emergency evacuation. Appropriate alarms must be sounded and pre-recorded messages activated. Ambulances should be called for standby and the security/usher staff should begin to calmly but firmly evacuate patrons. Security should also be sure no patrons re-enter the building, regardless of the reason.

The Facility Manager must take great care to clearly establish the chain of command when it comes to emergency evacuation. It must be clearly understood who has the right and responsibility to call for an evacuation. In most cities this responsibility is that of the ranking on-site member of the police bomb squad.

A way to ensure that proper procedures will be followed is to have a telephone bomb report form. If any member of the house or security staff takes a call during an event, this form or one very similar to it should be used and as much pertinent information as possible should be recorded and immediately conveyed to the event manager or police department.

Most people who actually put a bomb in a building want to be caught or want the bomb found before it goes off. If possible, keep the person talking because he/she may disclose the location of the bomb. Having the phone operator trained by the police bomb squad would be very helpful.

Preparation for emergency evacuation is absolutely critical. Drills should be conducted on a regular basis. A standardized routine should be developed for each type of event. Once the routine has been set, it should be typed and posted in strategic locations such as the office, the security room, the usher's locker room, backstage, lunch rooms and refreshment stands. The facility and its patrons are always vulnerable. The best defense is a plan carefully evolved to fit the facility and the organization. Being able to evacuate a facility in an emergency with a minimum of injury or loss of life is one of the greatest challenges and responsibilities.

§ 19-8. Search and Seizure.

The issue of search and seizure is a complex but important aspect of security and crowd management. Most facility managers believe the procedure is necessary in order to keep people from bringing beverage containers and weapons into facilities. But, each facility manager must be very cognizant of the requirements of the fourth amendment of the United States Constitution.

Normally, the event manager in conjunction with the facility manager and chief of police decide if a particular event (usually a rock concert) will draw a crowd of unruly patrons, many of whom will likely be in possession of bottles, cans, and other containers as well as assorted weapons and drugs. In such instances the facility's own security force and ticket takers must be supplemented by additional personnel to prevent these items from being brought into the facility. This relieves tension and protects people from being injured by objects used as missiles. But be sure to obtain sound legal advice from your attorney before you establish any procedures for search and seizure.

The September 1982 issue of *Auditorium News* (the official monthly publication of the International Association of Auditorium Managers) contained a very interesting article by Jerome O. Campane, a Special Agent of the FBI Academy, entitled "Amendment IV, The Fourth Amendment at a Rock Concert." The Article provides an enlightening update of the issue and offers some guidance on how to conduct a legal search and seizure operation. Campane indicates that the courts agree that civic authorities are entitled to take certain steps to prevent injury to the public and to provide protection for those who attend events by prohibiting the introduction of contraband and dangerous items. However, this cannot be done in a manner which violates a person's rights under Amendment IV, which states that "[t]he right of the people to be secure in their persons, houses, papers, and effects, against unreasonable searches and seizures, shall not be violated, and no warrants shall issue, but upon probable cause, supported by oath or affirmation, and particularly describing the place to be searched, and the persons or things to be seized." Therefore have an attorney provide you with written search and seizure guidelines — and perhaps even occasional on-site supervision.

Campane offers some practical advice on how to cope with the problem. For example, a notice on tickets and signs at your entrances will give the impression of voluntary consent. The availability of checkrooms for the deposit and safekeeping of large packages will also help, as will the elimination of festival seating which will avoid the rush through the turnstiles as doors first open, thus giving the security force a better opportunity to observe the patrons. When items are seized or arrests made, mass media publicity of the fact may help convince patrons not to bring such prohibited items to future events. Above all, Campane states, any procedure should be uniformly applied. It should not be employed only at rock concerts and only against teenagers. The facility manager should carefully document any incidents of violence and unruly behavior and apply this screening procedure at all events where such conduct is likely to take place. These procedures are obviously not all inclusive and again you are urged to meet with an attorney for specific guidelines regarding search and seizure procedures.

§ 19-9. Summary/Conclusion.

This chapter has provided the facility manager with a considerable amount of practical information that can be directly applied to his own operation. Because the business of facility management is exciting and because it is, therefore, easy to get caught up in the "glamour" of the events hosted, it is sometimes possible to lose sight of the most important responsibility — protecting the lives of patrons. By preparing for the worst, the facility manager will make each event a professionally managed, safe and enjoyable experience for the public and the performers. This, more than any other factor, will enhance such a manager's reputation and assure the success of a facility.

Chapter 20

ACTIVITY CENTERS

By

Geoffrey Miller

§ 20-1. Introduction.

There are hundreds of variables which make each manager's job different and unique in the area of facility management. There are certain characteristics and problems, however, which are common to all facilities. Budgeting pressures are forcing the owners and managers of activity centers to be much more creative on how the facilities are used. The days when the term "down time" was used are coming to a close. Increased traffic and use of the facility lead to the need for more efficient scheduling, security, supervision and maintenance. As facility management becomes more of a science and the emphasis is on efficiency, the trend is to give responsibility for the building to a single individual, the facility manager.

This chapter will attempt to discuss the important areas of operation for the facility manager. Policy development, planning, scheduling, personnel management, supervision, security and maintenance are areas which need constant attention by the facility manager. In addition, a brief examination of the shared facility in a collegiate setting can serve as a guide for what appears to be an indication of things to come.

§ 20-2. Policy Development and Implementation.

The activity center manager, whether he is opening a new facility or taking over one already in operation, is at an extreme disadvantage if operational policies have not been developed. If there are no policy guidelines, and decisions are left to the facility manager, it will lead to inconsistencies and inequities in the manager's decision-making process. For example, if there are no policies relating to the length of court time or reservation procedures for racquetball, the manager will inevitably make subjective decisions as disputes arise. Clearly, 95% of these disputes could be eliminated if established policies were listed.

Although fair and equitable policies take time and energy to develop, they are the basis of the activity-center manager's administrative operation. Once a policy is developed, the manager has something concrete to work with and also develops a rationale which can be explained to the public. If the policies are not in place, or if the policies are creating difficulties in the operation of the facility, it is imperative that a policymaking body be created to formulate new policies or change the existing ones. All too often these policies are decided upon without the input of the manager. It is important that the manager, who will be implementing these policies, have input and be involved in all policy decisions affecting the activity center.

271

Operational policies do not guarantee a problem-free facility, but it will improve the decision-making procedure. Administrators often fail to see the long-term ramifications of allowing exceptions to be made relating to policy. Once an exception is made for one facility-user, other users will inevitably be seeking the same treatment and beseeching the manager to go even further. *Take the time to formulate fair policies and then enforce them with no exceptions.* If users complain about a specific policy, ask them to formalize the complaint. Take the formalized complaint through the established decision and policymaking process. It is easier to change a policy than to continuously make exceptions.

§ 20-3. Scheduling and Planning.

Planning and organization are two of the central characteristics necessary for success. Although the routine duties of day-to-day operations may dominate the activity center manager's time, short-term and long-range planning can make the scheduling process less stressful and the job more enjoyable.

When preparing a schedule for the activity center, the manager must be organized and must establish (and be prepared to defend) priorities that allow one group to have access to the facility over another. In the case of the purely recreational facility, this prioritization process may not be as essential. However, most managers are dealing with a number of different program offerings. Either way, policies need to be established which clearly define the priority structure. For instance, Guilford College owns and operates the Physical Education Center, but leases time to the local YMCA. The college has requests for physical education classes, varsity intercollegiate practices and contests, and intramural offerings. The YMCA has class offerings and its membership has need of open recreational space. It is obvious that a need exists for a set of priorities that the manager can use to schedule each of the areas in the facility.

Once the priorities are agreed upon and set, the logical way to proceed is to obtain requests for space from each constituency. If communication is poor between the various groups competing for space in the facility, the more difficult it becomes for the manager to schedule efficiently. Every effort must be made to encourage communication and the meeting of scheduling deadlines. See the Appendix, at the end of this chapter for a form that is color coded which must be submitted two weeks in advance of the date for which reserved time is being requested. Depending on the number of spaces available (i.e., pool, racquetball courts, weight room, gymnasiums, seminar rooms, etc.) and the number of requests received construct an activities calendar board on a monthly and yearly basis. The board, displayed in a prominent place in the manager's office, can be a tremendous help in answering spontaneous questions relating to new requests for space and for rentals, particularly those that come in by phone and need immediate answers. A chalkboard, divided in grid form by masking tape, is an effective way to maintain and display the monthly schedule. By placing the board directly across the room, it can be referred to at any time by the manager or his staff. A master calendar notebook should also be kept close at hand so that the whole year's calendar is always at the manager's fingertips.

Ultimately, it is up to the manager to implement the priority system and schedule available spaces. Inevitably, there are conflicts or request overlaps, and it is important that the manager detect these as soon as possible and inform the respective groups so they can adjust and make alternate plans. It is also important to save the original request forms to avoid misunderstandings about what was originally requested.

Once the schedule has been developed based on the request forms, open space can then be determined and opened up for recreational space or rentals. Whenever possible, one area is kept open at the P.E. Center for recreation to accommodate the large number of students and YMCA members who use the facility. As a way of helping the "spontaneous user" of the facility, devise a recreation sheet which lists when spaces are open for free play on a monthly basis. This sheet is available at a check-in or equipment desk, or sent in the mail to all the individuals who use the activity center. This sheet is particularly helpful during the busy months for activities such as basketball (December, January, and February), and minimizes ill will that is associated with patrons coming into the facility and finding no space open for recreation and exercise. Communication is essential when gathering the information to put together a schedule, but it is imperative to communicate that information to the various constituencies who use the facilities.

A final concern of the manager in the scheduling process is rentals. A decision must be made by the policymaking body, about rental requests. Who can rent the facility? What about liability insurance? What fees will be charged? What kind of staffing arrangements need to be made for the rental period? These are valid questions and need to be handled.

In theory, all rental groups should have equal access to the facility. It may be prudent, however, for your policymaking body to define the qualifications for rental. If there are restrictions, they need to be made very clear. For instance, many nonprofit activity centers are reluctant to rent to groups who plan to use the facilities for a fund-raising activity. It is important to issue a contract to rental groups with specific terms regarding the nature of the request and the fees to be charged. The rental group must furnish proof of suitable insurance to indemnify the activity center against any liability arising from the use of the facility. In this day and age of multi-million dollar lawsuits, the manager must pay close attention to adequate and suitable insurance for all rental groups. A rate schedule should reflect the real costs that include utilities, labor, and the "wear and tear" of the facility. It is prudent to charge on an hourly basis for one half day use and add a full per diem charge. It is important to make necessary arrangements for adequate staffing which is well-trained to supervise the rental activity. It is a mistake to allow the rental group to provide staff, because control of the facility is lost.

§ 20-4. Personnel Management and Supervision.

Many factors influence the manager's leadership style, but no role is more important than that of the organizational leader. In any situation, qualified individuals must be chosen who have a sense of pride and responsibility for their job and the facility. An administrator's behavior and use of authority in directing employees are critical factors in determining the effectiveness of the leadership style or pattern. Heinz Weihrich points out, in his article in the April, 1979 edition of *Management Review,* that a leadership pattern is a function of balance between the "use of authority by the manager" and the "area of freedom for subordinates." Many managers, particularly those in collegiate environments, are required to handle a number of diverse areas of responsibility. This balance becomes crucial in those situations in which the facility manager needs to rely heavily on his subordinates.

Individual managers ultimately decide upon a leadership pattern or style that depends upon the number of employees and the structure of the organization. Beyond "style" there are a few steps which are critical to effective personnel management. It is imperative to formulate accurate and sufficient job descriptions for each of the positions on the staff. A job description not only provides a means of evaluating an employee's performance, but it prevents disagreements or misunderstandings that undocumented conversations frequently create. Since the job description is discussed by both parties, communication will be enhanced, and a pattern will be set for future discussions on job responsibilities and performance. As a job description changes, it is essential to update and share these alterations with the employees. It is helpful to use a job description with student and work-study employees. For those in facilities where student employees are a possibility, or necessity, a detailed job description is very helpful. Students are frequently preoccupied with other matters and the way to gain attention is through a contract or job description, signed by both the employee and manager, outlining duties and responsibilities. The development of job descriptions for each position is tedious, but time well-spent at the front end of the facility operation. It will effectively reduce the number of misunderstandings between the manager and the employees.

Another essential element of personnel management is the supervision of a facility and its operations through the permanent staff. If the activity center includes a pool or natatorium, supervision is a high priority. A pool can be a dangerous place or an "attractive nuisance," as well as a health hazard if it is not staffed adequately and professionally. The activity center manager cannot take responsibility for the day-to-day operation of the pool and maintain other facets of the managerial duties. The obvious key to safety and efficient management of a pool is the selection of a qualified and conscientious individual to run it. The pool manager should have flexibility to perform pool maintenance, schedule lifeguards, establish rules of operation, and order essential equipment without the burden of constantly clearing everything through the manager. Weekly or bi-weekly meetings with the aquatics director to review and discuss any particular items which may arise is recommended. It is through these meetings that emergency procedures, lifeguard regulations and maintenance procedures can be defined.

The supervision of the other areas in the facility may not be as vital as the pool, but it is still important to the day-to-day operation of the facility. It is important to employ a staff member in the building at all times who is mobile (not tied to a desk or phone) who can handle the spontaneous problems which inevitably arise. An activity center locker room can be a prime area for abuse and/or theft. The wrong kind of shoe or equipment can easily damage a synthetic or wood floor, racquetball court, tennis court, or other areas in the center. In addition, there are times when certain kinds of free play or activity are not acceptable because of a class conflict. These problems need to be handled by the facility manager or someone on the staff to maintain the facility and keep it attractive for people to come and enjoy.

§ 20-5. Security.

The kind of security the activity center chooses is largely dependent upon budget and the facility's design. The activity center manager must make the decision about security early in the operation of the facility, keeping in mind the experience preferred by the user of the facility. In the planning stages of a facility, get advice from security experts and incorporate their suggestions into the building design. Whatever the system agreed upon, the public's experience is a vital consideration.

For instance, an outside service can be hired, but the manager must weigh the pros and cons of the impact of a uniformed attendant versus a non-uniformed individual to perform the security. Frequently, a non-uniformed employee can check I.D. cards for admittance and also lend a warmer and more hospitable greeting to those who come to use the facility. In addition, this individual can perform other functions such as switchboard operation and typing. If an electronic system for check-in is affordable, the manager must also decide before purchasing whether there will be personal contact with the user of the facility.

If a receptionist is used, consider the requirement of photo-I.D. cards instead of ones with only the name, address and expiration date. Although the choice of photo-I.D. cards results in greater capital expenditure at the front end of the operation, the cards will clearly pay for themselves in the long run as they diminish abuse and therefore ensure that the only people using the facility are those who have a right to do so. With the receptionist system, it is essential that all other entrances be closed off and that emergency exits be secured so that they are only used during emergencies. This is particularly relevant when the facility includes a pool or natatorium. Depending upon the situation, the frustration of keeping up with exit doors may be a continuous hassle. However, the chances are good that your facility is something people want to get into and, as the cliche states, "where there's a will there's a way." The public is going to try to enter your facility in any way possible. As manager, do everything possible to direct all traffic through the main entrance and past the building's receptionist.

Give keys only to those who absolutely need them for opening and closing, or equipment check-out. This is sound advice and will prove to be helpful. The manager needs a set of master keys, as does his assistant and possibly one other staff member. If a receptionist is present during the hours of building operation, it is possible to set up a key check-out system where other staff members, instructors, and maintenance personnel can obtain a set of master keys. By keeping tight control of keys, the activity center manager can more efficiently control the facility. Whatever system you decide upon, be conscious of how little time it takes for "lost" keys to be copied and subsequently require the changing of all your locks.

§ 20-6. Maintenance.

The maintenance and upkeep of the facility is a vital part of the activity center manager's job. The way a building looks and the standards that are set for its maintenance have a great deal to do with the public's total experience in the facility, and, in many cases, has a large bearing on whether the public decides to continue to use the facility. In fitness centers, spas, and racquetball clubs where the operation is contingent upon the selling of memberships, the maintenance considerations become even more critical.

A well-chosen janitorial and maintenance staff can add to the success of the manager. It is important for the manager to take daily tours through the facility to note any problems or potential trouble spots. Many managers carry a small hand-held tape recorder as they inspect the facility and make comments as they go. The items can be listed afterwards into immediate or long-range project categories and then shared with the maintenance staff. Take into consideration any "down" periods when traffic in the facility is limited, so that major maintenance or painting operations can be scheduled during those periods. Also, periodic meetings with the maintenance staff can assist in developing preventive maintenance schedules which will help to avert major problems or shut downs which might interfere with the smooth day-to-day operation of the facility. In situations where the maintenance is performed by an outside group or a college maintenance staff which has other responsibilities besides the facility, the manager needs to keep accurate records of work that is requested and be flexible in making preparations for the work. Regardless of the particulars of each individual situation, the activity center manager must be sensitive to and involved with the maintenance and efficient upkeep of the facility for which he is responsible. Anything less than a conscientious effort in this area can soon result in not only the rapid deterioration of the facility but also in deterioration of the relationship between the building staff and those who use the facilities.

§ 20-7. General Operations.

In summary, create a checklist for the everyday operation of the activity center. This checklist cannot encompass all the particulars of each manager's situation, but it can be a helpful guide for those who are willing to pick up on general suggestions. The items include the following:

1. Be visible, accessible, and willing to deal in a prompt and professional manner with problems that come up.
2. Make certain at the start of each day that the receptionist, maintenance person, or the staff member responsible for opening up has checked on the operation of the essential equipment that affects space temperatures, hot water in the showers, pool temperature, and

similar duties. Two-thirds of the complaints a manager receives are related to things which directly affect the public's experience at the facility. A routine check every morning will enable the manager to prevent potential problems.

3. Each morning, check the daily building schedule for special events or anything that could potentially alter the normal routine. On Mondays, check the whole week's schedule in similar fashion. If the facility is used as a back-up in inclement weather, there will be times when it will be essential to make a decision about going to a "rainy day" schedule. This is particularly relevant when there are outdoor tennis courts, programs that are taught outdoors, or athletic teams which need to have space indoors for practice in bad weather.

4. Check on phone messages, mail, injury report forms, or particular problems from the day before and prioritize and follow up in the appropriate manner.

5. Set aside a period of time according to the day's calendar, without the interruption of the phone, to complete paperwork. Failure to discipline time and keep up with the paperwork associated with administrative duties can be problematic. A part of this time should be devoted to updating current schedules and working on long-range scheduling plans, particularly if the facility is used by a number of different constituencies who need some advance notice of changes and/or alterations. Establish scheduling deadlines and enforce them.

6. In the morning, set up appointments that are necessary during the day with staff, maintenance people, aquatics director, sales representatives and other publics. Keep enough time between appointments to pick up on any spontaneous situations that may develop which need immediate attention.

7. Before leaving the office at the end of the day, communicate with the person(s) on the staff who will be remaining until the facility is closed. Be sure to advise them of any special changes in the schedule or areas that need attention.

§ 20-8. The Shared Facility.

A cooperative-based facility which was planned and built with consideration for several constituencies is an example of shared arrangement that is becoming common throughout the United States. Four years ago Guilford College, a four-year liberal arts institution, and a local branch of the Metropolitan YMCA of Greensboro, North Carolina, entered into an arrangement for cooperative use of a facility.

The "town and gown" athletic center was conceived when representatives from the college and the local YMCA realized that each was considering building its own separate facility within a four-mile radius of each other. The college had decided to construct a new building to supplement its forty-year-old gymnasium which was inadequate and failed to meet the needs of the students. The Guilford College Community Branch of the YMCA, operating out of an elementary school, with little equipment and limited programs, also was trying to meet pressing needs for a building to house its operations. Conservative estimates predicted that it would take the YMCA close to 10 years to schedule and carry out the capital fund drive necessary to finance a $2.5 million structure. The initial contacts from college administrators answered the YMCA's needs and it marked the beginning of years of research and planning. Both groups realized the waste of resources for the community to build two expensive sport/recreational facilities with two separate administrative staffs, since the buildings would be vacant part of the time.

The careful planning which followed helped create a structure that is both unique and functional in design. In addition to renovating the old gymnasium and creating additional locker room space, a $4 million structure was constructed and connected to the old facility. The 64,581-square-foot structure includes a 25-meter, six-lane pool with a separate diving tank, a weight room, locker and shower facilities, four handball and racquetball courts and a field house with three regulation basketball courts that can be converted to use for tennis and volleyball. There is seating for 2,500 persons.

The end result is a contractual situation where the college owns and operates its Physical Education Center facility, and then leases time and space to the YMCA based on 40% of the operating cost. The rent includes all utilities, maintenance, equipment and a percentage of the salary of staff people who serve both institutions such as the building director, front desk receptionists, lifeguards and equipment desk employees.

In similar situations, a full commitment by both institutions, particularly the staffs, is an absolute must. There is little chance for success if anyone is not fully committed to the belief that the decision to share the facility is best for both institutions. With this in mind, all parties involved in the relationship need to maintain sensitivity and flexibility necessitated by the uniqueness of the situation.

Secondly, there is a distinct need for planning and putting everything in writing. The planning process includes asking the endless list of "what if" questions and establishing specific guidelines for priority usage. Putting everything in writing helps to keep all the related boards and committees informed and ensures that all policies are correctly interpreted before becoming effective. This includes the drafting, development and eventual signing of a contract between the two groups which covers the specifics of budget, budget review, staff, insurance and payment schedules.

Finally, it is important to employ a building director to oversee the operation and scheduling of the facility. The facility director is necessary to provide an objective approach to scheduling, and he or she can eliminate possible conflicts, ensure a more functional use of the facility, and administrate the operation of the building and its staff.

The joint utilization of the Physical Education Center has not been without its scheduling, security and coverage complications, but the cooperative arrangement has unquestionably resulted in the following accomplishments:

1. The center, open for 92 hours per week, is fully staffed and utilized with very little "down" time. The building is open a great deal more than either group could afford through separate staffing.

2. The joint utilization serves to bring the community and the college into closer contact through a variety of scheduled programs and intercollegiate events. The citizens of the community come onto the campus and therefore feel a part of the college through the YMCA. For example, the YMCA is encouraged to enter teams in the college intramural leagues, and the college offers football and basketball season tickets at a reduced rate to YMCA members.

3. Although it is difficult to assess the actual cost savings, each group is undoubtedly saving a great deal compared to the cost to operate separate buildings. This is accomplished through the sharing of the daily operational costs (staff, pool maintenance, utilities, housekeeping supplies, work-study student labor, athletic equipment and towels).

4. The YMCA is able to offer and supervise summer programs in which college students and the college community may participate without having to supply a full complement of staff. Due to the operation of these programs, many summer jobs are available to students in summer school and those living in the area.

Both the college and the YMCA not only endorse this concept of shared facilities, but also highly recommend it to any groups where this type of cooperation might be feasible. With the rising cost of construction and maintenance of athletic facilities, it is expedient for all to work together to reduce costs. To the YMCA, the cooperative agreement is vital as it provides a home for its members and programs. To the college, the arrangement is a way of providing expanded hours and a first-class facility to its students, staff and community. This situation is the first example of a cooperative venture planned from the beginning. The practicality of the venture represents a possible option to the traditional use of sports facilities in the past.

§ 20-9. Summary/Conclusion.

Budgeting pressures and increased use of activity centers place additional burdens on the facility manager, necessitating greater efficiency in planning and overseeing total use.

The facility manager must formulate or have a strong voice in formulating a fair policy as to use. Once in force, the policy must be adhered to by all users. Complaints must be formalized before policy changes are considered by the manager.

While the manager must deal with day-to-day matters, careful long- and short-range planning is essential to a smooth, ongoing operation.

The scheduling of space is critical, with priorities clearly defined and followed. An excellent way in which the manager can both demonstrate to a client and give quick answers to requests for space is to maintain master sheets and a large chalkboard in his/her office for easy referral. Once legitimate requests for ongoing space needs have been plugged into the schedule, and time and space are allotted for the "spontaneous user," that information should be printed and made available to all users of the facility. The facility's policymaking body must sharply define qualifications and fees for rental of space. The facility manager must provide adequate staffing for events staged by rental groups; this insures control of the facility.

The facility manager must, by his/her actions, set a "style" of leadership which should filter down throughout the staff. Job descriptions for subordinates should be written out and discussed with potential employees to avoid misunderstandings as to expectations of either party. This is especially true when a manager in a college setting hires students.

Since it is impossible for the manager to personally supervise all activities in the facility, he/she must employ extremely capable and dependable persons for key areas. This is particularly true if the facility has that "attractive nuisance," a swimming pool. Also, it is important to employ a staff member who is not tied to a desk or phone and who can handle problems as they arise.

A facility's budget and design should determine its security program. In planning security measures, get advice from experts, and incorporate their suggestions into the building design. Consider pros and cons of uniformed versus non-uniformed security personnel. Choose identification or membership cards which best suit your budget and physical layout. Keep close reign on keys for efficient control. "Lost" keys can be copied quickly and may necessitate the changing of all locks.

The activity center manager must be sensitive to and involved with the maintenance and efficient upkeep of the facility. If the facility is not clean and well-kept, it will neither attract nor hold users. Plan ahead for upkeep such as painting and refurbishing. Remember that the use of outside maintenance firms will require scheduling well in advance.

The effective manager must be accessible to deal with problems that arise; check with employees about "comfort" items such as space and water temperatures; be prepared for special events and the eventuality of putting rainy days schedules into effect; check messages and calendar of events; make appointments with staff and other publics; before leaving for the day, check with staff who will work until they close the facility for the night.

Before entering into a venture in which a facility is to be shared by two organizations, proceed with caution. Visit a facility such as the one at Guilford College, where the college owns the facility and leases time and space to the YMCA. From the beginning of talks, get everything out in the open, and when there is agreement as to sharing and operation, have everything in writing. Then, chances are excellent that a successful cooperative venture awaits.

Appendix

P. E. CENTER SPACE REQUEST FORM

Date of Request: _____

NAME OF SPORT OR GROUP: _____

PERSON REPRESENTING GROUP: _____

DATES REQUESTED: FROM _____ TO _____

TIMES REQUESTED: _____

SPACE(S) NEEDED: _____

NUMBER OF PARTICIPANTS: _____

SPECTATORS: YES ____ NO ____ ESTIMATED NUMBER _____

SPECIAL DETAILS: _____

_____

_____

LAUNDRY NEEDS: _____

TRAINING ROOM NEEDS: _____

_____

PERSON(S) RESPONSIBLE FOR TAKE DOWN AND/OR CLEAN UP: _____

_____

_____

SPACE MUST BE REQUESTED AT LEAST TWO WEEKS IN ADVANCE

Chapter 21

THE FACILITY MANAGER AS
CO-PROMOTER OF EVENTS

By

James Oshust

§ 21-1. Introduction.

The expression "to promote" or "to co-promote" is often used incorrectly. Any facility that charges a percentage rental, or that derives the majority of its business from a percentage of event ticket grosses is in fact a "semi-partner," in a manner of speaking, with the lessee. The facility and its management are in fact involved in the event. They are, along with the promoter, striving for the greatest amount of gross ticket sales possible. The only difference appears to be in the attitude and awareness of the lessor in the lessee (promoter) expense side of the ledger.

§ 21-2. Contractual Relationships.

Among the possible contractual relationships between lessor and lessee are the following:

A. *Co-promotion.*

In co-promotion, most often, a larger rental percentage is garnered by the facility, and within that larger percentage the facility's management has agreed to bear certain costs. Reasonable examples could be a 15 to 20% rental, with the facility charging no additional monies for box office services, purchase of tickets, stagehands or maintenance, etc.

True, there is some gamble, since the show's attendance might be disasterously poor and the additional percentage may turn out to be well below what it cost to provide those previously guaranteed services. Yet, there is the other side of the coin when a show does very well and the three to eight percent margin gross is far more than normally would have been charged the lessee for these services, leaving management with an appreciable amount of additional revenue.

B. *A Promotion or Promoted Event.*

In a promoted event the facility actually engages in guaranteeing or purchasing outright the event in question. Possibly a 60-40, or 50-50 split is incurred, but the facility may actually have to put some of the money up in advance for deposits for the act's services, or during the settlement finds itself paying more out than its incoming share of the gross ticket receipts might have been. Like any business gamble, however, these are the alternatives, win or lose.

C. *Buying or Creating Events.*

It is possible for a facility to buy or create an event which utilizes no middle person or has no involvement with the promoter, where the relationship is directly with the act or service or agency. A facility may also develop events such as a large "flea market" in an exhibition hall where the partners of the facility, private citizens, actually do the physical work and utilize their expertise. The facility provides the back-up service crews, utilities, space and fiscal guarantees. Then the two groups share all surpluses above all in pre-agreed expenses. In certain cases, where the facility provides all the personnel to operate an event it in fact becomes the lessor and lessee, one "in toto."

The facility manager must accept this fact: the arrangement agreement determines the role and thereby the responsibilities. He or she gives up certain prerogatives as the pure "lessor figure," and must accept some of the responsibilities, the difficulties, complexities, work level and efforts of the promoter or show booker. Details that previously were never the concern of the facility manager now become part of the required list of things to be done. The evening of the event there is no "guaranteed rent" or lack of liability. The bottom line of the settlement becomes extremely important for it truly indicates whether the facility has "won or lost."

It is vital that once the manager agrees that his facility will co-promote, or promote, or in some other fashion risk monies or possible revenues, that the manager understands that he has assumed the role of a partner, producer or promoter. One should not be overly impressed by the fact that some buildings will often "co-promote" or be recognized as management known to "promote" many events. To do so is to assume a role and an obligation that may not be desirable. Such a role assumption is to join into a very close relationship with another individual, organization or activity. An observer once remarked that in his hometown it was often said that certain marriages were made in heaven but what confused him was that the divorce court was still located on the first floor of the courthouse. Such is true with any partnership for it is necessary for anyone entering into such a relationship as an event partner to recognize that too often the expression friendship is confused with or considered to be synonymous with partnership.

A partnership is a legal entity created by joining, according to the law, two mutual interests. The law says nothing about the two groups or individuals being compatible, likable, capable of being friends with one another or having anything other than a legally endowed relationship. So be careful when selecting a partner.

§ 21-3. Cautions in Co-Promotion.

The following things should be considered before entering into co-promotions:

Determine if in fact a partnership with another individual or entity, company or building is a possibility. State statutes or local ordinances may preclude such a relationship. Many facilities are owned by cities which are in themselves municipal corporations and as such are creatures of the state.

Such entities may prohibit one department of the city from entering into any type of agreement with another non-municipally controlled entity outside the jurisdiction of the government in question.

Before asking the city attorney or assigned legal representative about this matter, prepare a "brief" of sorts. It should explain in concise terms what is being proposed, how many such activities, the extent of such possible involvement, the desired end results, and how such involvement would vary from your current practices or procedures.

Participate in the writing and developing of any agreement between management and another entity. It is not necessary to be versed in the "legalese" of modern contract law, but it is important to assure the document will not expose you to the unexpected. If the arrangement is to promote an event, will the relationship be as the buyer of the product and/or artist and/or service; or as the distributor of that talent or service to the general public; or is the role one of a vehicle for the artist and/or act, service or promoter to appear or to be used in the facility?

Develop an atmosphere of mutual understanding between management and your staff as well as other pertinent governmental agencies or individuals essential to security endorsement for such "involvement." Make certain they understand the purpose for the involvement and the benefits to be realized. Perhaps a small-scale involvement would be best, serving as a sample of the type activity, rather than a large promotion that could lose several thousands or more dollars, and thus ruin any future participation in such activities. Make each and every member of the management staff an integral part of the "co-promotion" or "promoting" effort.

Regardless of the type of facility, its structure or organizational design, a co-promotion or partnership exists both in the sharing of loss as well as the sharing of any profit. Be cautious of those very "nice terms" wherein 50% of all the proceeds are offered. It is possible that the contract contains provisions that are contrary to assumptions. The difference between reality and expectancy can be expensive.

For example, a young building manager signed a "promotion agreement with a small family-styled show." The terms were excellent inasmuch as they reflected a 50-50 split after agreed-upon advertising costs, facility costs and other items. In his desire to do well, the young manager exceeded the advertising budget by some $1,500 but felt that surely the increased business generated by the sixth performance justified the action. What the young manager found was that he had actually committed himself for payment of at least three meals for the company of some 30 persons, engagement, and the $1,500 additional advertising expense. The promoter had not agreed to share the costs.

Furthermore, the "co-promotion" contract called for certain standard fees to be paid by the building-partner, which included not only local stagehands, but all technical and nonperforming personnel in the company — far greater than the so-called "heads of departments" as might be charged by the ice show or circus or other such major sustaining family events now on the road. When the final settlement was computed, the young manager recognized that although he had received 50% of the revenue, he had in fact absorbed some

80% of the costs, almost a third of which were actually show-related costs and should have been paid by his partner. In this fashion the partner may have received a lesser amount than he might have on a "standard contract" rate, but his partner acquired a contract where the building picked up almost 50% of the show's ongoing operational costs. The net available to the show was far higher than the building's standard contract deal.

It is possible to give an appearance of having been co-promoters of an event when actually serving as a highly skilled professional and comprehensive specialist in the handling of certain details for the lessee. In this role a facility can perform all of the advertising and much of the promotion and publicity duties for the show and be paid for the services. Also the facility arranges for all staffing, stagehands, special material requests, catering if desired and will even handle certain financial arrangements such as submitting necessary artist's payment checks, divisions or split of the revenue to the pertinent parties concerned, including sound and lighting company billings. It is possible to provide extended services like stage and production requirements and other special needs of the event. In this way the facility is very much involved in the event, desires its success greatly and still reaps the greatest amount of revenue for the least amount of risk. This system has been quite popular with a number of promoters since it lessens their initial out-of-pocket expense, modern-day credit requirements and particularly their personnel's time to "work the city."

In any such arrangements, however, the needs of the lessee should be carefully spelled out. Facility management should address itself to responsibility for certain tasks and the methods of reimbursement and compensation, particularly in the case of event cancellation. If the facility has systems or procedures for the fulfilling of lessee needs, management is in a much better position to write those types of terms necessary to protect the facility from unnecessary loss or imprudent acceptance of liability.

§ 21-4. Need for Guidelines.

Although there is no sure formula for success in the fields of partnerships and co-promotions, the following cautions might be of assistance when dealing with the obstacles of inference, irrationality, emotion, public pressure, economic concerns and the very nature of the facility business — that of providing a forum for the presentation of increasingly popular spectator events.

A. *Know the Proposed Associate.*

Such firms as Better Business Bureau, Dun & Bradstreet, fellow facility managers, various legal authorities, police departments, governmental investigative agencies, the trade journals and court records are all sources of information concerning who or what you are being asked to join with on a particular venture.

B. *Require the Prospective Partner or "Associate" to Submit Information Concerning His or Her Background.*

The use of an application for lease form is proper since it allows you the chance to review pertinent data which constitutes the entity who wishes to join with the facility in partnership or co-promotion arrangement.

C. *Take Sufficient Time to Consider and Implement a Partnership.*

Schedule the proposed event eight, ten or more weeks in the future and longer if possible. Don't accept the ploy, "You've got to move now or you will lose the event." Instead of making a hasty decision, offer to rent the facility at a standard card rate, and adopt procedures that allow for the normal introduction and implementation of such an event. If the event is so good, the procedure is more than adequate. Don't trade proven practice for "opportunity" represented to you by some individual of unknown quality.

D. *Seek Legal Advice.*

As has often been stated, "The value of law lies not in the happiness it creates but rather the misery and the suffering it prevents." This is even more substantive in this instance because a partnership, co-promotion or promotion agreement constitutes a legally acceptable tie between two parties in the eyes of the court. Any resulting litigation will be fought in the courts, and by attorneys and all the data and information will be submitted in compliance with existing codes, ordinances, statutes and within the framework of judicially-required procedure and practice.

E. *Participate in the Formation of the Contract.*

This is absolutely necessary so as to clearly define for the local legal counsel, those things that should be addressed. Once such an agreement has been developed and practiced, and procedures have been tested by time and situation, agreements without constant attendance by your attorney are possible. Yet, if a potential partner suddenly decides to vary from an accepted norm, contact your legal advisor.

F. *Insistence Upon Communications With All Parties Involved in an Event Is Imperative.*

If building *A* is contracting with promoter or individual *B* to co-promote or partner with or assists in promoting an event featuring individual *C,* who may be represented by agency *D,* who may be working through the artist's personal representative individual *E,* make sure all those individuals or companies with whom the facility is, in fact, sharing the responsibility for possible loss, perform their functions properly by defining each party's role and detailing such understanding in writing.

G. *Remember the Thin Line That Divides the Permanent Position as Facility Manager and the Assumed Role as Partner or Co-promoter or Promoter, or Agent of an Event.*

Most importantly, do not try to wear two hats at the same time. Particularly, do not try to be all things to all people and to "have it your way" regardless of what happens. If it is necessary to act in the capacity of a facility manager in certain instances, then so define those areas in the agreement.

Furthermore, let the staff know that obligations accepted under the agreement must be fulfilled.

It is important to develop guidelines for all such relationships. Institute "stop guards" in the event plans go awry. Set fiscal limitations as to how much money may be drawn from the box office, who is to pay what portion of the performer's salary, when, and who is to be billed for or responsible for certain activities and materials or supplies, and what shall be the framework and sequence of time regarding the settlement of the show. It is impossible to maintain all the prerogatives of facility management and not be liable for any criticism and/or financial obligations that are inherent in co-promotion, promotion or partner arrangements for any event.

§ 21-5. Special Event Promotion.

Finally, there is the "special event" promotion that actually refers to one of the most important roles building management may assume. Aside from all the discussions of the traveling concert tours, "road shows," "major star events," there is often a very strong need for your involvement in those events that cannot muster or do not have the type of direction and/or impetus to allow them to be successful on their own.

The facility manager is an entertainment leader, director, expert and developer as well as activity implementer for the community. Groups, civic clubs, officials of government, novice promoters and others will seek advice, consultation and assistance. One important service is to help local groups resist the challenge and lure of promoting an event in the entertainment field for fund-raising purposes if such promotion is totally impractical, destined for failure, or totally out of character with the abilities of the group in question. The truly enjoyable part of the job is to help various groups acquire, develop and implement events within their fiscal resources, their promotional abilities and organizational needs.

From a selfish standpoint it is simply good business to provide such assistance. Expertise and encouragement can give the facility another event — one which is oriented to the community and can prove very successful not only from a revenue standpoint but from "polishing" if not increasing the professional image of the facility.

§ 21-6. Summary/Conclusion.

Like all such complex activities the facility manager must determine the ground rules acceptable to both parties. He must document the ground rules in writing. And, most important of all, he must adhere to the ground rules on a continuing basis. Inconsistency is the fatal flaw that will ruin any good promotion. There is no such thing as allowed inconsistency under the law. The law views inconsistency as the fault of one party or another in failing to meet his/her part of an agreement.

Co-promotions, promotions, partnerships and the development of certain events in the name of the facility should be approached as the most exciting and exhilarating part of the facility management profession. Despite the potential returns to be realized, cooperative ventures should be selected with great care. There are times when either the knowledge of certain subjects is insufficient, or financial odds are relatively in favor of the facility. At times the undertakings would become too great a burden. The number and kind of special arrangements to be entered into should receive very careful consideration. If you know your facility, understand your market area and have the confidence of your employer, the involvement in promoted or co-promoted events offers a challenge and a sense of accomplishment for all concerned.

Part 6

LEGAL MANAGEMENT

Chapter 22

RISK ASSESSMENT AND REDUCTION

By

Herb Appenzeller

§ 22-1. Introduction.

The sport manager has added a new responsibility to an already long list of duties: *risk assessment* or *risk reduction.* With unprecedented interest in sport participation, accompanied by a record number of lawsuits, it is essential that the sport manager understand the law as it applies to sport. Risk management, in simple terms, is the practice of assessing the risks inherent in a sport program by a safety audit. After the risks are identified, the sport manager should eliminate or correct the risks that exist in the program. A final step is to help transfer the risk by acquiring medical and/or liability insurance to protect the participants, personnel and the institution or program.

This chapter will consider: (1) Factors that influence liability; (2) recent trends in litigation; and (3) areas of concern for the sport manager. It will offer recommendations that are intended to reduce risks for the sport manager. It is unfortunate, but too often true, that while sport managers are vulnerable to litigation, they often lack the knowledge of the elements of liability, which is essential to operate a safe sports program.

Nancy Frank, a former coach at Greensboro College, designed a liability self-test for those people involved with sport programs to determine their knowledge in the elements of the law as it relates to sport. Her questions come from eight content categories that include: (1) terminology and principles; (2) equipment and facilities; (3) injuries and first aid; (4) activity preparedness; (5) travel and transportation; (6) insurance; (7) civil rights; and (8) supervision. Frank suggests that if the score on the self-test is low that the reader obtain material on the legal aspects of sport from periodicals and books. She also encourages attendance at in-service workshops in the area of liability to keep abreast of current trends in the law as they relate to sport. Frank believes that a basic knowledge of the elements of law is necessary in the daily operation of a sport program. A self-test with correct responses to questions is located in the Appendix at the end of this chapter.

§ 22-2. Factors That Influence Liability.

Sport managers need to recognize and give attention to five factors that can lead to litigation. These include: Ignorance of the law; ignoring the law; failure to act; failure to warn; and expense.

Ignorance of the law is often a leading cause of sport-related litigation. Several examples are illustrative of the problem. In 1973 Congress enacted the Rehabilitation Act into law which has been called the Civil Rights Act for Handicapped People. In 1977 Congress passed the Education For All Handicapped Children Act (Public Law 94-142) which, like the Rehabilitation Act, prohibited discrimination based on handicapping conditions in physical education and sports. Prior to the passage of these two landmark laws, the American Medical Association (AMA) set guidelines for disqualification from certain contact sports for conditions such as uncontrolled diabetes, jaundice, cardiovascular conditions and absence of a paired organ. Although the guidelines were merely recommendations, many physicians and others responsible for the operation of sport programs accepted and enforced them as mandatory requirements.

As a result, many sport personnel still prohibit individuals with disabilities from sport participation, clearly in opposition to federal law. Each year countless athletes with disabilities are forced to seek judicial redress to obtain compliance with established laws.

In 1977 the American Academy of Pediatrics went on record opposing the use of the trampoline in physical education, recreation and sport programs. The Academy based its edict on the fact that while the number of trampoline-related injuries was not unusually large, the number of crippling injuries was significant. Many sport organizations joined together to devise safety guidelines for the participant and instructor in an effort to keep the trampoline in their programs. The American Alliance for Health, Physical Education, Recreation and Dance issued guidelines that, if followed, should reduce the possibility of injury and subsequent liability. Unfortunately many sport managers and other personnel who use trampolines do not know these safety guidelines exist and continue to offer programs that do not follow them, subjecting themselves and others to potentially dangerous situations.

Many people associated with sport programs choose to ignore rules, regulations and laws until they are forced to comply by court order or the threat of a lawsuit. Two examples point out the problem. A large military base received millions in federal aid since it was an impacted area and therefore subject to close scrutiny in the operation of its school programs. School officials, however, admittedly ignored the law regarding Title IX and sex discrimination in its schools and publicly stated that they would not comply until the court forced them to follow the law.

Most states have codes regarding safety guardrails for bleachers in various sport facilities. There is also a national code designed to protect spectators who use bleachers. The unusually large number of bleachers at sports facilities without the required guardrails is proof that the law will be ignored in many instances until a lawsuit is threatened or after an accident occurs.

Failure to act is a leading factor in liability for the sport manager. Robert Waterman, Jr., co-author of the best-seller *In Search of Excellence,* states that one of the most important characteristics of an excellent company is simply *"They Act!"* Most sport managers have good intentions but often lack the ability to act until a serious injury or accident occurs. Two examples illustrate this fact.

A high school athletic director in Kansas reported that he attended an in-service workshop on liability in the sports program. He was determined to inspect the facilities upon his return to school. He reported, however, that he got busy and failed to act on the inspection until it was too late. A spectator at a track meet was hit in the head by a discus thrown into the stands. A Kansas court awarded the injured spectator $100,000 in damages, finding the location of the discus area to be dangerous for spectators who were in the stands nearby. It ruled that the athletic director and school were at fault and guilty of negligence.

A college athletic director requested that the dark bottom of the indoor swimming pool be painted a light color so supervisory personnel could observe swimmers in the pool. The athletic director volunteered to paint the pool's bottom if paint could be purchased, but his request was denied for an alleged lack of funds. On the day following his request, the pool was painted when a student, at a neighboring college, was found at the bottom of its pool by a group of swimmers in an afternoon class. The student had drowned in a morning class but due to the dark bottom of the pool went undetected until later in the day.

The ability to act is one of the top priorities of the safety conscious sport manager.

Failure to warn is one of the key issues in sport litigation today. Although little attention was given to warnings in the past, recent court cases changed all that.

James Sunday, a 20-year-old skier, was seriously injured when his ski became entangled with either a small bush or brush on a novice ski trail in Stratton, Vermont, *Sunday v. Stratton Corp.,* 390 A.2d 398 (Vt. 1978). Sunday, a permanent quadriplegic since the injury, sued the ski resort for negligence in trail maintenance. The Vermont Superior Court awarded him $1.5 million in damages. The major insurance companies that insured the Vermont ski resorts thereafter threatened to cancel all liability policies if the State of Vermont failed to take action to relieve the operators of the ski resorts from the full responsibility for the participants' safety. Vermont depends heavily on revenue from the ski industry and, as a result of the crisis, the Vermont legislature took immediate action by enacting a law known as an "assumption of risk" statute. The statute's intent is to "relieve the ski slope operator of total responsibility and place the burden of safe skiing on the participant."

Due to the enormity of the award in *Sunday,* many ski resorts have changed their advertisement from one boasting of safe trails and quality maintained slopes to signs that warn the skier that skiing can be hazardous to one's health.

In another area, the football helmet has received criticism in recent years and has been the target of numerous lawsuits. In 1980 it was reported that over 100 helmet-related cases alone were pending in the courts with total claims estimated to be over $300 million. The problem is two-fold: First, companies may refuse to gamble on expensive lawsuits and stop producing helmets; second, for those who manufacture helmets, skyrocketing insurance costs for product liability may result in helmets that cost more than high schools or colleges can afford.

The seriousness of the problem is demonstrated by recent court cases involving helmet-related injuries. In these instances the plaintiffs claimed that the key issue in the case was the manufacturer and school officials' failure to warn that catastrophic injury was possible in the sport of football.

A Texas court awarded Mark Daniels, a high school football player, $1.5 million for a crippling injury he received when the top of his helmet caved in while he was making a tackle, *Rawlings Sporting Goods v. Daniels,* No. 6257, Civil Court of Appeals, Tenth Judicial District (Waco, Texas, 1981). The court emphasized the importance and necessity of warning participants in sport activities of the dangers involved in the sport. The Texas court declared that "the failure to warn was negligence" and added that "a product that does not include a warning is dangerously defective."

In Seattle, Washington, Christopher Thompson was seriously injured when he used his head as a battering ram when he was about to be tackled. He claimed at the trial that neither his coach nor the helmet manufacturer properly warned him of the danger of catastrophic injury connected with the helmet. A Washington jury awarded Christopher, a permanent quadriplegic, a landmark $6.4 million. The jury based its award on the fact that the plaintiff had not been warned of the possibility of serious and permanent injury.

Samuel Adams and Mary Ann Bayless (Ref. 1), legal scholars at Washington State University, suggest ways to issue warnings for sport activities that include:

1. Spell out to participants in very specific terms the dangers involved in sports activities.
2. Require staff members to be aware of the latest safety techniques relevant to each activity.
3. Check staff members' knowledge of and proof of adequate conditioning, lead-up and progression in each activity taught.
4. Place an emphasis on injuries that are possible if proper technique is not used in the activity.

Adams and Bayless conclude that it is important to keep records of any material, films, guest speakers or any resource used to communicate the risk of sports participation to the participants.

Ray Perkins, football coach at the University of Alabama, tape-records his talks to his athletes regarding sport safety and warnings. Perkins realizes the need to issue warnings and inform participants of the risks involved in sports participation and the need to keep a record of the warning. His technique is sound procedure in a day of unprecedented litigation in sport.

Expense is another area which, when sport managers face a financial crisis or are unwilling to appropriate funds, the maintenance and inspection of equipment and facilities will inevitably suffer. When this happens, expensive lawsuits may result as illustrated by two cases.

A worker in a high school gymnasium tried to get onto a platform from a step ladder. He grabbed the railing around the platform but it collapsed causing him to fall to his death. *Woodring v. Board of Education of Manhasset Free School District,* 435 N.Y.S.2d 52 (1981). A New York jury awarded his wife $1,400,000 when it discovered that a nut and bolt which should have secured the railing was not in place and that the school failed to provide a program of preventive maintenance or inspection.

An errant puck at a college ice hockey facility struck an eleven-year-old boy who was returning to his seat after a trip to a concession stand. *Benjamin v. State,* 453 N.Y.S.2d 329 (1982). The boy sued the state of New York for its failure to provide protective fencing to ensure the safety of spectators at the facility. The court found that the lack of a protective fence caused the boy's injury and awarded him $24,000 in damages.

It is important that the sport manager resist the temptation to "let things slide" because of a lack of funds or unwillingness to spend money to inspect and maintain equipment and facilities. The cost of inspection and maintenance may be much less than a single award by a court.

§ 22-3. Recent Trends in Litigation.

There are seven trends that have implications for the sport manager. These include the fact that:

1. Today's average citizen is better informed than ever before of individual rights and the law. There is such a prevailing attitude that every injury should be compensated by insurance companies, manufacturers and school systems that society believes have endless financial resources. This attitude and awareness of the law leads to litigation and a future that legal authorities predict will be the most litigious ever.

2. Enormous damage awards are the rule today and million dollar awards are common.

3. All 50 states have reportedly modified the doctrine of governmental immunity with exceptions, insurance, tort claim acts and claim procedures that do not go through the judicial system to resolve conflicts.

4. There is movement toward acceptance of the doctrine of comparative negligence rather than contributory negligence; 39 states reportedly have adopted comparative negligence by 1985 and others are expected to adopt it in the future.

5. Lawsuits dealing with individuals with disabilities continue to escalate faster than those involving discrimination based on race, religion or sex.

6. Lawsuits for injuries involving alleged negligence may be taken out of the negligence area in favor of the constitutional law arena. Legal authorities speculate that lawsuits will be filed under the Civil Rights Act of 1871 when governmental immunity is claimed as a defense by state and local governments. As a result, state and local governments may be compelled to bear the entire cost of liability since Section 1983 of the Civil Rights Act prohibits any action against the federal government.

7. Sport managers will be held to a higher standard of care in the operation of their programs than ever before as the court is placing added responsibility and accountability on the sport manager.

§ 22-4. Areas of Concern for the Sport Manager.

John Weistart and Cym Lowell, writing in the *Law of Sports,* point out that:

> The area of the law of sports which has received the most frequent judicial analysis, and which has produced a correspondingly large body of decisional authority, is the liability which may result from injuries sustained in sports activities. The issues that are raised by the liability cases are actually not very broad, and the question presented by any given case is quite likely to fall within a very narrow applicable legal principle. (Ref. 2)

On the basis of many cases litigated in this area, it is safe to conclude that four areas present concern for the sport manager. These include a lack of supervision, incompetent personnel, defective equipment and unsafe facilities.

A. *Supervision.*

Legal scholars estimate that 80% of all court cases involving alleged negligence for sport injuries deal with some aspect of supervision. The sport manager is expected to provide adequate supervision to insure a safe and efficient operation of the sport program.

Three recent court cases reveal the court's attitude toward the sport manager's responsibility to those under his/her direction.

A tenured administrator in Yonkers, New York, was responsible for supervising the district's interscholastic athletic program. *Monaco v. Raymond,* 471 N.Y.S.2d 225 (1984). A student with a history of heart illness died while playing football. An investigation revealed that the boy played football without parental permission or a pre-participation physical examination. Although the examination was required, the school which the deceased attended and other schools in the district did not comply with the regulation.

The administrator was relieved of his supervisory duties with the interscholastic sport program and reassigned as Director of the Yonkers Education and Cultural Arts Center. A letter of reprimand was put in his file that said in part:

> This is an official reprimand for your failure to ensure the implementation of the rules and regulations for the operation of the interscholastic program in the Yonkers public school system. There is no question but that your position clearly required the overall supervision and evaluation of the program to ensure that state and district policies were, in fact, implemented. That was not done, and the responsibility for it was yours.

The reprimand continued: "Never again shall you have any responsibility, directly or indirectly, for any physical education, interscholastic or athletic program in the Yonkers public schools."

The court reasoned that the board's action was necessary in such a serious situation, and steps had to be taken "to ensure that a life will not be lost again." It denied the administrator's petition by concluding that: "There is no room in the hearts of the bereaved parents for the hurt feelings of the petitioner. The public outrage over the needless death far overshadows his belated complaint of a slap on the wrist."

It then favored the school district when it dismissed the petition and said: "A failure to ensure that others complied with certain rules, the violation of which was not charged to petitioner, can hardly be construed to constitute a stigma of 'constitutional proportions requiring a formal hearing.'"

In *Larson v. Independent School District No. 314*, 289 N.W.2d 112 (Minn. 1980), the court awarded over $1,000,000 to a student injured in a gymnastics activity. It found the instructor guilty of negligence but also included the administrator as guilty of negligence for failing to properly supervise the instructor.

In Michigan, a high school principal and athletic director were sued for allegedly breaching their duty to a fifteen-year-old boy who was severely injured when weights fell on him. *Vargo v. Svitchan*, 301 N.W.2d 1 (Mich. 1981). The boy accused the administrator of negligence for failing to supervise his coach, correct ventilation in the weight room and failing to observe rule violations for illegal summer football practice. The boy charged the school's athletic director with negligence for failing to supervise the sports program. The Michigan court noted that the athletic director had the responsibility of enforcing the rules and supervising activities because of his specialized training in sports. It also reasoned that the athletic director had the authority to eliminate unsafe practices engaged in by the coaches under his direction.

B. *Personnel.*

It is unfortunate, but too often true, that administrators employ incompetent personnel to work in sport programs. Dr. Robert Turner, a leader in youth sport in North Carolina, comments on the problem of the untrained youth sport coach when he states:

> Annually, thousands of willing volunteers become coaches of youth sports teams. Their knowledge of a particular sport may stem from having been an active player, a bench warmer, or just from observing the sport. Regardless of why they were selected, few will know much about how children acquire physical skills or their maturation process. Nor will many of these volunteer coaches have much knowledge of the psychological and sociological aspects related to coaching children.

Turner continues with a warning that applies to all administrators:

> No longer can youth be handed over to well-intentioned adults who make inadvertent errors that can have life long effects on the child, e.g., errors in skill teaching, weeding out the poor players, turn youngsters away from fun and healthful activity, and cause serious physical and emotional problems. (Ref. 3)

There are times when well-meaning people volunteer to coach an activity in which they are inadequately prepared. This can lead to trouble. Take this example.

Castle Heights Military Academy officials announced that their wrestling instructor had resigned and the wrestling program would have to be eliminated, *Stehn v. Bernarr McFadden Foundation, Inc.*, 434 F.2d 811 (6th Cir. 1970). However, one of the faculty members volunteered to help though he had no experience coaching wrestling.

Lowery Stehn, an eighth grade boy, received crippling injuries during a wrestling match. The instructor allegedly taught the student a new hold but not a method of escape or defense of the hold. During the match, Lowery's opponent used this new hold and as a result the plaintiff suffered a severe injury in which the spinal cord was severed. The key question at the trial was the qualifications of the coach. A jury considered the evidence presented and then returned a verdict in favor of the paralyzed youth. The award of $385,000 was reported to be the largest award by a federal court in Tennessee in more than a decade.

C. *Equipment and Facilities.*

It is evident from the number of cases that go to court that there is a wide variety of sport equipment that, along with unsafe facilities, presents hazards to the sports participant. Sport equipment and facilities are the basis of much controversy and litigation involving both continues to escalate.

C. Thomas Ross, a trial lawyer and co-author of *Sports and the Courts Quarterly* suggests that sport managers ask themselves these questions: Has your program met the duty of reasonable care to all who use the equipment and facility? Are the equipment, facility and premises in reasonably safe condition and is the conduct of those on the premises properly supervised?

Ross observes that in numerous cases the courts have ruled that the coach, administrator or supervisor of a facility have met their duty to those who use the equipment and facility if they exercise reasonable care and maintain the premises in reasonably safe condition and supervise the conduct of those on the premises. He points out that the court consistently rules that the supervisor is not the ensurer of the participants' safety but that the injured party must prove that specific acts or omissions breached the duty. Participants must obey rules and customs of the sport.

Ross suggests several ways to prevent litigation regarding equipment and facilities that include:

> Those responsible for the operation of a sport program should set policies concerning the inspection of equipment and facilities on a periodic basis. The line of responsibility must be clearly defined and delegated so that a specific person is accountable for developing and implementing a policy of inspection, maintenance and reporting of the condition of sports equipment and facilities. The records of the safety audit should include the name, date and condition of the various areas of the sport program with recommendations regarding their use. (Ref. 4)

§ 22-5. Summary/Conclusion: Recommendations for the Reduction of Risks in Sport Programs.

1. Keep abreast of current trends in the law as they relate to sport. Attend workshops that deal with tort liability, sport medicine and injury prevention.
2. Designate a safety officer to conduct and assume the responsibility for a safety audit of the sport program. Develop a clear, written policy for identifying and correcting potential risks.

3. Correct or eliminate potential risks before allowing the program activity to begin or continue.

4. Transfer the burden and cost of risks in the program by acquiring medical and/or liability insurance to protect participants, personnel and the program itself.

5. Know and obey rules, regulations and the law as they apply to the sport program.

6. Do not wait for an accident or crisis to act. *Act now* and be prepared by careful planning and preventive action to provide a risk-free program.

7. Warn participants in the program of all potential dangers and risks.

8. Provide competent personnel to direct and supervise the sport program. Determine the number of supervisors by the activity, size and age of the group. Work closely with inexperienced or less qualified personnel. Eliminate high risk activities until qualified personnel is available.

9. Consult with a qualified attorney in planning the operation of the safety audit and overall program.

REFERENCES

1. S.H. Adams & M.A. Bayless, "Clean Specific Instruction Is Your Best Position," 8 *Athletic Purchasing and Facilities,* No. 8. (August 1982).

2. J.C. Weistart & C.H. Lowell, *The Law of Sports* (The Bobbs-Merrill Company 1979).

3. Robert Turner, "Certification of Coaches," *Youth Sports: A Search for Direction* (Sport Studies Foundation, Greensboro, North Carolina 1981).

4. C.T. Ross, "Equipment and Facilities," *Summer Law And Sports Conference — Proceedings* (Guilford College Press 1983).

Appendix

LIABILITY INVENTORY
FORM O

1. Which term represents a failure to exercise the reasonable care and prudence expected of a physical educator/coach?

    A. Anti-trust
    B. Negligence
    C. Tort
    D. Liability

2. If a *spectator* at your softball class/game is injured by a ball which comes through a noticeable hole in the backstop, which condition would apply?

    A. Negligence — failure to ensure the spectator's safety
    B. Negligence — failure to provide reasonably safe conditions
    C. Spectators assume the risks which are inherent to the activity
    D. Spectators assume the risk by choosing to attend the activity

3. Does the type of activity that your students participate in have any bearing on the degree of supervision required?

    A. Yes, potentially dangerous activities require closer supervision
    B. Yes, team activities require closer supervision due to the greater number of participants
    C. No, all activities are potentially dangerous and therefore should be supervised at all times
    D. No, the more dangerous the activity, the more risks the student must assume

4. Where can you find a written code that will tell you whether or not your actions are negligent?

    A. In the *Second Restatement of Torts*
    B. In your state statutes
    C. In *Sports and the Courts*
    D. No such code exists

5. When should physical examinations be administered to your student/athletes?

    A. Before the first day of practice
    B. After the first day of practice
    C. Before the first strenuous workout
    D. After the team has been selected

6. Which condition is *not* required for an interscholastic or intercollegiate athletic program to be in compliance with Title IX?

    A. Equal opportunity for all teams to use the facilities
    B. Equal opportunity for all athletes to receive adequate coaching
    C. Equal monies for overall operation of men's and women's programs
    D. Equal provision of medical and training services

7. Which statement best defines the statute of limitations?

    A. Legislation which limits the amount of a settlement
    B. Specified time limit for filing a law suit
    C. Behavioral expectations of a reasonable and prudent person
    D. Restrictions prohibiting a law suit from being appealed

8. What degree of training in emergency care is expected of a physical educator/coach?

    A. The completion of an advanced first aid certificate
    B. Satisfied the requirements for a first aid certificate
    C. The ability to recall and perform necessary first aid acts
    D. Knowledge required to secure immediate emergency treatment

9. A soccer player dives for a ball that is falling close to the line. The field has been lined with unslaked lime. As a result, the player suffers permanent eye damage. Which statement best describes the player's position?

    A. The player has the right to expect the field to be free from potential hazards
    B. The injury sustained was inherent in the game
    C. The player assumed the risk of injury by diving for the ball
    D. Both A and C

10. What statement best describes the status of the governmental immunity doctrine?

    A. It remains applicable in all states
    B. It is applicable unless abrogated by state legislation
    C. It is applicable for required school activities only
    D. It has been declared unconstitutional by federal legislation

11. For which activities should you be especially careful to warn of dangers and provide adequate instruction?

    A. Swimming and baseball
    B. Power volleyball and football
    C. Wrestling and gymnastics
    D. Archery and basketball

12. Where can you obtain liability insurance?

    A. Through the National Education Association
    B. From your independent insurance agent
    C. Through the American Alliance for Health, PE, Rec., and Dance
    D. From any of the above sources

13. What is the correct terminology for a condition which, by its mere existence could endanger one's well being?

    A. Tort
    B. Omission
    C. Nuisance
    D. Commission

14. How does "due process" apply to student/athletes?

    A. Due process does not apply to minors
    B. School personnel have the right to abrogate due process
    C. Due process is a constitutional right guaranteed for all
    D. A consistent legal precedent concerning student rights has not been established

15. You give a small group of college physical education majors permission to observe your volleyball class/practice. During the activity, an errant spike strikes the head of a spectator who was just lifting her head from taking notes. What defense would you claim if damages were sought?

    A. Act of God
    B. Assumption of risk
    C. Contributory negligence
    D. Comparative negligence

16. Which procedure is *not* a legal responsibility of school authorities in reference to equipment and facilities?

    A. To ensure the safety of the students using the equipment and facilities
    B. To periodically inspect the facilities and equipment and make needed repairs
    C. To foresee hazardous situations and forewarn students accordingly
    D. To keep premises free from hidden dangers and reckless conduct

17. What can you, as a professional, do to limit involvement in a liability suit?

    A. Avoid teaching high risk activities
    B. Conduct yourself in a prudent and professional manner
    C. Secure a liability insurance policy with appropriate coverage
    D. Consult your attorney as to what behavior constitutes negligent behavior

18. Who generally makes decisions concerning questions of fact in court cases where negligence is alleged?

    A. The jury
    B. The judge
    C. The clerk of court
    D. Any of the above depending on the situation

19. Which added precaution should be taken when using your personal vehicle to transport students?

    A. Secure written permission from parents to transfer any incurring liability
    B. Notify the school administration of the route you plan to follow
    C. Add a rider to your existing automobile insurance policy
    D. Require all passengers to have valid accident insurance

20. Do you think it is necessary to keep a written record of accidents that happen during activities you are conducting?

    A. No, a written record can be used against me in court
    B. No, if I witnessed the accident, a written record is unnecessary
    C. Yes, it should include all facts and judgments concerning the accident
    D. Yes, it should include only the facts describing the accident

21. Cases involving alleged inadequate supervision often stem from the claim that teachers/coaches assume the role of "in parentis loco." Which statement best describes this condition?

    A. The parent entrusts the child to the custody of the school and thereby waives the right to sue for any ensuing damages
    B. The school personnel has a duty to protect the student's welfare as they represent a parental replacement
    C. As a parental replacement, school personnel assume the responsibility for all student actions
    D. The parent and the school share equally the responsibility of providing the child with a safe environment

22. Which statement reflects the rights of a physically impaired student/athlete concerning participation in school sponsored activities, i.e., physical education, intramurals, athletics?

    A. Public Law 94-142 indicates that these students are to be permitted to participate to try out for an activity
    B. The physically impaired may participate if they have consent of both the family doctor and the school doctor
    C. The student may participate, but by doing so, relieves school personnel of any ensuing liabilities
    D. The student may participate only in noncontact sports

23. What combination of factors must exist before you can be accused of being negligent?

    A. You must owe a duty to the plaintiff and a breach of this duty must occur
    B. There must be a causal relationship between your conduct and the wrongdoing, and the plaintiff must suffer an actual loss
    C. Both A and B are required
    D. Either A or B would be adequate

24. Which philosophical orientation could create a potentially hazardous situation for your students?

   A. Requiring students to attempt all skills at least once
   B. Extending opportunities for students to assist in developing regulations for the class
   C. Planning activities so that each student can work independently without constant supervision
   D. Encouraging students to strive for specific skill levels

25. AAHPERD guidelines are often consulted when investigating a case involving adequacy of instruction. What position does AAHPERD take concerning the use of trampolines and mini-trampolines?

   A. Offer the activity only to students with above-average motor ability skills
   B. Offer the activity, but require all students to sign a form relieving you of any incurring liability
   C. Offer the activity as an elective and do not permit the somersault to be attempted
   D. Do not use this equipment at all; the risk of injury is too high

26. Which term represents a legal wrongdoing resulting in direct or indirect injury to person or property?

   A. Liability
   B. Tort
   C. Negligence
   D. Causative factor

27. Which behavior is recommended for the teacher/coach in the event of an emergency?

   A. Begin first aid treatment, then go for help
   B. Get another faculty member to supervise your students while you get help
   C. Send someone for help and begin first aid immediately
   D. Dismiss the other students at once and begin first aid

28. The courts often decide that drowning is not the result of supervisory negligence. Which factor contributes highly to water-related accidents?

   A. The possibility of bodily malfunction
   B. The victim's negligence
   C. The inherent dangers of swimming
   D. All of the above

29. A California college student was injured when he stepped on a loose basketball and crashed into an unpadded wall during intramurals. The court found the college to be 75% at fault and the student to be 25% at fault. What action allows for the proration of damages?

   A. Comparative negligence
   B. Contributory negligence
   C. Assumption of risk
   D. Misfeasance

30. If you make a quotable written statement about another member of the "sport community" which is false and endangers his/her reputation, what allegation could you face?

   A. Libel charges
   B. Nuisance charges
   C. Battery charges
   D. None, no wrongdoing has been committed

31. Assume that proper instruction and adequate warning about the hazards inherent in the activity have taken place. What does the participant assume?

   A. All risks of injury
   B. Risks inherent in the activity

C. Risks not covered by school insurance

D. No risks of injury

32. What principle recognizes the fact that, even though care and proper precautions have been taken, injuries are inevitable in physical activity?

A. Contributory negligence

B. Act of God

C. Assumption of risk

D. Comparative negligence

33. A 16-year-old student comes to your class, dresses for activity, but leaves before you begin the activity. The student leaves school property, is hit by a car and seriously injured. The parents initiate a suit against you alleging inadequate supervision. What would be your best defense?

A. Contributory negligence

B. Assumption of risk

C. Unforeseeable accident

D. Act of God

34. Supervision responsibilities include seeing that the area is free from hazards. What condition best represents an attractive nuisance?

A. A wrestling mat rolled up against the wall

B. A folded trampoline leaning against the wall

C. A basketball goal secure to the wall

D. Volleyball standards stored in the corner

35. Which obligation is school personnel *not* expected to fulfill?

A. Exercise reasonable and prudent care

B. Ensure the student's safety

C. Indicate hazards inherent in the activity

D. Provide adequate supervision

36. From what condition does liability insurance protect the teacher/coach?

A. The risk of extensive loss

B. The hazard of being sued

C. The damage to one's profession

D. Both A and B

37. Which method of transporting students is most desirable?

A. Instruct student to drive his/her personal vehicle

B. Contract a reputable common carrier

C. Utilize school vehicles with faculty drivers

D. Arrange for parents to transport students

38. Which defense does *not* depend on the establishment of the defendant's negligence?

A. Governmental immunity

B. Contributory negligence

C. Assumption of risk

D. Act of God

39. Which combination of factors should be most strongly considered when planning activities involving physical contact?

A. Height and weight of participants

B. Size and skill level of participants

C. Age and weight of participants

D. Height and age of participants

40. You remove a severely injured player from the field without awaiting medical assistance. What may you be guilty of?

    A. Malfeasance
    B. Misfeasance
    C. Comparative negligence
    D. Contributory negligence

41. Which statement best describes "save harmless" legislation

    A. Legislation which states that no harm is inflicted unless permanent damage is sustained
    B. Legislation which requires public buildings to maintain hazard free conditions
    C. Legislation which permits a school district to protect teachers from large financial loss
    D. Legislation which requires administrative personnel to purchase liability insurance for employees

42. What is the intent of Title IX?

    A. To force the men's and women's physical education departments to merge
    B. To enable the more established men's athletic departments to absorb the weaker women's programs
    C. To ensure equal opportunity for participation in school sponsored activities
    D. All of the above

43. An injury occurs during your absence from the activity area. Under what condition would the court hold you responsible for damages?

    A. If the proximate cause of the injury was reasonably foreseeable
    B. If the activity involved dangerous equipment
    C. If the accident was unavoidable
    D. If either A or B conditions exist

44. A student is in a position of potential danger. You recognize the peril, but fail to correct the situation. If an injury occurred, what principle would the student utilize in trying to prove your negligence?

    A. Comparative negligence
    B. Contributory negligence
    C. Attractive nuisance
    D. Last clear chance

45. What type of insurance always provides compensation for injury regardless of the negligence involved?

    A. Liability insurance
    B. Accident insurance
    C. Life insurance
    D. Disability insurance

46. What degree of supervision does the court expect you to uphold?

    A. That of a reasonable average person
    B. That of a reasonable parent
    C. That of a reasonable professional instructor
    D. That of a reasonable level corresponding to the instructor's age and experience

47. Which principle expects you to alleviate as well as anticipate harmful situations for your students?

    A. In loco parentis
    B. Proximate cause
    C. Foreseeability
    D. Respondeat superior

48. Which factors become more important when high risk activities are involved?

    A. Quality of equipment and qualifications of instructor
    B. Quality of instruction and size of the activity area
    C. Quality of equipment and size of the class
    D. Quality of instruction and qualifications of instructor

49. You allow a student to use a bow string that is worn because you were not appropriated any funds to upgrade the archery equipment. The student is injured as a result and brings suit against you. Where would you stand?

    A. You could be held liable as the accident was foreseeable
    B. You could be held liable for comparative negligence
    C. You could not be held liable because no funds were appropriated to upgrade the equipment
    D. You could not be held liable because the student assumes the risks inherent in the activity

50. A spectator is injured solely due to the nature of the activity being observed. What would the defendant claim?

    A. Charitable immunity
    B. Governmental immunity
    C. Act of God
    D. Assumption of risk

☐   Please check the box to the left if you would prefer that your answer sheet be omitted from the scoring and evaluative processes.

REMEMBER: You may submit your answer sheet anonymously if you wish. However, if you wish to know how you scored, be sure to fill out the information sheet attached.

ANSWER SHEET

DIRECTIONS: Place the letter corresponding to the best answer for each question in the appropriate blank.

1. _____	21. _____	41. _____
2. _____	22. _____	42. _____
3. _____	23. _____	43. _____
4. _____	24. _____	44. _____
5. _____	25. _____	45. _____
6. _____	26. _____	46. _____
7. _____	27. _____	47. _____
8. _____	28. _____	48. _____
9. _____	29. _____	49. _____
10. _____	30. _____	50. _____
11. _____	31. _____	
12. _____	32. _____	
13. _____	33. _____	
14. _____	34. _____	
15. _____	35. _____	
16. _____	36. _____	
17. _____	37. _____	
18. _____	38. _____	
19. _____	39. _____	
20. _____	40. _____	

LIABILITY INVENTORY ANSWER KEY

Item	Response		Item	Response
1	B		26	B
2	B		27	C
3	A		28	D
4	D		29	A
5	A		30	A
6	C		31	B
7	B		32	C
8	C		33	C
9	A		34	B
10	B		35	B
11	C		36	A
12	D		37	B
13	C		38	A
14	C		39	B
15	B		40	A
16	A		41	C
17	B		42	C
18	A		43	D
19	C		44	D
20	D		45	B
21	B		46	C
22	A		47	C
23	C		48	D
24	A		49	A
25	C		50	D

Chapter 23

CONTRACTING WITH SUPPLIERS, STAFF AND PARTICIPANTS

By

Charles Lynch, Jr.

§ 23-1. Introduction.

The sport manager must assume that "anything that can go wrong will go wrong," and provide accordingly. In order to protect against the unexpected, contracts are essential. Although faced with new transactions and factual patterns daily, many of the same protective devices will appear in all agreements. Each agreement must state clearly and concisely the basic terms of any matter agreed upon, and then provide a resolution for all anticipated or imaginable contingencies.

The sport manager must approach his job as the chief executive officer of a business. Sport has become big business and affairs must be conducted according to prudent business practices. This chapter is concerned with suppliers, staff and participants. It is not an exhaustive management treatise but merely a practical guide to alert readers to potential risks inherent in seemingly minor day-to-day transactions.

§ 23-2. Importance of Contracts.

The importance of reducing oral agreements or understandings to writing cannot be overemphasized. If a dispute arises, each party will have a different opinion about the details of an oral agreement. At a minimum, a letter to confirm an agreement with a space at the bottom for acknowledgement by the other party might well avoid any future misunderstandings. Of course, the letter should be well-written, to the point, and state in clear and concise terms the writer's understanding of the oral agreement.

§ 23-3. Suppliers and Contracts.

Realize that a business transaction is involved when dealing with outside suppliers. A supplier is any person or organization that contracts for supplies, services or events. Some of the primary areas of involvement with suppliers are merchandise and services, concessions, medical, agreements with other schools, joint facilities and leases.

A. *Merchandise and Services.*

When ordering merchandise, know the terms of delivery and payment as contained on the order form or other agreement. When merchandise is delivered, make sure it is carefully examined for defects. Check the terms of payment to see if discounts for early payment are available. Also check to see if merchandise may be returned, and if there are any maximum time limits on returns. When contracting for services, check the references of the service provider to make sure that he is capable of adequately performing the agreed-upon services. Get a list of references and check with the references. Be careful of persons who respond with "our standard contract." Normally, these form contracts are very unfavorable to the purchaser. Disputed matters will always be resolved against the purchaser thereby making careful review of these form agreements time well invested.

B. Concessions.

How are concessions handled at events? Are they provided by the department or is a concessionaire used? If an outside concession organization provides the service, is there a written agreement with the firm? One should exist, and it should be carefully prepared with a detailed description of the duties and responsibilities of each party. For example, suppose a spectator at an event is injured by the explosion of a pressurized soft drink container at a concession stand. Who is liable? You may be, whether or not you had anything to do with the accident. If the concessionaire is liable, does he have adequate liability insurance? Your agreement with the concessionaire should provide that the concessionaire will indemnify you against all damages due to accidents which occur at or around the concession stands. However, if the concessionaire has no assets out of which to pay for damages, or if the concessionaire is inadequately insured, what good is such an agreement? The agreement should require the concessionaire to maintain some minimum liability insurance amount, and to provide you with a copy of the required insurance policy evidencing coverage and naming you as an additional insured under the policy.

C. Medical.

Do you have a doctor present at all of your events? Are you required by law to have a doctor present at all of your events? If you do have a doctor available and present at all of your events, do you have an agreement with him or her? You should. The agreement should detail and describe the services to be provided by the doctor, the amount he or she is to be paid, and should include a schedule or list of the events requiring the doctor's presence.

If you do not have a doctor present at your events, should you? Perhaps you are reasonably close to medical treatment facilities, and you have ambulance service. If you have ambulance service, are the ambulance personnel trained in emergency medical services, and are they capable of handling athletic injuries, heart attack victims, and other similar traumatic injuries? Finally, do you have an agreement with your ambulance service? A short sample physician's agreement is included in Appendix 1 to chapter 7.

D. Agreements With Other Schools.

When you make up your athletic teams' schedules do you enter into a written agreement with each opponent, or do you merely confirm the dates and times by telephone? If your school, conference or association has a standard agreement which you complete by filling in the blanks, do you keep copies of the filled-in agreements for your files?

E. *Joint Facilities.*

If you share ownership or use of a facility with another school, do you have a written agreement defining the rights and responsibilities of each owner or user? Does the agreement adequately protect you if an accident occurs while the other party is using the facility? A carefully drafted agreement defining the terms of use, supervision required during use and the specific responsibilities of each party could be very important in the event of an injury at the facility.

F. *Leases.*

For each facility that you lease for your use, or that you lease to others, you should have a written lease agreement.

§ 23-4. Contracts for Staff.

At the end of each athletic season, our newspapers usually carry several articles about the firing of coaches. Frequently these articles disclose that the school or other employer must pay the coach's salary for the remaining years on his or her contract. Obviously, the coaches in these cases have written employment agreements with the schools providing for payment following termination by the employer. In the absence of a written employment agreement, the general law is that the term of employment is at the will of the employer, and may be terminated at any time without further liability for payment. For the protection of your school and your coaches, a written employment agreement should be prepared, and it should define the term, rate of pay, expectations and other matters agreed upon by the parties. The employment agreement may also include a listing of the fringe benefits provided for the coach. For most business executives these include insurance, both medical and life, retirement benefits, the use of an automobile, secretarial or other similar assistance and perhaps housing.

Common at the larger university level is the summer camp program, whereby the coach can operate a summer camp by leasing some or all of the school's athletic facilities. From the school's standpoint, the lease or other agreement with the coach should specifically eliminate the school's participation in the conduct of the summer camp. The coach should operate the camp entirely on his own, and the school should only act as a lessor of its facilities. It should not pay its personnel for working at the camp, and they should make separate employment arrangements with the coach. Again, the coach should be required to maintain adequate liability insurance coverage, naming the school as an insured, and provide the school with proof of the coverage prior to the effective date of the lease.

§ 23-5. Contracts With Participants.

A. *Scholarships.*

The most common form of written agreement between the school and its athletes is the scholarship form. If there is no written scholarship agreement, one should be prepared. The scholarship agreement should outline the basic requirements that the athlete must maintain to keep his scholarship. If the scholarship is a one-year annually renewable agreement, this fact should be disclosed prominently to the athlete. If the athlete is to be adequately protected, the school should provide the athlete with some medical insurance program, either paid by the university, or paid at the option of the athlete or his family. Most medical insurance policies pay only a percentage of the actual medical bills, and by having only a regular family policy on an athlete, a parent may not have full medical insurance. Therefore, an additional policy, purchased by the athlete or his family, or provided by the university, may provide improved medical coverage for the athlete.

B. *Injuries.*

If an athlete is injured due to lack of supervision or faulty equipment, does your school have adequate liability insurance? If so, does the insurance require you to make an annual report on the condition of your equipment and facilities? Who performs the inspection and certification to the insurance company? Do you have adequate amounts of insurance? Judgments are being handed down for millions of dollars. If your policy limits are the standard $100,000/300,000, then you may be inadequately insured in the event of an injury. Additional insurance is usually not as expensive as the base amount, and you may be able to purchase an "umbrella" policy providing coverage of a million dollars or more without significant additional expense.

C. *Club Sports.*

If your school has a club sports program, does the school participate in or attempt to control the club sports? Are playing fields or other facilities for the club sports to use merely provided by the school or does the school control and administer club sports as part of the program? The more control and supervision one has, the greater the need for insurance and adequate supervision for these sports. See the Appendix at the end of this chapter for guidelines for club sports.

§ 23-6. Do You Need an Attorney?

Consult with an attorney and choose an attorney based on his or her capabilities. The attorney must understand the needs of the sport manager and be experienced in dealing with matters which affect the sports program. Most laymen do not understand that all attorneys do not attempt to practice in all fields of law. In choosing an attorney, ask questions about his or her type of practice and areas of speciality. If the attorney's practice is devoted primarily to criminal law matters, it is doubtful that the attorney or sport manager would benefit by his serving as attorney for the program. Also, do not choose an attorney solely because he or she is a friend or neighbor or because he or she is a booster of the program. All of these are good qualities, but unless the attorney is capable and competent to handle the program's legal problems, the association will not be beneficial to either party. Invite the attorney to visit, show him around, and let him feel that he is a part of the program. Welcome his advice and opinions on all matters, even if it is occasionally contrary to what one desires. Do not be afraid to consult with the attorney because he will charge a fee. Selecting an attorney because he is the cheapest one in town may not be getting very good representation, since one gets about what one pays for. Have an understanding with the attorney about fees. He should discuss them frankly and fairly, including the billing system and expected terms of payment.

Do not try to be a lawyer. Do not assume that because a situation was handled in one way last year, that a similar situation will be handled exactly the same this year. If the law has changed, or if the circumstances are not exactly the same, then last year's solution may not work. Never simply retype an agreement which you have previously used and substitute names and dates. Often this procedure is employed in an attempt to save legal fees. Call your attorney, and discuss the situation in detail. Let the attorney decide on the appropriate course of action.

You should use the attorney in the planning stages of a proposed event or transaction, and you should avoid calling your attorney only after the "deal has been struck." Frequently, the attorney's advice at the planning or negotiation levels may lead to better results, and he can make suggestions which may be beneficial to both parties.

§ 23-7. Summary/Conclusion.

In order to reduce your legal risks, have a good understanding of the arrangements and affairs of all aspects of the sport program. Written agreements, however simple, are the only way that certainty can be achieved. Engage an attorney who is competent and who is experienced in handling contract matters and general business affairs. Consult with the attorney frequently, particularly during the planning stages of a transaction or an event. The attorney's advice can be invaluable and may save a great deal of time and money in the long run.

Appendix

FERRUM COLLEGE GUIDELINES
FOR CLUB SPORTS

In an effort to meet the need resulting from interest in sports and activities that are not offered on the intercollegiate or intramural level the college sanctions Sport Clubs. Said clubs are not a part of the athletic program but the outgrowth of an intramural program that seeks to provide an opportunity for each member of the Ferrum College community to participate in an activity on a level commensurate with his or her ability.

Should there be sufficient interest, an activity or sport will first be considered for intramural participation. In the event size prohibits intramural scheduling, an attempt to offer extramural competition will be examined along sport club guidelines. Geographic considerations will play a large role in the consideration for sanction of any club. Opponents should be easily accessible and selected on the basis of having goals that are compatible with those of Ferrum College and its institutional mission.

Because of limited space and facilities, sport clubs will be required to adjust practice schedules and events to suit schedules developed for activities of larger scope. The fact that fifteen students have shown an interest in team handball will not always justify regular use of a facility that can be used by groups of larger number, such as softball, touch football, or even free play.

Each student participating with a sport club must sign a statement certifying that, he or his family, possesses health insurance coverage at least comparable to student health insurance available here. Presumably this means that all members of sport clubs will have medical insurance coverage, which will provide for medical expenses incurred as the result of injuries sustained in athletic competition.

The college does not assume any responsibility to pay for or underwrite the cost of medical care given to members of sport clubs in connection with injuries sustained in club practice or competition. Nor does the college provide life or accident insurance coverage for students engaged in club activities that require them to travel away from Ferrum College. The clubs cannot expect the college to accept or be held to assume legal responsibility for injuries caused to third persons by the activities of any sports club or its officers or members while traveling by private automobile or by public transportation.

The important point is that members of sports clubs should understand that they — and not Ferrum College — will be responsible for any injuries they cause. Sport club members, including any coaches, who drive private automobiles to or from events should recognize that they cannot look to Ferrum College to bear or share any liability they may incur to a third person in the course of such travel. Indeed, members and particularly officers of the sport clubs should appreciate the possibility that they might be exposed to a lawsuit and even to liability for injuries to third persons, especially when they are accompanying the driver and sharing his expenses.

The college requires that individuals who drive vehicles for sport club events must certify that they have liability insurance equal to the minimum amounts required in his home state. Nothing prevents individual clubs from providing insurance for their members against liability to third persons, resulting from their operation or ownership of, or presence in, any vehicle being used for club travel.

MEDICAL AND LEGAL RESPONSIBILITIES

It is the responsibility of students who wish to participate in club sports to ascertain whether they have any health conditions which makes it inadvisable for them to participate. The college, therefore, assumes no responsibility for physical injuries or aggravation of existing health conditions.

When financial funding is available it will be distributed among sport clubs after an assessment of the various needs by the Director of Leisure Services. Sanctioned clubs will receive code numbers for budgetary needs. Request for payment will be routed through the Director of Leisure Services and all funds raised or donated will be deposited in the club account with receipts forwarded to the Director of Leisure Services.

DIRECTIONS FOR SANCTION

I. Students, faculty or staff members wishing to form Sport Clubs should contact the Director of Leisure Services Programs for direction and guidelines which would, upon approval of the Director of Leisure Services Programs, include the submitting of the following to the Athletic Committee.

    A. Constitution, to follow no particular format, but to include:
        1. Name of organization;
        2. Rationale of, or need for, the club;
        3. Purpose of the organization;
        4. List of officers and method of selection;
        5. Amount of dues, if any, and how and when collected;
        6. Projected enrollment limits, if any; and
        7. Method of selecting and recruiting members;
    B. A signed petition with full names and class designation of potential members.
    C. A signed letter from faculty/staff member indicating the willingness to sponsor such a club.
    D. An estimate of expenses which would include:
        1. Equipment,
        2. Officials,
        3. Uniforms,
        4. Travel,
        5. Insurance, and
        6. Other expenses,
    E. A list of possible sources of income.
    F. A projected playing schedule and list of potential opponents.

II. Upon approval by the Athletic Committee a club would become operational under the leadership of the approved faculty/staff representative who, along with club officers, will answer directly to the Director of Leisure Services Programs.

III. At the conclusion of each season and/or academic year, the Director of Leisure Services Programs will meet with the Athletic Committee to evaluate club performance and determine status for the coming season.

SPONSORSHIP

It should be understood that in many instances club sponsors will lack coaching experience. The prime requisite for sponsorship will be an interest in student welfare and a willingness to devote the time needed to see that the club has adequate faculty/staff supervision and proper liaison between the club and the Director of Leisure Services. Non-college personnel may assist in coaching, but the final responsibility rests with the sponsor in seeing that the club participates within the parameters set forth.

The following duties are the responsibility of the sponsor:

1. See that each student has an up-to-date (within the current year) physical on file at the student health center.

2. See that each sports club member meets eligibility requirements.

3. Explain the school medical insurance coverage of each participant.

4. Maintain open lines of communication with the Student Health Center and see that each member understands and abides by its policies.

5. See that a copy of the Sports Club Waiver form is signed by each member and on file with the Director of Leisure Services.

6. See that a copy of each member's Medical History form is up-to-date, signed and on file at the Student Health Center.

7. See that a copy of each member's Medical History form accompanies the club on and off campus.

8. See that a travel form is left with College Security and the College switchboard for off-campus trips.

9. See that an individual trained in CPR and emergency first aid is present at each practice and game.

10. Attend all practice games or see that a qualified faculty/staff member attends all practice sessions and contests.

11. Coordinate practice times, scheduling and travel arrangements with club officers and the Director of Leisure Services.

12. Give tentative approval and advise the Director of Leisure Services of all fund-raising projects.

13. Assist club members in the development of a constitution.

14. Assist club members in submitting a year-end report to the Athletic Committee and Director of Leisure Services.

15. Inventory and collect all equipment at the conclusion of each season.

16. Inspect and give final approval for all equipment purchased by individuals to be used in sports club activities.

ELIGIBILITY

1. Sports Club membership will be restricted to those students who are currently enrolled as full-time students at the college.

2. No student shall represent a sports club for an off-campus activity while on academic probation. (Academic Probation is interpreted as follows: 1.30 GPA after the 1st semester of freshman year; 1.50 GPA after the freshman year; 1.80 GPA after the 1st semester of sophomore year; 2.00 for the previous semester after the completion of the sophomore year.)

3. Students on academic probation who meet National Junior College Athletic Association eligibility requirements may represent sports clubs for activities scheduled on campus.

4. Athletes who are currently participating on varsity teams will be ineligible for Sports Club competition.

5. Athletes who plan to try out for intercollegiate teams must secure approval from their varsity coach before participating on the sports club level.

6. In all cases the school physician will examine physicals and medical histories of sports club participants. The school physician's recommendations will be to the sponsor and Director of Leisure Services and will be the determining factor in eligibility.

FERRUM COLLEGE SPORTS MEDICAL HISTORY FORM

(PLEASE PRINT)

NAME _____ AGE _____
         Last   First   Middle   Nickname

Notify in Case of Emergency: _____
                        Name   Relationship
          Address _____

                      City   State   Zip
          Telephone: _____
                      Home   Business

Any history of serious illness or injuries with date of occurrence: _____
_____
_____

Any family history of TB, cancer, heart disease, etc. _____
_____

Any surgery and date of occurrence: _____
_____

Any allergies to medicines: _____
_____

Any present problem or complaint: _____
_____

Past athletic injuries: _____
_____

Any history of heat prostration: _____
Tetanus Toxiod: (Date) _____
Blood pressure: _____
Do you wear contact lens? _____ Do you wear glasses? _____
                        (yes or no)   (yes or no)
Medically able to participate in all sports: Yes _____ No _____

_____   _____
Player's Signature   Physician Signature

_____   _____
Parent or Guardian's Signature   Date

WAIVER

It is my intention to participate with the Ferrum College _____ Club. A copy of my physical exam and my medical history form is on file at the Student Health Center.

I give permission to the college physician to review both medical history and physical exam forms and determine my eligibility. I further grant permission to the club sponsor to carry a copy of my medical history form on off-campus trips and present it to medical authorities should it be needed as a result of my illness or injury.

The college policies concerning insurance coverage have been explained to me and I understand that I have the option to purchase additional insurance. At present I have a Health Insurance Policy with _____, numbered _____. It is comparable to the Ferrum College Health Insurance Policy.

I have read a copy of Ferrum College Guidelines for club sports and it has been explained to me by the club sponsor.

I, also, hereby, for myself and my agents, waive and release any and all rights and claims for damages I may have against Ferrum College for any and all injuries received by me in connection with this activity.

Signed: _____

Parent if under 18: _____

Club Sponsor: _____

FERRUM COLLEGE
SPORTS CLUB TRAVEL FORM

Club Sport: _____

Coach: _____ Adult Supervisor: _____

Destination: _____

Date and Time of Departure: _____

Date and Time of Arrival: _____

Date and Time of Return: _____ Depart:_____ Arrive: _____

    Where Staying: _____ Phone No. AC: _____

      Other Numbers Where Club Can Be Reached: AC: _____, AC: _____

Name of Driver: _____

Driver's License Number and State of Issuance: _____

Is Driver also the Owner of the Vehicle: Yes _____ No _____

If not, Name of Owner: _____

Age of Driver: _____ Student _____ Non-Student _____

Type of Vehicle and Year: _____

Tag Number and State: _____

Insurance Coverage: Name of Company _____

                       Policy Number _____

                       Expiration Date _____

                       Limits of Coverage _____

                       Name of Insured _____

Condition of Vehicle (poor, fair, good, excellent):   Tires _____

                                              Lights _____

                                              Brakes _____

                                              Wipers _____

                                              Other _____

Status of Passengers: Team Member _____

                       Student _____

                       Other _____

Driver's Previous Traffic Violations: _____

Signed: _____   _____

      Driver of Car   Club Sponsor

*NOTE: All vehicles are to return directly to campus and report to the sponsor at the gym. The sponsor is to notify the switch board and security that the group is back on campus.

COPIES OF THIS FORM ARE TO BE LEFT WITH
SECURITY AND THE SWITCHBOARD.

Chapter 24

THE LAW OF PUBLIC ASSEMBLY FACILITIES

By

James Oshust

§ 24-1. Introduction.

The current dilemma facing most personnel who manage public assembly facilities concerns the increasing list of laws that must be obeyed, requirements that must be met, codes that must be complied with totally, as weighed against the ever-increasing need to provide sensitive and responsive customer service for any and all activities in which a facility is engaged.

In certain cases, the decision is very clear-cut, having been formed by precedents in various legal cases. In the main, however, it normally comes down to a management decision, or at times, a lack thereof.

§ 24-2. Need for Legal Assistance.

In order to act within the law and still maintain services, the manager will need the assistance of an attorney. In order for him to make the best choices for actions to take, he will need to develop an understanding of the facility. Only when the legal counsel has been given sufficient information on the particular type of operation and some of the nuances that distinguish it from other similar operations, can he or she best prepare defense for an initiated legal action, offer substantive legal advice concerning a particular question, or provide ongoing direction and guidance in formulating rules and regulations in operational procedures.

The reader is cautioned that, like all aspects of society, the law itself changes. As social mores and conduct of society in general shift ever so slightly in one direction or another, so does the interpretation of the law; with these changes are the variations in the final judicial findings regarding any particular reflected issue brought before the court. Know the general concept of law. Stay on top of current industry standards and/or procedures found effective elsewhere. And most of all, ask for help early from those trained and schooled to provide appropriate legal consultation. To delay in requesting help, providing information or determining facts necessary for later decisions is to face potential disaster. At best, it can cast a shadow over the credibility of the operation and of the facility's position in the community.

§ 24-3. Access and Availability of Facility.

Access to and availability of facilities for various purposes has become an extremely sensitive item in certain areas of the country lately. A conflict in what was considered community standards and the legal aspects of access to a facility arose in Green Bay, Wisconsin in early 1983 concerning the imminent concert presentation of the then controversial rock star Ozzy Osbourne. The facility in Green Bay is operated under a management contract between a private group and the county. Local interests opposed the appearance of Osbourne and prevailed on county authorities to recommend to the management company that the existing contract for the concert be cancelled.

The management group's contract gave them total authority to handle all booking. Yet, trying to maintain a decent rapport with their client, the county, the management firm stated they would accede to the county officials' wishes if they, the county, took full legal liability for the decision. The county's corporation counsel, however, intervened saying that such a decision by either party was in direct conflict with existing law and applied constitutional freedoms. Fortunately for all concerned, Ozzy Osbourne reportedly became ill at an earlier concert elsewhere and the event was cancelled by the promoter.

In another instance, a facility was to be rented by a somewhat unusual group of individuals, by current social standards, for the purpose of holding a "Gay Beauty Contest." Local church and school groups protested violently; this event was cancelled due to a lack of ticket sales and inability of the promoter to provide necessary deposit funding.

At another facility there were doubts as to whether the building could be rented to a group that advocated policies very similar to those espoused by the Communist Party, and other groups, whose past history had indicated less than favorable local support in many urban areas of the United States. Again, that group's proposed meeting never materialized due to lack of sufficient funding and the logistics of providing necessary security requirements.

In all cases, however, the question arose — what right does a public assembly facility have to restrict or, if desired, to bar presentation of an event or availability to an individual for a public program? One person in an entertainment-industry meeting in early 1984 quipped, "You have no rights to stop them — and your ability to do so deteriorates from that point on."

When a facility is designed and constructed to serve the purpose of housing groups of individuals in attendance at a meeting, trade show, an entertainment presentation, dramatic production, music concert or similar programs, it does not matter who owns the facility and what its normal day-to-day use is. The example that follows will possibly contribute to an understanding.

Wholesome University has built a basketball arena which also houses athletic department offices. The facility is used for the school's varsity basketball games, volleyball, commencements, occasional artistic presentations of school groups like the university's symphonic choir and orchestra, and the daily physical education programs. During the summer, however, the facility sits vacant. Students are gone, sports activities are absent and the university has been called upon to make it accessible possibly for rock concerts. There are a certain number of major stars who tour the area from time to time. Since the facility holds 7,500 to 12,500 or more, it becomes a candidate for the staging of many types of artists or groups.

Although the facility is not intended as a profit-making structure, it suddenly comes into its own when it is found that there is not a competitive or like facility within miles of the campus. In addition, the university's financial advisors, recognizing the inflationary spiral, express admonitions to the university administration concerning the need to find funds for yearly operations and at some time in the future, needed repairs and/or additions. Thus with the spector of increasing deficit facing the facility, devices, such as rock show promotors, major artists, the overnight event, etc., for acquiring needy and speedy funds become an attractive possibility.

There is sufficient parking; the university has the manpower and the facilities with which to provide for the events. A large enough consuming public exists in and around the university area to assure fairly consistent success. Now what shall the university do?

The growing inclination, of course, is to provide the facility, making it available for such profit-making events, normally within certain predetermined conditions. Regardless of these conditions, once a facility is offered for such public use, it cannot be doled out in a miserly fashion. It cannot be acceptable one day to host "Kenny Rogers" because his is one of those types of acts or events the community will enjoy, and on the other hand discourage or, simply put, refuse to deal with legitimate promoters who may wish to bring in "The Blasters," even though "The Blasters" have had some reported problems in other parts of the country.

To forestall the playing of "The Blasters," one must also give up "Kenny Rogers," and in turn, depending on the nature of inherent litigation, must cease all such operations. This may be what a university feels it will have to do. But, once out of the entertainment game, they must stay out. For to re-enter would be in fact to become "selective." This is one of the most serious complaints leveled against facilities today. What a facility, its community, that community's leadership, or the operators of the facility feels is "normal" and "acceptable" to local community standards and needs may not, in the eyes of the court, be broad or general enough in its scope to preclude the claim of First Amendment rights ostensibly being exercised by those requesting dates or usage in the facility.

A program of usage should be consistent with the style of the facility. A theater, upholstered and boasting such refinements as chandeliers, extensive wood paneling and carpeting throughout, has a right to restrict those types of activities which are not considered normal for its type of decor. Rock concerts, trade shows, and other events that might be considered injurious to the facility's interior and equipment can be refused on legally justifiable grounds.

A symphony orchestra often finds little compatible with the large basketball arena. Theater productions are difficult to stage in large-roofed buildings having no built-in "grid" or suspension system for the hanging of sets. All these are physical matters and very easy to resolve.

§ 24-4. Access to Records, Booking Schedules and Operational Details.

When any facility "goes public," so do many of its records. There are certain protections given the privately owned and operated building. Certain university facilities have a greater degree of protection than do those outwardly owned and operated by cities, counties and states. Yet, any claims regarding availability of dates or violation of First Amendment rights or overly-restrictive policies place the facility in the position of possibly being required to reveal certain documents. This could include booking schedules, most financial data, and operational procedures. Any stated policy or consistent procedure should be put in writing, and should be reviewed by an ongoing monitoring process. To merely stipulate that something exists as a policy or something else is a standard method of achieving a certain end is insufficient when faced with the potential for litigation.

Privacy is a word once considered the definition of a right intrinsic to everything one did and inalienable in all aspects of personal societies. That is no longer true today. The courts have ruled that if one person's or group's privacy creates a situation or allows a hindrance to exist that diminishes or prohibits another individual's or group's right to needed information, then that prior bastion of privacy may be severely intruded upon.

§ 24-5. Access to Premises.

Courts have ruled that access to the premises of any public assembly facility shall be granted under conditions which form a rather large umbrella encompassing numerous types of protests, solicitation and public commentary. This is not to say that anyone may enter upon the premises of any facility at any time to do whatever they wish; however, in order to protect guarantees of free speech, the courts have stated that access to the general populace cannot be severely restricted or unnecessarily hindered. If the facility is located well within the confines of a secluded campus area, and there is little daily traffic, or its location in fact is quite isolated from normal public contact, it may experience little or no confrontational incidents.

A. *Sale of Items.*

It should be remembered, however, that one of the primary rules prohibiting the development of any contact with the general public or attending patron at an event concerns the sale, merchandising or distribution of any type of material which is in direct conflict to the operation of the facility in question. More simply put, the coliseum that has granted a promoter or his acts or performers the right to sell T-shirts, can ban nonlicensed sellers of such goods from the premises. Food stands can be prohibited on the premises whether they are for the sale of a product or for the giving away of samples.

B. *Distribution of Written Materials.*

The distribution of handbills, leaflets and other such written materials can be restricted so long as the restrictions do not in themselves stop the supplier from coming on the premises and having at least what is considered by the court a "reasonable degree of access" to passing patrons or general public.

C. *Soliciting Funds.*

The question of soliciting for funds is at best difficult. Most facilities prohibit any solicitation for funds either on premises or inside the facility. Once inside the physical structure of the building, management policies supersede the previously broad powers allowed by First Amendment criteria to all citizens. What we have been discussing are things that would, could, shall or might take place on the physical grounds or "premises" of a building, on the escarpment leading to the doorway and the sidewalks surrounding the property and/or facility.

D. *First Amendment Rights.*

The law is clear regarding First Amendment rights granted an individual only because that particular constitutional amendment is so very broad in its interpretive scope. Our forefathers did not designate place nor time nor attitude. It might be best to remember that an overt attempt to regulate excessively, to restrict by imposition of hindrances, or to impede by ignoring requests, creates a basic ground on which most litigation is founded.

The soliciting of funds can be restricted from the facility itself and its immediate environs. As to the soliciting on the premises, this is best handled through a clear understanding and interpretation of existing local ordinances. As for the distribution of leaflets and other types of written material, this clearly falls within the First Amendment rights of all individuals. If, however, such activities bar, hinder, impede or create the atmosphere thereof as concerns the access of any individuals to and from the entry portals of a facility, then such activities can be controlled by management or local law enforcement agencies.

It is helpful to designate areas for such individuals to stand. Furthermore, there should be certain simple procedures by which those desiring such rights inform the facility that they intend to protest or use that particular facility's event as a public forum. However, a conscientious attempt to provide such groups these alternatives must still exist. Be specific about procedures concerning solicitations, handbilling and other such methods of protest or desired access to transient public. Have copies of such regulations or procedures available for distribution to interested parties who may wish to gather on premises or utilize the area for their form of public demonstration. Such procedures should be made a part of any formal record kept at the highest level of authority such as the city clerk's office, county commissioners' office, dean of student activities office, superintendent of facilities office, or the office of the facility and/or university's legal counsel.

§ 24-6. Search and Seizure.

Much has been written about this subject. At the present time, there appears to be no truly definitive case pending regarding search and seizure or methods of surveilling customers attending events to preclude unwanted objects such as glass containers, alcohol, weapons and similar objects. This does not mean, however, that the question has been resolved. It merely lies in abeyance due to the pressure of other legal matters that have arisen in the industry. It should be noted that when situations arise wherein there shall be those that will protest methods by which facility personnel check individual patrons coming into a building, the courts will again be asked to intervene.

The following items can be included in anyone's list or inventory of suggested procedures:

1. All checks, searches, close surveillance, requests for the checking of baggage, parcels, purses or whatever, should be done by civilian-clothed individuals rather than uniformed police officers.

2. The language of any and all prohibitions should be very plainly marked at each and every portal and distributed in a fashion so as to clearly reflect the essence of the prohibition, and the methods of its implementation.

3. Courteous, clear, but direct conversation with the patrons being questioned regarding suspicious items, bulges in clothing, or parcels is far more effective than the blunt direction of requests or demands to search when reasonable cause may not exist.

4. Review the procedure with every individual that may be concerned — event staff, management personnel, legal counsel and law enforcement officers. Continually monitor application of procedure at each and every occasion.

§ 24-7. Crowd Control.

The amount of security forces necessary to provide for the well-being of the patrons and participants in any event cannot be found on any chart of standards. It is not part of any handbook or authoritative research material. It is principally a matter of management's judgment based on given circumstances, past history, information gleaned from the industry regarding like facilities and situations — and very possibly, a certain degree of luck.

Security is vital not only to control an unruly crowd and to protect of the event's participants, but also to provide needed help in the event of major emergencies and, at times, some basic customer services. Certain law enforcement detachments have individuals trained in paramedic services. Others can provide preliminary fire protection support as well as radio systems allowing a communications network often far more sophisticated than the facility can afford or find practical to utilize at all times.

At no time can management of the facility and its owner ever give up the right to reasonable levels of security personnel for all events, including their positioning, and specific duties. To relinquish these rights is to endanger the safety and welfare of the patrons who are the primary responsibility of facility management.

§ 24-8. Availability of Required and Desired Accouterments.

A. *Patrons with Disabilities.*

Much is written today about providing seating for the disabled, ramps for the use of wheelchairs, and particularly, parking facilities for the disabled. Developing and providing facilities for disabled patrons is just good business. Many of these individuals have been kept from attending events not only because of personal physical difficulties but also, and more importantly, because of the lack of adequately modified facilities.

Federal and state governments have written volumes of regulations and procedures regarding such situations. In simple terms, those with basic physical handicaps, but with the mental alertness to provide their own thought processes independent of other assistance, need parking facilities, ramp access for wheelchairs and/or crutches, and minimization of difficulties in utilization of restrooms. The government has and can provide architectural plans for those desiring to construct new or renovated existing facilities.

Only recently have those with severely limited hearing been "heard," as it were. Recent technical developments allow facilities, particularly smaller theaters, to be adapted for the hearing impaired. The process is fairly simple. It involves the installation of an electronic coil or wiring system by which signals can be transmitted to separate receiving units utilized by the patron. Or in some cases, it can actually raise certain elements of sounds so as to be more defined to those utilizing hearing aids.

It is important, however, that the facility manager be aware of these new developments and, when funds become available he or she should implement whatever system meets both budgetary and technical limitations existing in the facility in question.

Investigate, recognize, develop and implement any and all procedures that will aid the disabled — it is good business, it is a worthwhile effort, and it expresses a sensitivity of management toward the potential patron who must remain the most important part of any program.

B. *Emergency Medical Care.*

Recognition of the emergency care needs of any group of attending or participating patrons should come as a result of review and consultation with qualified preventative and emergency medical care specialists.

Categorize possible patrons as to age, emotion potential, and consider the nature and duration of the event. Proper equipment and medical personnel can be expensive, but certainly worthwhile.

There may be pressure concerning the expense of acquiring technically sophisticated cardiopulmonary equipment. The maintenance of even basic emergency care supplies, bandages, splints, medicines, stretchers and oxygen tanks can severely stretch the most carefully prepared budget. Yet the "landlord" must be prepared for the worst — or at least the tragic possibility. Heart failure, pulmonary complications, sprained or broken limbs are constant spectors when any large group gathers.

Coordinate on-site facilities with the closest permanent medical facilities. Develop response codes and assess the emergency medical care needs of patrons.

The type of accident reporting system used is vitally important. Clear-cut lines of organization normally define who does what. This may be fine for most management situations — until an accident occurs or a medical emergency is at hand. During such a crisis the natural inclination of sensitive man to sympathize, to commiserate, to reach out and help becomes dominant. When the emergency at hand has passed, the cold reality of administrative need and potential legal requirement takes precedence, often revealing a lack of information on what has most recently taken place.

Remember that proper response to those in need includes appropriate record-keeping. Review all accident and medical reports. Critique pertinent staff. Learn from these incidents since they provide the most graphic example of what might exist that portends hazard or indicates need for possible change.

§ 24-9. Summary/Conclusion.

There exists no simple answer to the numerous legal and socio-political questions that will arise regarding the operation of any public assembly facility. If you look for the all-encompassing formula to create the proper mix between professional management needs and the often fickle nature of public demand you will find none.

What you can use is a practiced discipline in dealing with every situation, every problem, every opportunity. Accept the preeminence of law as that cohesive element required in any society. Communicate your needs clearly, concisely and sincerely so as to acquire the broadest, most effective audience. Understand that flexibility and mobility in the blade of the fencing foil adds a dimension of strength and a capacity for endurance. It has been written that civilization hinges on the habit of obedience to criminal law and to some lesser degree civil law. Although this respect for civil law is less constant and not as engrained, it is still no less important. Professional management that strives for the better in whatever is undertaken requires patience, skill and ethical stamina. Less than this precludes the success of any worthwhile venture.

Chapter 25

PLAYER CONTRACTS FOR PROFESSIONAL
TEAM SPORTS

By

Glenn Wong

§ 25-1. Introduction.

The general manager of a professional team-sport franchise must deal with
a number of different contracts while running his operation. These include
player contracts, coach and manager contracts, front office employment
contracts, facility lease contracts, radio and television contracts, minor league
player contracts, winter league player contracts, waivers and releases of
liability and others. The leagues and teams use standard contracts to deal
with some of these areas, while in other areas the contracts are negotiated
and drafted on an individual basis. The focus of this chapter is on the club-
player contract negotiations in professional team sport. The important
documents for the general manager dealing in player contract negotiations
are the standard player contract, the collective bargaining agreement, the
league constitution, bylaws and rules. The first two impact most directly on
the player-contract negotiation area. Therefore, the discussion is divided into
three sections: the standard player contract; the collective bargaining
agreement; and additional contract amendments. Other contracts that a
general manager of a professional sport team may deal with are discussed
briefly under the heading *"Other Contracts."* It should be emphasized that
this chapter is designed to give the reader an overview of some of the different
elements of professional sport player contracts. It is not intended as a
comprehensive discussion of an extremely complex area.

§ 25-2. The Standard Player Contract.

Each major professional league has its own standard-form player contract,
and it is generally included as part of a collective bargaining agreement. A
brief discussion follows concerning some of the similarities and differences
that are found in the standard player contracts. The following clauses are
likely to be similar:

A. *Termination Clause.*

This is the clause under which most players are cut, waived or released
from the club. The most common reason for releasing, waiving or cutting a
player is for lack of sufficient playing skill. In other words, the player who is
competing with other players for a position on the team is deemed, in the sole
opinion of the club, to have insufficient skill and ability. This clause often
results in litigation, where the player feels that he has been terminated while
injured. The player contends that he has not been terminated for lack of
sufficient playing skill, but that he was injured and was not able to
demonstrate his abilities.

329

B. *Physical Condition.*

A player agrees to report in good physical condition and to keep himself in good physical condition during the season. This clause has been used in a few instances to terminate a player who was overweight or out of shape. This clause may have been used to deal with players with drug or alcohol problems. However, most professional leagues have resorted to a specific drug policy to deal with problems.

C. *Renewal or Option Clause.*

All leagues have a renewal or option clause in a standard player contract. The clauses vary from league to league, and in some situations, the renewal or option clause is mandatory (e.g., National Basketball Association rookie contract and the North American Soccer League). At one time, a renewal or option clause was found in all standard player contracts. However player unions in most situations made these clauses negotiable, and therefore they may either be included or excluded.

D. *Filing.*

Player contracts in all professional team sport leagues are filed with the league office. A commissioner or president of a league then has 10 days to disapprove the contract, if he deems the contract to be in violation of any league rule.

E. *Compensation.*

This clause sets forth the salary that is paid to a player. Additional compensation is provided for in the collective bargaining agreement (discussed in § 25-3 *infra*) and may be provided in additional contract clauses (discussed in § 25-4 *infra*). Minimum compensation levels are set forth in the collective bargaining agreement.

F. *Payment.*

The salary is generally paid during the regular playing season. For example, a NFL player who earns $160,000 per year will be paid $10,000 per week for the 16 weeks of the regular season. The player is not paid during the off-season. During the pre-season, the collective bargaining agreement generally provides for compensation on a weekly basis. Post-season pay is additional compensation, apart from the salary. Some leagues, generally those in the formative stages have attempted to pay the players over the entire year, rather than during the regular playing season. This assisted the owner's cash flow situation and in at least one situation (Women's Basketball League) resulted in players not being paid because the team declared bankruptcy.

G. *Other Activities.*

A player agrees not to participate in outside activities that may involve a significant risk of injury. There have been a number of cases where a player has been injured in the off-season as a result of playing another sport. If the club knows the player is participating in an outside activity with a significant risk of injury, the club has the right to have the player stop participating. If the player is injured in such an activity, he may have breached his contract and may not be entitled to future contract rights (such as guaranteed pay). The player may be able to protect himself by requesting permission from the club to participate in an outside activity. A club that is aware that a player has participated in a certain outside activity in the past, which the club deems is no longer in the club's and player's best interests, may negotiate to include a clause in the contract specifically preventing the player from participating in that activity.

H. *Rules.*

A player agrees to abide by the club's training rules.

I. *Assignment.*

A club is given the right to assign, sell, exchange or transfer a player to another club.

J. *Publicity.*

A player grants the club the authority to use his name and picture for publicity and promotional purposes.

K. *Grievance Procedure.*

This clause designates the procedure by which the club and a player may resolve a dispute. The details of the grievance and arbitration clause are setforth in the collective bargaining agreement. The club and player may have a dispute as to whether the club has properly terminated the player, whether the club has properly compensated the player, whether the club has provided the fringe benefits to the player as provided in his contract or in the collective bargaining agreement, whether the player has achieved the incentive performance bonus clauses in his contract, and many other issues. There have been at least 300 cases which have been decided by an arbitrator in professional basketball, football and baseball. Hundreds of other grievance cases have been filed, but were either dropped or settled.

L. *Uniqueness Clause.*

The player represents that he has extraordinary and unique skill and ability and that any breach of the contract will cause irreparable injury to the club. This clause is an extremely important one in professional sports today and throughout history. The uniqueness clause allows the first club to prevent a player from playing for a second club in another league, when the first club is able to prove a valid and binding contract. The uniqueness clause has been invoked against Napolean Lajoie, Rick Barry, Dick Barnett, Lou Hudson, Billy Sims and many others.

M. *Collective Bargaining Agreement.*

All professional team sport leagues, with the exception of the United States Football League (USFL), have a collective bargaining agreement. However, the USFL is unionized and the management and the union are negotiating an agreement and hope to reach an agreement before the 1985 season. The collective bargaining agreement usually includes an article concerning the standard player contract.

While there are many similarities in the standard player contract, there are several differences which should be noted:

1. The National Football League uses a series of one-year contracts. An NFL player who signs a contract for a period of three years signs a series of three one-year contracts. Other professional team sports would use a three-year contract. This means that the National Football League player will sign three different contracts for 1984, 1985 and 1986. The National Basketball Association player will sign one contract for 1984 to 1986. A major reason for the difference is the National Football League's collective bargaining agreement on injury protection.

2. The National Basketball Association actually has three standard player contracts: rookie — single season; veteran — single season; and, rookie or veteran — two or more seasons for rookie — single season contract).

3. The North American Soccer League, because it has both indoor and outdoor seasons, has different variations for the term and services of the player. For example, a player can sign a contract for either the indoor or outdoor season, or for both.

In conclusion, the standard player contracts used in professional team sports have many similarities in the types of clauses contained in the contracts. However, there are some differences in the types of clauses and also in the content of the clauses. A review of standard player contracts used in other professional leagues, such as the World Football League, the American Soccer League, the Women's Basketball League, the World Hockey Association and the Major Indoor Soccer League, reveal many of the same aforementioned clauses, although again there are differences in content.

While the standard player contract is important, what has become more important in this day of increased negotiating leverage and salaries for the players, is the collective bargaining agreement and the individually negotiated additional amendments.

§ 25-3. The Collective Bargaining Agreement.

A collective bargaining agreement is an agreement by and between the management (the clubs) and the union (as representative of the players). The collective bargaining agreement details the terms and conditions of employment. A professional team-sport collective bargaining agreement is different from most nonsport agreements in that the agreement sets forth the minimum terms and conditions of employment. This allows the player the ability to negotiate on an individual basis above and beyond the minimums set forth in the collective bargaining agreement and the standard player contract. This differs from the general practice in the labor sector, whereby the collective bargaining agreement sets forth the terms and conditions of employment and employees are not allowed to negotiate additional benefits on an individual basis. Therefore, employees in similar job positions, with similar backgrounds and/or experiences are paid the same wages or salaries. For example, all secondary school teachers within an administrative unit with a masters degree and five-years experience are paid the same salary. In professional team sport, not all quarterbacks, second basemen, guards and wings are treated or paid equally.

As in standard player contracts, a comparison of collective bargaining agreements in professional team sport shows a number of similarities and differences. However, there are vast differences in the collective bargaining agreements, particularly in the content of the different articles. A detailed comparison of the collective bargaining agreements would be too lengthy a process for this chapter, therefore a brief discussion of the typical articles found in a professional team sports collective bargaining agreement follow. The focus is on those clauses which most directly impact on a player's individual contract negotiations.

A. *Free Agency.*

A free agent is defined as a veteran player who has fulfilled his contractual obligations with his current club. In basketball free agency in some cases, may be obtained after one year. In football, free agency may be obtained in two years. The longest period of time before a player can obtain free agency status occurs in baseball, where a player must have six years of major league service, in addition to fulfilling his contractual obligations, before being a free agent. In most sports, a free agent can negotiate with any other club in the league. However, in baseball, there is a reentry draft which may limit the number of teams a free agent can negotiate with.

B. *Right of First Refusal.*

The right of an original club to match an offer obtained by a free agent from a new club. Basketball and football (NFL) have the right of first refusal.

C. *Compensation.*

An original club is granted the right to be compensated for the loss of a free agent. Both football (NFL) and baseball allow an original club to be compensated. Football's compensation is in the form of draft choices and based on the salary offered to a free agent by a new club. Baseball's compensation formula is complicated, and the compensation varies in accordance with the statistical category (by positions) the free agent falls within. If a free agent falls within the top 20% of his statistical category, he is deemed a Type "A" player and the original club is entitled to select a player from a pool of players left unprotected by 21 clubs. Clubs which lose a Type "B" free agent are entitled to a draft choice.

D. *Grievance Arbitration.*

This article sets forth a dispute-resolving procedure for any disputes between a player and a club involving the standard player contract and the collective bargaining agreement. Disputes arising out of other agreements, such as the Constitution or bylaws may also be arbitrated, provided they pertain to the teams and conditions of a player's employment.

E. *Injury Grievance Arbitration.*

The National Football League has a separate injury grievance arbitration clause, which allows a player to bring a complaint claiming that he was terminated by a club while injured.

F. *Salary Arbitration.*

This article allows a neutral arbitrator to resolve disputes between players and clubs relative to salary. It is used in baseball and hockey.

G. *Minimum Salaries.*

The minimum annual salary that a club must pay a player included in all collective bargaining agreements. In some sports such as baseball, a minimum salary of $35,000 for the 1983 season applies to all players, regardless of their years of service in the league. However, in football, the minimum salary is determined by a sliding scale based on the number of years of service in the league. For example, for 1984, a rookie in the NFL must be paid at least $40,000 per year, while a 16-year veteran must be paid at least $200,000 per year. In the NBA, a rookie first-round draft pick who signs a one-year contract must have a minimum salary of $75,000 and a nonfirst-round draft pick's minimum salary is $65,000 for the 1984-85 season.

H. *Pre-Season Training Camps.*

The compensation for players during training camp and the earliest commencement date for pre-season training camps are set forth in this article. For example, in 1984, NFL rookies will be paid $400 per week and veterans $450 per week. In the NFL, pre-season training camp may not, as a general rule, begin before July 15th.

I. *Travel.*

This article sets forth the travel benefits a club must provide for players on road trips. This may include some specific guidelines for management. For example, in the NBA, clubs are required to make their best efforts to make the following arrangements for their players while they are "on the road":

1. To have their baggage picked up by porters.
2. To have them stay in first class hotels.
3. To have extra-long beds available to them in each hotel.
4. To provide first-class transportation accommodations on all trips in excess of one hour.

J. *Moving Expenses.*

A player who has been traded, assigned or obtained on waivers is provided moving and travel expenses for himself and his family.

K. *Meal Allowances.*

The players are given a per diem when they are on the road. For example, in the NFL for 1984, players will be given $7.00 for breakfast, $8.00 for lunch and $20.00 for dinner.

L. *Playoff Money.*

This article provides for the money to be received by players who participate in the playoffs. In some collective bargaining agreements such as baseball, a pool is established from gate receipts and players receive a percentage of the pool. For example, 36% of the pool goes to the World Series winner. In the National Football League, a player's share is predetermined and set forth in the collective bargaining agreement. For example, each qualifying player of the Super Bowl winner receives $36,000, while each loser receives $18,000. In the North American Soccer League, the outdoor playoff pool is $50,000 or 5% of the gross gate receipts.

M. *Insurance.*

These articles provide for medical, life, disability insurance coverage and dental plans for players.

N. *Pension Retirement Fund.*

A pension/retirement fund is established for the players and is usually funded by management. The players generally do not make direct contributions, such as deductions from salary. However, they may contribute indirectly, for example, by participating in an all-star game. In baseball the proceeds of the all-star game are contributed to the pension fund. In hockey, the Player's Association agreed to pay 50% of the cost of the increase in pension benefits. The Association would pay its share from its proceeds of all international hockey games.

O. *Termination Pay.*

A player who has been terminated from a club may be provided with termination pay. The amount of termination pay varies according to the league. In basketball, a player does not receive any termination pay if he is terminated prior to or on the 55th day of the club's season. If he is terminated on or after the 56th day, the player receives his full salary for the season. In football, a player with four or more years of service may be entitled to termination pay up to a maximum of $6,000. In baseball, a player is given 30-days pay if he is terminated prior to the regular season and 60-days pay if he is terminated during the regular season.

There are many other clauses contained in a professional sport collective bargaining agreement which a general manager must deal with. The articles vary depending on the sport and league involved. However, some of the articles which have not been discussed include: off-season training camps, exhibition games, days off/scheduling, limitation on deferred compensation, pay and cable television, the college draft, union dues check off, agent regulation, waivers and loans of players to minor league clubs, international games (hockey), game tickets, endorsements, apprentice players, temporary injury contracts, prohibition of no-trade contracts and all-star games.

In conclusion, the collective bargaining agreement is an extremely important document for the general manager. The variation in collective bargaining agreements among the different leagues is great and much more pronounced than the standard player contracts. In addition to the collective bargaining agreement, a general manager must also be aware of any arbitration decisions which have interpreted the collective bargaining agreement.

§ 25-4. Additional Contract Amendments.

Amendments to the contract, which have been negotiated in addition to the standard player contract and the collective bargaining agreement, have been a problem area for professional team sport contract negotiators. The major problems are that some of the clauses are vague, ambiguous or unclear.

There is a tremendous variety in additional contract amendments, and the number of additional contract amendments varies from contract to contract and from sport to sport. One trend in professional team sport is the use of standardized additional contract amendments. These standardized clauses are contained in the collective bargaining agreements in basketball and hockey, while the club's management council drafts standardized clauses in football. In basketball, for example, the standardized clauses, referred to as "allowable amendments" include amendments that provide for: a player to be compensated if he is injured while playing or practicing for the club; a player to be compensated despite failing, refusing or neglecting to maintain standards of good citizenship, good sportsmanship or obey the club's training rules; a player to be compensated despite his lack of skill; and a player to be compensated despite suffering a mental disability. In hockey, the collective bargaining agreement sets forth standardized clauses for certain amateur players, a player's option contract and a player's termination contract. In football, the club's management council has drafted a bonus clause standard form, which may be used by the clubs.

The free agent, journeyman or marginal player is not as likely to have many additional contract provisions, and the additional provisions he may negotiate are often standardized. The superstar player (or the player in a good bargaining position) has, in many cases, the leverage and ability to add unique and non-standardized clauses to his contract. When the standardized forms are not available, the clauses are drafted by management or the player's representative.

There have been some contracts which reportedly have run hundreds of pages, but most add no more than a page or two to the standard player contract. Listed and discussed below are a number of typical clauses that are added as amendments to the contract. This discussion will be only a brief overview of possible additional amendments, as imagination and creativity have resulted in some atypical and extraordinary clauses being drafted. The more typical clauses are discussed first.

A. *Performance Clauses.*

Plays (football); interceptions (football); sacks (football); games (baseball, football, and basketball); innings pitched (baseball); at bats (baseball); roster bonuses and percentage of the plays (football); honor teams and individual awards (football, basketball and baseball); team wins (San Antonio Spurs — basketball).

B. *Compensation Guarantees.*

1. *Skill Guarantee.* A player will be paid his salary in the event that the club deems that he does not have sufficient playing skill.

2. *Injury Protection Guarantee.* A player will be paid his salary in the event that he is unable to play because of an injury. This clause may be drafted so that a player will be paid only if the injury is football-related or may also include a nonfootball-related injury.

3. *Full Guarantee.* A player is paid regardless of skill, injury, mental disability, death, strike or any other event. One additional consideration concerning guarantees is how the contract is guaranteed. Most contracts are guaranteed by the club, that is, the business which owns the club. If the business is a corporation, then none of the stockholders of the corporation are personally responsible for the debts of the club if the club declares bankruptcy. Therefore some players, especially those that sign contracts with a new team or league, require some type of personal guarantee from the owner. This may take the form of a letter of credit or a personal services contract.

C. *Additional Monetary Compensation.*

1. *Attendance Clauses.* A player is paid for every spectator over a certain number of spectators.

2. *Weight Clauses.* Either a bonus payment if a player makes weight or a fine if a player does not make weight.

3. *Loans.* A player is loaned money at a low interest rate or no interest at all.

4. *Real Estate Partnerships.* A player is given a share of a partnership for the tax advantages and the possibility of future appreciation of the property.

5. *Annuities.* A club purchases an annuity for a player which gives a player a stream of income in the future.

6. *Publicity Clauses.* A player is paid for public relations appearances on behalf of the club. These appearances are over and above the appearances required in the standard player contract. For example, a player may be compensated for his participation in an off-season promotional campaign.

D. *Assignability Restrictions.*

1. *Full No-Trade Clause.* A player cannot be traded during the term of his contract.

2. *Partial No-Trade Clause.* Either a player cannot be traded for part of the term of his contract (i.e., he cannot be traded in the first year of his contract) or a player cannot be traded to certain teams.

3. *Buy-Out Provisions.* A club can buy the right to trade a player for an agreed upon amount.

E. *Nonmonetary Compensations.*

1. *Lodging on Road Trips.* A club provides a player a single room on road trips. Some collective bargaining agreements specify that there are two players to a room.
2. *Lodging During the Regular Season.* A club provides a player a house or apartment during the regular season.
3. *Transportation for a Player.* A club provides an automobile during the season.
4. *Transportation for the Family.* A club provides round-trip airline tickets for the player's family to attend games.

F. *Educational Clauses.*

Educational clauses provide for tuition reimbursement and a bonus to be paid upon graduation. They are most prevalent in baseball and the United States Football League (USFL), since baseball drafts college juniors and the USFL drafts college seniors in the middle of the academic year (January). Both baseball and the USFL have standardized language relating to education. Baseball's is found in the National Association rules and the USFL adds the clause to the standard player contract. The clauses may be modified or deleted by agreement of the parties. In other sports, educational clauses are negotiated on an individual basis.

G. *Charitable Contributions.*

These vary tremendously and include the establishment of charitable foundations, scholarships, donations, and contributions. In some cases the contribution is based on a player's performance. For example, a baseball player may contribute $100 to a charitable organization for each home run that he hits.

Listed and discussed below are some of the atypical or extraordinary additional amendments to contracts which are found in a few professional team sport contracts:

1. *Weight Clauses.* Although this clause was discussed above, many feel that it falls into the "extraordinary" category.
2. *Lodging.* Reportedly there was a basketball player who had a clause in his contract requiring that the team provide him with a single room and a waterbed on road trips. His room also had to be on a different floor from his teammates.
3. *Uniform Numbers.* The selection of a certain uniform number.
4. *Employment of Players.* Some players have negotiated employment clauses into their contracts, whereby the player will work for an owner's business after retiring from the game. Ted Turner, owner of the Atlanta Braves and a cable television network, has included this type of clause in some player contracts.

5. *Employment of Relatives.* Some contracts with players have included the hiring of a relative as an employee, usually as a scout, for the team.

6. *Free Agency.* Some players have negotiated clauses in their contracts which have changed the clause defining either free agency, right of refusal or compensation from those in the collective bargaining agreement.

7. *Buy-out Provisions.* If a club releases a player with time remaining on his contract, then it must pay a player a termination fee. However, the termination fee is usually less than the salary amount. For example, the last year of a player's contract calls for a salary of $1,000,000. If the club chooses to terminate the player, it must pay him $250,000. This clause is most prevalent in Major League Baseball.

There are two trends in dealing with additional contract terms and conditions in professional sport. The first is the adoption of standardized language that must be incorporated into the contract. The most progressive sport in this approach is the National Basketball Association.

The second trend is the better preparation of contract negotiators through information sharing and educational sessions. Major League Baseball is in the process of computerizing salary information, while the National Basketball Association has already done so. The most progressive, however, is the National Football League, which since 1981 has held labor relations and contract negotiation seminars at Harvard University. These sessions have included the use of Harvard Business School case studies in the labor relations and contract negotiation areas. They have also included a simulated football negotiation exercise called Headball. In addition, the National Football League Management Council has reviewed all contracts and compiled a list of individually negotiated contract clauses that were either vague, ambiguous or unclear.

§ 25-5. Other Contracts.

There are a number of other contracts a general manager might deal with. In some situations, a standard form contract is a starting point, while in other situations an individually negotiated and drafted contract may be the norm.

A general manager in baseball and hockey who deals with a minor league system must be familiar with minor league contracts and a working agreement with a minor league team. Professional baseball is governed by the National Association Agreement. In addition, baseball is unique among professional team sports in that certain players play Winter League Baseball and a standard player contract is used for those players. In addition, the general manager must deal with employees, manager's, and coaches. A general manager must also deal with waivers and releases of liability with respect to facilities, concessionaires, spectators and players.

A league, as representative of the member clubs, also negotiates marketing, licensing and promotional contracts with the business sector. As a general rule, the clubs give up most of their licensing rights to the league. A general manager may be involved in negotiating contracts for the remaining marketing and licensing rights. A league is also responsible for negotiating national television and radio contracts, and the contracts for umpires, referees and officials. The contracts for these individuals are generally negotiated through collective bargaining and not on an individual basis. The management council, sometimes apart from the league, represents the clubs for purposes of collective bargaining.

The final contract areas are stadium leases and television and radio contracts. Since each agreement is unique, these are generally negotiated on an individual basis, obviating the need for standard form contracts.

§ 25-6. Summary/Conclusion.

A mistake in the contract negotiation area can be a severe blow to a professional team sport organization. The resulting adverse publicity from a mistake can hurt a club by losing a player and also gate revenues. Sometimes a mistake is never known to the public, but has resulted in giving a player leverage to demand a trade. A club makes the trade, but may not receive full value for a player and the public wonders why the club made the trade.

Mistakes have occurred in the past. Many of these situations have resulted in arbitration cases. The contract interpretation cases involving "Catfish" Hunter and Carlton Fisk in baseball resulted in both players being declared free agents. Also, the case of Rudy Hackett in basketball resulted in an arbitrator's decision which found that Hackett's contract was "guaranteed" by the first team, and that the contract law principle of mitigation of damages did not apply. Therefore, Hackett was allowed to keep the salaries he received from two different teams for the same season.

There have also been a number of arbitration cases involving a player who was cut from a club for "lack of sufficient playing skill." In several of these cases, a player was successful in arguing that he was cut for reasons other than a "lack of sufficient playing skill." For example, basketball player Ken Charles contended that he was cut because of his high salary. The arbitrator agreed with Charles and awarded him the balance of his salary for the season in which he was improperly terminated. However, it is interesting to note that the 1984-87 North American Soccer League collective bargaining agreement permits the cutting of a player for financial reasons.

Some final thoughts concerning general managers and professional team sport contracts. The standard player contracts, collective bargaining agreements and additional contract amendments in other sports are important to a general manager for two reasons.

First, a general manager may be dealing with a player who has a contractual obligation with another league or another sport. The Boston Celtics in the NBA are probably very familiar with Major League Baseball's standard player contract and collective bargaining agreement, having litigated the Danny Ainge case with the Toronto Blue Jays. Ainge had a baseball contract with Toronto and wanted to play baseball in Boston. General managers of NFL teams are quite familiar with the USFL standard player contract, and vice versa. The Detroit Lions and the Houston Gamblers, who were involved in the Billy Sims case, and the Buffalo Bills and the Birmingham Stallions who were involved in the Joe Cribbs case, fall into this category. The Sims case involved a player who had signed contracts with both the Lions and the Gamblers. The Cribbs case involved a claim by Buffalo that it had the right to match the contract offer made to Cribbs by Birmingham.

Second, the knowledge of other league's contracts and collective bargaining agreements may give a general manager a new idea or approach in contract negotiations. The allowable amendments and other standardized forms used in other leagues should be time and litigation tested. In addition, it would help the general manager to have background information on arbitration decisions and court decisions which have interpreted the contract and the collective bargaining agreement.

It is easy to see why some argue that general managers need also to be lawyers. While this combination may have some advantages, and it is found on some professional sport clubs, it is not a necessity. It is also not easy to find an individual with a sport law background and the expertise with all the other areas, such as player personnel and business matters that a general manager must deal with. The majority of clubs rely on a general manager who knows and understands the standard player contract, collective bargaining agreement, constitution, bylaws and other legal documents. In some instances a general manager may need legal assistance, such as in the drafting of an additional contract amendment, an interpretation of an arbitration decision or an interpretation of a legal decision in another sport (such as a drug case or eminent domain case). In such instances the general manager then uses the legal counsel for the club.

Index

A

B

C

COMPUTERS—Cont'd
  Introduction, §17-1.
  Reasons why computerization is avoided, §17-2.
  Sizing equipment to applications, §17-7.
  Spreadsheets, §17-6.
  Summary, §17-8.
  Word processing, §17-6.

CONCESSIONS.
  Marketing events and services for spectators, §10-6.

CONTRACTS.
  Facility manager as co-promoter of events, §21-2.
  Player contracts for professional team sports.
    Additional contract amendments, §25-4.
    Collective bargaining agreement, §25-3.
    Conclusion, §25-6.
    Introduction, §25-1.
    Other contracts, §25-5.
    Standard player contracts, §25-2.
    Summary, §25-6.
  Suppliers, staff and participants.
    Conclusion, §23-7.
    Importance of contracts, §23-2.
    Introduction, §23-1.
    Need for an attorney, §23-6.
    Participants, §23-5.
    Staff, §23-4.
    Summary, §23-7.
    Suppliers, §23-3.

                              D

DEFINITIONS.
  Personnel.
    Personnel management, §1-2.
    Professional and hourly employees, §1-3.
  Sport marketing, §9-2.

                              E

EMERGENCY MEDICAL SERVICES FOR CROWDS.
  Conclusion, §8-8.
  Duty to provide an emergency medical capability, §8-2.
  Emergency medical systems in action, §8-5.
  Introduction, §8-1.
  Planning for emergency medical response, §8-6.
  Program complexity, §8-7.
  Scope of treatment.
    Other facilities and state laws may dictate, §8-4.
    Standards and guidelines, §8-3.
  Summary, §8-8.

EMERGENCY PROCEDURES MANUAL.
  Event management, §19-7.